Pro SQL Server 2005 Reporting Services

Rodney Landrum
and Walter J. Voytek II

Pro SQL Server 2005 Reporting Services

Copyright © 2006 by Rodney Landrum and Walter J. Voytek II

All rights reserved. No part of this work may be reproduced or transmitted in any form or by any means, electronic or mechanical, including photocopying, recording, or by any information storage or retrieval system, without the prior written permission of the copyright owner and the publisher.

ISBN-13 (pbk): 978-1-59059-498-8
ISBN-10 (pbk): 1-59059-498-3

Printed and bound in the United States of America 9 8 7 6 5 4 3 2

Trademarked names may appear in this book. Rather than use a trademark symbol with every occurrence of a trademarked name, we use the names only in an editorial fashion and to the benefit of the trademark owner, with no intention of infringement of the trademark.

Lead Editor: Tony Davis
Technical Reviewer: Trish Middleton, Chris Rausch, Thomas Rizzo
Editorial Board: Steve Anglin, Dan Appleman, Ewan Buckingham, Gary Cornell, Tony Davis, Jason Gilmore, Jonathan Hassell, Chris Mills, Dominic Shakeshaft, Jim Sumser
Project Manager: Sofia Marchant
Copy Edit Manager: Nicole LeClerc
Copy Editor: Kim Wimpsett, Julie McNamee
Assistant Production Director: Kari Brooks-Copony
Production Editor: Laura Cheu
Compositor and Artist: Kinetic Publishing Services, LLC
Proofreader: April Eddy, Linda Seifert
Indexer: Broccoli Information Management
Cover Designer: Kurt Krames
Manufacturing Director: Tom Debolski

Distributed to the book trade worldwide by Springer-Verlag New York, Inc., 233 Spring Street, 6th Floor, New York, NY 10013. Phone 1-800-SPRINGER, fax 201-348-4505, e-mail orders-ny@springer-sbm.com, or visit http://www.springeronline.com.

For information on translations, please contact Apress directly at 2560 Ninth Street, Suite 219, Berkeley, CA 94710. Phone 510-549-5930, fax 510-549-5939, e-mail info@apress.com, or visit http://www.apress.com.

The information in this book is distributed on an "as is" basis, without warranty. Although every precaution has been taken in the preparation of this work, neither the author(s) nor Apress shall have any liability to any person or entity with respect to any loss or damage caused or alleged to be caused directly or indirectly by the information contained in this work.

The source code for this book is available to readers at http://www.apress.com in the Source Code section.

To all the victims of hurricanes Dennis, Katrina, and Rita,
which ravaged the Gulf Coast during the 2005 hurricane season.
Rodney Landrum and Walter J. Voytek II

Contents at a Glance

Contents

About the Authors

 **RODNEY LANDRUM** is an MCSE working as a systems engineer, DBA, and data analyst for a software development company in Pensacola, Florida, that specializes in applications for the health-care industry. He writes software reviews and feature articles for numerous magazines, including *Windows & .NET Magazine, SQL Server Magazine, Connected Home, T-SQL Solutions, Microsoft Certified Professional Magazine*, and *Electronic House*.

 **WALTER J. VOYTEK II (JIM)** is the CEO and president of HealthWare Corporation, a Microsoft Certified Partner, which specializes in information technology solutions for the health-care industry. He has worked in information technology for more than 30 years and in health-care IT for nearly 20 years. He has spoken publicly at several national conventions and also speaks for HealthWare in a variety of settings each year. As the founder and chief software architect for HealthWare, Jim has been instrumental in the design and development of HealthWare's award-winning solutions based on Microsoft technologies.

About the Technical Reviewers

 **TRISH MIDDLETON** is a professional software developer with more than 15 years of experience. She is currently focused on C#, HTML, XSLT, XML, and SQL Server while developing a Web application for Travis Software. She obtained her MCSD and MCDBA last year while taking a sabbatical from the corporate world. Outside of computers, Trish likes to run, rollerblade, do yard work, and do home improvements. When she isn't doing those things, she's playing with her three dogs—Toppsin, Backspin, and Juliet.

 **CHRIS RAUSCH** has been a software engineer for the *Sheridan Press* for more than eight years and has more than eleven years' programming experience. Chris has developed for the Unix/Solaris and Windows platforms, creating Web applications and GUI-driven Windows applications using multiple languages, data stores, and protocols. Most recently, he has accepted the role of project manager for several digital technology projects.

 **THOMAS RIZZO** is a director in the SQL Server group and an 11-year veteran at Microsoft. Beyond his work in SQL Server, Thomas has worked in various server groups at Microsoft, including Exchange, SharePoint, and BizTalk Server. He is also the author of books about programming using Microsoft's collaborative technologies, and he recently coauthored *Pro SQL Server 2005* (Apress, 2005). You can reach Thomas at thomriz@microsoft.com.

Acknowledgments

I would first like to thank my father, who, when I was 13, wanted me to be a systems analysts like him. I didn't know what that was exactly, but I knew that there were computers involved. And computers meant games. When he bought my first Atari, with a 300-baud modem and a Microsoft Basic Programming cartridge, I knew his intentions were good. Fifteen years later, when I had become the modern equivalent of a systems analyst, he didn't stop me from getting an Atari tattoo, though he laughed the whole way through. So, I want to thank my dad for his investment in my future and for his continuing encouragement.

I cannot thank enough my mother, Faye, for her support while I was writing this book and during many other times. Knowing that I had three small children, a full-time profession, and a book to write on a tight deadline constantly made her ask, "How do you do it?" I can say now, "Not without you, Mom!"

I would also like to thank Karla, who has been a constant source of inspiration and encouragement, keeping me heads-down at the computer when I would rather have been shooting pool—and for understanding while I worked on Chapter 2 in the train station in Madrid while on vacation.

Jim, thank you for being the coauthor of this book. I enjoyed all the book meetings. You did an excellent job.

I also would like to thank Eric Doverspike, who turned me on to the creative uses of ISNULL. Eric is a dedicated .NET programmer with the sort of sound work ethic that I envy. I wish I could get to work as early as he does. But 5:30 a.m. is sleepy time.

Finally, I would like to thank everyone at Apress who played important roles in shaping the book. It's immensely better, thanks to all your careful attention. Special thanks go to Tony Davis, lead editor, and Tom Rizzo, technical reviewer, whose thoughtful comments not only helped the book but made me a better writer. Thanks to Laura Cheu, who, under a pressured deadline, kept everything moving swiftly forward and brought it all together. Hats off to the copy editors, Kim Wimpsett and Julie McNamee, who leapfrogged over many hurdles to insure—I mean, *ensure*—the text made sense.

You all did a great job!

Rodney Landrum

I would like to thank Rodney, my coauthor, because without him I would not have been involved with this book at all. We have been colleagues for many years, and it has been a pleasure working with him. Having already written another book with Rodney and knowing the quality of his writing, doing this book with him was an easy choice.

I would also like to thank my father, who introduced me to the world of electronics when I was still very young. His interest in digital electronics would prove to be the spark that set me on my path to a career in information technology. I remember so clearly the day he brought a book home called *Digital Computers Made Simple*. I read it and thought to myself how exciting it was that a machine could be built and programmed to do so many different things. I could see so many possibilities, and at that point I knew I was hooked.

My first exposure to computer technology started about the time the Intel 8008 became available. With my father's help, I was able to procure one of these early microprocessors, and it became the basis for the first microcomputer I ever built. Using these early technologies, I built and entered several computer systems in science-fair projects throughout my high-school years, eventually competing at the international level.

My corporate career began early when I started my first company while still in high school. Today I am the CEO of HealthWare Corporation, a company that provides information technology to the health-care field. I am also partners in several other businesses with interests ranging from technology to real estate.

I would like to thank my wife, Kathi, who has put up with the long hours that it took to write the book. She is a wonderful companion who understands me well and always provides support and encouragement for any endeavor I undertake.

I would also like to thank my mother, who encouraged me all those years in school when I was participating in science fairs. Thanks to my sister, who always tells me she gave up her computer technology genes so I could have them. And to the rest of my family, friends, and colleagues who supported me and my wife, Kathi, throughout the process of writing this book.

A very big thank you goes to HealthWare Corporation and all of its employees and customers. They have been instrumental in my career and have provided inspiration for writing the book.

Special thanks go to Bruce and Cindi Yarbrough, who welcomed me into their home when hurricanes forced us to move HealthWare's data center operations to Atlanta. Thank you also to my nephew Ethan for introducing me to gaming on Microsoft's Xbox while I was there.

Thanks also go to Apress and the wonderful people involved with this project for their important roles in getting this book to print: lead editor Tony Davis; project manager Sofia Marchant; technical reviewers Chris Rausch, Trish Middleton, and Tom Rizzo; copy editors Kim Wimpsett and Julie McNamee; production editor Laura Cheu; indexer Kevin Broccoli; proofreaders April Eddy and Linda Seifert; comp house Kinetic Publishing Services; and any others involved with their important roles in getting this book to print.

Special thanks go to Tom Rizzo, the SQL Server product manager at Microsoft, for answering many questions for us during the course of our writing and for putting us in contact with other resources within Microsoft when needed.

Walter J. Voytek II

Introduction

At its core, the process of designing reports hasn't changed substantially in the past 15 years. The report designer lays out report objects, which contain data from a known data source, in a design application such as Crystal Reports or Microsoft Access. He or she then tests report execution, verifies the accuracy of the results, and distributes the report to the target audience.

Sure, there are enough differences between design applications to mean that the designer must become familiar with each particular environment. However, there's enough crossover functionality to make this learning curve small. For example, the SUM function is the same in Crystal Reports as it is in Microsoft Access as it is in Structured Query Language (SQL).

With Microsoft SQL Server 2005 Reporting Services (referred to as SSRS throughout the book), there is, again, only a marginal difference in the way reports are designed from one graphical report design application to another. So, if you do have previous reporting experience, your learning curve for SSRS should be relatively shallow. This is especially true if you come from a .NET environment, because the report designer application for SSRS is Visual Studio 2005 or the application included with SQL Server 2005, Business Intelligence Development Studio (BIDS).

Having said all this, several differences set SSRS apart from other reporting solutions:

- It provides a standard reporting platform based on Report Definition Language (RDL), which is the XML schema that dictates the common structure of all SSRS reports. This allows for report creation from any third-party application that supports the RDL schema.

- SSRS is an integral part of the SQL Server 2005 release.

- SSRS offers features out of the box that in other products would be expensive additions to a basic deployment. These features include subscription services, report caching, report history, and scheduling of report execution.

- SSRS, being a Web-based solution, can be deployed across a variety of platforms.

This book was written in parallel with a real SSRS deployment for a health-care application, so it covers almost every design and deployment consideration for SSRS, always from the standpoint of how to get the job done effectively. You'll find step-by-step guides, practical tips, and best practices, along with code samples that you'll be able to modify and use in your own SSRS applications.

What This Book Covers

From designing reports and stored procedures in Chapters 2–4, to deployment, management, and security processes in Chapters 6–9, the book uses a standard real-world theme to show how we chose to work with SSRS. Throughout, you'll find tips and tricks that we discovered while working closely with SSRS. The book also covers extending SSRS functionality with custom code in Chapter 5. In addition, we will demonstrate almost all the enhancements that are included with the SQL Server 2005 version of SSRS, including multivalued parameters, interactive sorting, and an entire chapter devoted to the ad hoc Report Builder application.

The following is a chapter-by-chapter breakdown to give you a feel for what the book covers:

Chapter 1, "Introducing the Reporting Services Architecture": This chapter introduces SSRS and discusses some of the driving forces behind our company's adoption of this technology. We then take a detailed look at the component pieces of the SSRS architecture, including Report Manager, BIDS, and the SSRS report server and databases. We describe how these work together to provide an effective reporting solution. We will also highlight all the new features and enhancements to the latest version of SSRS for SQL Server 2005. We finish with installation and configuration instructions.

Chapter 2, "Report Authoring: Designing Efficient Queries": The foundation of any report is the SQL query that defines the report data. In this chapter, we examine the query development process and show how to build and test high-performance queries for business reports. We also show how to encapsulate such queries in parameterized stored procedures to benefit from precompilation and reuse.

Chapter 3, "Using Report Designer": This chapter explores BIDS in detail, demonstrating the use of all the major embedded elements of SSRS within that environment. It shows how to create data sources; how to add report parameters, filters, and expressions; and provides an in-depth look at the layout section for report design.

Chapter 4, "Building Reports": Having covered query and report design basics, we now walk you through the process of building a full business report, including interactive features such as document maps, hyperlinks, and bookmarks.

Chapter 5, "Using Custom .NET Code with Reports": This chapter shows you how to customize your reports using .NET code, either by embedding Visual Basic .NET code directly in your report or by using a custom .NET assembly. We discuss and demonstrate each technique and its pros and cons.

Chapter 6, "Rendering Reports from .NET Applications": This chapter shows how to control the rendering of your reports programmatically in a variety of supported formats, either via URL access or by using the Web services API.

Chapter 7, "Deploying Reports": SSRS provides several means of deploying reports: using the Report Manager interface, using VS .NET, using the rs command-line utility, or writing code using the Web services API. This chapter demonstrates and explains each of these techniques.

Chapter 8, "Managing Reports": This chapter examines the many facets of SSRS report management, including content management, performance monitoring, report execution auditing, and control. It shows how to perform each of these tasks effectively, using built-in tools such as Report Manager, the new Report Server Configuration Manager, and command-line utilities, as well as using custom .NET management tools.

Chapter 9, "Securing Reports": This chapter introduces several important components of SSRS security, namely, data encryption, authentication and user access, and report auditing. This chapter also shows how to use each of these components in a secure SSRS deployment.

Chapter 10, "Delivering Business Intelligence with SSRS": In our work, we found that by integrating SSRS with many of the other components of the business intelligence (BI) platform, we were able to provide all the necessary information to our employees wherever they were and whenever they needed it, thus dramatically improving our overall business strategy. In this chapter, we demonstrate how we set about integrating SSRS with BI components such as CRM, SharePoint Portal Server, and Analysis Services.

Chapter 11, "Performing Ad Hoc Reporting Using Report Builder": In the final chapter, we will demonstrate the much anticipated Report Builder application, a Web-based report design tool for end users to build their own reports. The reports are created using report models as data sources. We will show how to build and deploy a report model and tap into it with Report Builder.

In each chapter, we've tried to touch on every aspect of SSRS in enough detail to allow you to translate the concepts into your own applications. Our intention was to provide truly practical, useful information on every page and not to parrot material that's adequately covered in Books Online (BOL). To that end, concepts such as cascading parameters and designing reports with hierarchical data using the LEVEL function aren't covered, because you can find adequate explanations and working examples in BOL.

We believe this book will serve as both an introduction and a step-by-step guide through many common tasks associated with SSRS, while also offering concepts and solutions that we've been developing ourselves for our own applications.

Who This Book Is For

We coauthored the book with the intention of demonstrating how to use SSRS from multiple vantage points. As a data analyst and engineer, Rodney goes through the report design and deployment processes using standard SSRS tools such as Report Designer and Report Manager. As a .NET developer, Jim takes on the role of showing how other developers can extend SSRS by creating custom Windows Forms applications, as he explains the SSRS programming model.

Source Code

In this book, we use a subset of a real database designed for a health-care application that we developed. You can find that prepopulated database (which we named Pro_SSRS, for the book), the data mart database and cube file used in Chapter 10, the completed RDL files, queries, stored procedures, and .NET application projects, as well as full installation instructions, in the Source Code section of the Apress Web site (http://www.apress.com).

CHAPTER 1

■ ■ ■

Introducing the Reporting Services Architecture

When Microsoft announced in 2003 that it was going to release SQL Server Reporting Services (SSRS) as a SQL Server 2000 add-on, a frenzy of excitement ensued. The product was originally slated for release with SQL Server 2005, so the early release was a welcome event for many. Our software development company decided to embrace SSRS early on and was fortunate to work with Microsoft during the beta phases. In January 2004, the month SSRS was released to manufacturing (RTM), we deployed it immediately. We intended to migrate all of our existing reports (which had been developed on as many as five reporting applications and platforms over the past ten years) to SSRS. We can sum up the reason for the seemingly rapid decision in one word: *standardization.*

Just as Microsoft wanted to create an industry standard with Report Definition Language (RDL), the Extensible Markup Language (XML) schema that dictates the common structure of all SSRS reports, we wanted to provide a standard reporting solution to our customers. Even in the first version of the product, SSRS delivered almost all the features we needed. Thanks to its extensibility via SSRS's Web service, we could programmatically add other features that weren't already directly supported. In addition, Microsoft was committed to enhancing SSRS over time. Even prior to SSRS for SQL Server 2005 (SS2005), Microsoft provided valuable enhancements such as client-side printing in service pack releases.

That brings us to present day, to the SSRS enhancements that have been incorporated into the long-awaited release of SQL Server 2005. SSRS has taken its place as a key component in the latest release of SQL Server and can no longer be thought of as just an add-on. The new features in SSRS are extensive (we provide an overview of these features shortly), and in most cases the incubus for their inclusion in the SSRS for SQL Server 2005 release was direct user feedback. Throughout the book, we will demonstrate each of these new features as we show how to build reports and applications. Furthermore, we'll explore how SSRS integrates with other new features in SSRS of SQL Server 2005 and how you can utilize these features to build comprehensive and effective business intelligence (BI) and Web reporting solutions.

Understanding the Benefits of SSRS

The decision of our company to migrate immediately to SSRS was based on the following perceived benefits for the company and for our customers:

Standard platform: In addition to providing a standard realized with the RDL, our development teams had been using Visual Studio .NET (VS .NET) as their main development environment. Because SSRS reports were currently developed within this platform, we wouldn't need to purchase additional development software. Our clients would need to purchase only a low-cost edition of a designer—Visual Basic (VB) .NET, for example—to gain the benefit of developing custom reports themselves. In SQL Server 2005, Business Intelligence Development Studio (BIDS) is included as a free, alternative report designer. Because it is based on Visual Studio 2005 (VS 2005), report designers who learn to design reports with BIDS can move to the full VS 2005 environment anytime with no additional training.

Cost: SSRS is an integral part of SQL Server 2005 and is available in many editions, from Express to Enterprise. When you purchase SQL Server, you get SSRS as well.

Web-enabled: Because SSRS is a Web-based reporting solution, a single deployed report is accessible to a variety of clients, from the browser to custom Windows Forms. Also, because reports are accessed via Hypertext Transfer Protocol (HTTP) or HTTP Secure (HTTPS), you can view reports from any location that has access to the SSRS Web server, which no longer requires reports to be installed locally with heavy client applications.

Customizable: SSRS provides a .NET Web service as a front end and as such can be accessed programmatically to extend the delivery of reports beyond the browser. As .NET programmers, we knew we would want to build custom applications to render reports where we could control the look and feel of the report viewer. We show one such application in Chapter 6, which covers report rendering.

Subscriptions: Having the ability to deliver reports through e-mail or a file share and processed during off-peak hours, which was offered with SSRS subscription abilities, was a huge advantage for our company and our clients. We show how to set up two different kinds of subscriptions, standard and data-driven, in Chapter 8.

As you'll see, SSRS is a full reporting solution that encompasses many levels of professional expertise, from report design to database administration. In many organizations, especially small- to medium-sized ones, information technology (IT) professionals are asked to perform many jobs. They write a query and design a report in the morning, perform database backups or restores in the afternoon, and update all the systems before heading home.

Fortunately, during external deployment of SSRS to our clients and internal deployment for my software development company, I (Rodney) have worn each of these hats on a day-to-day basis. I have been entrenched in every deployment phase. By developing efficient stored procedures, designing reports, testing security, and maintaining deployed reports as a content manager, I have witnessed the day-to-day operation of SSRS from many perspectives.

In addition to those roles, I have also been responsible for our company's overall strategy for building solutions to analyze and transform the data that's gathered through both our own and other third-party applications. To that end, an essential part of my job was integrating SSRS into the overall BI strategy that incorporated the following:

- Disparate data sources such as Analysis Services Cubes and SQL Server relational databases

- Applications and tools such as Microsoft Excel and Business Scorecards

- Document management systems such as Microsoft SharePoint Portal Server

We'll dive into the details of such integration projects in Chapter 10, which is devoted to BI.

SSRS represents another world—a world that an administrator who uses standard management tools doesn't typically witness. That is the world of the software developer who can extend and control SSRS programmatically, building custom report viewers and deployment applications. In this book, as you work through each step of building a reporting solution for health-care professionals, we'll demonstrate how an administrator can accomplish the task with built-in tools, as well as how a developer can create an application to provide enhanced functionality.

SSRS IN CONTEXT: GREEN BAR, ANYONE?

Before we begin our breakdown of the overall SSRS platform, I (Rodney) will share a personal experience that illustrates one of the many challenges that SSRS addresses. That is, the story shows that creating an environment where the method in which the data is delivered to users is often as crucial as the data itself. Users want easy and fast access to data in an intuitive but powerful interface. SSRS overcomes this challenge of changing the way users work by delivering reports in applications that are already familiar to most users: browsers and e-mail clients.

Jumping back in time a few years—well, 12 years—when I started down the path of what is now described correctly as IT, I took a job as an intern in the government sector. I should have known by the *Data Processing Center* banner over the door to my interviewer's office that I wasn't exactly stepping into the modern digital age. I was offered the lowly position of mainframe computer operator, which I took eagerly despite that I knew I would be eating boiled eggs and tomato soup for the foreseeable future. On the first day, I was introduced to two assemblages of technology that my father, who also worked in data processing (DP), introduced me to in the early 1980s: a vault full of reel-to-reel magnetic tapes and box after box of green bar paper. In time I came to both appreciate and loathe the rote task of, every night, printing thousands of pages of reports that I knew would only be scanned by a few people and then discarded. I say that I appreciated the task because every so often I would be visited by a programmer who wrote one of the reports. We'd talk about the time it took to write the report, why he constantly had to update the reports, and who was asking for the updates (typically a high official). We would also commiserate about the fact that generating such a report each night was a complete waste of valuable resources. I could only hope he meant me.

One day I heard a rumor that my beloved Data Processing Center was going to be absorbed by another government body. I learned, as many did, that sweeping changes would affect my position. New supervisors came in and surveyed the inherited archaic technology landscape. What happened was astounding in many regards. The banner over my former boss's door was the first to be altered; with the stroke of a paintbrush we were now *Information Resources*. The new regime didn't think "computer operator" was a good title for me anymore. In less than the time it takes to print 3,000 checks, I became a "data specialist," and I could now eat spaghetti with real meat sauce.

I bided my time, awaiting a new system that would mean I could take the reins in my new administrative position and stop hauling the green bar. A new system was duly purchased, and I was elated. Finally, I thought, they'll bring in a modern networked system that will have online report delivery technologies. On the day the hardware was delivered, I looked in awe at my—technically, their—new IBM RS6000. Fortunately for everyone except me, the new printer that was delivered accepted the same green bar paper that we had stockpiled for years to come!

This story demonstrates that often the benefits of new technologies go unrealized because of the habitual nature of the workers who are forced to adopt that new technology. Users who relied on the Data Processing Center were used to receiving their 200-page reports each morning and tossing them by noon. If the reports weren't discarded, they were bound, bundled, and hauled to the basement for future reference. It had been done that way for years. It seemed that only the people who appreciated the work that went into the reports—the programmers and computer operators—understood the ridiculousness of the practice.

In the ensuing years, I had a number of positions, all of which involved delivering data in myriad reporting technologies, using a plethora of data stores. One day it was scrubbing data from Indexed Sequential Access Method (ISAM) files; the next day saw me pulling data from a Unix-based Oracle database. With the blessing of Open Database Connectivity (ODBC), data was accessible in almost any format.

Eventually I began work with Microsoft SQL Server 6.5 and have remained there through versions 7.0 and 2000. Over the latter years, Microsoft released a variety of applications that made my job significantly easier while offering much in the way of data delivery. A notable example was the introduction of Online Analytical Processing (OLAP) Services in 7.0, which became Analysis Services in 2000. However, one item that always seemed just out of reach was a client application that could be used to effectively deliver the data contained within these new technologies. Sure, Excel could tap into OLAP cubes, and Data Analyzer was a promising addition, but these were expensive applications that required local installations. Surely a Web-enabled reporting application would be available soon, right?

This brings me to the present, where SSRS has been unveiled and is holding its own as a prime contender in the reporting market space. SSRS has been available as an add-on to SQL Server 2000 for more than a year now. It met or exceeded my expectations as a version 1 product in most areas. Yet, from reading the public newsgroups and through my own experience, it was obvious that Microsoft needed to address a number of shortcomings. A couple of the SSRS enhancements, such as client-side printing functionality and SharePoint Web Parts for Reporting Services, made their way into the two service packs that have been released for SSRS for SQL Server 2000. However, many other features are specific to SQL Server 2005. In the following two sections, we'll cover first the new SSRS features and then the enhancements to Microsoft's BI platform, with which SSRS can be fully integrated (as we will demonstrate throughout the book).

SQL Server 2005 Reporting Services Enhancements

The following are the most significant enhancements made to the SSRS technology that have emerged since version 1.

Report Builder/Data Modeler

The Report Builder application, a new feature to SSRS for SQL Server 2005, is a local, ad hoc, report-designing application that is intended to be used more by report consumers than by report developers. The business logic and underlying data structures are created as a data model by an administrator who is familiar with the source data. With the Report Builder application, the user can create and publish reports based on available models. Chapter 11 covers how to build and deploy a data model as well as create reports with the Report Builder application.

Multivalue Parameters

SSRS 2000 supported report input parameters, allowing for the autogeneration of report parameters from query or stored procedures parameters, drop-down selectable data values, and default values. However, it soon became evident that the inability to select more than one value at a time to pass into the report was a serious limitation. What if you needed to see, for example, 2003 and 2004 data from a list of available values such as "2002,2003,2004"? In SSRS for SQL Server 2000, you could see 2003 *or* 2004 *or* all the years, but 2003 *and* 2004 was not an available option. SSRS for SQL Server 2005 addresses this limitation. We will cover multivalued parameters in Chapter 4.

Enhanced Expression Builder

Expressions are the core components of any SSRS report. With expressions it is possible to selectively control not only the content but also the desired behavior of report. Knowing this, Microsoft has included an enhanced expression editor in SSRS for SQL Server 2005, replacing the limited version in the previous release. The expression builder in SSRS for SQL Server 2000 was little more than a textbox for code entry. Now the expression builder includes a categorized list of available functions, such as String and DateTime functions, as well a built-in IntelliSense that validates the expression as it is being typed.

Graphical MDX Query Builder

Multidimensional Expressions (MDX), used to query OLAP data cubes, is a robust language that when used effectively can derive information that would be impractical to do with Transact SQL (T-SQL). However, MDX is a complex language with strict syntactical requirements, and thus MDX queries can be tricky to formulate. In SSRS for SQL Server 2000, MDX was supported, but the queries could not be created graphically. SSRS for SQL Server 2005 includes a graphical MDX query builder that you will use in Chapter 10 when designing your Analysis Services application.

Embeddable SSRS Controls

The ability to embed controls in custom applications makes it easier for developers to integrate SSRS into their projects. SQL Server 2005 includes freely distributable controls that you can use for Windows Forms development and ASP.NET Web Forms development. These controls provide additional benefits to developers, such as the ability to render reports while disconnected from the SSRS. We will cover SSRS controls in Chapter 6.

Rich Client Printing

SSRS has always had the capability to deliver reports in a variety of formats, but not all of them were print-ready. Reports rendered in Hypertext Markup Language (HTML), for example, provided interactive features such as drilling down, but printing large reports rendered in the browser was not printer-friendly. Often, sections of the report would be truncated or paginated incorrectly. You could create delivery extensions with SSRS for SQL Server 2000 to print directly to a client printer. With SSRS for SQL Server 2005, this functionality is built in.

Interactive Sorting

The ability of users to sort report data after rendering provides another level of interactivity that, potentially, mitigates the need to deploy multiple reports. SSRS for SQL Server 2005 allows report developers to define interactive sorting, which you will explore in Chapter 4.

SSRS and Business Intelligence

Because SSRS is but one component of Microsoft's BI platform, we'll now cover other new features and enhancements to SQL Server 2005 that will form an integral part of your overall reporting solution.

Business Intelligence Development Studio (BIDS)

BIDS is a limited version of Visual Studio 2005 that is included with the SQL Server 2005 base installation. With BIDS, developers can create entire projects for each of the supported components of SQL Server 2005, including SQL Server Integration Services (SSIS), SQL Server Analysis Services (SSAS), and of course SSRS. We will use BIDS throughout the book to show how to design and deploy SSRS reports and Analysis Services projects.

SQL Server Management Studio (SSMS)

With the new SQL Server Management Studio (SSMS), Microsoft has taken a big step toward consolidating within one environment many of the tools that in previous versions of SQL Server would have been executed individually. SSMS replaces Enterprise Manager and Query Analyzer, offering a much more elaborate set of tools for creating and managing SQL Server objects and queries. In addition to managing SQL Server and Analysis Services servers, administrators can use SSMS to manage instances of their SSRS reporting servers. In the previous version of SSRS, this level of control was available graphically through the browser-based Report Manager or a custom application.

We will show how to use both SSMS and Report Manager throughout the book for different tasks. We will show how to use SSMS, for example, to test query performance, a task done previously with Query Analyzer. In addition, we will show you how to use the browser-based Report Manager to view published reports, set security permissions, and create subscriptions. Both applications share functionality for managing SSRS; however, Report Manager is often preferable to SSMS because it does not require a local installation. You can access Report Manager from a browser anywhere on your network. You would need to have access to the installed SQL Server 2005 client tools in order to use SSMS.

SharePoint Web Parts

SharePoint, either in Microsoft SharePoint Portal Server (SPS) or in Windows SharePoint Services (WSS), has become one of Microsoft's most successful products. SSRS for SQL Server 2005 provides tighter integration with SharePoint by way of Web Parts that connect directly to SSRS reports on the report server. Chapter 10 covers how to incorporate these controls into a BI application.

Exploring the SSRS Architecture

You've probably heard the expression that the devil is in the details. You'll be drilling into those details throughout the book, right down to the data packets that SSRS constructs, as you explore each aspect of SSRS from design to security. For now, let's pull back to a broader vantage point—the 10,000-foot view—and look at the three main components that work together to make SSRS a true multitier application: the client, the report server, and the SQL Server report databases. Figure 1-1 shows the conceptual breakdown of the three component pieces.

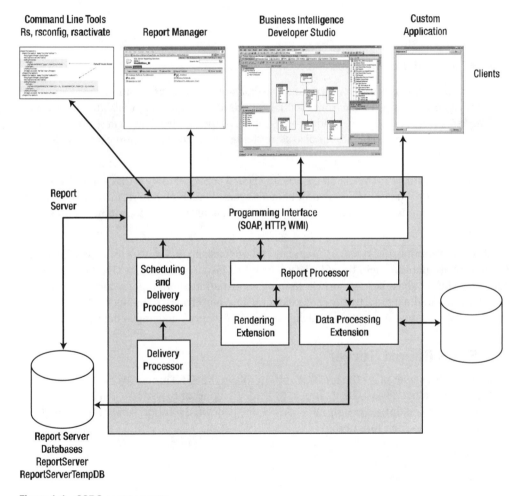

Figure 1-1. *SSRS components*

Here, the data source and the SSRS databases, ReportServer and ReportServerTempDB, are separate entities; the data source is the origin of the data that will populate the reports; and the report server databases store information about the reports. Both the data source and the report server databases can physically be located on the same SQL Server, assuming the data source is a SQL Server database. The data source can be any supported data provider, such as SQL Server, Oracle, Lightweight Directory Access Protocol (LDAP), or Analysis Services. It's possible to configure a single server to act as both the SSRS report server web service and report server database as well as the data source server. However, this isn't recommended unless you have a small user base. We'll show how to monitor the performance of the SSRS configuration and build a small Web farm, post-installation, in Chapter 8.

SSRS Databases

The SSRS installation creates two databases:

ReportServer: This is the primary database that stores all the information about reports that was originally provided from the RDL files used to create and publish the reports to the ReportServer database. In addition to report properties (such as data sources) and report parameters, ReportServer also stores folder hierarchy and report execution log information.

ReportServerTempDB: This database houses cached copies of reports that you can use to increase performance for many simultaneous users. By caching reports using a nonvolatile storage mechanism, you make sure they remain available to users even if the report server is restarted.

Database administrators can use standard tools to back up and restore these two databases. An additional database might be added after the initial installation of SSRS: the RSExecutionLog database. This database stores more discernable information about report execution, such as the user who ran the report, the time of execution, and performance statistics. We'll cover creating the RSExecutionLog database and discuss report execution logging in detail in Chapter 8.

The SSRS Report Server

The SSRS report server plays the most important role in the SSRS model. Working in the middle, it's responsible for every client request to render a report or to perform a management request, such as creating a subscription. You can break down the report server into several subcomponents by their function:

- Programming interface

- Report processing

- Data processing

- Report rendering

- Report scheduling and delivery

SSRS Web Service Interface

The programming interface, exposed as .NET Web service application programming interfaces (APIs) and uniform resource locator (URL) access methods, handles all incoming requests from clients, whether the request is a report request or a management request. Depending on the type of request, the programming interface either processes it directly by accessing the ReportServer database or passes it off to another component for further processing. If the request is for an on-demand report or a snapshot, the Web service passes it to the Report Processor before delivering the completed request to the client or storing it in the ReportServer database.

■**Note** On-demand reports are ones that are rendered and delivered directly to the client, while snapshots are reports that are processed at a point in time and delivered to the client through e-mail, to the client through file shares, or (if configured) directly to a printer.

The Report Processor

The Report Processor component is responsible for all report requests. Like the programming interface, it communicates directly with the ReportServer database to receive the report definition information that it then uses to combine with the data returned from the data source, which is accessed via one of the data processing extensions.

Data Processing

SSRS supports four data processing extensions to connect to data sources. These are SQL Server, Oracle, OLE DB, and ODBC. When the data processing component receives the request from the Report Processor, it initiates a connection to the data source and passes it the source query. Data is returned and sent back to the Report Processor, which then combines the elements of the report with the data returned from the Data Processor extension.

Report Rendering

The combined report and data is handed off to the rendering extension component to be turned into one of several supported formats, based on the rendering type specified by the client (we cover rendering in depth in Chapter 6):

- *HTML*: Default rendering format, supporting HTML versions 4.0 and 3.2.

- *Portable Document Format (PDF)*: Format used to produce print-ready reports using Adobe Acrobat Reader. SSRS doesn't require that you have an Adobe license to render in PDF, which is a great benefit to customers. All you need is a PDF reader.

- *HTML using the Office Web Components (OWC)*: Can be used for rendering reports that are designed to take advantage of the extended features of OWC, such as a pivot table or chart. HTML for OWC has been depreciated in SSRS 2005 and needs to be enabled post installation. We show you how to do this in Chapter 8.

- *Excel 2002 and 2003*: Service Pack 1 of SSRS supports Excel 97 and later.

- *XML*: Other applications or services can use reports that are exported to XML.

- *Comma-separated values (CSVs)*: By rendering to a CSV file, you can further process the report by importing it into other CSV-supported applications such as Microsoft Excel.

- *MIME HTML (MHTML)*: You can use this format, also known as a *Web archive*, to deliver reports directly in e-mail or to deliver them for storage, because the report contents, including images, are embedded within a single file.

- *Tagged Image File Format (TIFF)*: Rendering image files using TIFF guarantees a standard view of the report, as it's processed the same way for all users despite their browser settings or versions.

Scheduling and Delivery

If the request from the client requires a schedule or delivery extension, such as a snapshot or subscription, the programming interface calls the Scheduling and Delivery Processor to handle the request. You can generate and deliver report snapshots based on a user-defined or shared schedule to one of two supported delivery extensions: an e-mail or a file share. Note that SSRS uses the SQL Server Agent to create the scheduled job. If the SQL Server Agent isn't running, the job won't execute. We'll cover creating subscriptions and snapshots based on shared schedules in Chapter 8.

Client Applications

SSRS includes several client applications that use the SSRS programming interface, namely, its Web service APIs, along with URL access methods to provide front-end tools for users to access both SSRS reports and configuration tools. These tools provide report server management, security implementation, and report-rendering functionality. The tools are as follows:

- *Report Manager*: This browser-based application ships with SSRS and provides a graphical interface for users who need to view or print reports or to manage report objects for their workgroups or departments. We cover Report Manager in detail in Chapter 8, which covers managing SSRS.

- *BIDS*: This tool provides an integrated environment for developing SSRS reports. We introduce BIDS in Chapter 3 and step through building reports in this environment in Chapter 4.

- *Command-line utilities*: You can use several command-line tools to configure and manage the SSRS environment, including `rs`, `rsconfig`, `RSKeyMgmt`.

- *Custom clients*: These VB .NET Windows Forms and Web applications call the SSRS Web service to perform such tasks as rendering reports and managing report objects. SSRS includes sample application projects that you can compile and run to extend the functionality provided by the main tools listed earlier. In Chapters 6 and 7 we show how to develop your own custom applications: a report viewer and a report publisher.

- *Reporting Services Configuration Manager*: Previously, SSRS relied on command-line utilities or on direct modification of config files for changing many of the properties of the SSRS installation. SSRS for SQL Server 2005 includes a new tool designed specifically to change many of these properties in a graphical environment.

When thinking of a Web-based application, the natural inclination is to think *Web browser*. Even though other front-end tools, such as SSMS and BIDS, connect to the report server, a Web browser plays an important role in providing the graphical interface for users who view or print reports or remotely manage the report server for their workgroups or departments.

Report Manager

Within Report Manager, users can render reports, create report subscriptions, modify the properties of report objects, and configure security, as well as perform a host of other tasks. Users can access Report Manager by simply opening their Web browser and navigating to a URL of the form `http://Servername/Reports`. Figure 1-2 shows Report Manager in action, with a listing of reports in a folder deployed specifically for clinicians.

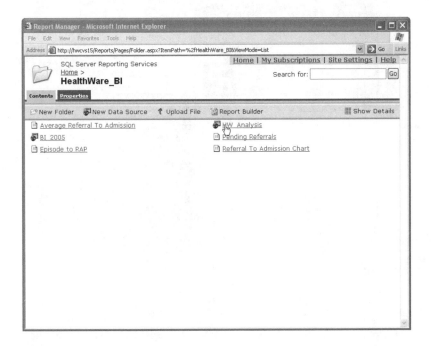

Figure 1-2. *The Web-based Report Manager application*

Business Intelligence Development Studio (BIDS)

The browser is only one of several clients that can use the SSRS Web service. In fact, BIDS is a client when it interacts with the Web service to deploy reports and data sources. BIDS offers a graphical design environment that report developers use to produce the RDL files that SSRS uses for deploying and rendering reports.

■**Note** Because RDL is a defined standard, you can use any design application that supports the creation of RDL files. Other third-party report designers are available, and many more are forthcoming.

By defining the base URL and folder name in a BIDS report project, you can deploy the RDL files that are created directly to the report server while in design mode. The base URL is of the form http://*Servername*/ReportServer. We'll cover the entire BIDS design environment in Chapter 3, including most available report objects. We'll also describe the RDL schema that defines every aspect of an SSRS report. Figure 1-3 shows the BIDS design environment, also called an integrated development environment (IDE), with a report loaded in design mode.

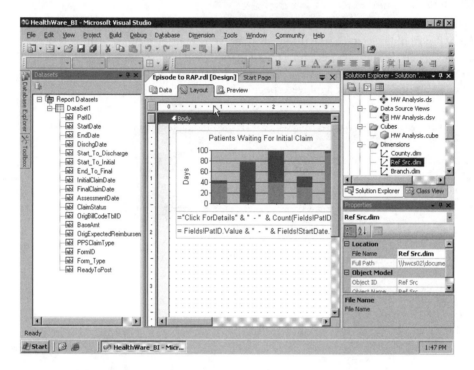

Figure 1-3. *BIDS environment*

Command-Line Utilities

In addition to graphical applications such as BIDS and SSMS, SSRS provides several command-line utilities that are considered Web service clients. The tools have the added benefit of being automated by using built-in task scheduling in Windows. SSRS includes four main command-line utilities:

- rs: Processes report services script (RSS) files that are written with VB .NET code. Because you can access the full SSRS API via the code in the script, all SSRS Web service methods are available.

- rsconfig: Configures the authentication methods and credentials for how SSRS connects to the ReportServer database. rsconfig also sets the unattended SSRS execution credentials for SSRS.

- RSKeyMgmt: Manages the encryption keys that SSRS uses to store sensitive data securely, such as authentication credentials. Chapter 9 covers how to use rskeymgmt.

Custom Clients

The final types of clients are those custom designed to access the SSRS Web services. We've built several such applications for our own company, such as a report viewer and report publisher. Third-party commercial applications exist that provide extended functionality. Other clients, such as the new Report Builder application, is a good example of building not just a report-rendering form but an entire design application that connects directly to the report server and can be installed using standard ClickOnce technologies from within the browser.

Installing and Configuring

You can install SSRS—like Analysis Services, Integration Services, and Notification Services— as part of the main SQL Server 2005 installation. When installing SSRS, you can choose which components to install and also specify the initial configuration settings. You can see the components available within the SSRS install portion of SQL Server 2005 in Figure 1-4; these include both server and client components.

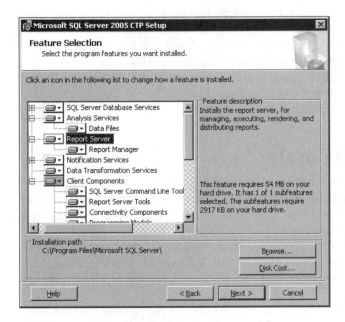

Figure 1-4. *Installation of SSRS components*

Server components include the report server Web service, ReportServer databases, and Report Manager. When installing the server components, you may have the option of configuring the installation to connect to an already existing SSRS database. By choosing this option, the instance of SSRS you're installing joins a Web farm of other SSRS servers, all using the same ReportServer database.

Note The standard edition of SSRS doesn't provide support for setting up Web farms. Throughout the book, we'll be using the Developer edition of SSRS, which provides support for Web farms and for another enterprise feature: data-driven subscriptions.

Client components include the administrative command-line tools mentioned previously, such as `rs` and `rsconfig`, as well as documentation, samples and the Reporting Services Configuration Manager.

As noted, the install process also allows you to set your initial SSRS configuration. For example, you can do the following:

- You can choose security settings, such as whether the report server will use HTTP, use HTTPS, or use both.

- You configure a Simple Mail Transfer Protocol (SMTP) mail server to handle the delivery of subscriptions.

After you install SSRS, you can modify the configuration settings you chose during the install in a few ways. For example, after reviewing performance data, you might decide that the report server needs to connect to an existing Web farm. You can perform this task using the `rsconfig` utility or using the graphical Report Services Configuration Manager.

You can reconfigure the security settings or the mail server by directly modifying the `RSReportServer.config` file. We'll cover using these tools, modifying the configuration file settings, and gathering performance measures in Chapters 8 and 9.

Deploying SSRS Securely

Security ranks as one of the highest priorities for businesses today. Providing customers and employees with a secure and reliable computing environment is not only good practice but in many cases it's a requirement, mandated by stringent federal regulations. In our case, this meant adherence to the Health Insurance Portability and Accountability Act (HIPAA), which requires policies and procedures to be in place to guarantee that confidential patient information is securely transmitted and accessible only by those with the authority to view it. To that end, we have to ensure that the data we transmit over a network connection, especially the Internet, is encrypted at its source.

SSRS is a role-based application that provides access to the objects it stores through the use of defined roles, such as content browsers who may only view reports and report data. The roles that SSRS provides are associated with Windows-based login accounts, so SSRS relies on Windows as its primary source of authentication. It is possible to extend the security model for SSRS to support other methods of authentication, such as forms-based authentication whereby users can log in with accounts maintained outside Windows to access the report server. Since SSRS has multiple authentication points—namely, at the report server level through IIS and the data-access level, SQL, or Windows authentication—specific security risks exist when altering the default Windows roles-based security model. For one, IIS would need to be set up to allow anonymous access. Another is that SSRS can support only one security extension at a time. In other words, a single SSRS report server either can be extended to support a nondefault authentication model or can remain in default Windows authentication, but not both simultaneously. Depending on your level of need for custom security—say, for example, you need to deploy SSRS on an Internet-facing server, or your application already supports forms authentication, and it would be too difficult to work within the constraints of Windows authentication—then you might need to consider a custom security extension. Our needs were such that we could easily incorporate SSRS into an existing Windows authentication model.

In this book, we'll cover two deployment scenarios:

- Intranet deployment using Virtual Private Network (VPN) and firewall technologies to allow access to the SSRS report server

- Internet-hosted application that uses Terminal Services to connect securely to an SSRS report server

In Chapter 9, we'll walk you through securing the SSRS deployment models with technologies that provide the required encryption levels and user authentication. In addition to the two models that we will cover, we will also briefly discuss ways to integrate a forms-based authentication method that will allow clients to connect directly to SSRS via the Internet.

Summary

Having created and deployed numerous projects with SSRS for SQL Server 2000, we have been anxiously awaiting, along with the rest of the SQL Server community, the release of SQL Server 2005 and the promised enhancements to SSRS. Though SQL Server 2005 has been a long time coming, SSRS was fortunately released ahead of its anticipated schedule, so it has been tested for more than a year. As you work through the book, we will point out enhancements where applicable, but our aim, as with the first edition of the book, is to show how to take advantage of advanced features, provide useful examples, and, mostly, put SSRS to work in a real-world environment where the user who will be working with the reports and applications that you deploy will have the final say on the solution's success.

CHAPTER 2

∎∎∎

Report Authoring: Designing Efficient Queries

SSRS provides a platform for developing and managing reports in an environment that includes multiple data sources of information. These data sources can include both relational data (for example, SQL Server, Oracle, MySQL, and so on) and nonrelational data (for example, Active Directory, LDAP stores, and Exchange Server). Standards such as ODBC, OLE DB, and .NET facilitate the retrieval of data from these disparate data stores, so as long as your system has the relevant drivers, SSRS can access the data. In the SSRS report design environment, configuring a dataset that drives the report content is the first step of the design process.

However, before we introduce the many elements of the report design environment, it's important to begin with the heart of any data-driven report—whether it's Crystal Reports, SSRS, or Microsoft Access—and that is the query. With any report design application, developing a query that returns the desired data efficiently is the key to a successful report.

In this chapter, we will describe the following:

- The health-care database that is the target of the reporting queries in this book—you cannot design efficient queries unless you understand the design of the data. We'll also describe an easy way to familiarize yourself with your data when the full schema details are not available.

- How to design basic but effective SQL queries for reporting purposes; we'll create queries based on real-world applications, the kind that report writers and database administrators create every day.

- How to use SSMS to gauge query performance; the initial query defines the performance and value of the report, so it's important to understand the tools required to create and test the query to ensure that it's both accurate and tuned for high performance.

- How to transform the optimized query into a parameterized stored procedure. This gives you the benefit of precompilation for faster performance and the benefit of the procedure being centrally updated and secured on SQL Server.

Introducing the Sample Relational Database

Throughout the book, we'll show how to design and deploy a reporting solution and build custom .NET SSRS applications for a SQL Server–based health-care application using relational tables and stored procedures. The application was originally designed for home health and hospice facilities that offer clinical care to their patients, typically in their homes. The Online Transactional Processing (OLTP) database that powers this application, and the one we'll use for examples in this book, captures billing and clinical information for home health and hospice patients. The database that we will use is called Pro_SSRS and is available for download in the Source Code area of the Apress Web site (http://www.apress.com) with instructions available in the ReadMe.txt file on how to restore the database in preparation for use in this and subsequent chapters.

Introducing the Schema Design

Over the years, the application has had features added, and the database schema has been altered many times to accommodate the new functionality and to capture data that is required. This data is needed not only to perform operational processes such as creating bills and posting payments to the patient's account but also to provide valuable reports that show how well the company is serving its patients. Because these types of health-care facilities offer long-term care, our customers need to know if their patients' conditions are improving over time and the overall cost of the care delivered to them.

The database that was ultimately designed for the application consists of more than 200 tables and has many stored procedures. In this book, you'll use a subset of that database to learn how to develop reports that show the cost of care for patients. You'll use eight main tables for the queries and for the stored procedures you'll begin using to build reports in the next chapter. These tables are as follows:

- Trx: The main transactional data table that stores detailed patient services information. We use the term *services* to refer to items with an associated cost that are provided for patient care.

- Services: Stores the names and categories for the detailed line items found in the Trx table. Services could be clinical visits such as a skilled nurse visit, but they could also include billable supplies, such as a gauze bandage or syringes.

- ServiceLogCtgry: The main grouping of services that are similar and provide a higher-level grouping. For example, all visits can be associated with a "Visits" ServiceLogCtgry for reporting.

- Employee: Stores records specific to the employee, which in this case is the clinician or other service personnel such as a chaplain visiting a hospice patient. An employee is assigned to each visit that's stored in the Trx table.

- Patient: Includes demographic information about the patient receiving the care. This table, like the Employee table, links directly to the Trx table for detailed transactional data.

- Branch: Stores the branch name and location of the patient receiving the care. Branches, in the sample reports, are cost centers from where visits and services were delivered.

- ChargeInfo: Contains additional information related to the individual Trx records that is specific to charges. Charges have an associated charge, unlike payments and adjustments, which are also stored in the Trx table.

- Diag: Stores the primary diagnoses of the patient being cared for and links to a record in the Trx table.

Figure 2-1 shows a graphical layout of the eight tables and how they're joined.

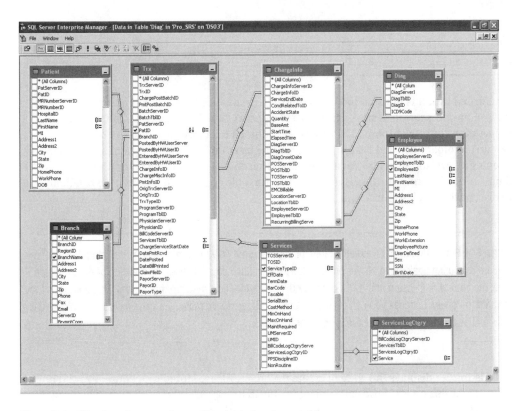

Figure 2-1. *Viewing the sample application's database tables*

Knowing Your Data: A Quick Trick with a Small Procedure

For every report writer, familiarity with the location of the data in a given database can come only with time. Of course, having a database diagram or schema provided by a vendor is a useful tool, and we have the luxury of that here, but this isn't always available. One day, faced with the dilemma of trying to find the right table for a specific piece of missing data, we decided to put together a stored procedure, which we named sp_FieldInfo. It returns a list of all the tables in a specific database that contains the same field names, typically the primary or foreign key fields. For example, in the health-care database, if you wanted a list of fields that contained the PatID field (the patient's ID number that's used to join several tables), you would use the following command:

```
sp_fieldinfo PatID
```

The output would be similar to that shown in Table 2-1.

Table 2-1. *Output of* sp_fieldinfo

Table Name	Field Name
PatCertDates	PatID
PatDiag	PatID
PatEMRDoc	PatID
Trx	PatID
Patient	PatID
Admissions	PatID

Armed with this information, you could at least deduce that, for example, the patient's physician information is stored in the PatPhysician table. However, often table and field names aren't intuitively named. When we encounter a database such as this from time to time, we run a Profiler trace and perform some routine tasks on the associated application, such as opening a form and searching for an identifiable record to get a starting point with the captured data. The Profiler returns the resulting query with table and field names that we can then use to discern the database structure.

Tip SQL Server Profiler is an excellent tool for capturing not only the actual queries and stored procedures that are executing against the server but also the performance data, such as the duration of the execution time, the central processing unit (CPU) cycles and input/output (I/O) measurements, and the application that initiated the query. Because you can save this data directly to a SQL table, you can analyze it readily, and it even makes good fodder as a source for a report in SSRS.

Listing 2-1 displays the code to create the sp_fieldinfo stored procedure. You can find the code for this query in the code download file in the SQL Queries folder. The file is called CreateFieldInfo.sql.

Listing 2-1. *Creating the* sp_fieldinfo *Stored Procedure*

```
IF  EXISTS (SELECT * FROM sys.objects WHERE object_id =
OBJECT_ID(N'[dbo].[sp_FieldInfo]'))
DROP PROCEDURE [dbo].[sp_FieldInfo]
Go
CREATE PROCEDURE sp_FieldInfo
(
 @column_name nvarchar(384) = NULL
 )
AS
SELECT
```

```
        Object_Name(id) as "Table Name",
        rtrim(name) as "Field Name"
FROM
        syscolumns
WHERE
        Name like @column_name
```

Introducing Query Design Basics

Whether you're a seasoned pro at writing SQL queries manually through a text editor or someone who prefers to design queries graphically, the end result is what matters. Accuracy, versatility, and efficiency of the underlying query are the three goals that designers strive to achieve. Accuracy is critical; however, having a query that's versatile enough to be used in more than one report and performs well makes the subsequent report design task much easier. For scalability and low response times, efficiency is paramount. A great report that takes 15 minutes to render will be a report your users rarely run. Keep the following goals in mind as you begin to develop your report queries:

The query must contain accurate data: As the query logic becomes more complex, the chance of inaccuracy increases with extensive criteria and multiple joins.

The query must be scalable: As the query is developed and tested, be aware that its performance might be entirely different as the load increases with more users. We cover performance monitoring with simulated loads in Chapter 8. However, in this chapter we'll show how to use tools to test query response times for a single execution in order to improve performance.

The query should be versatile: Often a single query or stored procedure can drive many reports at once, saving on the time it takes to maintain, administer, and develop reports. However, delivering too much data to a report at once, to support both details and a summary, can impact performance. It's important to balance versatility with efficiency.

Creating a Simple Query Graphically

Query design typically begins with a request. As the report writer or database administrator (DBA), you're probably often tasked with producing data that's otherwise unavailable through standard reports that are often delivered with third-party applications.

Let's begin with a hypothetical scenario. Say you receive an e-mail that details a report that needs to be created and deployed for an upcoming meeting. It has already been determined that the data is unavailable from any known reports, yet you can derive the data using a simple custom query.

In this first example, you'll look at the following request for a health-care organization:

Deliver a report that shows the ten most common diagnoses by service count.

Assuming you are familiar with the database, the query design process begins in SSMS, either graphically or by coding the query with the generic query designer. Both methods are available within SSMS.

■**Note** We'll cover setting up the data source connection required for building an SSRS report in Chapter 3. For now, you'll connect directly to the data with the available query design tools within SSMS. It is important to mention that though you are designing the query within SSMS, similar tools are available within the BIDS so that you can create your queries at the same time you create your report. We chose SSMS in this case because it contains lists of database objects that you may need to reference as you begin to develop the query.

We'll show how to design the query with the graphical tool to demonstrate how the underlying SQL code is created. You can access the graphical query designer by right-clicking anywhere in the new query window within SSMS and selecting Design Query in Editor (see Figure 2-2).

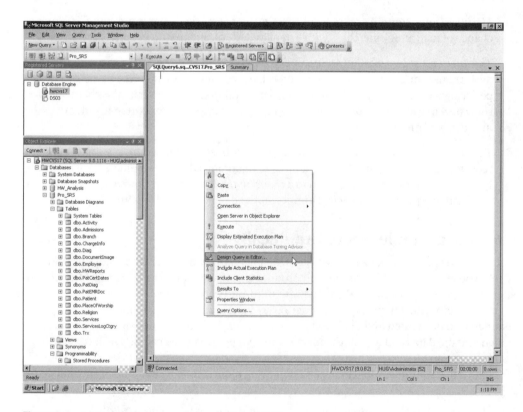

Figure 2-2. *Accessing the query design tool in SSMS*

After you open the query designer, you can perform tasks such as adding and joining additional tables and sorting, grouping, and selecting criteria using the task panes (see Figure 2-3).

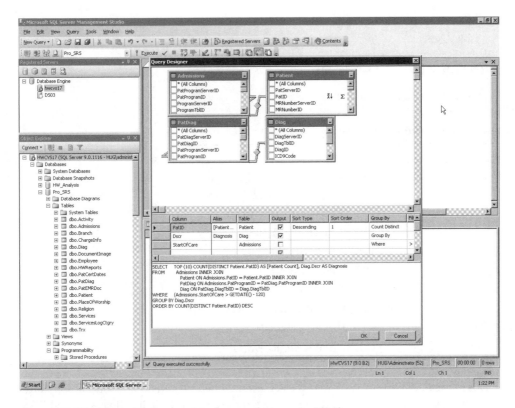

Figure 2-3. *Working with the graphical query designer in SSMS*

This initial query is a relatively simple one; it uses four tables joined on relational columns. Through the graphical query designer, you can add basic criteria and sorting, and you can select only two fields for the report: a count of the patients and a specific medical diagnosis. You can order the count descending so that you can see the trend for the most common diagnoses. You can directly transport the SQL query that was produced to a report, which we'll show how to do in Chapter 4. Listing 2-2 shows the query produced. You can find the code for this query in the code download file in the Source Code area of the Apress Web site (http://www.apress.com) in the SQL Queries folder. The file is called Top10Diagnosis.sql.

Listing 2-2. *The SQL Query Produced Using the Graphical Query Designer to Return the Top Ten Patient Diagnoses*

```
SELECT
    TOP 10 COUNT(DISTINCT Patient.PatID) AS [Patient Count], Diag.Dscr AS
    Diagnosis
FROM
    Admissions INNER JOIN
    Patient ON Admissions.PatID = Patient.PatID INNER JOIN
    PatDiag ON Admissions.PatProgramID = PatDiag.PatProgramID INNER JOIN
    Diag ON PatDiag.DiagTblID = Diag.DiagTblID
```

```
GROUP BY
     Diag.Dscr
ORDER BY
     COUNT(DISTINCT Patient.PatID) DESC
```

Table 2-2 shows the output of this query.

Table 2-2. *Sample Output from the Top Ten Diagnoses Query*

Patient Count	Diagnosis
206	ABNORMALITY OF GAIT
134	BENIGN HYPERTENSION
116	BENIGN HYP HRT DIS W CHF
104	PHYSICAL THERAPY NEC
89	DECUBITUS ULCER
85	DMI UNSPF UNCNTRLD
77	ABNRML COAGULTION PRFILE
72	CHR AIRWAY OBSTRUCT NEC
65	DMII UNSPF NT ST UNCNTRL
63	CONGESTIVE HEART FAILURE

This particular query has a small result set. Even though it's potentially working with tens of thousands of records to produce the resulting ten records, it runs in less than a second. This tells you that the query is efficient, at least in a single-user execution scenario.

This type of query is designed to deliver data for quick review by professionals who will make business decisions from the results of the data. In this example, a health-care administrator will notice a demand for physical therapy and might review the staffing level for physical therapists in the company. Because physical therapists are in high demand, the administrator might need to investigate the cost of caring for physical therapy patients.

Creating an Advanced Query

Next, we'll show how to design a query that reports the cost of care for the physical therapy patients. The goal is to design it in such a way that the query and subsequent report are flexible enough to include other types of medical services that can be analyzed as well, not only physical therapy. This query requires more data for analysis than the previous query for the top ten diagnoses. Because you'll process thousands of records, you need to assess the performance impact.

The design process is the same. Begin by adding the necessary tables to the graphical query designer and selecting the fields you want to include in the report. The required data output for the report needs to include the following information:

- Patient name and ID number

- Employee name, specialty, and branch

- Total service count for patient by specialty

- Diagnosis of the patient

- Estimated cost

- Dates of services

Listing 2-3 shows the query to produce this desired output from the health-care application. You can find the code for this query in the code download file in the SQL Queries folder. The file is called EmployeeServices.sql.

Listing 2-3. *Employee Cost Query for Health-Care Database*

```
SELECT
    Trx.PatID,
    RTRIM(RTRIM(Patient.LastName) + ',' + RTRIM(Patient.FirstName)) AS
    [Patient Name],
    Employee.EmployeeID,
    RTRIM(RTRIM(Employee.LastName) + ',' + RTRIM(Employee.FirstName)) AS
    [Employee Name],
    ServicesLogCtgry.Service AS [Service Type],
    SUM(ChargeInfo.Cost) AS [Estimated Cost],
    COUNT(Trx.ServicesTblID) AS Visit_Count,
    Diag.Dscr AS Diagnosis, DATENAME(mm, Trx.ChargeServiceStartDate) AS
    [Month],
    DATEPART(yy, Trx.ChargeServiceStartDate) AS [Year],

FROM
    Trx INNER JOIN
    ChargeInfo ON Trx.ChargeInfoID = ChargeInfo.ChargeInfoID
    INNER JOIN  Patient ON Trx.PatID = Patient.PatID INNER JOIN
    Services ON Trx.ServicesTblID = Services.ServicesTblID JOIN
    ServicesLogCtgry ON
    Services.ServicesLogCtgryID = ServicesLogCtgry.ServicesLogCtgryID
  INNER JOIN
    Employee ON ChargeInfo.EmployeeTblID = Employee.EmployeeTblID INNER JOIN
    Diag ON ChargeInfo.DiagTblID = Diag.DiagTblID INNER JOIN
    Branch on TRX.BranchID = Branch.BranchID
WHERE
    (Trx.TrxTypeID = 1) AND (Services.ServiceTypeID = 'v')
```

```
GROUP BY
    ServicesLogCtgry.Service,
    Diag.Dscr,
    Trx.PatID,
    RTRIM(RTRIM(Patient.LastName) + ',' + RTRIM(Patient.FirstName)),
    RTRIM(RTRIM(Employee.LastName)  + ',' + RTRIM(Employee.FirstName)),
    Employee.EmployeeID,
    DATENAME(mm, Trx.ChargeServiceStartDate),
    DATEPART(yy, Trx.ChargeServiceStartDate),
    Branch.BranchName
ORDER BY
    Trx.PatID
```

The alias names identified with AS in the SELECT clause of the query should serve as pointers to the data that answers the requirements of the report request. Again, knowing the schema of the database that you'll be working with to produce queries is important, but for the sake of the example, the joined tables are typical of a normalized database where detailed transactional data is stored in a separate table from the descriptive information and therefore must be joined. The Trx table in Listing 2-3 is where the transactional patient service information is stored, while the descriptive information of the specialty services such as "Physical Therapy" is stored in the Services table.

Other tables, such as the Patient and Employee tables, are also joined to retrieve their respective data elements. You use the SQL functions COUNT and SUM to provide aggregated calculations on cost and service information and RTRIM to remove any trailing spaces in the concatenated patient and employee names. You can use the ORDER BY PATID clause for testing the query to ensure that it's returning multiple rows per patient as expected. It isn't necessary to add the burden of sorting to the query. As you'll see in the next chapters, sorting is handled within the report. Dividing the load between the SQL Server machine that houses the report data and the report server itself is important and often requires performance monitoring to assess where such tasks as sorting, grouping, and calculating sums or averages for aggregated data will be performed. If the report server is substantial enough to shoulder the burden and is less taxed by user access than the actual data server, it might be conceivable to allow the reporting server to handle more of the grouping and sorting loads.

Testing Performance with SQL Server Management Studio (SSMS)

Now that you have developed the query, you'll look at the output to make sure it's returning accurate data within acceptable time frames before moving on to the next phase of development. You can see the results of the output from SSMS along with the time it took to execute the query in Figure 2-4. You can further modify the query directly in SSMS if desired. However, one of the best features of SSMS you'll notice is the ability to view quickly both the number of records returned and the execution time. Once you do that, the next step is to create the stored procedure.

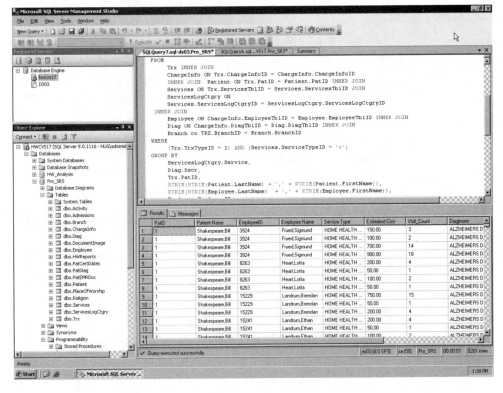

Figure 2-4. *Viewing the query execution output in SSMS*

You now have the data the way you want, and the query is executing in an average of one second. To verify the execution times, run the query 15 times in sequence from two different sessions of SSMS. Execution times will vary from one to two seconds for each execution. For 5,201 records, which is what the query is returning, the execution time is acceptable for a single-user execution. However, you need to improve it before you create the stored procedure, which you will want to scale out to accommodate hundreds of users, and begin building reports.

Looking at the Execution Plan tab in SSMS will give you a better understanding of what's happening when you execute the query. In SSMS, click the Display Estimated Execution Plan button on the toolbar. When the query is executed, the Execution Plan tab appears in the Results pane.

The Execution Plan tab in SSMS shows graphically how the SQL query optimizer chose the most efficient method for executing the report, based on the different elements of the query. For example, the query optimizer may have chosen a clustered index instead of a table scan. Each execution step has an associated cost. Figure 2-5 shows the Execution Plan tab for this query.

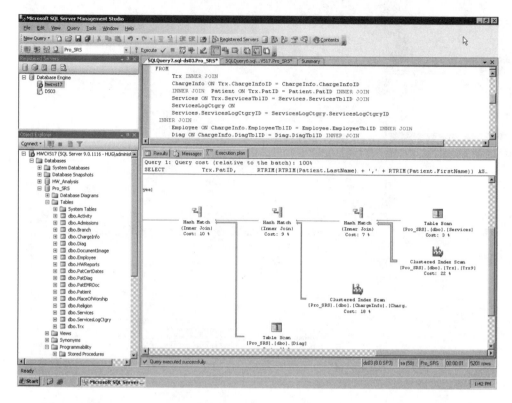

Figure 2-5. *Viewing the Execution Plan tab displayed in SSMS*

The query took one second to execute, and from this execution plan it's easy to see which section of the query had the highest cost percentage. The WHERE clause in the query had a 22 percent cost when determining the TrxTypeID value and the service type. For reference, the TrxTypeID integer field specifies the type of financial transactions as charges, payments, or adjustments. You're concerned only with the TrxTypeID value of 1, representing charges. For the service type, you're interested only in "V," representing visits, and not in other types of billable services, such as medical supplies. If you could get the cost of the WHERE clause down to a lower number, the query might improve the overall performance.

Optimizing Performance: Dividing the Load

Because SSRS and T-SQL share many data formatting and manipulation functions, you can choose in which process—query or report—these functions should be used. You can choose to have the query handle the bulk of the processing. This limits the number of rows that the report has to work with, making report rendering much faster. Alternatively, you can limit the selectivity of the query, allowing it to return more rows than are possibly required. You can then have the report perform additional filtering, grouping, and calculations, which allows the query or stored procedure to execute faster. With many users accessing the report simultaneously, having the report share the processing load also limits the impact on the data source server, in this case, SQL Server.

In this query, based on initial benchmarking, we've determined we'll remove the portion of the WHERE clause that specifies that the query should return only service types with a value of "V" for visits. Instead, we'll let the report filter out any service types that aren't visits. When you remove the service type criteria from the query and reexecute it, you can see that the overall execution time remains constant at or is less than one second, and the cost of the WHERE clause goes from 22 percent to 13 percent. Also, it's important to note in the performance analysis that the record count went up by only 54 records, from 5,201 to 5,255 by removing the "V" from the WHERE clause. You can see this in the lower-right corner of Figure 2-6.

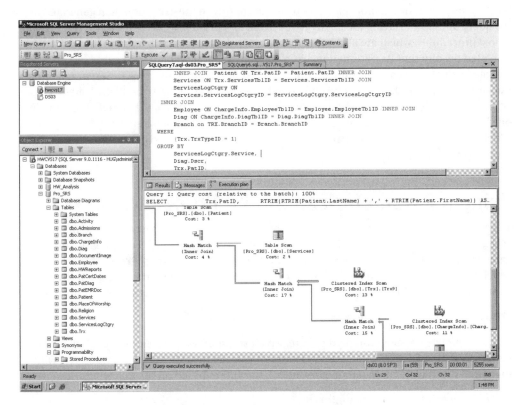

Figure 2-6. *Viewing the execution plan with the modified query*

To take advantage of a report filter, you need to add a field—Services.ServiceTypeID—to the SELECT portion of the query, like so:

```
Select
...
Branch.BranchName AS Branch ,
Services.ServiceTypeID
```

You will use the additional field Services.ServiceTypeID as the filter value in the report that you will be designing. By proceeding in this fashion, even though you're returning more rows than you might need for a particular report, you also gain the benefit of using this same base query for other reports when you eventually make it a stored procedure, which you will do in the following sections. Other reports might need to show service types other than visits, and this query will serve this purpose as well with only slight modifications to the report. For example, you might need to investigate the cost or quantity of supplies (a service type of "S") used by employees. You can use this same query and stored procedure for that report as well.

The query as it stands, now including the ServiceTypeID as a value in the SELECT clause and not as criteria, is ready to begin its life as a stored procedure. Queries serve many purposes and are good to develop reports with, as you'll do in Chapter 4. However, encapsulating queries in stored procedures is typically the preferred method of deployment for several reasons. Stored procedures, like ad hoc queries, execute according to the execution plan generated by the query optimizer. Having the ability to reuse the execution plan saves time and resources. Stored procedures, which are also beneficial because they're precompiled, can reuse an execution plan despite that its parameters, which are passed to it when it's executed, might have changed values. You can centrally maintain stored procedures on the SQL Server machine, unlike ad hoc queries that might be embedded in an application or in the RDL file in this case. When the underlying schema of a database changes, you can update the stored procedure in one location, whereas embedded queries all need to be modified separately for each report in which they reside. In the next section, we'll show how to create a stored procedure based on the employee cost query.

Using a Parameterized Stored Procedure

You can use SSMS to produce the code to create a stored procedure based on the employee cost query and also to drop it (if the stored procedure already exists in the database). In the database where you create the procedure, simply right-click the Stored Procedures folder, which is under the Programmability folder, and select New Stored Procedure. This opens a window that contains a sample CREATE PROCEDURE command for the new stored procedure.

```
CREATE PROCEDURE <Procedure_Name, sysname, ProcedureName>
```

To complete the new stored procedure, which you should name Emp_Svc_Cost, you simply need to paste in your SELECT statement. However, you can provide optional parameters with the stored procedure. These parameters limit the result set based on the following criteria:

- Service time (year and month)

- The branch where the employee works

- The individual employee

- The type of service

To create parameters for a stored procedure, you add the variable names preceded by @ characters and provide the appropriate data types and initial value; the initial value for all the parameters is NULL, as Listing 2-4 shows. You can find the code for this query that creates the stored procedure Emp_Svc_Cost in the code download file in the SQL Queries folder. The file is called CreateEmpSvcCost.sql.

Listing 2-4. *Creating the* Emp_Svc_Cost *Stored Procedure*

```
IF EXISTS
(
    SELECT name from sysobjects
    WHERE name = 'Emp_Svc_Cost'
)
    DROP Procedure Emp_Svc_Cost
GO
CREATE PROCEDURE [dbo].[Emp_Svc_Cost]
@ServiceMonth  Int=NULL,
@ServiceYear Int=NULL,
@BranchID Int=NULL,
@EmployeeTblID Int=NULL,
@ServicesLogCtgryID char(5)=NULL
AS
SELECT
    Trx.PatID,
    RTRIM(RTRIM(Patient.LastName) + ',' + RTRIM(Patient.FirstName)) AS
    [Patient Name],
    Branch.BranchName,
    Employee.EmployeeID,
    RTRIM(RTRIM(Employee.LastName) + ',' + RTRIM(Employee.FirstName)) AS
    [Employee Name],
    Employee.EmployeeClassID,
    ServicesLogCtgry.Service AS [Service Type],
    SUM(ChargeInfo.Cost) AS [Estimated Cost],
    COUNT(Trx.ServicesTblID) AS Visit_Count,
    Diag.Dscr AS Diagnosis, DATENAME(mm, Trx.ChargeServiceStartDate) AS [Month],
    DATEPART(yy, Trx.ChargeServiceStartDate) AS [Year],
    Services.ServiceTypeID
FROM
    Trx INNER JOIN
    Branch on Trx.Branchid = Branch.BranchID INNER JOIN
    ChargeInfo ON Trx.ChargeInfoID = ChargeInfo.ChargeInfoID
    INNER JOIN  Patient ON Trx.PatID = Patient.PatID INNER JOIN
    Services ON Trx.ServicesTblID = Services.ServicesTblID INNER JOIN
    ServicesLogCtgry ON
    Services.ServicesLogCtgryID = ServicesLogCtgry.ServicesLogCtgryID INNER JOIN
    Employee ON ChargeInfo.EmployeeTblID = Employee.EmployeeTblID INNER JOIN
    Diag ON ChargeInfo.DiagTblID = Diag.DiagTblID
WHERE
    (Trx.TrxTypeID = 1) AND
    (ISNULL(Branch.BranchID,0) = ISNULL(@BranchID,ISNULL(Branch.BranchID,0)))
AND
    (ISNULL(Services.ServicesLogCtgryID,0) = ISNULL(@ServicesLogCtgryID,
        ISNULL(Services.ServicesLogCtgryID,0)))  AND
    (ISNULL(Employee.EmployeeTblID,0) = ISNULL(@EmployeeTblID,
        ISNULL(Employee.EmployeeTblID,0))) AND
```

```
--Case to determine whether Year and Month were passed in

        1=Case
            When ( @ServiceYear is  NULL) then 1
            When ( @ServiceYear is  NOT NULL)
            AND @ServiceYear = Cast(DatePart(YY,ChargeServiceStartDate) as int)
Then 1
        ELSE 0
        End
AND
        1=Case
            When (@ServiceMonth is NULL)  then 1
            When (@ServiceMonth is NOT NULL)
            AND @ServiceMonth = Cast(DatePart(MM,ChargeServiceStartDate) as int)
Then 1
        ELSE 0
        END
GROUP BY
        ServicesLogCtgry.Service,
        Diag.Dscr,
        Trx.PatID,
        Branch.BranchName,
        RTRIM(RTRIM(Patient.LastName) + ',' + RTRIM(Patient.FirstName)),
        RTRIM(RTRIM(Employee.LastName)  + ',' + RTRIM(Employee.FirstName)),
        Employee.EmployeeClassid,
        Employee.EmployeeID,
        DATENAME(mm, Trx.ChargeServiceStartDate),
        DATEPART(yy, Trx.ChargeServiceStartDate),
        Services.ServiceTypeID
ORDER BY
        Trx.PatID
GO
```

Using Case and ISNULL to Evaluate the Parameters

In the previous query, you added several new criteria to the WHERE clause for evaluating the
parameters. You used the ISNULL function and a CASE statement to evaluate the values of the
database fields and parameters.

```
        (ISNULL(Branch.BranchID,0) = ISNULL(@BranchID,ISNULL(Branch.BranchID,0)))
        1=Case
AND
        When ( @ServiceYear is  NULL) then 1
        When ( @ServiceYear is  NOT NULL)
        AND @ServiceYear = Cast(DatePart(YY,ChargeServiceStartDate) as int)  then 1
        ELSE 0
        End
```

At first the logic for these evaluations might seem confusing, but remember that as long as the criteria are equal, results are returned. This is true through the entire WHERE clause because it's evaluated with AND. This is easier to understand with the following sample statement:

```
SELECT * from Table1 WHERE 1 = 1
```

In this statement, all rows are returned, because 1 always equals 1. It doesn't matter that you aren't comparing values from the table itself.

For the ISNULL function, you look to see whether the value of a database field—BranchID, for example—contains a NULL value, and if so, ISNULL replaces NULL with zero. The right side of that equation looks to see whether the @BranchID parameter was passed in as NULL; if so, then the value for @BranchID is set to the value of BranchID in the database table and equals every row. If the @BranchID parameter is passed to the stored procedure as a value—say, 2 for the branch Nested Valley—then only BranchID 2 is returned because BranchID = @BranchID = 2. This evaluation is performed when there might be NULL values in the field because NULL values can't be compared with standard operators such as =.

For fields that always have non-NULL values such as service dates, you can evaluate those with a CASE statement in the WHERE clause. For the two time values, Service Year and Month, you use similar logic as with the ISNULL evaluations. If the parameters @ServiceMonth and @ServiceYear are passed in as NULL to the stored procedure, then the stored procedure returns every record, and the CASE statement sets the equation to 1 = 1. If the parameters contain legitimate values, such as 2004 for the year, the CASE statement is set to 1 = 1 only when the parameter value equals the database value. Otherwise, the CASE statement is set to the equation to 1 = 0, and the record is skipped.

Testing the Procedure

The next step is to grant execute privileges for the stored procedure in SSMS by navigating to the database Pro_SSRS and then expanding the folder to Programmability. From here, select Stored Procedures, then right-click Emp_Svc_Cos, and finally select Properties. A Permissions property page will allow you to add the public role and grant execute permission to any group or user you desire. In this case, click Add on the Permissions page, find Public in the list of available users, and grant the Execute permission. (We're sure the humor of this wasn't lost on the developer, who knew someone would grant a public execution.)

■**Note** The test server on which we're developing the reports is an isolated and secure system. Typically, granting execution privileges to the public role isn't recommended. We'll lock down both the stored procedure and the report in Chapter 9.

You can now test the procedure directly in SSMS with the following command:

```
EXEC Emp_Svc_Cost
```

Because you have allowed NULL values for the parameters, you don't explicitly have to pass them in on the command line. However, to test the functionality of the stored procedure, you can pass in the full command line with the appropriate parameters; for example, you can pass all services rendered in September 2003, like so:

```
EXEC Emp_Svc_Cost 09,2003,NULL,NULL,NULL
```

Executing the procedure in this way returns 321 records, and the results verify that, indeed, only services in September 2003 were returned in a fraction of a second (see Figure 2-7).

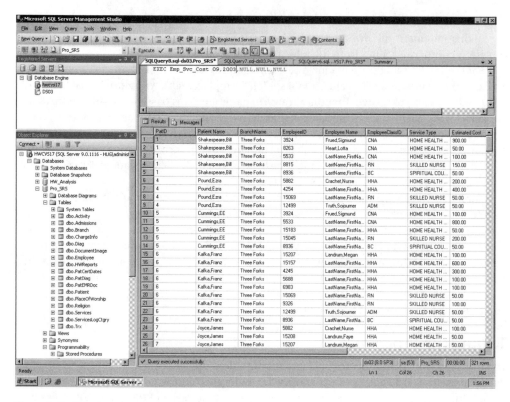

Figure 2-7. *Viewing the results of* Emp_Svc_Cost *with year and date parameters*

Summary

In this chapter, you began to design the essential part of a report: the query and stored procedure. By using stored procedures, you gain the benefits of central administration and security and also gain the ability to execute compiled code to return the dataset instead of a stand-alone query. You can develop queries in conjunction with the report, using the built-in query tools within SSRS. However, it's best to deploy the report with a stored procedure.

A report request and the target audience are the deciding factors when determining the layout and default rendering of the report. However, even though reports are often designed to answer a specific need, if they're based on the same tried-and-true stored procedures, with similar parameters and groupings, the data will be accurate across all reports. You can then focus the design time on the report itself and not on rewriting queries.

■■■

CHAPTER 3

Using Report Designer

The professional lines between system administrators, DBAs, and developers are blurring. Products often are extensible through code or at least have the potential to create functionality that goes well beyond the out-of-the-box offerings. SSRS is such an application. The days of the Microsoft Management Console (MMC) are numbered and will be overshadowed by the new interface on the block, the IDE. Actually, the IDE isn't new at all, as any developer will tell you. However, system administrators, DBAs, and even report designers have to become familiar with this new way of working. As you're probably already well aware, you can create reports in SSRS within Visual Studio 2005 or BIDS. This is a boon for developers, because now they can use the same IDE, if they choose Visual Studio 2005 over BIDS, for report creation and application development. For the rest of us, creating reports in Visual Studio 2005 presents a learning curve. SQL Server 2005, with the delivery of BIDS and SSMS, has essentially the same environment not only for report creation but also for Integration Services (formerly Data Transformation Services) packages, query design, database design and management, and almost all tasks currently associated with SQL Server and Analysis Services. So, now that you have developed your queries and stored procedures, you can turn your attention to the tools available to report designers when SSRS is installed.

In this chapter, we'll show how to set up and explore the BIDS IDE using the embedded elements of SSRS within that environment. To that end, we'll walk you through the following tasks to familiarize you with the tools of report design before showing how to create a full-blown SSRS report in the next chapter:

- Introducing the elements of BIDS

- Describing the role of RDL in SSRS with sample code from the various report objects it controls

- Creating a data source and dataset

- Defining query and report parameters

- Discussing report pagination

- Introducing and defining expressions and filters and explaining how you can use them together to control report content and formatting

- Creating data region samples: the List, Table, Rectangle, Matrix, Chart, and Image

- Implementing two simple tips for creating report templates and printing labels

Everyone learns differently—some like to follow a step-by-step guide to a known conclusion, and some like to view a completed report to see the specific components of its design. Because of this, we will take both approaches in this and subsequent chapters. Specifically, we'll show you how to build each sample from the ground up, and we'll also point you to the completed sample in the Source Code area of the Apress site (http://www.apress.com) so that you can analyze the report as you read through the steps to achieve the end result.

We provide all the data sources, reports, and projects you will work with in this chapter in a solution called Pro_SSRS. You can open this solution in both BIDS and Visual Studio 2005. You'll find detailed instructions in the Source Code area on the Apress site for installing the samples for each chapter. This chapter will focus primarily on the IDE of BIDS and for clarity provide a step-by-step guide to familiarize you with BIDS, including how to use SSRS-specific report objects such as Lists, Tables, and Charts. At the point when you begin creating these specific report examples, you will have two reports, a starting-point report and a completed report sample for each object (which we will point out at the beginning and end of each main section). This way, you can step through the procedure to produce the output in the starting-point report and then open and compare the end result to the completed report.

Exploring the Elements of BIDS

In BIDS, one or more *projects* contain all the reports and shared data sources. In addition to physically and logically grouping reports together, a project also maintains properties that are specific to that project. These properties allow the project to work independently of other projects. All projects that you create are themselves contained within a *solution*.

We'll now show how to create a project and a solution. Open BIDS, and select File ➤ New ➤ Project on the menu bar. This displays the New Project dialog box. Under Project Types, select Report Server Project, which is in the Business Intelligence Projects folder. The project name defaults to Report Project1 if this is the first project you've created. The location of the project can be a local drive or a network location. In this case, make it C:\Pro_SSRS\Reports.

By default, the solution is named according to the project name, in this case Report Project1, as shown in Figure 3-1. If you check the Create Directory for Solution box, you can append a new directory to the base location. In this case, choose Solution1.

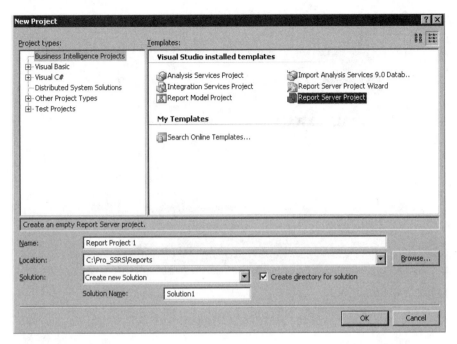

Figure 3-1. *New Project dialog box*

After you click OK, both the project and solution are created, and you can create report items and data sources within the project.

However, first you should add two important property settings to the project: the target folder in which to deploy the reports on the SSRS server and the SSRS server URL.

You can set these properties via the Solution Explorer, which displays the solution and the projects it contains, as well as all the reports and other objects the individual projects might contain. You can access the Solution Explorer by clicking View ➤ Solution Explorer on the menu bar. In the Solution Explorer, highlight the project, and select Project ➤ Properties from the menu; alternatively, right-click the project, and select Properties. The TargetReportFolder property controls the folder that's created to store the deployed reports and data sources on the SSRS server. The TargetServerURL property is the URL to the SSRS Web server. As you can see in Figure 3-2, the TargetServerURL property is in the form http://*servername*/ReportServer. In this case, the SSRS Web server is localhost.

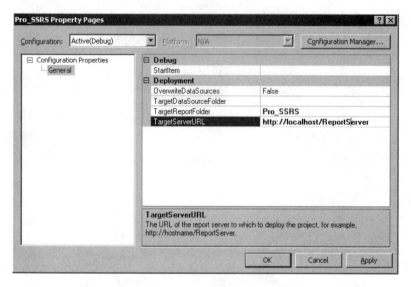

Figure 3-2. *Project properties*

Setting Up a Basic IDE

Now that you have a new solution and a new project to contain the reports you'll build, it's time to get personal. As report designers, you're going to spend many hours gazing at the pixels that are your creations. Therefore, it's important to set up the environment exactly the way you want it. The ideal setup for designing reports is a personal choice. Some prefer high-resolution display settings with every available design toolbar always in view within the environment. Others prefer undocked toolbars and a dual monitor set up at a lower resolution. Whatever your preference, BIDS makes it easy to manipulate the design tools within the IDE to personalize your configuration. In addition to the Solution Explorer, covered in the previous section, you can use several common tools within the IDE to design reports:

- The Toolbox is where you find all the report objects covered in this chapter, such as the Matrix and Table data regions. Data regions are the defined report objects within the SSRS report design environment that contain the field values from the data source.

- In the Properties window, you set the values for the various formatting and grouping properties for report items.

- The Error List window is important when troubleshooting report errors. Mismatched data types and invalid use of functions are common issues that arise when designing reports. The Error List window is the place to see the details of these errors.

- Finally, the Fields window holds the datasets and the field information you've defined for the report.

Figure 3-3 shows a custom layout for designing reports in SSRS. All the toolbars are dockable anywhere within the IDE, or they can extend beyond the main IDE to their own location on the desktop. Having this setup typically requires a high-resolution configuration—1152×864 or higher—to be most effective. In this case, the Toolbox is undocked, and the Solution Explorer and Properties toolbars are docked on the right side of the report design grid. The toolbars can autohide when not in use, which again is a personal preference. BIDS, as well as the full Visual Studio 2005 environment, now has a dock position map that assists in precisely placing the dockable item.

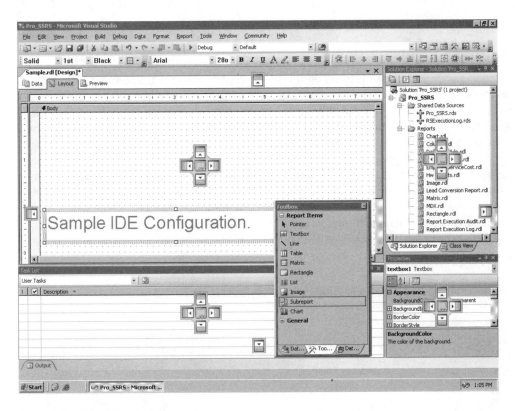

Figure 3-3. *Sample IDE configuration*

Understanding Report Definition Language (RDL)

RDL is the standard to which all reports created with the embedded SSRS tools in Visual Studio 2005 adhere. SSRS uses the RDL file that's stored in the ReportServer database to render the report through the Web server. RDL is an XML-based schema that defines each element of a report, such as formatting, dataset information, grouping and sorting, and parameters and filters. As you add items to the report, the RDL code changes to include each addition.

In the IDE, this is typically invisible to the user, as it takes place in the background. However, at times you might need to modify the RDL directly to make global changes using a find-and-replace method. We've had to do this several times when a parameter or field name changed in a source stored procedure. Within Visual Studio 2005, while working on a report, you can view the RDL code directly at any time by pressing F7.

Because RDL is a standard, you can create it with any report designer that supports it. Currently Visual Studio 2005 and BIDS are the main report designers for SSRS, but as more and more companies embrace RDL, other report designers will become available. In fact, in SQL Server 2005, Microsoft has introduced the Report Builder application that lets end users design and publish their own SSRS reports. Chapter 11 covers the Report Builder application and its components.

Throughout this chapter, we'll present the RDL sections of the report objects on which you are working to show how the RDL is updated while designing a report. The complete RDL schema is available at http://schemas.microsoft.com/sqlserver/reporting/2005/01/ reportdefinition.

Adding a Report

To add a new report to your project, right-click the Reports folder in the Solution Explorer, select Add, and then New Item. Notice that you have the option of adding an existing item as well. This option is useful if you already have a report to add to a project or if you've built a template report file as a base starting point. We'll show you how to add a template in the "Using a Report Template" section of this chapter.

For now, select Report in the Add New Item dialog box, and then click Add to add the report named Report1.rdl to the project. Double-clicking the newly added, blank report opens it in the design environment. By default the report is named Report##.rdl, where ## is the next available report number in sequence. At this point, the report is a blank slate. As with any report that contains data from a data source, the first step is to create one or more datasets. Figure 3-4 shows the IDE, including the Solution Explorer and Toolbox with the report design objects.

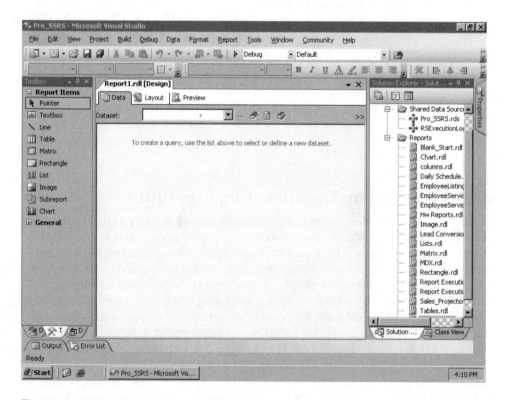

Figure 3-4. *BIDS IDE with* Report1.rdl *loaded*

Setting Up Data Sources and Datasets

Each report created in SSRS contains both a data source and a dataset. A data source not only defines the type of connection that is established to the data, whether it's SQL Server, Analysis Services, or Oracle, but it also defines the specific connection properties, such as the server and database name. A dataset, on the other hand, is the data, rows, columns, and fields that are returned from the data source. The dataset is created by building a query that retrieves information from the data source. This query, as in the case of a SQL Server data source, can take the form of a text-based query embedded directly in the report, or it can be a stored procedure.

In Chapter 2, you created a stored procedure called `Emp_Svc_Cost` that contains employee and patient visit information. Because it includes detail records that can be aggregated in several ways, enough information is in this stored procedure to demonstrate how you can use many of the report objects. Therefore, you'll use that procedure as your dataset as you work with most of the report objects in this chapter. For other report objects, such as the image report object, you will in fact use direct queries instead of the `Emp_Svc_Cost` stored procedure.

Creating a Data Source

Each report can use one or more data sources. Reports that use the same data source—for example, one that connects to a specific SQL Server database—can use what is referred to in SSRS as a *shared data source*. Shared data sources are published along with the report and can be modified on the report server after deployment. In the report designer, shared data sources contain several properties that you must configure before you can use them.

Let's step through the process of creating the shared data source for the stored procedure `Emp_Svc_Cost`. First, right-click Shared Data Sources in the Solution Explorer, and select Add New Data Source; the Shared Data Source dialog box will appear. Second, click the Edit button in the dialog box to create the connection string. In this case, you know that the server that contains your source database and stored procedure is located on the local SQL Server, so you can type **localhost** as the server name. The data source property defaults to Microsoft SQL Server (SqlClient). After you type **localhost** as the server, you can choose the `Pro_SSRS` database from the database drop-down selection. In this case, because the database is configured to use both Windows and SQL authentication, choose the Use Windows Authentication option. If you choose to use SQL authentication, you can also choose to store the SQL username and password. Generally, Windows authentication is the preferred method of authentication because it has a single point of login for users. (Chapter 9 covers authentication for deployed reports.) Figure 3-5 shows the data source connection properties. If you choose, you can test the connection by clicking the Test Connection button.

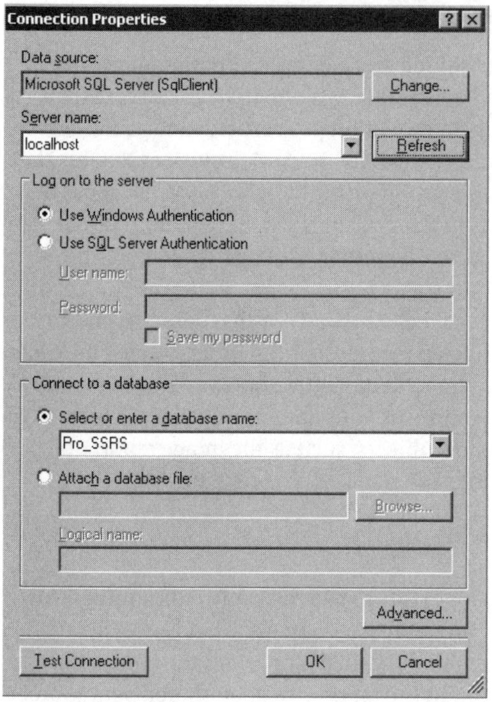

Figure 3-5. *Data source connection properties*

You now have a shared data source. Notice that the name of the shared data source has defaulted to the name of the database, Pro_SSRS. You can rename this after creating it by right-clicking it and selecting Rename.

In practice, we've developed all our reports using an identical data source name. However, because each of our online customers had a database that uniquely identified them, we designed an application that reset the database properties in the data source after it was published. In this way, we could use the same reports against the same database schema, but we could deploy the reports to multiple customers on the same report server.

In this example, the data source file you created has an .rds extension and is stored and published separately from the report. You can open an .rds file in a text editor, because it's an XML file that defines the connection properties you just created graphically. Listing 3-1 shows the Pro_SSRS.rds file.

Listing 3-1. Pro_SSRS.rds *File*

```
<?xml version="1.0" encoding="utf-8"?>
<RptDataSource xmlns:xsd=http://www.w3.org/2001/
XMLSchema xmlns:xsi="http://www.w3.org/2001/XMLSchema-instance">
```

```
<Name>Pro_SSRS</Name>
<DataSourceID>8665c4ac-17ca-436c-be19-334a1fa55274</DataSourceID>
<ConnectionProperties>
  <Extension>SQL</Extension>
  <ConnectString>data source=localhost;initial catalog=Pro_SSRS</ConnectString>
  <IntegratedSecurity>true</IntegratedSecurity>
</ConnectionProperties>
</RptDataSource>
```

Creating a Dataset

Regardless of whether you've developed a query or stored procedure in an application other than BIDS or whether you're beginning it now within the report, your next step is to proceed to the Data tab to create your first dataset. In this example, you're using a stored procedure that is already complete and tested, so half the battle is done.

On the Data tab, select <New Dataset...> in the Data Set list, which opens the Data Set properties dialog box. Each dataset defaults to a name of the syntax, DataSet##, where ## is the next unused number in sequence. You will then choose the data source you created in the previous step, Pro_SSRS. In the Command Type drop-down list, change the default, Text, to Stored Procedure. In the Query string textbox, input the name of your stored procedure, **Emp_Svc_Cost**, as shown in Figure 3-6. Finally, enter **Pro_SSRS_DS** for the name of the new dataset, and click OK to complete the dataset configuration.

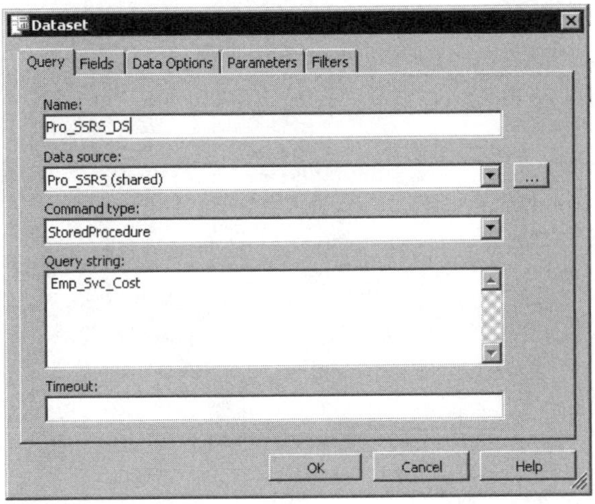

Figure 3-6. *Dataset properties*

When you click OK, the generic query designer automatically opens to the Data tab. From here you may execute the query and review the results by clicking the Run button on the Data tab's toolbar. When the stored procedure is executed, any parameters that have been defined are created, and before data is returned, you must supply the parameter values. In the case of this stored procedure, define five parameters: @ServiceYear, @ServiceMonth, @BranchID,

@EmployeeTblID, @ServicesLogCtgryID. The available default values for the parameters, when the stored procedure is executed on the Data tab, are either NULL or Blank. A Blank value is different from a NULL value in that it can be an empty string. A NULL value indicates that the value is nothing. NULL values can't be evaluated with non-NULL values. In Chapter 2 you built logic into the stored procedure to handle NULL parameter values so that when the user doesn't supply a value, the query returns all records. If the user selects a specific value, only the records that match that parameter value are returned. Execute the stored procedure with NULL values, and make sure you're getting the results you expect. You can see the results of the stored procedure execution in Figure 3-7.

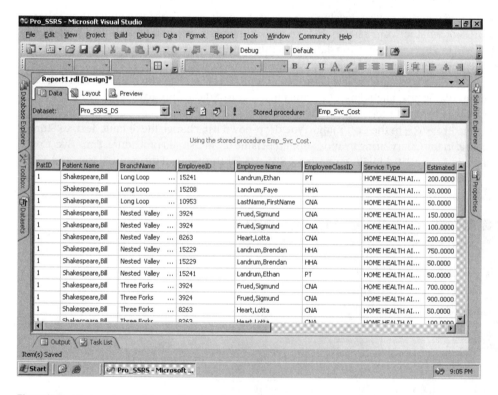

Figure 3-7. *Data returned from the stored procedure*

Note When prompted for the parameter values, Blank is the default value. To have the stored procedure execute without a data type error, you must select the value of NULL.

An SSRS report can use multiple datasets at one time. This extends the flexibility of your reporting, in that you can provide more data to the user in a single report. Multiple datasets are also useful for populating parameter drop-down lists, which you will do in Chapter 4.

However, having too many datasets could affect a report's performance, so it's important to make sure the execution times for each result set are within acceptable ranges.

The RDL file for each report contains a section for each dataset defined for the report. Listing 3-2 shows a sample of the RDL for the dataset you've defined in this chapter.

Listing 3-2. *Dataset Section of RDL*

```
<DataSet Name="Pro_SSRS_DS">
  <Fields>
    <Field Name="PatID">
      <DataField>PatID</DataField>
      <rd:TypeName>System.Int32</rd:TypeName>
    </Field>
    <Field Name="Patient_Name">
      <DataField>Patient Name</DataField>
      <rd:TypeName>System.String</rd:TypeName>
    </Field>
    <Field Name="BranchName">
      <DataField>BranchName</DataField>
      <rd:TypeName>System.String</rd:TypeName>
    </Field>
    <Field Name="EmployeeID">
      <DataField>EmployeeID</DataField>
      <rd:TypeName>System.String</rd:TypeName>
    </Field>
```

When creating a dataset, several additional tabs contain other configuration properties:

- *Fields*: Defines additional fields such as calculated fields or fields that aren't automatically defined with the data source. You derive calculated fields from an expression.

- *Data Options*: Sets several options specific to the data as it's retrieved from the data provider, such as case sensitivity and collation.

- *Parameters*: Defines the query parameter values for the dataset and the order in which they're evaluated. Stored procedures with declared parameters automatically generate the query parameters in SSRS.

- *Filters*: Defines filter values for the dataset that you can use when the report is executed.

Creating Other Data Sources

One exciting aspect of SSRS is its ability to query multiple data source types in addition to SQL Server. Any ODBC or OLE DB provider can be a potential data source for SSRS as well as XML, SSIS, and SAP. For a simple example of using a data source other than a SQL Server database, let's look at the OLE DB Provider for Microsoft Directory Services. Creating the data source to Analysis Services is similar to the SQL Server one you created earlier, with the difference being selecting OLE DB as the data source and selecting OLE DB Provider for Microsoft Directory Services for the OLE DB provider in the data source properties.

By using a direct LDAP query, you can generate field information for use in SSRS like so:

```
SELECT cn,sn,objectcategory,department
  FROM 'LDAP://DirectoryServerName/OU=OuName,DC=Company,DC=Com'
```

The query uses a standard SQL dialect that returns the common name, surname, object category (computer or person), and department from Active Directory. The field names are automatically created and can be used like any other data field for a report.

You must take a couple caveats into consideration when querying Active Directory, as well as other data sources that don't support the graphical query designer in SSRS:

- Query parameters aren't supported directly in the query. However, you can define and use report parameters in the query—referred to as a *dynamic query*—and also to filter data.

- Because a graphical query designer isn't available, you need to develop the query in the generic query designer by typing the query directly and testing. This requires knowledge of Active Directory objects and names.

Tip Several tools are available to assist in managing Active Directory, such as Active Directory Application Mode (ADAM); LDP, an Active Directory tool included with the Windows Support Tools; and ADSIEdit, a graphical Active Directory browser included with the Windows Support Tools.

Setting Parameters

Parameters in SSRS come in two flavors, *query parameters* and *report parameters*, and the two are often tied together closely.

You use a parameter that's based on a SQL query or stored procedure to limit the record set returned to the report, typically in the WHERE clause of a query. In the source query, you define parameters by prefacing the parameter's name with an @ symbol, such as @MyParameter. Within SSRS's query design tools, this does two things. First, it forces the query to prompt for the value of the parameter when it's executed. Second, it automatically creates the other parameter: the report parameter by the same name. With stored procedures, such as Emp_Svc_Cost, which you created in the previous chapter and have used here, any parameters that have been defined are also automatically created for the report.

It is also possible to have report parameters that are disassociated from a query or stored procedure. For example, you could have a report parameter that controls a report's behavior or layout properties. When you use a report parameter in this way, it's often linked to a report *filter* or is used in an expression that controls a property value of a report item. In Figure 3-8, you can see the Report Parameters property dialog box with the automatically generated parameters from the Emp_Svc_Cost stored procedure that you just set up for your report. To get to the Report Parameters dialog box, with the Data or Layout tab in focus, select Report ➤ Report Parameters from the menu. Report parameters are used within a report, both for setting criteria for datasets and for controlling report design layout elements, which you will do in detail in Chapter 4.

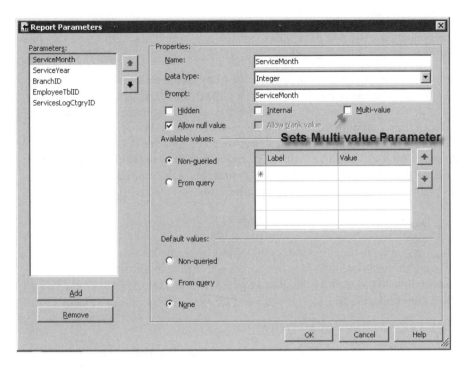

Figure 3-8. *Report Parameters dialog box*

Figure 3-8 also shows the Multi-value checkbox. This is a new feature in SSRS for SQL Server 2005. In the previous version, SSRS for SQL Server 2000, multivalue parameters were not available. Multivalue parameters allow users to select all values or combinations of values to be used within the report to limit the data that is displayed. When multiple values are chosen, these are passed to the query or stored procedure as a string array. It is important to note that multivalue parameters require the following special considerations when implementing in your reports:

Does not accept NULL *values*: This is important when deciding which parameters to make multivalued, as it will influence the design of the underlying query or stored procedure. In this case, you built logic into the Emp_Svc_Cost stored procedure to accept NULL values and return all data when NULL was passed in from a parameter. You will have to modify this stored procedure to work with multivalue parameters.

Will be evaluated as a String: Since a multivalue parameter returns a comma-separated string, you will need to also consider the data type assignment for the stored procedure parameters since the report parameter and the query or stored procedure parameter need to be the same data type to work properly.

Affects performance: Multivalue parameters are best utilized when there is a relatively small list of values. Choosing to allow users to select a range of years—for example, "2003,2004,2005"—is much better than allowing them to select 1,000 patients based on their IDs, as these will all be passed into the stored procedure as a comma-separated string value to be evaluated with the In clause.

Cannot be used in filters: Unlike single-value or nullable parameters in SSRS, multivalue parameters can be used only to pass back to the query or stored procedure, so using them to limit with report filters is not possible.

Requires string manipulation logic in stored procedures: Stored procedures do not evaluate multivalue parameters correctly, so using IN (@MyReportParameterArray) in a stored procedure, for example, will not return the expected result. This has been an issue with SQL for a long time, and numerous ways, both good and bad, exist to work with multivalue string arrays with stored procedures. User-defined functions (UDFs) or dynamic SQL are two possible choices. In Chapter 4, when we show how to build a deployable report, we will discuss how to use a special UDF that parses the multivalue report parameter into a table that will work effectively to limit the result set to exactly what is expected.

Setting Up Filters

Like parameters, report filters can limit the results of data on a report; however, you don't necessarily have to use them in conjunction with a parameter. In fact, filters, which can be defined at many points in the report, evaluate an expression and filter the results based on that evaluation. Filters take this form:

```
<Filter Expression> <Operator><Filter Value>
```

An example of a filter is one that limits the data on a report to a specific user or that is based on user input from a parameter value.

Chapter 9 demonstrates how to use a filter that limits the report based on a built-in Global collection, which includes the username of the person executing the report. Filters are beneficial in that once the report is rendered, you can use them in conjunction with parameters to limit the data in the report without requerying the data source. In Figure 3-9, you can see a filter that limits the data displayed based on a parameter called User. The logic is this: if the parameter value for User is equal to a field value of User, then include only those records where they match and otherwise include all records. Parameters and filters are included as elements of an RDL report file.

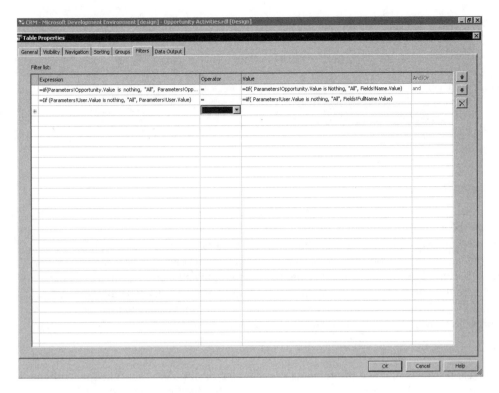

Figure 3-9. *Sample filter on a table data region*

Listing 3-3 shows the sample RDL elements.

Listing 3-3. *Parameter and Filter RDL Elements*

```
<ReportParameter Name="User">
  <DataType>String</DataType>
  <Nullable>true</Nullable>
  <DefaultValue>
    <Values>
      <Value>= nothing</Value>
    </Values>
  </DefaultValue>
  <AllowBlank>true</AllowBlank>
  <Prompt>User</Prompt>
  <ValidValues>
    <DataSetReference>
      <DataSetName>User</DataSetName>
      <ValueField>fullname</ValueField>
      <LabelField>fullname</LabelField>
    </DataSetReference>
  </ValidValues>
</ReportParameter>
```

```
<Filter>
  <FilterExpression>=Iif (Parameters!User.Value is nothing, "All",
    Parameters!User.Value)</FilterExpression>
  <Operator>Equal</Operator>
  <FilterValues>
    <FilterValue>=iif( Parameters!User.Value is nothing, "All",
      Fields!FullName.Value)</FilterValue>
  </FilterValues>
</Filter>
```

Expressions

Throughout this section, you'll use fields from the dataset to create sample report segments. Because the values from the fields are derived from *expressions* that are essentially VB .NET code, we will cover them now because they play a crucial role in the report design process.

You can use expressions to produce a value for any report item that uses them. In SSRS, you can assign expressions to almost any report property, from formatting such as color or padding to the value of a textbox. A simple expression such as that of a field assignment is commonly used while designing reports. In fact, every time you add a field to an area of a report, it's automatically converted to an expression, like so:

`=Fields!FieldName.Value`

An expression is signified by prefacing its content, typically a VB .NET function, with the equal sign (=). You can also concatenate expressions with other functions and literals. We will show several examples of expressions throughout the book. We will list several sample expressions here and show how to assign them to report items:

- `=Parameters!ParameterName.Value`: Used to assign the value of a parameter to a report item such as a textbox or cell in a table.

- `=IIF(Fields!FieldName.Value > 10, Red, Black)`: You use the IIF function for conditional expressions. In this case, it would set the color for a property, such as the text color to red, if the value of `FieldName` was greater than ten.

- `=Fields!FieldName1.Value & " " & Fields!FieldName2 .Value`: Used to concatenate the value of two fields.

- `=Avg(Fields!FieldName.Value)`: Aggregate functions such as `Sum`, `Avg`, `Min`, and `Max` that return the average value of the fields.

- `=RowNumber(Nothing)`: Used to maintain a running total for the row numbers in a report. Nothing in this case is a scope parameter passed to the function indicating a grouping or dataset. The scope parameter could be a group name or dataset, in which case a new row count would begin at the end of each group or dataset.

In SSRS for SQL Server 2005, the expression builder application that is used inside the report development environment was rebuilt to give it the type of functionality that is required to assist users in easily creating useful expressions. The former incarnation of the expression builder, released with SSRS for SQL Server 2000, was little more than a text-entry box, with limited report object selections. Report designers needed to be intimately familiar with VB

.NET functions or spend time muddling through help files to find the appropriate syntax. With the new expression builder, most of the common functions are listed, along with their syntax; in addition, they are categorized based on their type, that is, Text, Conversion, and Date & Time. This makes it much quicker to find the right function and place it as part of the expression you are building. Another great feature that developers have become accustomed to, and frankly should not have to live without, is IntelliSense, which is a contextual, in-line command completion feature. As you can see in Figure 3-10, as you are typing the expression (in this case a field value expression from your stored procedure), you are prompted with all the possible selections based on that expression. Once the expression is complete and syntactically correct, you can click OK, and the expression will become a part of the report object where you have associated it. If any syntax errors exist, these will be evidenced by a standard red underline that indicates a problem. Hovering the mouse over the red underline will display the type of error; in most cases "Invalid Syntax."

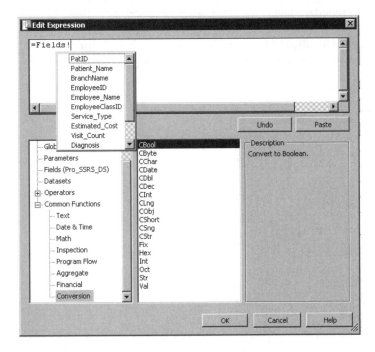

Figure 3-10. *Assigning an expression*

Laying Out a Report

Now it is time to delve into the area in the IDE in which you'll probably spend the most time: the Layout tab. The real creative magic begins here, and we don't mean because a wizard or two might be involved.

Based on the report request and target audience, the look and feel of each report might be entirely different. One user might expect drill-down functionality, and other users might need full, detailed listings of data for printing. Whatever the case, SSRS provides many tools in the Toolbox for building high-quality reports quickly and efficiently that can be immediately deployed from within the report designer. In the following sections, you'll take the sample data and put it to use as you explore the functionality of each of the available tools and data regions.

For each object we demonstrate, we'll give the graphical representation of the design environment as well as its RDL counterpart. Note that defined sections of the RDL file contain every aspect of a report, from the general layout to pagination. This is important because often it's easier to work directly within the RDL file to make alterations to a report. As we show how to adding functionality to the sample report projects, we'll point out sections of the RDL files where the graphical report design is converted to code.

Setting Up Pagination

To begin, look at the general report properties for the new report. While on the Layout tab, select Report and then Report Properties from the drop-down menu on the toolbar.

Five tabs are in the Report Properties dialog box; for now you're concerned with the Layout tab. As you can see in Figure 3-11, the Layout tab contains property settings for pagination, such as number of columns, page width, and margins. Because a number of reports will be printed in landscape format, set the page width to 11 inches and the page height to 8.5 inches. Leave all the margins at 1 inch.

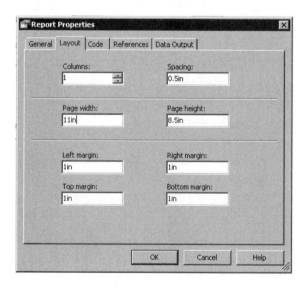

Figure 3-11. *Report Properties Layout tab*

The margins play an important role in printing. We can say with some embarrassment that we had some initial issues when configuring reports to print on a single sheet, even though we thought we had set the margins and the page width and height correctly. The issue turned out to be a combination of these settings and the size of the design grid. The general formula for calculating the correct pagination settings is as follows: the right side of the design grid needs to be equal to or less than the page width, minus both the right and left margin sizes. So, in this case, for a width of 11 inches with margins of 1 inch each for right and left, the design grid needs to be no wider than 9 inches. If you ever have any issues with printing blank pages, or with data going to a second page, the issue is most likely caused by the design area. Because the design area expands automatically as you add report objects such as data regions, you might exceed the width without realizing it until you print the report.

The Layout tab also contains a Columns setting, where you can specify the number of columns. We use multicolumn reports frequently in our industry, primarily for printing labels. Later in the "Creating a Multicolumn Report for Printing Labels" section, you'll create a multi-column report to do just that.

Using Report Objects

In this section, you will look at the report objects to see their basic functionality and also learn how you can tap into each one's unique versatility when developing reports. At this point, if you have not already done so, open the Pro_SSRS solution that we have provided with starting points and completed samples as you read through the individual object sections. We will cover the following report objects:

- *List*: This is a free-form container object for a single data grouping.

- *Table*: This is used for tabular reports with rows and columns but provides single or multiple date groups.

- *Rectangle*: Like the List, the Rectangle is a container; however, it does not provide any data groupings.

- *Matrix*: This report object, like the Table, provides multiple grouping levels; however, data is laid out in a cross-tab or pivot-style report.

- *Chart*: SSRS provides many chart styles that can be incorporated with other report objects such as the Table or Matrix or used as a stand-alone report.

- *Image*: This report object can embed standard format images, such as JPEG or TIFF, directly in a report. You can embed images directly in report, say for a company logo, or pull them directly from a database table.

Implementing a List

The List data region is one of the two free-form container objects that allow a single grouping of data. The other free-form data region is the Rectangle, and the two are similar in that they can contain other report objects and data regions. Free-form data regions don't constrain the layout of fields to a fixed format; the person creating the report is responsible for aligning the objects.

Because the list contains a grouping level, you can use the List data region only with a single dataset. Note that the List data region displays one record at a time from the dataset based on this grouping. By default, no grouping is assigned to a list.

To learn how you can use the List data region with the Emp_Svc_Cost stored procedure, which returns detail records for the number of visits for patients, you add a list to the design area and drag fields from the dataset into it. You use Employee_Name, Patient_Name, Visit_Count, and Estimated_Cost to show total visits and cost for each patient/employee combination.

In the Pro_SSRS solution, the list sample's starting-point report is called List Start. The List Start report has a data source and dataset, called emp_svc_cost, already defined for the localhost server, which should match your environment if you are using BIDS to connect to your local SQL Server 2005 server.

To begin, open the List Start report, and click the Layout tab. To add the List report object to the report, double-click List in the Toolbox. The List control is automatically added to the upper-left area of the design grid. Grab the lower-right corner of the list and drag it down until it is approximately 7 inches by 2 inches.

Next, select the Datasets toolbar, expand the emp_svc_cost dataset, drag these fields to the design area, and place them in the List data region:

- Patient_Name

- Employee_Name

- Service_Type

- Estimated_Cost

- Visit_Count

You will next add the Sum function to the Visit_Count and Estimate_Cost fields so that each field will be of the syntax =Sum(Fields!fieldname.Value). If you added a grouping level to the list, which you will do shortly, the Sum function would have been automatically added to these fields. Next, you will size the fields so that when you're finished, the report looks like Figure 3-12. As is obvious, you aren't concerned with beauty at this point but functionality.

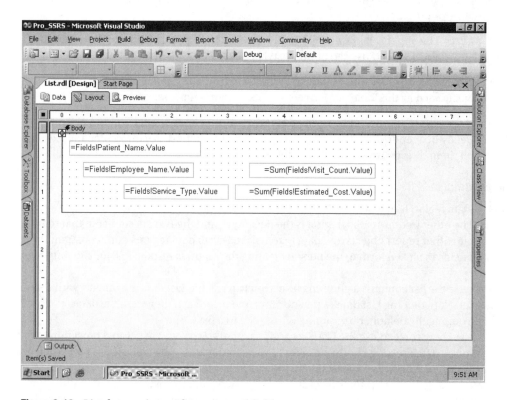

Figure 3-12. *List data region with ungrouped fields*

When you click the preview button, the report will generate and display visit information for each patient and employee (see Figure 3-13). Notice that the sum of the fields Visit_Count and Estimated_Cost is the same for each record, which is reflective of the values for the entire record set. In other words, the stored procedure returned 13,028 total visits for all the patients at a total cost of $642,551.1336. Each sum amount is the same for all patients and employees because you have not as yet defined any grouping for the list itself. You will do that next.

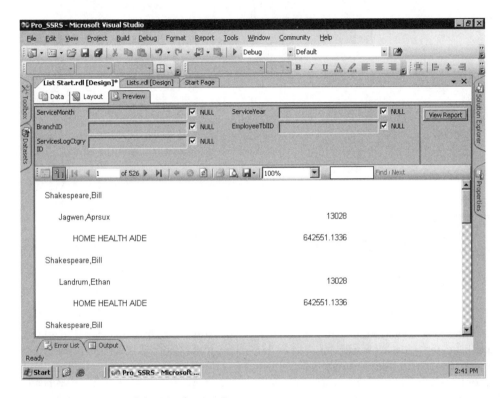

Figure 3-13. *Preview of the List data region*

To add the grouping, click the Layout tab, right-click inside the List data region, and select Properties. This opens the List Properties dialog box. Next, click the Edit Details Group button, and add two fields in the Group On area—Patient_Name and then Employee_Name—as group expressions. The preview of the new list with grouping levels now shows the correct number of visits for each patient and employee combination. However, notice that in Figure 3-14 the now familiar Bill Shakespeare is showing up multiple times with 37 visits for the employee Sigmund Freud and eight visits for employee Lotta Heart, for example. What you really want to see is Bill Shakespeare once with all the employee and visit information grouped in the figure. You could remove the grouping for the employee from the list, but that would cause the report to group all the patient's visits under a single employee and reflect the data inaccurately. In this case, you need to use a nested list that contains its own grouping level for employees. You do this by adding another List data region to the existing data region. This should force each detail record for the employee to show yet have it still be contained within the individual patient group.

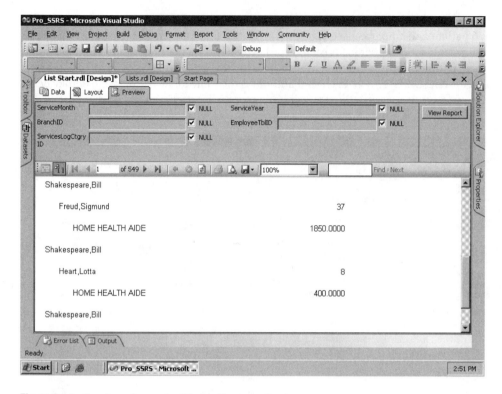

Figure 3-14. *Previewed report with duplicate patient*

To add a nested list, you need to rearrange the layout somewhat. The first step is to add another list to the initial list by clicking the List data region in the Toolbox as you did previously and sizing the new list into the existing list, which you will refer to as *list1*. Next, move all the fields from list1, except for the Patient_Name field, into the new nested list, which you will call *list2*. The report layout looks like Figure 3-15. Also notice that we have added a Line object from the Toolbox at the bottom of list1 to distinguish where the groups will break in the report. Next, go to the properties of the new list2, assign the same dataset, and add the grouping for Employee_Name as you did in the previous step by clicking the Edit Details Group button. Finally, it is important that you remove the Employee_Name grouping from list1, which will force the nested grouping levels that you desire, namely, Patient_Name in list1 and Employee_Name in list2.

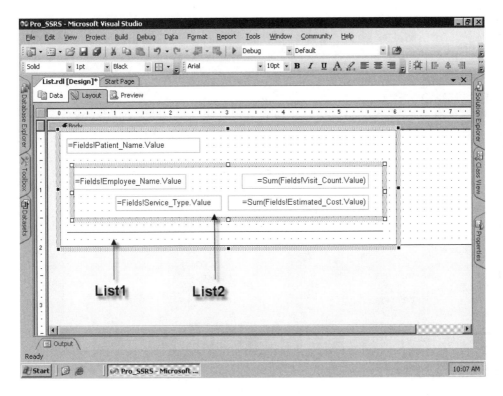

Figure 3-15. *Report layout with two lists*

Now, when you preview the report with the two lists—list1 grouped by Patient_Name and the nested list2 grouped by Employee_Name—you can see that multiple employees are associated with a single patient, with each employee displaying the correct total number of visits and estimated cost (see Figure 3-16). The line will separate the grouped results, showing where the main List data region is repeating.

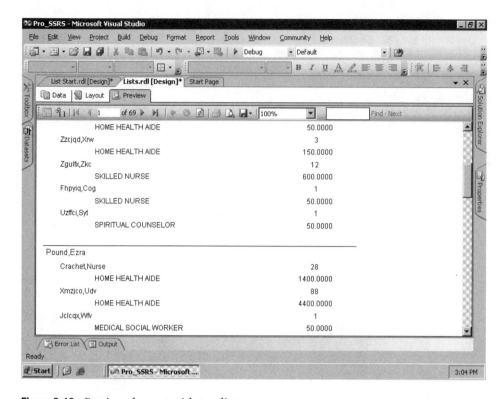

Figure 3-16. *Previewed report with two lists*

You can see the section of the RDL file that shows a sampling of the List data region you just created in Listing 3-4. Notice in the XML schema that the `<List>` element encapsulates everything that has been graphically added to the List data region, including all formatting, grouping, and the nested list.

Listing 3-4. *RDL List Section*

```
<List Name="list1">
      <Style>
        <BorderStyle>
          <Bottom>None</Bottom>
        </BorderStyle>
      </Style>
      <Height>1.625in</Height>
      <Top>0.25in</Top>
      <Grouping Name="list1_Details_Group">
        <GroupExpressions>
          <GroupExpression>=Fields!Patient_Name.Value</GroupExpression>
        </GroupExpressions>
```

```
</Grouping>
<Width>6.875in</Width>
<DataSetName>Pro_SSRS_DS</DataSetName>
<ReportItems>
  <List Name="list2">
```

■**Note** To access the full RDL file from within BIDS, while on the Layout tab, select View and then Code on
the drop-down menu. If you are working in Visual Studio 2005, press F7 and use Shift+F7 to toggle between
Code and Designer modes.

The completed report for the List object is called Lists.rdl in the Pro_SSRS project.

Implementing a Table

The Table data region provides a means of organizing data into tabular rows and columns with
possible multiple grouping levels. Every Table data region has, by default, a row that contains
detail records as well as table headers and footers. You can group tables on individual fields
from a single dataset or with expressions that might combine multiple fields. Tables make it
easy to make a report uniform because of the structured nature of the table. Fields from the
dataset are simply added to a cell within the table, and when the report is rendered, it's automatically formatted. This is in contrast to the List data region that provides much of the same
functionality as tables but requires manually positioning and aligning fields. As you'll see in
this example, it's often useful to combine data regions such as a Table, Rectangle, or List to get
both free-form control and structure simultaneously.

The starting-point report for the Table report object that we will demonstrate in this section is available in the Pro_SSRS project in the Source Code area for the book on the Apress
site. It is called Table Start.rdl. Open the Tables Start.rdl file in BIDS to begin.

As you did with the list, you will begin on the Layout tab and double-click the Table in the
Toolbox. This adds a table that's the exact width of the design area, with each of the three
columns equally divided in width. You could have sized the table by dragging it into position
in the design area if you didn't want the table to encompass the entire design area.

Next, drag the same fields you used for the list example to the detail row of the table. In
the list example, you used the fields Employee_Name, Service_Type, Estimated_Cost, and
Visit_Count as detail information and Patient_Name for the group. To add the four fields to the
detail row, you need to add a fourth column to the table. You accomplish this by right-clicking
the bar at the top of the middle column and selecting Insert Column to the Right. You now
have four equally sized columns to which you can drag the four fields so that the report
appears as it does in Figure 3-17, with the fields placed in the detail row of the table. You will
wait to add the Patient_Name field until you add a grouping level. Notice that the column
headings for each of the fields are added automatically when the fields are dropped into the
individual cells.

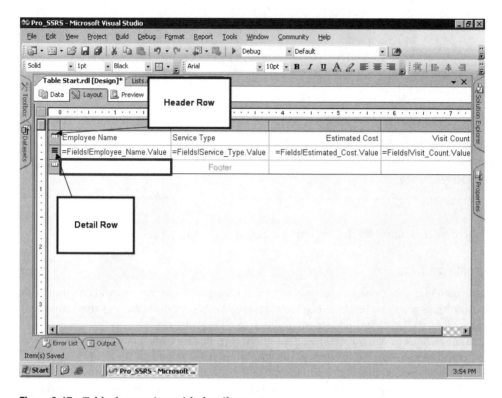

Figure 3-17. *Table data region with detail rows*

To add the Patient_Name field to the table so that the report has the same functionality as the list you created previously, you need to insert a group in the table. To do this, right-click the Detail button to the left of the detail row and select Insert Group. This opens the Grouping and Sorting Properties dialog box (see Figure 3-18). In the Group On section of the General tab, select =Fields!Patient_Name.Value in the drop-down list, which forces the grouping on the patient, and then click OK.

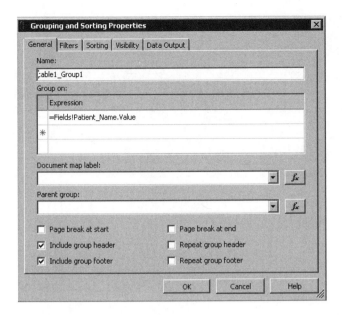

Figure 3-18. *Grouping and Sorting Properties dialog box*

■Tip Though you don't use it here, notice in Figure 3-18 that the group can contain a parent group. Parent groups are based on hierarchical data, such as an organizational chart. By assigning a parent group, you can use the Level function to create an expression that automatically recognizes the data's hierarchical relationships. The Level function is useful for formatting a report—for example, for indenting the lower levels to display that relationship correctly.

After you click OK in the Grouping and Sorting Properties dialog box, you need to add the Patient_Name field to the new grouping row that was created in the previous steps. To do this, drag the Patient_Name field to the header cell in the group, directly above the Employee_Name detail field. To distinguish the patient from the employee, make the Patient_Name cell bold. For clarity, delete each of the headers that were originally added when you added the detail row fields—click the cells of the header, and press the Delete key. Next, resize the columns so that the data is closer together. You can accomplish this either by dragging the right edge of each column to the left or by selecting the entire column and entering the desired width in inches in the Properties window.

Finally, you need to set an additional grouping level for the detail row, as you did for the header row that contains the Patient_Name field. Right-click the detail row button, select Edit Group, add =Fields!Employee_Name.Value to the Group On expression, and click OK. You also need to make sure the Estimated_Cost and Visit_Count fields have the Sum function applied to them—=Sum(Fields!Estimated_Cost.Value), for example—and then you can preview the report. When the report is rendered, it performs similarly to the list you created previously, as shown in Figure 3-19.

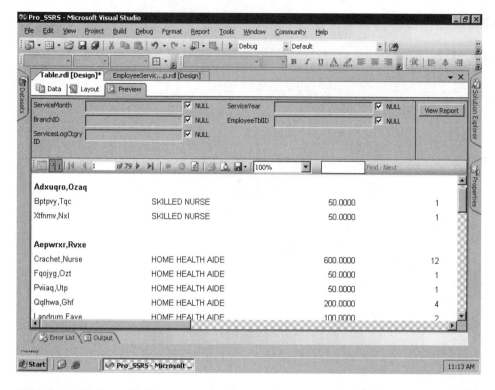

Figure 3-19. *Preview of table*

You could add more grouping levels to the table at this point if you need to, but for now you'll learn how to combine the table with the free-form rectangle to show how it's possible to extend beyond the structured nature of the table while maintaining multiple grouping levels.

The RDL listing for the table you've created will span many pages, so we have chosen, where appropriate, to include a section of the RDL output for each of the data regions. In Listing 3-5, you can see a complete <TableCell> section that would be a child node to the <TableCell>, <TableRow>, and ultimately the <Table> elements. The particular cell from the table that the RDL is referencing is the Patient_Name field that you added to its own grouping in the table. Notice also that the Patient_Name field has a section of RDL that defines CanGrow. By assigning the CanGrow property to a cell within the Table data region, it automatically expands to fit the length of the data that it contains. The opposite is true as well by assigning the CanShrink property.

Listing 3-5. *RDL Section for Table Data Region*

```
<TableCell>
  <ReportItems>
    <Textbox Name="Patient_Name">
      <Style>
```

```
            <PaddingLeft>2pt</PaddingLeft>
            <PaddingBottom>2pt</PaddingBottom>
            <PaddingTop>2pt</PaddingTop>
            <PaddingRight>2pt</PaddingRight>
            <FontWeight>700</FontWeight>
        </Style>
        <ZIndex>15</ZIndex>
        <rd:DefaultName>Patient_Name</rd:DefaultName>
        <CanGrow>true</CanGrow>
        <Value>=Fields!Patient_Name.Value</Value>
      </Textbox>
    </ReportItems>
</TableCell>
```

The completed report for the Table object is called Table.rdl and is in the Pro_SSRS project.

Implementing a Rectangle

The Rectangle data region, as discussed earlier, is similar to the List data region in that it's a free-form container object for report items. Like the list, it encapsulates all the objects into one defined area. So, when it's repositioned or deleted, the objects inside are also repositioned or deleted. Also, like all the other report objects and data regions we'll cover, you can position and scope the rectangle inside other data regions.

The Rectangle data region is more limited than the List data region, as it contains no grouping levels. You can group the objects or data regions that are placed inside a rectangle. You can use rectangles in several creative ways in an SSRS report. You will pick up where you left off on the previous sample, using the Table data region, and add a rectangle as a placeholder inside the table. This way, you can add a level of free-form design to the report while maintaining the structure afforded by the Table data region. In this example, we will also introduce the Textbox report object. A Textbox can contain literal string values such as a report title; it might also contain an expression. You use a Textbox object to add titles to the free-form objects that you place inside the rectangle.

The starting-point report for this section is called Rectangle Start.rdl and is available in the Pro_SSRS project in the Source Code area for the book on the Apress site.

To begin, open the Rectangle Start report, and follow these steps to add a rectangle to the entire detail row:

1. The first step is to drag a Rectangle data region from the Toolbox into the detail row that is extended in size in the Rectangle Start report. Notice that when the rectangle is added, it appears inside the table as a grid.

2. Next drag the two fields, Visit_Count and Estimated_Cost, from the emp_svc_cost dataset into the detail area. Place them vertically so that the Visit_Count field is above the Estimated_Cost field. Notice that SSRS automatically assigns the Sum aggregate function to the fields.

3. Next, drag two textboxes from the Toolbox into the rectangle to the left of the two fields you just added. The textboxes, which can contain expressions or literal strings, serve as labels. Inside the textboxes, type **Visit Count** and **Estimated Cost**, respectively.

4. Next, add formatting to the textboxes by selecting each textbox using the Shift key and then setting the color property to Firebrick and the font size to 12 point. You will also make the `Estimated_Cost` and `Visit Count` fields bold. You can find these settings on the standard formatting toolbar or in the Properties window. When complete, the report layout will look like it does in Figure 3-20.

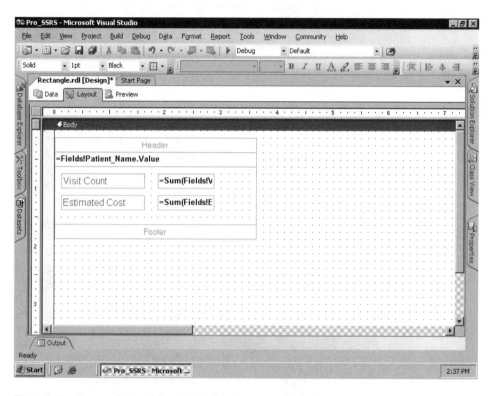

Figure 3-20. *Rectangle in table with formatting*

When you preview the report, the `Estimated_Cost` field doesn't appear to be in the correct format. The format should be currency. Each textbox contains formatting properties that you can set in several ways. While on the Layout tab, right-click the textbox that contains the sum of the `Estimated_Cost` data field, and select Properties. You can set the format for the textbox value on the Format tab of the Textbox Properties dialog box. By clicking the ellipsis button beside the Format Code field, you are presented with several available formats, with Currency being the one you will choose (see Figure 3-21). The default currency format with a code of "C" contains two decimal places. If you chose to do so, you can override this by choosing Custom and entering **C0** or **C1**, which would give you no decimal places or one decimal place, respectively. For this example, leave the default two decimal places.

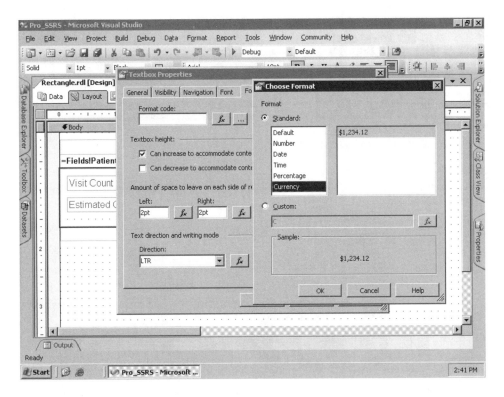

Figure 3-21. *Choose Format dialog box*

When you click OK and preview the report, you can see that you now have a single detail row that's formatted with vertically aligned textboxes with appropriate formatting, as shown in Figure 3-22. Using a rectangle in this manner allows more flexibility when adding several free-form elements to a report while still providing the multiple grouping levels of the table.

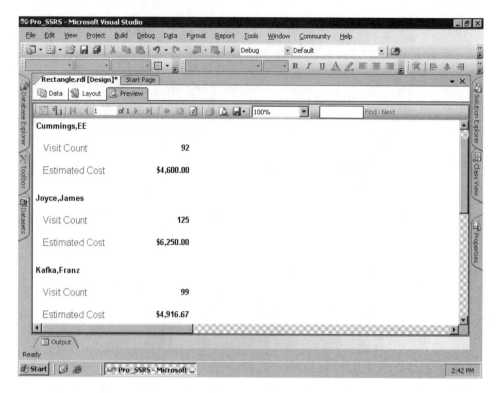

Figure 3-22. *Preview of table with formatting*

You can see the RDL output of the rectangle that you added to the table in Listing 3-6.

Listing 3-6. *RDL Output for Rectangle*

```
<Rectangle Name="rectangle1">
  <ReportItems>
    <Textbox Name="textbox2">
      <Style>
        <PaddingLeft>2pt</PaddingLeft>
        <FontSize>12pt</FontSize>
        <Color>Firebrick</Color>
        <PaddingBottom>2pt</PaddingBottom>
        <PaddingTop>2pt</PaddingTop>
        <PaddingRight>2pt</PaddingRight>
      </Style>
```

The completed report for the Rectangle object is called `Rectangle.rdl` and is located in the `Pro_SSRS` project.

Implementing a Matrix

You can use the Matrix data region to produce output formatted in rows and columns around aggregated measures. A matrix in SSRS is similar to a pivot table or a cross-tab report. You can group data fields in a matrix together with other fields, producing a natural summary and detail relationship. Simple single-level Matrix data regions with one column and one row provide valuable BI that you can deploy for quick analysis. However, to tap into the true benefit of a matrix, SSRS provides the ability to render the output in the interactive OWC format so that users can manipulate the matrix report for in-depth analysis. This is true for data derived from standard SQL queries or from data derived from an MDX query used with Analysis Services (covered in Chapter 10). For now, we'll introduce some of the properties of the Matrix data region and use the stored procedure, `Emp_Svc_Cost`, to populate it with the `Estimated_Cost` value for each patient over a period of time. You concatenate the field values for `Year` and `Month` to use for the column grouping section of the matrix and `Patient_Name` for the row grouping.

The starting point report for the Matrix object demonstrated in this section is available in the `Pro_SSRS` project in the Source Code area for the book on the Apress site. This report is called `Matrix Start.rdl`.

By default, only three cells are in a Matrix data region that defines Columns, Rows, and Data cells, as shown in Figure 3-23. You can use the fourth blank cell at the top left for a label or for an expression-and-parameter combination that can control the layout of the matrix itself. Chapter 9 discusses how to change the default static grouping of a matrix report by using a parameter value, where you use a matrix report to analyze SSRS execution statistics.

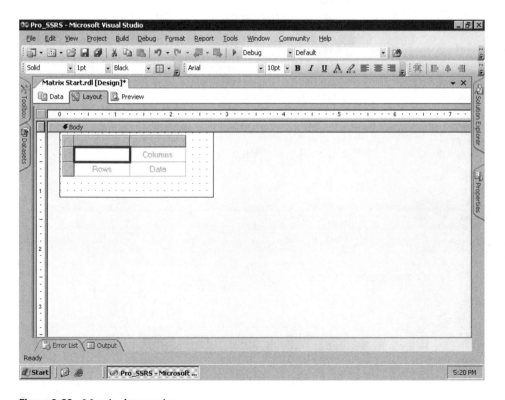

Figure 3-23. *Matrix data region*

With the `Matrix Start.rdl` report open, double-click the Matrix object in the Toolbox, which will automatically add a matrix to the design area of the report. Next, drag two fields onto the matrix, `Patient_Name` and `Estimated_Cost` from the `emp_svc_cost` dataset, which go in the Rows and Data areas, respectively. For the Columns area, define an expression that concatenates the `Service_Year` and `Service_Month` fields. The expression is as follows:

```
=Fields!Year.Value & " - " & Fields!Month.Value
```

You also use this expression to create a custom grouping with the combined fields. To group the Columns area on the expression, right-click the column field, select Edit Group, place the expression in the Group On section, and select OK. Next, left-align the `Estimated_Cost` field, and set the formatting to Currency, as demonstrated in the previous section. When you preview the report, you can see in Figure 3-24 that the matrix shows the estimated cost of care for the familiar patients for each month they had service.

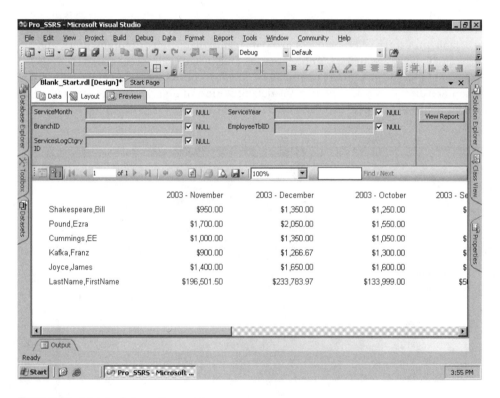

Figure 3-24. *Matrix data region preview*

You can see the RDL output of the matrix in Listing 3-7.

Listing 3-7. *Matrix RDL Listing*

```
<Matrix Name="matrix1">
  <Corner>
    <ReportItems>
      <Textbox Name="textbox1">
        <Style>
          <PaddingLeft>2pt</PaddingLeft>
          <PaddingBottom>2pt</PaddingBottom>
          <PaddingTop>2pt</PaddingTop>
          <PaddingRight>2pt</PaddingRight>
        </Style>
        <ZIndex>3</ZIndex>
        <rd:DefaultName>textbox1</rd:DefaultName>
        <CanGrow>true</CanGrow>
```

The completed report for the Matrix object is called `Matrix.rdl` and is available in the `Pro_SSRS` project.

Implementing a Chart

The Chart data region of SSRS, like the Matrix data region, allows multiple grouping levels from a single dataset. Instead of the column- and row-level groupings that the Matrix data region provides, the Chart data region uses Series, Categories, and Values. You can set many properties for a chart, and as with all other data regions, a chart can use expressions to define its properties. Also, like other data regions, you can place charts by themselves or scope them within another region such as a List or Table data region. For example, you could use a simple chart to show the overall visits by type of clinician, which in your stored procedure is determined by the `Service_Type` field. You could also add the chart to a cell in a table that's grouped by patient and time frame, such as Month and Year. The chart would show for each grouping a visit count for that patient over time. Let's add a chart to the report that uses the `Emp_Svc_Cost` stored procedure. For the chart, you will add three familiar fields, one for each chart area: Series, Categories, and Values will contain `Patient_Name`, `Employee_Name`, and `Visit_Count`, respectively.

The starting-point report for the Chart object demonstrated in this section is available in the `Pro_SSRS` project in the Source Code area for the book on the Apress Web site (http://www.apress.com). This report is called, creatively enough, `Chart Start.rdl`.

1. To begin, open the `Chart Start.rdl` report to the Layout tab, and click the Chart tool in the Toolbox to add the Chart object to the design area. After you add the Chart object, you can see each of the three areas of the chart that hold the fields you add.

2. Drag the `Visit_Count` field to the Drop Data Fields Here area.

3. Next, drag the `Patient_Name` field to the Drop Series Fields Here area.

4. Finally, drag `Employee_Name` to the Drop Category Fields Here area (see Figure 3-25).

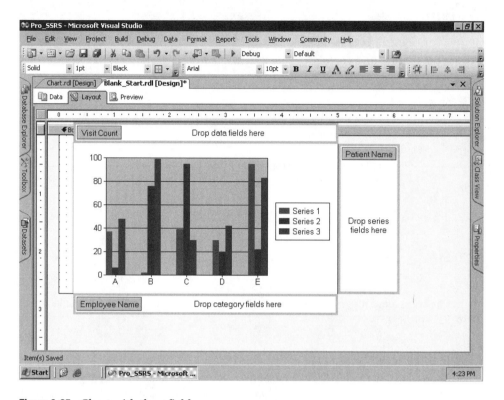

Figure 3-25. *Chart with three fields*

Before you preview the chart, let's look at its properties. By default, the chart is a column type. You'll modify several properties of the chart to add functionality and visual appeal. Right-click in the chart area on the Layout tab, and select Properties. On the General tab, change the Chart Type option to Bar, and set the Chart Sub-Type option to Stacked. Next, change the Palette option to Light. The properties should look like Figure 3-26.

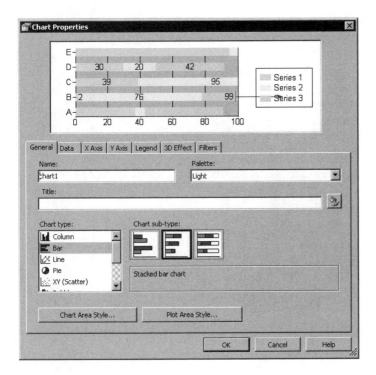

Figure 3-26. *Chart properties*

You might notice in Figure 3-26 that black numbers are in the chart. These don't appear by default. These are called *point labels* and can be set from the Data tab of the Chart Properties dialog box. On the Data tab, select the Edit button for the Values section of the chart. From the dialog box that displays, click the Point Labels tab, select the Show Point Labels checkbox, and set the label expression to be the same as the data itself, as follows:

```
=Sum(Fields!Visit_Count.Value)
```

Adding this expression puts data labels, or pointers, on the report so that users can easily discern what values are set for the data series. Finally, click the 3D Effect tab, and check the Display Chart with 3D Visual Effect box. You also choose Cylinder on the same tab and set the Horizontal Rotation to 20 degrees. You can now click OK and preview the chart, as displayed in Figure 3-27.

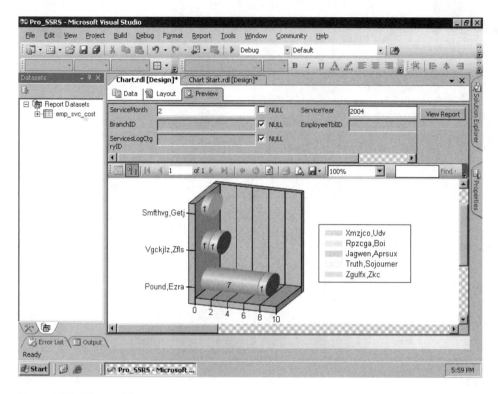

Figure 3-27. *Chart with custom properties*

■**Note** We chose to narrow down the list for visits that happened in 2004. This was intentional, as it limited the data to an easily viewable amount; otherwise, the chart would have been populated with too many patients and would appear jumbled. The `Chart Start.rdl` report has a default parameter value of 2004 as well, so your results will match.

You can see the RDL output for the chart you just created in Listing 3-8.

Listing 3-8. *Chart RDL Sample*

```
<Chart Name="chart1">
  <ThreeDProperties>
    <Enabled>true</Enabled>
    <Rotation>30</Rotation>
    <Inclination>20</Inclination>
    <Shading>Simple</Shading>
    <WallThickness>50</WallThickness>
    <DrawingStyle>Cylinder</DrawingStyle>
  </ThreeDProperties>
```

```
<Style>
  <BackgroundColor>White</BackgroundColor>
</Style>
```

The completed report for the Chart object is in the Pro_SSRS project and is called Chart.rdl.

Implementing a Image

Having images in a report can give it a polished look while extending its value as a resource. Fortunately, SSRS includes an image tool that can add images from a variety of locations and supports many standard image formats. Our health-care application stores many images in a SQL Server database as Binary Large Objects (BLOBs), as part of a patient electronic medical record (EMR). You can load any type of image into the database and associate it with the patient using a front-end image retrieval application. Once the image is in the database and tagged to a patient's identification number, which is a field in the database, you can use SSRS to display that image in a report. For this sample, you will continue with the theme of famous author patients and add their images to a simple report. The starting-point report for the Image report object is called Image Start.rdl. Since much of the report is constructed using objects you have already used, the starting point is already laid out with these object included. The dataset that is used for this report includes demographic information for patients who have their photographs stored in a database table called DocumentImage in the Pro_SSRS database. You can use the predefined dataset, called Get_Image, for the Image Start.rdl report, which simply returns patient demographic information for three patients along with their photos.

Begin by opening the Image Start.rdl report in the Pro_SSRS project and clicking the Layout tab. Next, select the Image tool from the Toolbox, and click into a blank area of the List data region that is already set up in this report. As you can see in Figure 3-28, you're presented with the Image Wizard when you add the Image tool to the list. You can choose several ways to retrieve images. For example, you could use an image that you've added to the project, or you could embed the image directly into the report. This option would serve you well if the report contained a single image that wouldn't be used again and was intended to be distributed to a variety of sources that might not have access to the image at any other location. Choose Database for the source image, and click Next.

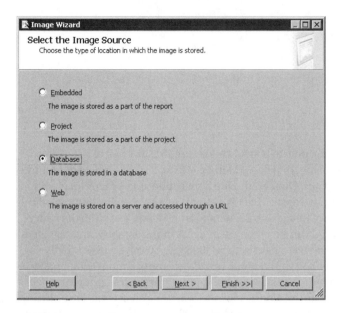

Figure 3-28. *Image Wizard source selection*

The next step of the Image Wizard is to select the dataset from where the image will be returned. The Get_Image dataset returns images that are associated with each patient. It contains limited fields for the sample, and you're retrieving only a patient photo to add to the list. However, if this were a real report, you could use other images that would be standard to a patient record, such as X-ray images or photos of a patient's wounds. Even scanned images of paper documentation or faxes could be stored in the database and effectively added to a full report. Figure 3-29 shows the selection of the image field and Multipurpose Internet Mail Extensions (MIME) type, such as BMP or JPEG. The images in this example are stored in JPEG format.

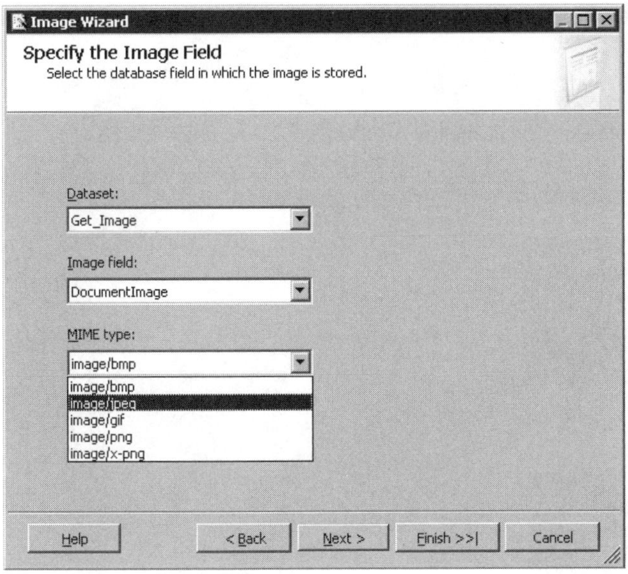

Figure 3-29. *Image field selection*

When you click Finish in the Image Wizard and preview the report, the two photo images are correctly associated to the patient, as shown in Figure 3-30.

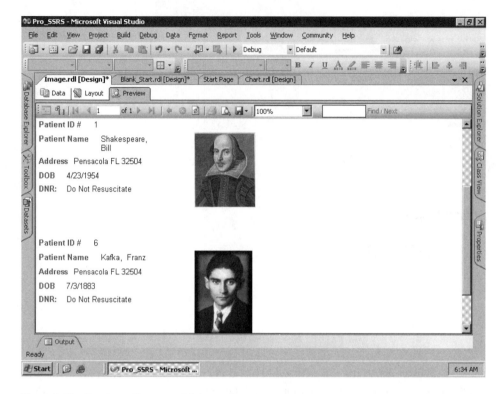

Figure 3-30. *Preview of report with images*

Listing 3-9 shows sample RDL elements for images.

Listing 3-9. *RDL Output for Image*

```
<Image Name="image1">
  <ZIndex>10</ZIndex>
  <Top>0.375in</Top>
  <MIMEType>image/jpeg</MIMEType>
  <Height>0.75in</Height>
  <Width>0.75in</Width>
  <Source>Database</Source>
  <Style />
  <Value>=Fields!DocumentImage.Value</Value>
  <Left>2.875in</Left>
  <Sizing>AutoSize</Sizing>
</Image>
```

The completed `Image` object report is called `Images.rdl` and is located in the `Pro_SSRS` project.

Implementing Two Simple Report Design Tips

For a version 2 product, SSRS provides invaluable tools that cover most of the bases when designing distinctive, interactive, and flexible reports. However, a few—we'll call them *desirable*—features weren't included in the available versions of SSRS. In this case, we're referring to the lack of support for report styles or templates. Though SSRS does include some templates in the Report Wizard, which we cover in the next chapter, you have no way to select a template for a blank report. In other words, you need to create every report from scratch from a blank design, and you need to apply the styles as you build the report. For reports that have a similar look and feel, this can be repetitive and time-consuming. You can use the following two tips to add some level of the desired functionality.

Using a Report Template

To address this lack of support, we've created our own template reports. These reports are built to the point of having predefined parameters—which are standard across all the reports—as well as predefined groupings. Also, you can add any formatting such as standard color patterns and report titles, defined by a global collection value ReportName, to the template file or files. Once you create the template files, you can copy or paste them into the project as starting points for new reports. Or, if you place them in the correct folder, they're available when the designer opts to add a new report. Simply by placing the template RDL file into the location Drive:\Program Files\Microsoft Visual Studio 8\Common7\IDE\PrivateAssemblies\ ProjectItems\ReportProject when you add a new report to the project, the template file is available like any other report or wizard. You can see this in Figure 3-31, where the template file is called Custom_Report_Template.

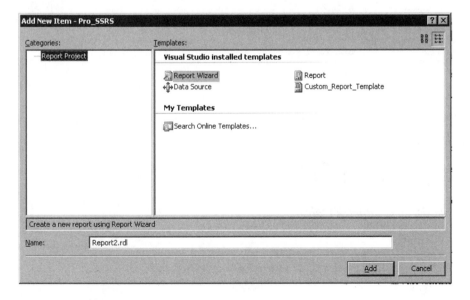

Figure 3-31. *Report template file selection*

Creating a Multicolumn Report for Printing Labels

The second tip deals with a need that's similar to styles and templates. Our company has many reports that produce labels using standard label forms. We noticed that when we began looking at SSRS to deliver this functionality, we happened upon the best way to produce data-driven labels: using multiple columns. We discussed multiple columns previously when looking at the Report Properties dialog box. Setting multiple columns for a report forces the data to be placed on a single multicolumn page. This "snaking" effect is perfect for labels. Figure 3-32 shows the output of a report we created using four columns with a single List data region that contains patient address labels. The list was sized to be 2 inches by 1 inch, with appropriate spacing set between the columns. The data shows the familiar author patients with other patients represented by LastName, FirstName. We've modified these name field values in the database for security reasons; however, these are legitimate individual database fields.

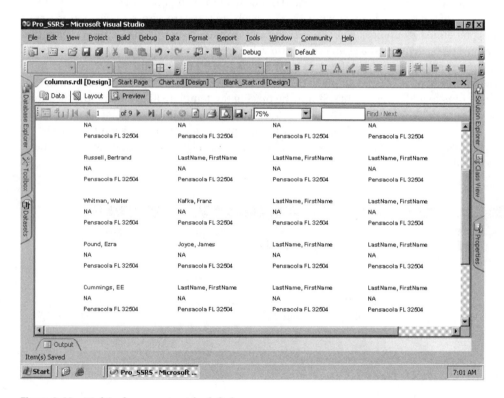

Figure 3-32. *Multicolumn output for labels*

Summary

In this chapter, we covered a big chunk of the BIDS IDE and the tools you'll use to build a reporting solution. You learned that each report consists of defined elements that are based on a defined schema in the RDL, which gives SSRS the advantage of standardization. We covered the report objects that make up reports and viewed their properties and functionality. You also saw for each object how the graphical design components are directly translated to RDL through the design process. Now that you're more comfortable with the design environment, you'll learn how to use it to design and deploy some real reports. In the next chapter, we'll show how to take a step-by-step approach to adding these report items to a report that was designed as part of an SSRS migration for our health-care application.

CHAPTER 4

∎∎∎

Building Reports

In the previous chapter, you laid the foundation for your first report by creating a query and subsequent stored procedure. You also learned about the fundamental elements used to build reports and are now familiar with the design environment. So, it is time to put all the pieces together and begin building reports. You can easily apply the concepts in this chapter to any company that uses SQL Server and relational database systems. This chapter will focus primarily on creating a reporting solution based on data from a SQL Server health-care database; it will use many of the available report elements in SSRS.

The report you will be creating in this chapter is called the Employee Service Cost report. This report will utilize the same query and stored procedure, Emp_Svc_Cost, that you have been working with since Chapter 2 to provide the report data. As a reminder, the query returns detail records that represent services, such as a skilled nurse or home health aide visit, performed for patients. Each type of service has an associated cost for the health-care company. This report, when complete, will show important cost points based on associated data provided by the query, such as the patient's diagnosis, the employees who performed the services, the date of each service, and the branch location of the patient. By grouping and sorting the report at these cost points, the user will be able to see the cost of services from the individual patient all the way up to the branch location, which might serve hundreds of patients. You will group and calculate the cost amount at each level.

Specifically, in the following sections, you will create the Employee Service Cost report initially with the Report Wizard, which produces a report based on predefined selections, and then from scratch. We will show the process of using the wizard for demonstration purposes only and therefore will not continue with the report that it produces. For the report you build from scratch, you will add all the features that the Report Wizard can add plus much more. The following list highlights the design goals for the Employee Service Cost report:

- Step through adding a base report that uses the Table data region based on the dataset you defined for the Emp_Svc_Cost query.

- Add several basic formatting elements to the report.

- Add interactivity to the report with document mapping, visibility, hyperlink actions, and interactive sorting, which is a new feature of SSRS for SQL Server 2005. Both document mapping and hyperlink actions allow the user to navigate to defined locations either within the report or outside the report, such as a Web site. In this chapter, you will use visibility properties within your report to expand and collapse report items from summary to detail. Interactive sorting gives an SSRS report versatility by allowing it to be sorted, in much the same way Microsoft Outlook allows sorting by clicking column headers.

- Add parameters to the report automatically by changing the dataset from a query to a parameterized stored procedure. You will also add other datasets to populate the parameters defined by the stored procedure.

- Learn how to use multivalued parameters using a modified stored procedure and UDF.

- Add a filter to the Table data region to show only service types that are visits.

- Add a Chart data region for the top ten diagnoses to the report.

- Add the final touches to the report, such as a page header and footer, title, and page numbers.

In addition, as you begin to work more closely with report and query parameters, you will learn how to use a new feature of SSRS for SQL Server 2005: multivalued parameters. As mentioned in previous chapters, multivalued parameters require special consideration when designing the underlying query, so in this chapter you will use a modified version of your stored procedure that takes advantage of a UDF; this will teach you how to best utilize this new and much anticipated feature.

In the preceding chapters, we covered the steps for creating the solution, project, and data source that your report will use, so we will not cover these steps again here. We will, however, show how to use the same data source properties to connect to the health-care database where the data for your report resides. The same database also contains the stored procedure you created in Chapter 2, `Emp_Svc_Cost`, that you will use later in this chapter.

Creating a Report with the Report Wizard

In many scenarios, the Report Wizard is a fast method for creating a basic report that can be further enhanced before deployment. The Report Wizard is suitable for reports that are primarily data listings that do not require much special formatting. In this section, you will step through the Report Wizard to create the Employee Service Cost report before designing the same report manually.

To open the Report Wizard in your report project, right-click the `Reports` folder in the Solution Explorer and select Add New Report. The first wizard screen defines the data source. For this example, check New Data Source; however, you also have the choice to use a shared data source that has already been defined as part of the project. Supply the same data source information as you did in the previous chapter to connect to the health-care database. The connection string should look similar to the following:

```
Data Source=localhost;Initial Catalog=Pro_SSRS
```

The next screen in the wizard defines the query. Paste the query you created in Chapter 2 into the Query String area (see Figure 4-1). You can open this query from the `Query` folder in the code download for the book. The file is called `Report_Wizard_Query.sql`. Clicking the Query Builder button launches the graphical query designer.

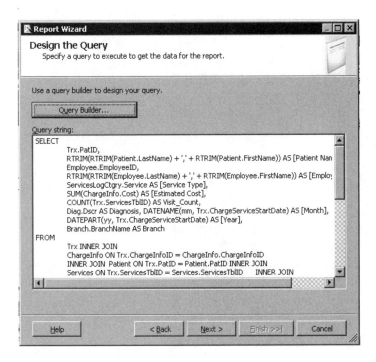

Figure 4-1. *Pasting the query in the Query String area*

■Note The query designer in the Report Wizard does not support stored procedures or other nonstandard SQL queries, such as LDAP, which you will use later in this chapter.

The next screen of the Report Wizard asks whether the report should be in tabular or matrix form. Selecting Tabular will trigger the wizard to provide grouping information on the next screen; selecting Matrix will provide a similar screen for rows and columns instead of groups. For this example, select Tabular then click Next and choose the grouping and detail layout to show Year as the primary group, with Month, EmployeeClassID, and Employee_Name next. For details, you want to see the patient-specific information—Diagnosis, Visit_Count, Estimated_Cost, and Service_Type—as shown in Figure 4-2.

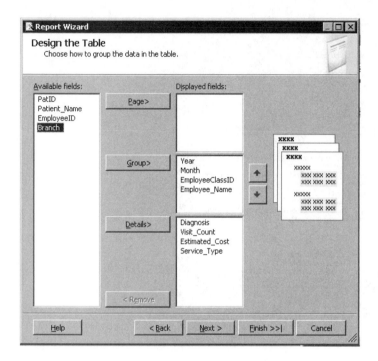

Figure 4-2. *Report Wizard group and details selections*

Once you have grouped the data that will be in the report, the next two screens are primarily for formatting. Here you can specify whether you want the report to have a stepped or block layout, as well as whether the report will include subtotals and provide drill-down functionality. You can also choose a custom style for the report.

■**Tip** You might notice that the wizard is similar in appearance to the one provided for Microsoft Access. Access and SSRS share many of the same features, and the Access report format is currently the only supported format that can be automatically converted to RDL. A caveat exists, though, when converting: any Visual Basic for Applications (VBA) code you have written in Access will not migrate to SSRS. You will have to rewrite that functionality.

For now, choose Stepped with No Drill-Down Functionality, apply the Corporate style to the report, click Next in the wizard, and change the name from the default, ReportX, where X is the next number in sequence of created reports, to Employee Cost Report. Next, check the Preview Report box, and then click Finish. After a few moments, the resultant report appears. Though at first glance it appears to need many cosmetic changes, such as extending the size of the several columns such as Employee Name and Diagnosis and formatting the Estimated Cost column for currency, the report is at least functional. It would need a good deal of work to get it the way you want, and assuming you accepted one of the default styles, this would be a good starting point for modification, as shown in Figure 4-3.

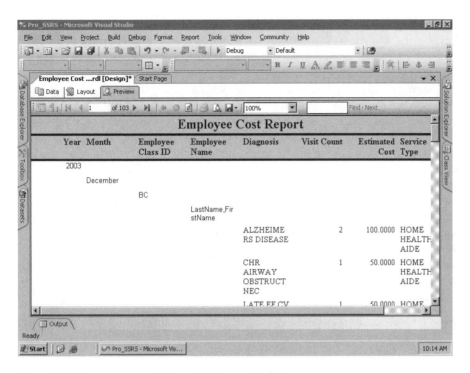

Figure 4-3. *Report generated from the Report Wizard*

To fully take advantage of the flexibility of SSRS and the report design environment of BIDS, let's create the same report from scratch.

Building Reports from Scratch

When working with a blank report, the first decision will be to choose which data regions to use in the body of the report. This decision is driven mostly by the type of data you are working with and by the report audience. For example, a chief executive officer (CEO) might not be concerned with details, preferring to see summary information about the status of the business products and services, and therefore would be more inclined to view a matrix report with column and row totals. However, in the initial report, you will be working with the Table data region because you want to show the interrelationships between patients and employees with multiple groupings in tabular rows, not columns.

In this section, you will follow specific steps to get your report to a basic starting point by adding a Table data region, and then you will continue to add formatting and functionality. When you are finished, the report will contain many SSRS features, including interactive drill-down and navigation links, custom formatting, interactive sorting, populated drop-down parameters, and a chart that displays the top ten diagnoses by cost. You will finish the report by adding several design touches, such as page numbers and execution times. You will also examine how to modify the report to work with multivalue parameters.

For this project, you will add a new report from the Solution Explorer and create
a dataset that uses the same query from the previous section of this chapter for the Report
Wizard. For ease, we have included the starting-point report in the Pro_SSRS project. The
EmployeeServiceCost_Start report already has the datasets and initial query defined for the
localhost SQL Server, which should match your environment. You will begin by using just
the basic query and not the stored procedure. The dataset you will use to begin with in the
EmployeeServiceCost_Start report is called Emp_Svc_Cost. Later in the "Setting Report Parameters
with Stored Procedures" section, you will modify the dataset to use the stored procedure and
see how the parameters defined in the stored procedure will automatically create the report
parameters.

In the following sections, you will go through several steps to add functionality to a single
report. The steps are provided so that you can walk through the process of building the report,
starting with the EmployeeServiceCost_Start report; however, at several intervals, you may
choose to open one of the several sample reports that reflect the completed steps. If a report is
available, we will point it out in the text.

With the EmployeeServiceCost_Start report open in BIDS, move to the Layout tab. The
following steps get you to your starting point in the report, where you will begin to apply more
advanced formatting and logic:

1. Drag the Table report element to a blank section of the design grid.

2. Right-click the center table column, and select Insert Column to the Right.

3. Drag the last three fields—Employee_Name, Estimated_Cost, and Visit_Count—to the
   three last three columns on the detail row in the order listed. Notice that the column
   headings—Employee Name, Estimated Cost, and Visit Count—were automatically
   created for you for each field dragged to the detail row. You will leave these here for
   now and add formatting in the following sections.

4. Edit the Visit_Count and Estimated_Cost field expressions to be sums, as in
   =Sum(Fields!Estimated_Cost.Value).

5. Right-click the detail row, and select Insert Group.

6. In the Group On ➤ Expression drop-down list, select =Fields!Diagnosis.Value. Uncheck
   the Group Footer checkbox for the Diagnosis group. Enter **Diagnosis** for the group
   name, and select OK. Drag the field Diagnosis into the first column of the new Diagnosis
   group header.

7. Perform steps 5 and 6 for ServiceType and PatientName, replacing the Group On
   expression with their respective field values for step 6, =Fields!Service_Type.Value
   and =Fields!Patient_Name.Value. Enter **ServiceType** and **PatientName** for the respective group names, uncheck Group Footer, and click OK. Drag the respective fields
   Service_Type and Patient_Name into the first column of each of the groups you just created.

8. Right-click the detail row, and select Edit Group. In the Group On drop-down list,
   select =Fields!Employee_Name.Value.

After these eight steps, the report is starting to take form, as you can see in the preview.
Though not yet aesthetically appealing, it displays the data in the appropriate, hard-fixed
groupings and is tabulated so that it is easy to discern the detailed service information, such
as the cost and counts of services for each patient (see Figure 4-4).

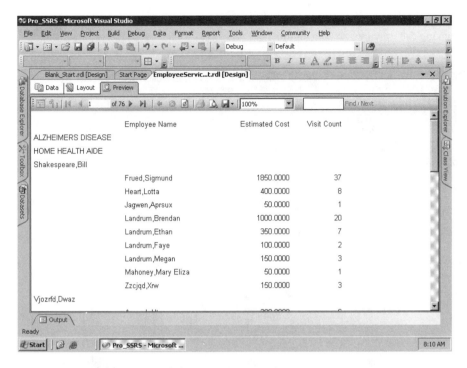

Figure 4-4. *Employee Service Cost report details and groups*

Formatting the Output

You can modify several quick and easy report properties to add a more professional look and feel to the report:

- Border Style

- Format

- Padding

By using the Shift or Control key, or by clicking and dragging the mouse, it is easy to apply report properties to many cells simultaneously. For the Employee Name, Estimated Cost, and Service Count header cells, you will add a border to the bottom, separating the record header from the actual data. First, highlight the three header column cells by holding down the Control key and clicking each cell. Next, open or expand the Properties window. The Properties window contains a Border Style property for each area of the selected cells—top, bottom, left, and right. For this example, select Solid for the bottom border.

With the Properties window still open, click the Estimated Cost detail row cell. Format the cell in the Properties window to be currency by adding the formatting command C0 for the Format property.

Two of the groups inside the report, Service Type and Patient, would be more distinguishable if they were indented. You can select each group cell individually and in the Properties window modify the Padding property from the default of 2 points to 10 points for Service Type and 15 points for Patient Name.

After you apply the formatting, you can immediately see how these changes affect the output by clicking the Preview tab (see Figure 4-5).

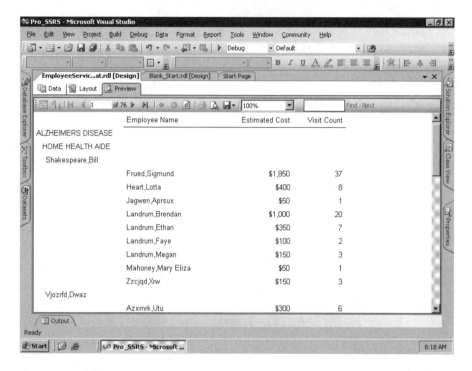

Figure 4-5. *Report output with formatting*

The EmployeeServiceCost_Format.rdl report in the Pro_SSRS project has the three formatting elements applied.

Adding Subtotals

Having subtotals at each grouping level makes the report much easier to read for the user. This is especially true if the report will have interactive drill-down features, as yours will have. Adding subtotals to the groups is as easy as dragging the fields that will be summed to the appropriate position in the table. When fields are dragged into a grouped row, the Sum function is automatically applied to the field expression, as in =Sum(Fields!Diagnosis.Value). The same applies to the detail row if any detail grouping is defined. For this report, you have defined a group for the Employee_Name field in the detail row. This forces the report to calculate the sums of the Estimated_Cost and Visit_Count fields for each employee. For this report, this is all that is required, but for many other reports you will be creating, you will need to include the detail records for a more granular analysis.

In preparation for adding interactivity to the report, you will sum the Estimated_Cost and Visit_Count fields at all grouping levels by dragging the two fields to the Estimated Cost and Visit Count locations in each group heading row—in this case, for Diagnosis, Service Type, and Patient Name. You should also make the topmost grouping, in this case the Diagnosis field, bold by holding the Control key and clicking to highlight each of the Estimated Cost and Visit Count values in the Diagnosis group and then clicking the Bold button on the toolbar. With the bold formatting applied, the summed values at the group level will be easy to distinguish from the detail row values. You should also format the `Estimated_Cost` field to be currency as you did previously for the detail row.

The output of the report, which you can see by selecting the Preview tab, has much more valuable information now for each grouping. For Alzheimer's disease, for example, you can now see that there were 1,249 services for a total estimated cost of $62,350, and the bold formatting helps visually separate the values. The patient Bill Shakespeare (whose name is indented because of the padding you applied to the Patient group) is an Alzheimer's patient and has had 82 of the 1,036 home health aide visits. You can further see each employee's visit count and the cost for this patient in the detail rows (see Figure 4-6).

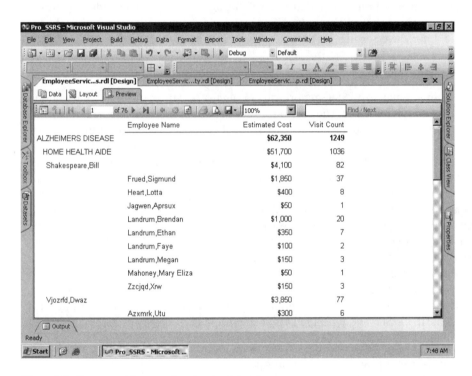

Figure 4-6. *Report with grouping level subtotals*

The `EmployeeServiceCost_Subtotals.rdl` report in the `Pro_SSRS` project includes subtotals.

Adding Interactivity

Regardless of the audience for a particular report—whether it is a decision maker interested in on-screen summarized data or a knowledge worker who needs the ability to print reports—interactivity within the report makes navigating to specific information easier and more efficient. You can provide interactivity within an SSRS report in several ways. You will be working with four basic types of interactivity in the following sections:

- *Document mapping*: Provides a navigation pane within the report with values based on a field or grouping.

- *Visibility*: Adds interactivity to a report by hiding and showing report items based on user input.

- *Interactive sorting*: This is a new feature of SSRS for SQL Server 2005 that allows users to interactively select how the report data will be sorted.

- *Hyperlink actions*: Allows the user to click a report item that is linked to a location within the same report or external to the report.

The different rendering formats provided with SSRS, which are covered in detail in Chapter 5, accommodate viewing and printing reports to meet the needs of different types of workers. However, this produces a limitation in that some of the functionality of one rendering format is not available in other formats. This is most evident when working with interactivity, as you will see in the "Interactive Sorting" section.

Document Mapping

Creating a document map in an SSRS report will present users with an integrated navigation pane when the report is rendered. The user can select an item in the navigation pane, which will cause the report to jump to the position where that item is located. In the example report, for instance, a user might be interested in viewing information about Alzheimer's patients. You can create a document map for the Diagnosis group in the report so that when the user selects Alzheimer's from the navigation pane, the report will automatically skip to that section; in other words, the user will not have to manually search through the report to find the desired information. You can also add document maps at multiple levels, creating a hierarchical selection in the navigation pane. Keeping with the example, you can add a document map to the Service_Type group in addition to the Diagnosis group; the user can then expand Alzheimer's in the navigation pane to see all the types of services—home health aide, for example—that have been performed for each diagnosis.

You create document maps by adding an expression to the Document Map Label property available for individual report items or for groups. By following these steps, you will add a document map label to the Service_Type and Diagnosis groups:

1. On the Layout tab, right-click the entire row for the second-level grouping, which is the Service_Type group, and select Edit Group.

2. On the General tab of the Grouping and Sorting properties dialog box, select =Fields!Service_Type.Value in the Document Map Label drop-down list and click OK.

3. Complete steps 1 and 2 for the Diagnosis group, which is the first-level grouping above Service_Type. Select =Fields!Diagnosis.Value for the Document Map Label option.

Now when you preview the report, the navigation pane will automatically be displayed on the left side of the report. The preview, which is in HTML by default, displays in one of the rendering formats that supports document mapping, such as PDF (see Figure 4-7).

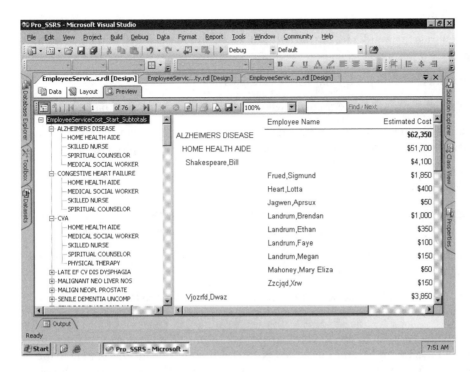

Figure 4-7. *Report with navigation pane from document map*

The `EmployeeServiceCost_DocumentMap.rdl` report in the `Pro_SSRS` project includes a document map.

■**Note** Adobe Acrobat views document mapping as bookmarks when the report is rendered in PDF. Bookmarks in SSRS perform a different function altogether. They are embedded within the report, and report items are assigned bookmark links.

Visibility

Another feature of SSRS is the ability to show or hide areas of the rendered report based on user input. Often users want to see only summary information on a report but be able to drill into the summary data to see the detail information if necessary. Report designers might make two reports, a summary and a detail report, which have to be updated and maintained separately. The reports are often based on the same query. Fortunately, SSRS's ability to show or hide report data does away with the need to create separate reports. The visibility properties for report items control showing and hiding report items.

Let's assume you have distributed your report to your intended audience, and they have come back with "suggestions" for how to improve the report—this is real-world reporting, after all. They indicate they would like to see the following:

- Summary totals for the visit count and the estimated cost of each diagnosis when the report is first rendered, but with the ability to drill to the detail of the patient and employee if warranted

- The number of patients who have a specific diagnosis

- The number of individual employees who have provided care for these patients

With SSRS this is fairly straightforward, and you can knock out an improved report quickly. You just need to follow these design steps before modifying the visibility properties:

1. On the Layout tab, right-click the entire Employee Name column, and select Insert Column to the Right.

2. Highlight and delete the Employee Name column header text. With the drill-down feature you will be adding with visibility properties, this column header will no longer be needed.

3. Enter **Employee Count** and **Patient Count** as the new column header text in the second and third columns, respectively.

4. Resize the second and third columns in the table from right to left so that they are approximately 1 inch each.

5. Highlight every cell in the Service Type, Patient Name, and Details rows. You can accomplish this by holding down the Control key and clicking the row marker to the left of the first column in the table. Once all the rows are highlighted, select an 8-point font size from the formatting toolbar.

You can control the visibility state of report items, hidden or visible, by setting visibility property values. You can hide report items at any level in the report and toggle their visibility property values when a user clicks the + or – icon to show or hide them. The toggle point of the hidden items is another report level, such as a group. In this example, you would like to hide every level except the `Diagnosis` and `Service_Type` fields but give the user the ability to show or hide the details. To begin, hide every group except Diagnosis and Service_Type. The steps to accomplish this are as follows:

1. Right-click the detail row icon, and select Edit Group.

2. On the Visibility tab, select Hidden.

3. Check Visibility Can Be Toggled by Another Report Item.

4. In the Report Item drop-down list, select `Patient_Name`. If `Patient_Name` is not displayed in the drop-down list, you may have to type it in.

5. Perform steps 1 through 4 for the Patient group, selecting or typing **Service_Type** as the toggle report item.

The other two requests were to be able to see the patient and employee totals for each diagnosis. You can add an expression, `CountDistinct`, to the report that will count each unique patient and employee and calculate the amounts at the diagnosis level. The syntax used for the patient count is as follows:

```
=CountDistinct(Fields!FieldName.Value)
```

By adding the CountDistinct expression for the field PatID (which you know to be unique per patient) as well as for the field EmployeeID, it will be much easier to see at a glance how many patients with a specific diagnosis have been cared for.

Place the following two expressions for the Diagnosis group in the cells just below the Employee Count and Patient Count header cells:

```
=CountDistinct(Fields!EmployeeID.Value)
=CountDistinct(Fields!PatID.Value)
```

Though the report is still similar to the noninteractive report, with the drill-down additions it will look much different when previewed (see Figure 4-8).

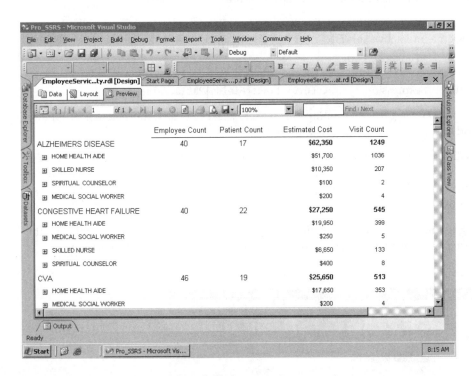

Figure 4-8. *Report with interactive drill-down*

The EmployeeServiceCost_Visibility.rdl report in the Pro_SSRS project includes the visibility properties.

Interactive Sorting

It never fails when deploying a report to a large audience: someone will ask that the report be sorted in a certain way that usually differs from the way it was originally designed. When this scenario happens, typically the report designer is torn between creating a second, almost identical report with custom sorting to appease the requestor and placing the request in queue for a future enhancement to the report. A new feature of SSRS for SQL Server 2005, interactive sorting, alleviates this need and allows users to sort the report at runtime on any number of fields that have been defined to use this functionality.

In the sample report, you know that you have a broad audience that may use this report for different purposes. A chief financial officer (CFO), for example, may want to view the report to see which diagnosis has the most number of visits, while another user may need to understand how many patients have a certain diagnosis and would like the report sorted by patient count and not visit count. In this section, you will add interactive sorting to the report to meet these two needs, knowing that it is possible to sort the report in any other criteria if it is requested without having to create additional reports based on a user subdivision.

Since you know that the interactive sorting you will apply to your report will be patient count and not visit count, all you have to do is add this criteria to each of the textboxes where the users will click to change the sorting based on their needs. Add the interactive sorting to the Patient Count and Visit Count header cells by following these steps:

1. On the Layout tab, right-click the Patient Count header textbox, and select Properties. Click the Interactive Sort tab.

2. Check the Add an Interactive Sort Action to This Textbox box.

3. In the sort expression, type **=CountDistinct(Fields!PatID.Value)**.

4. For the Data Region or Grouping to Sort area, select Choose Data Region or Grouping, and select Emp_Svc_Cost in the drop-down list.

5. In the Evaluate Sort Expression in this Scope area, select Choose Data Region or Grouping Diagnosis in the drop-down list, and click OK. This tells the sort to count all the distinct patient IDs and sort this at the data level. The expression will be evaluated in the Diagnosis group.

6. Right-click the Visit Count header cell, and perform steps 1 through 5, replacing the sort expression with =Sum(Fields!Visit_Count.Value), as shown in Figure 4-9.

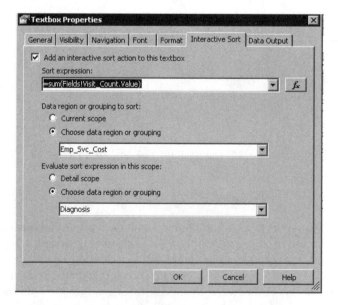

Figure 4-9. *Interactive sort properties for the visit count*

When you view the report with the new interactive sorting expressions in place, you can see the automatic addition of a selectable sort icon in the Patient Count and Visit Count header fields, as shown in Figure 4-10. When a user clicks this icon in the browser, the report will automatically resort to showing either the most or least number of patients per diagnosis or the most or least number of visits per diagnosis. Figure 4-10 is showing the diagnosis with the most number of patients, which is Physical Therapy NEC with 103 unique patients diagnosed with this illness. The user could also choose to sort the report in ascending or descending order by the number of visits.

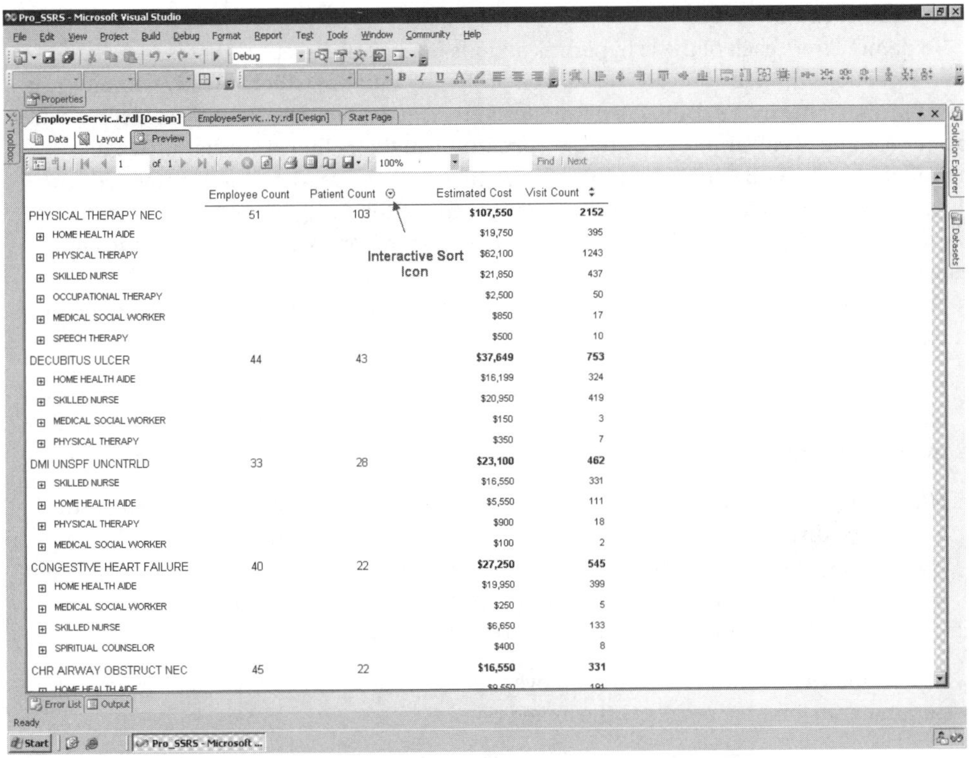

Figure 4-10. *Report sorted interactively to show the number of patients*

Interactive sorting is a textbox property and is typically used on column headings in a Table or Matrix data region. A single textbox can control sorting for one or more data regions as long as they are within the same scope or grouping. For example, it is possible to sort multiple tables that are nested within a List data region.

The `EmployeeServiceCost_InteractiveSort.rdl` report in the `Pro_SSRS` project includes interactive sorting.

Hyperlink Actions

Having the ability to link one report item, such as the contents of a textbox, to another report or URL adds another valuable level of interactivity in SSRS. By adding hyperlinks to an SSRS report, users can work with the report as they would an application or a Web page, making their tasks more efficient. In this section, you will learn how to add several links or actions to your reports to aid users in linking to other reports and locations, such as a company intranet site.

You can associate three basic actions with values in a report:

- Jumping to a bookmark

- Jumping to a URL

- Jumping to a report

You can find these on the Navigation tab of the report items that support these actions, such as textboxes and images.

To demonstrate each of these hyperlink actions, we will use a report that is more suited to hyperlink actions than the one you have been designing thus far, which already contains one level of interactivity in the drill-down functionality. The next report, Employee Listing, will provide a simple list of employees, grouped according to their clinical specialty. Two reports are available in the code download for the Employee Listing report. One is provided with only the dataset created so that you can step through the following procedures to create the report. It is called EmployeeListing_Start.rdl. The other report is a complete version called EmployeeListing.rdl.

You will add the three interactive hyperlink actions to the report to deliver the following features:

Bookmark: When the employee name is selected, the report will jump to a bookmarked location within the report that contains more details about the employee, such as the number of patients they have seen.

URL: You will also set up a link to the employee's department Web site, based on the employee's discipline or clinical specialty. You will also use a report parameter that you will set up specifically for the purpose of selecting the employee's branch location. When users select a branch location from a drop-down list provided with the report parameter, they will be taken to their own department's intranet site.

Report: You will add a link to your Employee Service Cost report that will pass an EmployeeID parameter to limit the results of the linked report.

The completed Employee Listing report will contain two Table data regions, one for summary information and one for detailed information about the employee's visits. You will add the hyperlink actions to the summary portion of the report, which will be the first page the user sees. Listing 4-1 shows the query for the dataset that delivers employee information. For this report, you will limit the employees to a known set, as shown in the WHERE clause, to keep the report small. Also, you will add a date range with two parameters, @DateFrom and @DateTo, that you will create and utilize later. The EmployeeListing_Start.rdl report contains default values for a date range from January 1, 2003, to the current date using the Now() function.

Listing 4-1. *Employee Listing Query*

```
SELECT
    Employee.EmployeeID, Employee.LastName,
    Employee.FirstName,
    Employee.EmployeeTblID,
    Employee.EmploymentTypeID AS EmploymentType,
    Employee.HireDate,
    Discipline.Dscr AS Discipline, Patient.LastName AS
    patLastname, Patient.FirstName AS patFirstname,
    Trx.ChargeServiceStartDate,Discipline.DisciplineID
FROM
    Employee INNER JOIN
    Trx INNER JOIN
    ChargeInfo ON Trx.ChargeInfoID = ChargeInfo.ChargeInfoID ON
    Employee.EmployeeTblID = ChargeInfo.EmployeeTblID INNER JOIN
    Discipline ON Employee.DisciplineTblID =
    Discipline.DisciplineTblID INNER JOIN
    Patient ON Trx.PatID = Patient.PatID
WHERE
    (Trx.ChargeServiceStartDate BETWEEN @DateFrom AND @DateTo)
```

To begin, open the EmployeeListing_Start.rdl report. The steps to produce the initial basic report as shown in Figure 4-11 are straightforward, with only a few pointers needed. First, you will be using a Table data region again, so simply drag the table to the report area on the Layout tab. Second, add a column to the default three columns of the table. Next, add the following fields onto the detail columns: EmployeeID, LastName, HireDate, and DisciplineID. The employee DisciplineID field references an employee's clinical specialty, such as Home Health Aide or Skilled Nurse. For the employee name, because the fields have been padded with spaces, you will want to use the rtrim function to concatenate the LastName and FirstName fields into one field that will replace the LastName field that you added to the second column and then change the header to Employee Name.

```
=rtrim(Fields!LastName.Value) & ", " & rtrim( Fields!FirstName.Value)
```

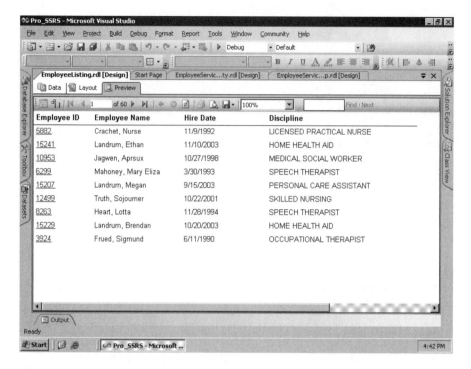

Figure 4-11. *Employee Listing report with hyperlink actions*

Additionally, when using dates, the default format is to include the date and time values, even if there is no time associated with the date. The hire date might look like this, for example: 10/20/2003 12:00:00 AM. By selecting the properties of the Hire Date cell, you can change the format from the default to a more standard format, such as 10/20/2003, excluding any time value. The format code for this date is d.

Next, because you are returning detail records, with more than one per employee, you need to group the detail row itself using the value of the Employee_Name field. You can do this by right-clicking the detail row and selecting Edit Group. In the Group On expression field, add the same trimmed employee name as shown in the previous code line. Now when you preview the report, you have your list of employees to which you can add hyperlink actions. Finally, force a page break after this table so you can add a detailed table that will be used as a bookmark link. To add a page break to a report, simply right-click to get to the table properties in the upper left of the table. On the General tab, select Insert a Page Break After This Table.

Adding a Bookmark Link

In this section, you will add a bookmark link to the Employee_Name field in the Employee Listing report that, when clicked, will jump to a defined location within the report. In this case, you will not add another Table data region to the report to contain detail information about employee visits. Bookmarks ease the navigation burden on large reports when users are looking for specific information. As discussed previously, summary and detail information can exist within the same report; in the case of adding a bookmark, you are not hiding the data so much as moving it to another location within the same report. The net effect for the user is the same, however, in that they control when they see the detail information.

To add a bookmark to the Employee Listing report, first follow the procedure to drag a new table element to the Layout tab. Next, add the patient name and the trimmed employee name. For this table you will want to group by the employee name, so right-click your detail row and select Insert Group. You will use the same trimmed expression as the group value expression, as follows:

```
=rtrim(Fields!LastName.Value) & ", " & rtrim( Fields!FirstName.Value)
```

On the General tab for the grouping, select Page Break at End, which will force the detail line for each employee to start on a new page. Next, add the date field that represents when the service was performed, =Fields!ChargeServiceStartDate.Value, to the third column, and format the date as you did earlier.

Now when you preview the report, the summary employee listing will appear on the first page, and the detail records that show the employee visits will appear on each subsequent page.

Next, you will add a BookmarkID field to the Employee_Name field in the detail row in the table. By right-clicking the field and selecting Properties ➤ Advanced, you can view the Navigation tab that controls all three hyperlink actions. In the BookmarkID field, you will again add your trimmed employee name expression. This will serve as the pointer record for the bookmark link you will now create.

To create the bookmark link, you will perform the same steps to get to the Navigation tab for the Employee_Name field in the first table. In the Hyperlink Action section of the tab, select Jump to Bookmark and paste in the trimmed employee name expression you used for BookmarkID.

■Tip Hyperlink actions do not automatically change the formatting of the field to indicate an associated hyperlink. You can manually change the color and add underline formatting so that the user knows to click the link.

When you preview the report, as shown in Figure 4-12, you see the detailed information for the selected employee, in this case Sojourner Truth, presented on page 2; the first page of the report is the Employee Listing table, where you clicked on the bookmark link in the Employee_Name field.

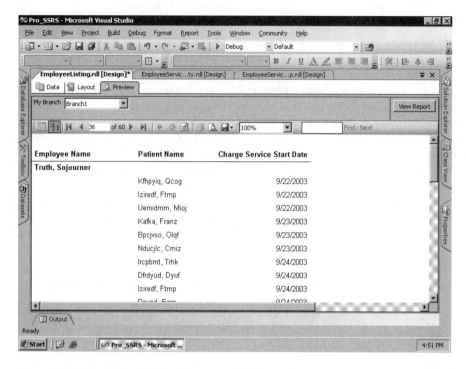

Figure 4-12. *Employee visit detail report called from a bookmark link*

Adding a URL Link

URL links connect a report to information stored in other locations, such as a Microsoft SharePoint site or the Internet. Like bookmark links, URL links are defined on the Navigation tab and can be applied to many report items. As discussed in Chapter 3, in almost every value field that is used in SSRS, expressions define the contents. In the case of the URL, you will build an expression that will define the HTTP location, using a combination of the literal URL and a field value from the dataset.

For example, let's assume that for each employee discipline a home page on your intranet site is designed specifically for that discipline. An employee who is a home health aide would have a `DisciplineID` of HHA, and your Web site designed for home health aides would be at `http://webserver1/hha`. Assuming that the same is true for each discipline, it would be easy to add a URL link for each discipline to your report.

Just as you did for the bookmark link for `Employee_Name`, let's open the Navigation tab for the `Discipline` field. Select Jump to URL, and add the following expression:

```
="http://webserver1/" & Fields!DisciplineID.Value
```

When the `DisciplineID` field is selected within the report, the browser will open and connect to the site of the specific employee's discipline—for example, HHA for the home health aides site or RN for the registered nurses site.

Building the URL Link with a Report Parameter

Taking the concept one step further, if you had multiple Web servers at different locations or branches, you would not want to hard-fix the Web server name in the URL string. By using a report parameter to select the server name based on the branch location, it would be possible to control the Web server portion of the URL string that you created in the previous example. Let's step through this procedure. Figure 4-13 shows what the Report Parameters dialog box should look like.

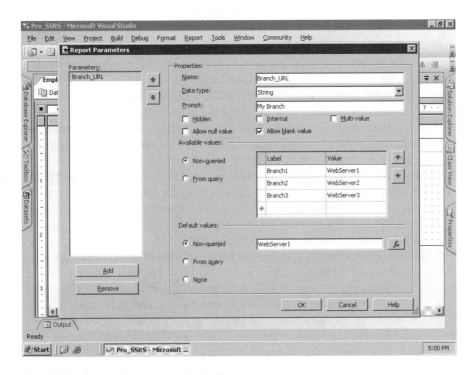

Figure 4-13. *Report Parameters dialog box*

Follow these steps:

1. While on the Layout tab, select Report ➤ Report Parameters from the menu bar.

2. Click Add, and enter **Branch_URL** for the parameter name.

3. Enter **My Branch** for the prompt.

4. In the Available Values section, enter the following labels/values: **Branch1** = **Webserver1**, **Branch2** = **Webserver2**, and **Branch3** = **Webserver3**.

5. Set the default value to be `Webserver1`.

6. Return to the Navigation tab for the `Discipline` field, and apply the new expression `="http://" & Parameters!Branch_URL.Value & "/" & Fields!DisciplineID.Value`.

7. Preview the report. Notice that you have a new parameter drop-down list called My Branch that was set to Branch1 based on the default value of `Webserver1`.

■**Note** Many expressions and report items are case-sensitive inside the Visual Studio environment. Often, if you receive an error indicating that a value is not valid, it will turn out to be that the case was incorrect.

With the URL location assigned to be that of the parameter Branch_URL, whenever a different branch is selected from the drop-down list, the appropriate server for that branch will be selected.

Jumping to a Report

Quite possibly the most useful hyperlink action in SSRS is the ability to link to another report, called a *drill-through report*, from a specified location within the current report. You have been working on two reports in this chapter, learning about many of the elements available. Now let's tie the two reports, Employee Listing and Employee Service Cost, together by creating a hyperlink from one to another. You will also pass a parameter value along with the hyperlink to narrow the results of the Employee Service Cost report when it is called from the Employee Listing report. The parameter value will be EmployeeID.

To add the hyperlink action that links to the Employee Service Cost report, return to the Navigation tab, this time from the EmployeeID textbox within the Employee Listing report. After clicking the Jump to Report button, a drop-down list appears with all the reports that are available in the current solution. If the report has already been deployed to the report server and is not in the current solution, you can use the relative path based on the target server that is defined in the project. In this example, the target server is http://hwc04/reportserver. You could add the relative path to any report on the report server. In this case, select the EmployeeServiceCost.rdl report, and then click the Parameters button. Choose the parameters that are populated when the report is selected; later in the "Setting Report Parameters with Stored Procedures" section, we will show how to add these parameters to the report. Choose EmployeeTblID as the parameter, and assign its value as =Fields!EmpTblID.Value, which is a field in the Employee Listing report that has a corresponding value to the EmployeeTblID parameter. After applying the new action, if the EmployeeID textbox is clicked when previewing the Employee Listing report, the Employee Service Cost report will be called and the parameter passed, thus narrowing the dataset for that report to only that selected employee.

In addition to interactive sorting, another feature in SSRS has been long-awaited: the ability to have a Date control added as part of the report automatically when a datatype of DateTime is added as a report parameter. In SQL Server 2005, this is an enhancement that, though it was possible to easily code a Date control in a custom .NET form, many report designers wanted a standard control for their users in the browser. To see this new Date control, add a single line to your Employee Listing report query. This will be an addition to the WHERE clause as follows:

```
Where ChargeServiceStartDate Between @DateFrom and @DateTo
```

After you add this line to the query, two report parameters are created, DateFrom and DateTo. If these parameters are set as string values, which by default they are, changing them to a datatype of DateTime in the Report Parameters dialog box will force them to display a graphical date picker control, as shown in Figure 4-14. Now when you run the report, you can actively select the service dates that will automatically narrow down or expand your employees in the Employee Listing report.

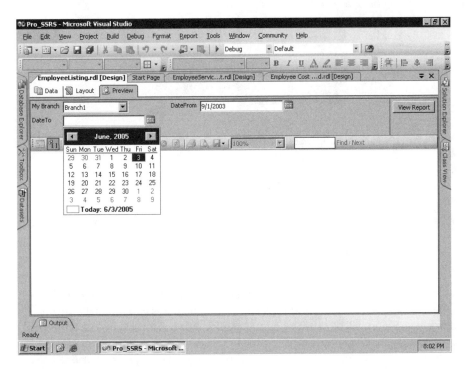

Figure 4-14. *Long-awaited date controls for report parameters*

Adding Hyperlink Formatting and Tooltips

Before you save the new Employee Listing report, let's add two formatting properties that will make the link more obvious as well as provide feedback on what will happen when the link is selected. The first task is to simply make the EmployeeID field resemble a hyperlink. Select the field, and apply an underline and color format of blue (see Figure 4-15).

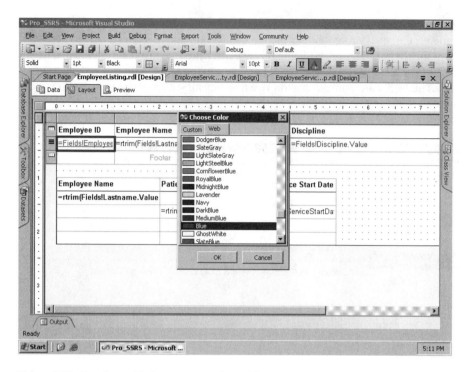

Figure 4-15. *Employee Listing report with visible hyperlinks*

Next you will add a tooltip to the same field. Tooltips appear whenever a user hovers the cursor over the field, and they provide additional information. In this case, you will use one simply to show which report will be called when the EmployeeID box is clicked—the Employee Service Cost report. The ToolTip property is located in the Misc section of the Properties window. After selecting the field, open the Properties box, and enter **Employee Service Cost** as the tooltip. Notice that the tooltip, like most other values, can be an expression as well as a literal string.

■Note Tooltips will not display in preview mode; the report must be deployed before they can be viewed in the browser.

It is possible to assign multiple parameter selections as input for the drill-through report. Now that you are linking to the Employee Service Cost report, which will have multiple parameters, let's take a closer look at how parameters and filters work together to deliver data to a report.

Setting Report Parameters with Stored Procedures

In Chapter 3, we introduced parameters and explained how you can use them within reports and queries to limit the results returned from the data source. To this point you have been working with a query instead of a stored procedure to build reports, but we have only touched the surface of how you can use parameters within SSRS. Parameters get their values primarily from user input and are most often associated with a dataset; they are used to limit the amount of data returned. When a parameter is used in this way, it is called a *query parameter*. Query parameters that are part of a dataset, such as a SQL query or stored procedure, automatically generate report parameters within SSRS.

In this section, you will modify the dataset of your Employee Service Cost report to use a parameterized stored procedure instead of a query. By default, report parameters generated from stored procedures do not have populated drop-down lists of data for users to select, so in this section you will also populate the report parameter lists with valid data for user-selectable input. Finally, you will see how SSRS works with NULL parameter values and how to generate a NULL value for the parameter. This will become especially important when retrieving data for your SSRS report, as we will explain later in this section.

You will return to the stored procedure you have already created, called Emp_Svc_Cost, which, as you might recall, will deliver the same dataset as the SQL query you have been using. The stored procedure has the added benefit of accepting all the parameters you want to use in the report. SSRS will automatically create the report parameters from the stored procedure. Let's quickly review the parameters that will be passed into the report from the stored procedure:

- BranchID

- EmployeeTblID

- ServiceMonth

- ServiceYear

- ServiceLogCtgryID

To create the parameters automatically for your Employee Service Cost report, which is currently using a nonparameterized query, you will simply change the dataset for your report to be the stored procedure.

Open the EmployeeServiceCost_SP report from the project included in the code download. On the Data tab that has the dataset Emp_Svc_Cost, you can click the ellipsis button (...) next to the Dataset field to open the Properties window. In the Command Type drop-down list, change the value from Text to Stored Procedure. Next, type the name of the stored procedure, **Emp_Svc_Cost**, in the Query String window. When you click OK and then execute the query in the generic query designer, you are prompted to input parameters (see Figure 4-16). Since the stored procedure is designed to accept NULL values, change the default input value in the Define Query Parameters dialog box from Blank to NULL, and click OK to complete the execution. If you do not select NULL instead of Blank, the query will fail with an error message, "Failed to convert string to Int32."

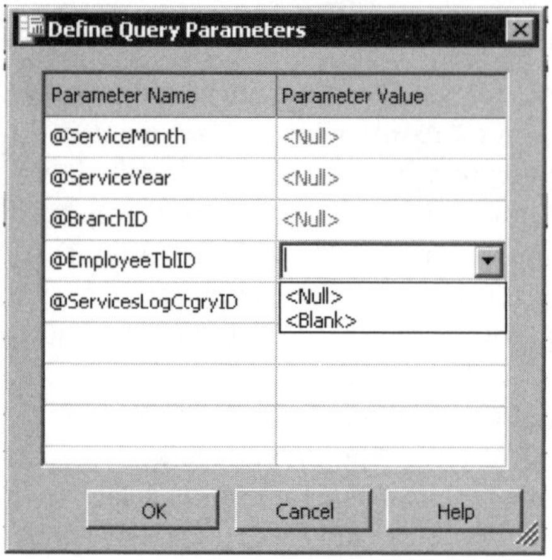

Figure 4-16. *Parameters required for the stored procedure* Emp_Svc_Cost

In the Report Parameters Properties box, you can see that the report parameters were automatically created from the stored procedure. Though SSRS did correctly assign the datatype for each parameter, integer, and string, it did not automatically set the field to allow NULL values (see Figure 4-17). For the purpose of this report, which expects NULL values as possible parameters, it is important that the Allow Null Value checkbox is selected for each parameter so that when the report is previewed, NULL will be the default value, and the NULL checkbox will be automatically checked so that the report executes without requiring user input.

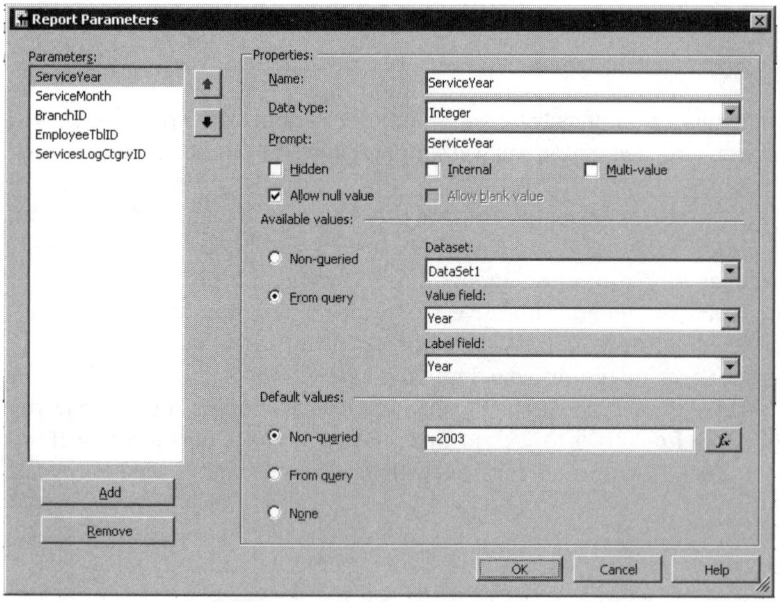

Figure 4-17. *Report Properties dialog box, showing the* Allow Null Value *field*

Default parameter values will also need to be manually configured. If no default parameter value is assigned to an available parameter, the report, when rendered or previewed, will not process the incoming data until a user supplies a value. Previewing the report without modifying the parameter selection reveals that the user would need to enter a value for each parameter that has no default value assigned. The user would not be able to choose from a list of values but would have to enter them manually. This is unacceptable because the user will not always know the correct values; good examples of this are the `EmployeeTblID` field that is used to select a specific employee and the `BranchID` field used to retrieve the branch name.

The first step is to provide valid query-assigned values for the parameter drop-down lists. It would be beneficial to provide a view of the report in preview mode prior to adding descriptive parameter values from a new dataset (see Figure 4-18). Notice that there is a `NULL` checkbox selected next to the parameter selections. The `NULL` checkboxes appear when the parameter allows `NULL` values, as you set earlier, and there are no other available values.

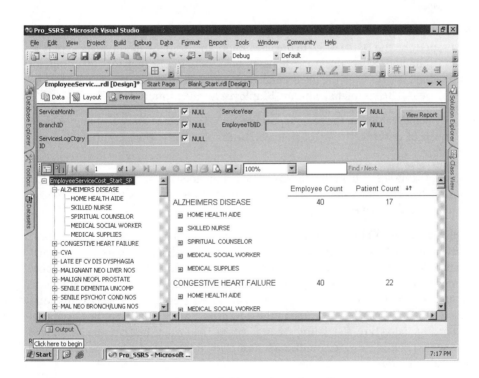

Figure 4-18. *No parameter values available via drop-down list*

The following list of procedures will add two datasets to populate the Branch and Employee drop-down lists for the parameters:

1. On the Data tab, create two new datasets, `Employee_DS` and `Branch_DS`, by dropping down the Dataset list and selecting New Data Set. For both datasets you create, you will add simple queries that will return the IDs and names for the employee and the branch. Notice in the `WHERE` clause of the employee query that you are including only a known set of employees for simplicity.

```
--Query for Employee Parameter
SELECT
    EmployeeTblID,rtrim(rtrim(employee.lastname) + ',' +
    rtrim(employee.firstname)) as Employee_Name
FROM
    Employee
WHERE (Employee.EmployeeTblID IN
(32, 15, 34, 44, 129, 146, 159, 155, 26))

--Query for Branch Parameter
SELECT
    BranchID, BranchName
FROM
    Branch
```

2. After you have created the datasets with the previous queries and verified that they execute properly on the Data tab, go to the Layout tab, and from the menu select Report ➤ Report Parameters. Select the BranchID parameter, and enter **Branch** for the prompt for clarity, as you will be selecting the branch name in the drop-down list. Do the same for the EmployeeTblID parameter, entering **Employee** for the prompt.

3. In the available values for the branch parameters, select From Query, and then select the Branch_DS dataset. The Value field will be BranchID, and the Label field will be BranchName.

4. Follow the same steps to modify the Employee parameters, assigning Employee_DS and choosing the Value and Label fields as EmployeeTblID and Employee_Name, respectively. When finished, select OK.

5. Finally, on the Layout tab you will add a grouping for Branch Name to the table in the report so that as the parameters are selected, you can see that the report is specific to a branch. To do this, right-click on the button to the left of the Table Header row, above Diagnosis, and select Insert Group. This will make the Diagnosis group, formerly the first group, now the second group and will add a new group. Assign the expression value of =Fields!BranchName.Value to the new group, and click OK in the Grouping and Sorting dialog box. Next, drag the BranchName field from the Datasets window to the new first column row for the Branch group you just created. Also, make the field bold, and resize the font to 12 points.

The report will now have populated drop-down lists for the available parameter values, as shown in Figure 4-19. Notice that for the two parameters where you have added available values, the NULL checkbox has disappeared.

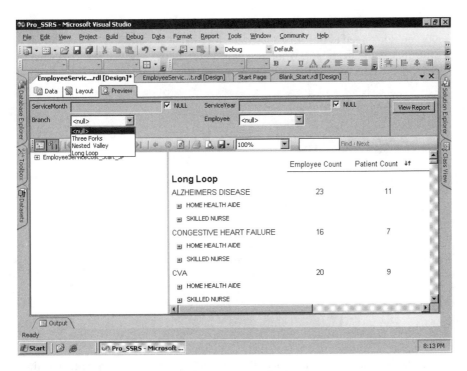

Figure 4-19. *Report with populated parameter selections*

You could perform the same steps for the `ServiceLog CtgryID` parameter and provide a valid drop-down list from the table values. However, since you may also be viewing the report in a custom report viewer that will also accept parameter values, this particular parameter value is of little use to you now for direct user input. That being the case, it will be beneficial to take advantage of another new and much needed feature, the ability to hide parameters. This functionality was added in Service Pack 2 for SSRS for SQL Server 2000 and is available in 2005 as well. Sometimes a parameter can and should be populated by events other than user input. In these instances, users will only be confused by seeing these additional parameters. In the Report Parameters dialog box, select the `ServicesLogCtgryID` property, and check the Hidden box. It will also be beneficial to modify the time-based parameters (`Service Year` and `Service Month`) for this report. Time-based values are often tricky to deal with because of the special formatting needs of the DateTime datatype, which can store years, months, and days as well as hours, minutes, and seconds. The procedures for setting up the `Service Year` and `Service Month` parameters with valid values is almost identical to the `Branch` and `Employee` procedures covered earlier, with the exception that the `Service Year` needs to default to the current year and not `NULL`.

The first step is to create a dataset for the `Service Year` and `Month` parameters based on the service date, which is the field `ChargeServiceStartDate` in the stored procedure. You will use the `DatePart` and `DateName` functions in the two queries to derive valid values. The valid values for the dates are contingent upon their existence in the table, so, for example, if your data contained values for 2003 and 2004, only those two years would show up in the drop-down list. Populating the date values in this way precludes the user from having to enter a date and also prevents the report designer from having to hard-code year and month values into the report.

Listing 4-2 shows the two queries that drive the parameter values. Unlike with SSRS for SQL Server 2000, you don't need to pass in a NULL value in the dataset, as SSRS for SQL Server 2005 supplies the NULL value by default when the parameter allows NULL values. This was a limitation with the previous version that has been addressed.

Listing 4-2. *Parameter Value Queries*

```
SELECT
     DISTINCT DatePart(yy,ChargeServiceStartDate) as Year
FROM
     TRX


--Query to Derive Month
SELECT
     DISTINCT  DatePart(mm,ChargeServiceStartDate) as DateNum,
     DateName(mm,ChargeServiceStartDate) as Month
FROM
TRX
ORDER BY
DatePart(mm,chargeservicestartdate)
```

To finish the report, add the Service Year field to the report, formatting it with a distinct color (in this case, dark salmon), and then resize the field to 12 points. Before you preview the report, it is important to set the default value for the year so that a valid Service Month selection is not based on the default Service Year field of NULL. This could potentially have undesired results; in other words, the user might select January and assume that it means January for the current year, when in fact it would be all occurrences of January.

To make the Service Year parameter default to the current year, go to the Report Parameters dialog box and set the Default Value option to the following expression:

```
=cint(DatePart("yyyy",Now()))
```

You can preview the report and provide parameter values (see Figure 4-20).

■Note Most of the data in the Pro_SSRS database is from 2003 and 2004. If the current year is defaulted to a different year, the data you see may not be the same as that shown in Figure 4-20.

The EmployeeServiceCost_Parameters.rdl report in the Pro_SSRS project includes populated parameters.

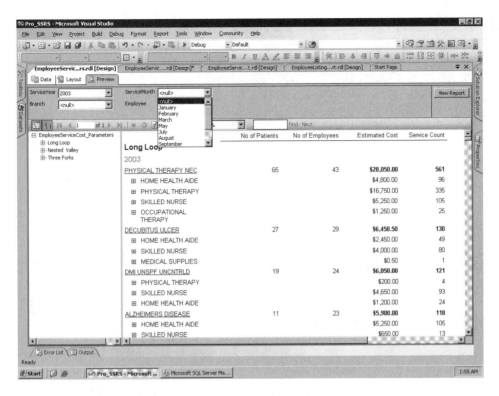

Figure 4-20. *Report with valid year and month values*

Applying a Filter

You might recall from Chapter 2 that you enhanced the performance of your stored procedure, Emp_Svc_Cost, by removing the criteria that looked only at visits. You will now apply a filter to the report to take the place of the original query criteria so that only visits will be displayed.

You can use *filters* to exclude values from a report after the results have been returned by the query. Filters, in that sense, will prevent a requery; however, the full dataset will be returned to the report. In the example in Chapter 2, you knew that a limited number of excess rows would be returned. You should use filters when a query parameter is not supported by the data provider or with report snapshots. You should also use filters in reports that address a specific request or solution and that are based on the same stored procedure as other reports, because you can use filters without modifying an existing stored procedure. Here is a simple filter expression applied to the Table data region of your report that will exclude any rows that are not visits:

```
=Fields!ServiceTypeID.Value = "V"
```

To add the filter expression, on the Layout tab right-click the upper-left section of the table, and select Properties. On the Filter tab, enter the previous expression so that it looks like Figure 4-21.

Figure 4-21. *Filter dialog box to exclude nonvisits*

Adding a Chart

SSRS provides a Chart data region that has a style similar to Microsoft Excel. Charts can be scoped within the current dataset or can use their own dataset. For this example, you will add a stacked bar chart to the beginning of the report that will show the top ten diagnoses and a count of the number of services for each diagnosis. This will essentially mirror the data provided in the report thus far. This report thus far is now also grouped by Branch, which will automatically separate the values in the Branch group you have defined. You will want to emulate this for your chart. You have only three branches in this particular dataset, so the result should be in line with the details of the report. Follow these steps to add the chart to the report:

1. On the Layout tab, click and drag the table you have already defined to make room for the chart.

2. Click and drag the Chart data region to an area above the table.

3. Right-click anywhere on the chart, and select Chart Type ➤ Bar ➤ Stacked Bar.

4. Using the same `Emp_Svc_Cost` dataset defined for your report already, drag the `Visit_Count` to the Data area of the chart.

5. Drag the `Diagnosis` field to the Category area of the chart.

6. Drag the BranchName field to the Series area of the chart.

7. Resize the chart so that it aligns with the table below it. You can select both report elements, and on the toolbar select the Make Same Width icon.

8. Right-click the chart, and select Properties. On the Data tab, select Edit in the Category groups for chart1_CategoryGroup1. Because you want to make the report show only the top ten diagnoses, you need to add a filter to this grouping. You will use the Top N operator to make this happen, as shown in Figure 4-22, based on the top ten diagnoses by a sum of the visit count.

Figure 4-22. *Filter value for top ten diagnoses*

Finally, you can preview the report. Sometimes a report needs a chart up front for a quick view of the data prior to analyzing the details. Someone perusing this report might find it interesting in the chart, for example, that the Physical Therapy NEC diagnosis seems to be more prolific in the Nested Valley branch. This initial preview might warrant more investigation that can be gleaned from the details in the report. In Chapter 10, when we discuss Analysis Services and SSRS, we will go into more detail about analyzing and reporting on these data trends.

When previewed, the report should look like Figure 4-23.

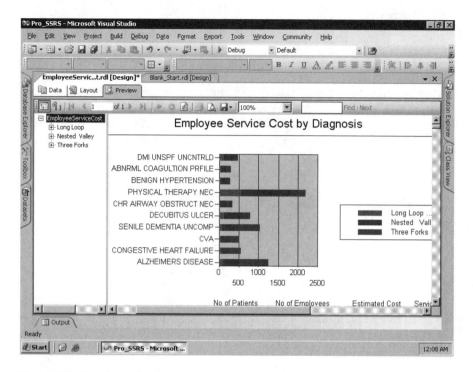

Figure 4-23. *Employee Service Cost report with a chart*

The Chart data region has many properties that you can apply, as covered in Chapter 3; however, the appearance of the stacked bar is suitable for your report and can be deployed as is.

Adding the Final Touches

In many projects, the final touches can be quite time-consuming. You now have the Employee Service Cost report to the point where it is functioning the way you expect and has had formatting applied to some extent during development. You have only a few final elements to apply before you call the report complete and before it's ready to deploy to your SSRS Web server for production:

- Adding a page header and footer
- Adding a report title
- Adding page numbers
- Adding the report execution time

To add a page header and footer to the report, select Report ➤ Page Header and Page Footer. This will add the two new sections to the report where you will add the values that will print on every page.

In the Toolbox, you'll see two report items, a textbox and a line, that you can use in the page header and footer sections. First drag two textboxes to the header and one to the footer. Then align one of the header textboxes to be the same width as the table, enter your report title as **Employee Service Cost by Diagnosis**, change the font size to 16 points, and apply bold formatting. Next, drag a line into the header section, and position it between the chart and the report title textbox you just created.

In the second textbox in the header section, add the following expression based on global parameters as defined in the Edit Expression window:

```
= "Page" & "   " & Globals!PageNumber & " of  " & Globals!TotalPages
```

Finally, in the textbox in the footer, add the following expression for the report execution time:

```
=Globals!ExecutionTime
```

You are now ready to preview your report one last time before you deploy it to your users. This time, let's take a look at the final version in the browser (see Figure 4-24). This is what the report will look like when it has been deployed to the Web server. (We will discuss methods for deploying reports in Chapter 6.)

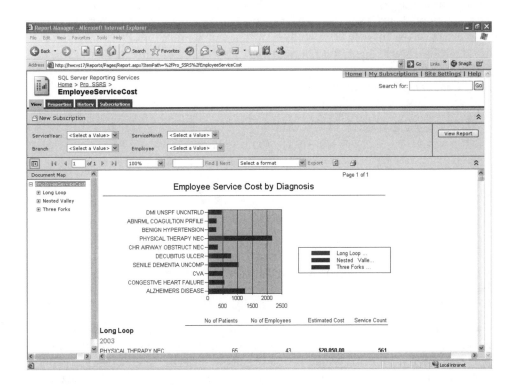

Figure 4-24. *Report rendered in the browser*

The completed report in the Pro_SSRS solution is called EmployeeServiceCost.rdl.

Working with Multivalued Parameters

Multivalued parameters are an enhancement to SSRS for SQL Server 2005 that is probably one of the most awaited features for an SSRS update. Having the ability to individually select values to feed into the report is a powerful feature that most other reporting applications take for granted and that was not available in SSRS for SQL Server 2000. Working with multivalued parameters to achieve the most usefulness from them, however, requires special design considerations, as mentioned in Chapter 3. The reason for this, especially when working with stored procedures, is that the multivalued parameters are passed back to the stored procedure as a string value. The only way to work effectively with multivalued parameters is to know that the query or stored procedure will evaluate all, one, or multiple values returned to it based on user selection. Because SQL Server does not evaluate a string in the same way it does a single value in a stored procedure, which honestly has been the bane of SQL developers for years, you have to go into multivalued parameters knowing that you will have to parse string values. For writers/logicians like ourselves, this is a fun game. For others, who have to develop reports with multivalued input parameters for a large audience, this can be a nightmare. Rest assured that once you understand string manipulation techniques, multivalued parameters will be a worthwhile time investment.

To accurately demonstrate how to work with multivalued parameters, which we will affectionately refer to as MVPs henceforth, let's take a copy of the Employee Service Cost report with the assumption that you will redesign it to accept the Year and Month parameters as multivalue. To begin, you will have to first modify your base stored procedure. Previously it was fine to evaluate the expression of your Year and Month parameters with the logic in Listing 4-3.

Listing 4-3. *Logic to Evaluate* Year *and* Month *Parameters Without MVP*

```
1=Case
        When ( @ServiceYear is  NULL) then 1
        When ( @ServiceYear is  NOT NULL)  AND @ServiceYear =
        Cast(DatePart(YYYY,ChargeServiceStartDate) as int)  then 1
    else 0
    End
AND
    1=Case
        When (@ServiceMonth is NULL)  then 1
        When (@ServiceMonth is NOT NULL)  AND @ServiceMonth =
        Cast(DatePart(MM,ChargeServiceStartDate) as int) then 1
    else 0
    END
```

However, now that you will be using MVPs, NULL values are not acceptable. The value of NULL in your logic was to select all values. This precluded you from accepting more than one value. For example, if you had the years 2002, 2003, 2004, and 2005 as valid values, you could either select all the values by selecting NULL or select only one value to narrow the data. You could not have selected 2003 *and* 2004. Now you can. The only way to effectively use MVPs is through the WHERE clause of the query or stored procedure, with parameters, that feeds the report data. You will have to take advantage of the IN clause of T-SQL to make the best use of MVPs. Unfortunately, though, it is not as simple as modifying the stored procedure to say

`Where value IN (@MyParameter)`, because SQL does not evaluate the `IN` clause as a string when using a stored procedure parameter. We can best explain this with the following example.

Let's say you make the `Year` and `Month` report parameters multivalued parameters. You can do this quite simply by checking the Multi-value box in the Report Parameters dialog box, as shown in Figure 4-25. Notice also that the Allow Null Value checkbox is unchecked. Allow Null Values cannot be checked if you want MVPs to work.

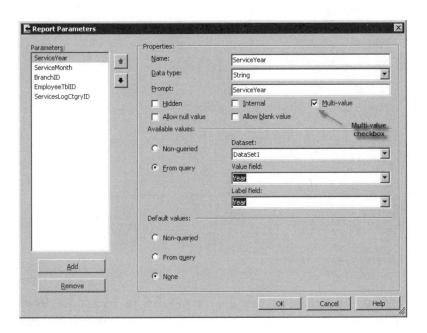

Figure 4-25. *Report rendered in the browser*

If you were to execute the report now, you would see, as you did in the previous example using a dataset to populate the available values, that you are able to select one or more or all values for the year and month options, as shown in Figure 4-26.

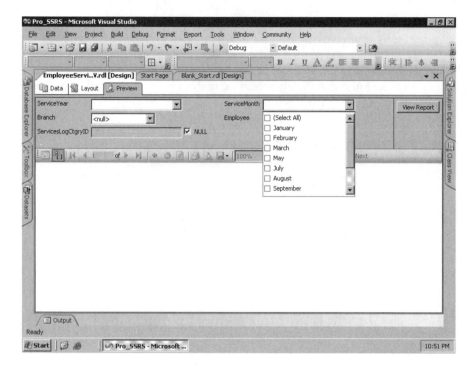

Figure 4-26. *Multiple parameter selection*

Because the values for the MVP will be returned as a string—taking the year, for example, as "2003,3004"—this will not work with the stored procedure logic that you have defined. You will need to modify the stored procedure to use the IN clause so that the value will be equivalent to the following expression:

```
WHERE
1=Case
```

```
      When Cast(DatePart(YYYY,ChargeServiceStartDate) as varchar(20)) in (@Year)
  End
```

The problem here is that the variable @Year will be evaluated as a string and not an integer as it is defined in the stored procedure. If you were to select a single value—2003, for example—this would be fine because SQL would correctly evaluate the single value within the IN clause. SSRS, however, when multiple values or Select All is chosen, passes a string such as "2002,2003,2004,2005". When evaluated within the stored procedure, the query will fail. You need to first change the datatype of Year and Month to be a character or string value. So, you will choose varchar(20) for your stored procedure and parse out the values as they are passed in. Using varchar(20) will allow you to select a wide enough range to cover the Year and Month value strings.

The best way to parse the string as it is returned from the report is another decision you must make both for performance and versatility. You have two effective methods for doing this, either dynamic SQL or a UDF. Creating dynamic SQL, which is essentially building a variable SQL expression using variables defined by user input, is cumbersome and syntactically challenging. Wrapping SQL statements within quotes and programmatically concatenating variables is time-consuming and often frustrating, yielding unpredictable results. What is worse is that it opens itself up to SQL injection hacks where users can interject values as strings that may execute statements that the developer did not intend. The best way to handle string values for MVPs is through a UDF to parse the individual values and feed these into the IN clause of the query. Knowing that the values will always be returned in a comma-separated string makes loading the values into an accessible table much easier by using a function designed for this purpose. This type of function is called a *table-valued function*, because the parsed rows of the input string are loaded into a table that can then be referenced as a subquery in the calling stored procedure. Let's take a look at a parsing function that you will use in your stored procedure while working with MVPs. Listing 4-4 defines the UDF called fn_MVParam. This function is in the Pro_SSRS database that you have been using.

Listing 4-4. fn_MVParam, *String-Parsing Function*

```
CREATE FUNCTION dbo.fn_MVParam(@RepParam nvarchar(4000), @Delim char(1)= ',')
RETURNS @Values TABLE (Param nvarchar(4000))AS
    BEGIN
    DECLARE @chrind INT
    DECLARE @Piece nvarchar(4000)
    SELECT @chrind = 1
    WHILE @chrind > 0
        BEGIN
            SELECT @chrind = CHARINDEX(@Delim,@RepParam)
            IF @chrind  > 0
                SELECT @Piece = LEFT(@RepParam,@chrind - 1)
            ELSE
                SELECT @Piece = @RepParam
            INSERT  @Values(Param) VALUES(@Piece)
            SELECT @RepParam = RIGHT(@RepParam,LEN(@RepParam) - @chrind)
            IF LEN(@RepParam) = 0 BREAK
    END
    RETURN
END
```

This function, when called from your Emp_Svc_Cost_MVP stored procedure, will return the parsed values from SSRS's multivalued parameter selection and allow you to use this as criteria for selecting data to include in the report. The key point of this function is that it uses several T-SQL functions itself, such as CHARINDEX, LEN, and LEFT, to populate the @Values table with the individual items from your report parameter string. The following modification to the base Emp_Svc_Cost stored procedure, as shown in Listing 4-5, will be required to make the Emp_Svc_Cost_MVP stored procedure effectively work with the MVPs.

Listing 4-5. *Modification to* WHERE *Clause for MVP*

```
1=Case

    When Cast(DatePart(YYYY,ChargeServiceStartDate)
      as varchar(20)) IN (select Param from fn_MVParam(@ServiceYear,','))  then 1
```

```
    else 0
    End
AND
    1=Case

    When Cast(DatePart(MM,ChargeServiceStartDate)
      as varchar(20)) IN (select Param from fn_MVParam(@ServiceMonth,',' ))  then 1
    else 0
    END
```

Notice that instead of saying IN (@Year), for example, which will not work, you are calling your function fn_MVParam. The function takes two values, the string and the delimiter. In this case, you are using a comma as the delimiter.

When the report is run and the new function is called, you can see that you can select one, two, any combination, or all values from the populated drop-down, and you know that your stored procedure will effectively handle the parsing, evaluating, and criteria to deliver only the data that you want to see in the report, as shown in Figure 4-27.

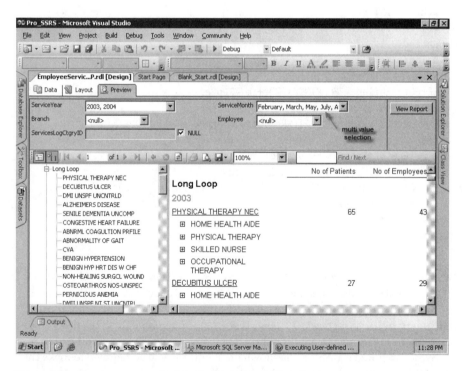

Figure 4-27. *Report generated with multiple selection criteria*

The completed report for multivalued parameters in the Pro_SSRS project is called EmployeeServiceCost_MVP.rdl.

Summary

It seems as if we have covered much ground in the actual design of a reporting solution with SSRS. However, at the same time, we have only scratched the surface of getting to the raw power and flexibility of SSRS. We have yet to show how to interweave custom assemblies to perform specific functions that go beyond basic expressions. You will also be working with other data regions in other parts of the book that we have not touched on here. Additionally, you have been working with only a small number of reports in this chapter; often in a business, especially when facing migrating existing reports to SSRS, you will be working with many reports simultaneously. Deploying, administering, and securing these reports are going to become critical next steps.

Luckily, a robust and flexible design environment is only one component of SSRS. In the upcoming chapters, you will deploy, secure, and analyze the performance of the reports you are designing here, using a variety of methods.

SUMMARY

CHAPTER 5

■ ■ ■

Using Custom .NET Code with Reports

SSRS 2005 offers software developers a variety of options when it comes to customizing reports through code. These options give software developers the ability to write custom functions using .NET code that can interact with report fields, parameters, and filters in much the same way as any of the built-in functions. To give just two examples, you can create a custom function that does the following:

Implements a business rule and returns true *or* false *based on the logic*: You can use such a function as part of an expression to change the value or style of a field based on the fields or parameters passed to the function.

Reads data from sources not otherwise available to SSRS 2005 directly: You can do this by having your custom code read data directly from the source. In this chapter, you will examine how to read data from an XML file. The sample code for this chapter also includes an example of reading data from a Web service. Although we won't cover it in this chapter, with SSRS 2005 you can also create custom extensions that will allow you to view data in the Report Designer as a data source.

In short, using custom .NET code gives developers the ability to extend the capabilities of SSRS 2005 far beyond those that are available out of the box.
This chapter will cover the following:

Custom code for use within your report using code embedded in the report: This method is the simplest way to add custom code to your report, and it deploys along with your report since it is contained in the RDL. However, it limits what you can do, must be written in VB .NET, and offers limited debugging support.

Custom code for use within your report using a custom assembly called by the report: This method is more involved to implement and more difficult to deploy, but it offers you nearly unlimited flexibility. Your custom code has the full power of the .NET Framework at its disposal and has the added benefit that you can use the custom assembly across multiple reports. You can also use the full debugging capabilities of Visual Studio while developing your custom assembly.

Generally, you will add custom code to your report when you need to perform complex functions and you need the capabilities of a full programming language to accomplish them. However, before you embark on writing custom .NET code, you should first evaluate whether using the built-in expression functionality can meet your needs.

Using Embedded Code in Your Report

Using embedded code is by far the easiest way to implement custom .NET code in your reports, for two main reasons. First, you simply add the code directly to the report using the Report Designer's user interface (UI) in either BIDS or Visual Studio. Second, this code becomes a segment within the report's RDL file, making its deployment simple because it is a part of your report and will be deployed with it.

Although it is easier to use, embedded code does have a few considerations that you should take into account:

Embedded code must be written in VB .NET: If you are a C# programmer or use some other .NET-compatible language as your primary development language, this may force you to use the custom assembly for all but the simplest of functions.

All methods must be instance based: This means the methods will belong to an instantiated instance of the Code object and you cannot have static members.

Only basic operations are available: This is because, by default, code access security will prevent your embedded code from calling external assemblies and protected resources. You could change this through SSRS 2005 security policies, but this would require granting FullTrust to the report expression host, which would grant full access to the CLR and is definitely not recommended. If you need these capabilities, use custom assemblies so you can implement security policies to grant each assembly only the security it needs. You will look at custom assemblies and how to set security for them in the "Deploying a Custom Assembly" section.

Before you run the included examples, make sure to read the ReadMe.htm file included with the sample code for this chapter. It is located in a file in the samples root folder. If you have the code open in Visual Studio, it will be under the Solution Items folder. It contains setup and configuration steps that are required before running the examples.

Let's take a look at how this feature of SSRS 2005 works by adding some embedded code to one of the reports you have already created. In this case, start with the sample Employee Service Cost report included with this chapter. It is a slightly modified version of the Employee Service Cost report you created in Chapter 4. We will show you how to use the embedded code feature to add a function that will determine whether you have exceeded a certain number of visits for a patient in a given time period. You will then use that function to determine the color of one of the text fields in the report to help draw attention to those specific patients.

> **■Note** In this chapter's example, we'll use a slightly modified version of the report created in Chapter 4 so that the employee report parameter will include an employee with patients who have exceeded the maximum number of visits. We've also set defaults for the report parameters to make sure the results included this patient.

Using the ExceedMaxVisits Function

Listing 5-1 is the full listing of the custom code that you will add to the Employee Service Cost report. It is a simple function, called ExceedMaxVisits, which determines whether a patient has exceeded a certain number of visits over some period of time. This allows you to identify cases for review to determine why they have such a high utilization of services.

Listing 5-1. *The* ExceedMaxVisits *Function*

```
Function ExceedMaxVisits(ByVal visitCount As Integer, ➡
    ByVal visitMonth As Integer, ➡
    ByVal visitYear As Integer) As Boolean

    ' Our businesses logic dictates that we need to know whether
    ' we exceed 240 visits per patient per visitYear
    ' or 20 visits per patient per visitMonth
    If (visitMonth = Nothing And visitYear <> Nothing) Then
        If visitCount > 240 Then
            Return True
        End If
    ElseIf (visitMonth <> Nothing) Then
            If visitCount > 20 Then
                Return True
        End If
    End If

    Return False

End Function
```

If you are following along with the code in the book, you will need to create a new Visual Studio 2005 BI project, as shown in Figure 5-1. If you don't have Visual Studio 2005 installed, you can create this first project in BIDS. For this example, call the solution Chapter 5 and the project Reports.

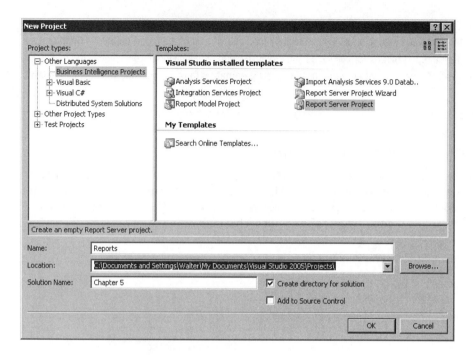

Figure 5-1. *Creating a Visual Studio BI project*

■**Note** For those of you who are not familiar with Visual Studio 2005 and/or BIDS, they are essentially the same IDE except Visual Studio 2005 adds full programming language support such as C# and VB .NET as well as other software development tools. Also note that both organize individual projects into solutions so you can keep related projects together.

To add the existing EmployeeServiceCost-NoCode.rdl file to your new project, right-click the Reports project, and select Add ➤ Existing Item, as shown in Figure 5-2. Alternatively, with the Reports project highlighted, select Project ➤ Add Existing Item from the menu. Next, browse to the location where you installed the Chapter 5 samples, and select EmployeeServiceCost-NoCode.rdl. You will also need to add the shared data source by adding an existing item and picking the Pro_SSRS.rds file.

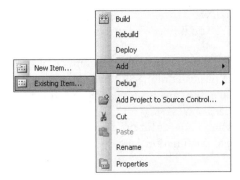

Figure 5-2. *Adding* `EmployeeServiceCost-NoCode.rdl` *to your project*

To add the code from Listing 5-1 to the Employee Service Cost report, first open the report by double-clicking it or by right-clicking it and selecting Open in the Solution Explorer. Next, with the report on the Layout tab, select Report Properties from the Visual Studio Report menu; alternatively, right-click within the report design area, and select Properties. On the Report Properties dialog box's Code tab, add the code from Listing 5-1 to the Custom Code box, as shown in Figure 5-3.

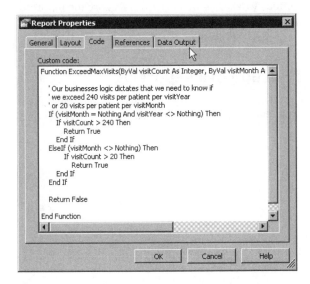

Figure 5-3. *Entering embedded code in the custom code editor*

■**Note** You must enter the function declaration (the first line) as a single line in the embedded code editor, or you will receive an error when you try to preview the report. In Listing 5-1, it is shown with returns but should be entered into the embedded code editor without them.

Now that you have defined your custom code, you'll want to use it to highlight the patients who have exceeded the maximum visit count. To do this, you need to access the ExceedMaxVisits method as part of an expression.

Methods in embedded code are available through a globally defined Code member. When a report's RDL file is compiled into a .NET assembly (at publish time), SSRS 2005 creates a global member of the class called Code that you can access in any expression by referring to the Code member and method name, such as Code.ExceedMaxVisits.

Listing 5-2 shows how to use a conditional expression in the Color property of a textbox to set the color of the text depending on the return value of the function call.

Listing 5-2. *Using a Conditional Expression*

```
=iif(Code.ExceedMaxVisits(Sum(Fields!Visit_Count.Value),
    Parameters!ServiceMonth.Value,Parameters!ServiceYear.Value),
    "Red", "Black")
```

The method ExceedMaxVisits determines whether the patient has had more visits in the time span than allowed and returns true if so or false if not. Using a Boolean return value makes it easy to use the method in formatting expressions, because the return value can be tested directly instead of comparing the returned value to another value.

When a patient exceeds the maximum visits allowed, ExceedMaxVisits returns true, which sets the value of the textbox Color property to Red, which in turn will cause the report to display the text in red. If the patient has not exceeded the allowable number of visits, then ExceedMaxVisits returns false, and the Color property is set to Black.

Using the ExceedMaxVisits Function in a Report

Now we'll walk you through how to actually add this expression to the report. First, select the field in the report to which you want to apply the expression. In this case, select the patient name textbox, as shown in Figure 5-4.

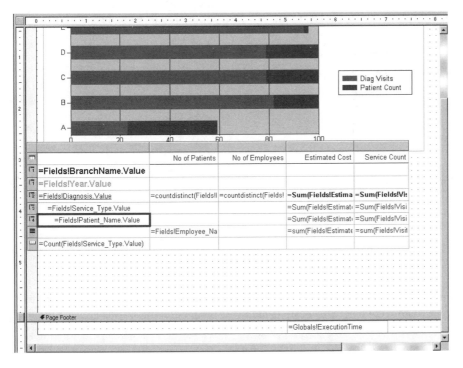

Figure 5-4. *Adding the expression to the report*

Second, with the textbox selected, go to the Properties window, and select the Color property (see Figure 5-5).

Figure 5-5. Color *property in the Properties window*

Next, click the down arrow, and from the list select Expression (see Figure 5-6).

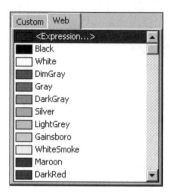

Figure 5-6. *Color selection list*

Now you will see the Edit Expression dialog box, as shown in Figure 5-7. Enter the expression using your custom code here. You can just type the expression in, or you can use the expression editor to insert the parameters that you need into your expression.

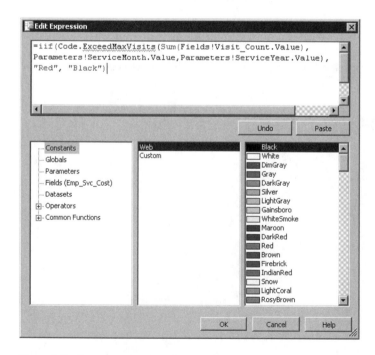

Figure 5-7. *Entering an expression in the expression editor*

You can now run your report, and the patient name will be displayed in red or black according to the business logic in the Code element of the report.

Now that you have modified the report to use the ExceedMaxVisits function, you can preview the report to see it in action. To do this, select the Preview tab, and select ServiceYear 2003, Branch Long Loop, Service Month November, and Employee Ywzvsl, Nnc. You should now see a report that looks similar to Figure 5-8.

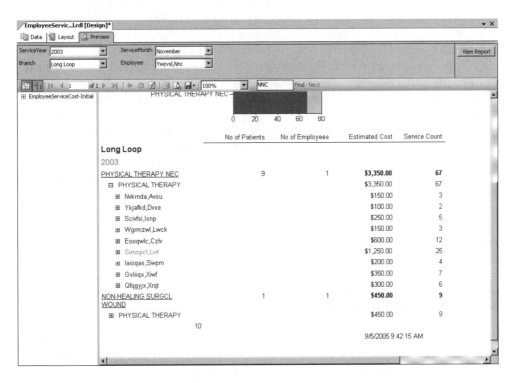

Figure 5-8. *Report with the embedded code*

Accessing .NET Assemblies from Embedded Code

The Code element of the report was primarily designed for basic use of the .NET Framework and VB .NET language syntax. Access to many of the framework namespaces is not included by default in the Code element. Referencing many of the standard .NET assemblies in your embedded custom code requires that you create a reference to it in the report. To do this, go to the References tab of the Report Properties dialog box, click the ellipsis by the References: Assembly name grid, and then select the appropriate assembly you want to reference. Note that, by default, these referenced assemblies will have only Execution permission.

Although it is possible to use other .NET Framework assemblies and third-party assemblies directly within the Code element of the report, as just described, it is highly recommended that you consider using a custom assembly instead. One of the primary reasons for this is security. By default, the Code element runs with Execution permission only, which means it can run but cannot access protected resources. If you need to perform certain protected operations, such as reading data from a file, you'll have to set the security policy for the code group named Report_Expressions_Default_Permissions to FullTrust. This code group controls permissions for the report expression host assembly, which is an assembly that is created from all the expressions found within a report and is stored as part of the compiled report. To set the security policy, you need to edit the policy configuration files of the report server and the Report Designer. See the "Deploying a Custom Assembly" section later in this chapter for the standard location of these files.

But making this change to the security policy is not recommended. When you change the permissions for the code that runs in the Code element, you also change the permissions for all reports that run on that report server. By changing permissions to FullTrust, you enable all expressions used in reports to make protected system calls. This will essentially give anyone who can upload a report to your report server complete access to your system.

If you need to use features outside the VB .NET language syntax, need additional security permissions, have complicated logic to implement, need to use more of the .NET Framework, or want to use the same functionality within multiple reports, then you should move your code into a custom assembly. You can then reference that assembly in your report and use the code through methods and properties of your custom class. Not only does a custom assembly allow you a lot more flexibility in the code itself, it also allows you to control security at a much more granular level. With a custom assembly, you can add a permission set and code group for your custom code just to that specific assembly without having to modify the permissions for all code that runs in the Code element.

You'll want to use custom assemblies for another reason. With embedded code, you do not have the benefit of developing the Code section of your report using the full Visual Studio IDE with features such as IntelliSense and debugging at your disposal. Writing code in the Code section of your report is not much different from working in Notepad.

However, you can work around this. If the code you choose to place in the Code element is more than just a few simple lines of code, it can be easier to create a separate project within your report solution to write and test your code. A quick VB .NET Windows Forms or console project can provide the ideal way to write the code you intend to embed in your report. You get the full features of the IDE, and once you have the methods working the way you want, you can just paste them into the code window of the report. Remember to use a VB .NET project, since the Code element works only with code written in VB .NET.

Using Custom Assemblies with Your Report

Custom assemblies are harder to implement but offer you greater flexibility than embedded code. The process of creating them is a bit more involved because they are not part of the report's RDL and must be created outside the Report Designer. This also makes them more difficult to deploy because, unlike the embedded code, which becomes a part of the report's RDL, the custom assembly is a separate file.

However, your hard work is repaid in many ways:

Code reuse: You can reuse custom code across multiple reports without the need to copy and paste code into each report. This allows you to centralize all the custom logic into a single location, making code maintenance much simpler.

Task separation: Using assemblies allows you to more easily separate the tasks of writing a report from creating the custom code. This is somewhat similar in concept to writing an ASP.NET application using the code-behind feature. This allows ASP.NET developers to separate the page markup, layout, and graphics from the code that will interact with it. If you have several people involved, you can let those who specialize in report writing handle the layout and creation of the report while others who may have more coding skills write the custom code.

Language neutrality: You can use the .NET language of your choice. Choose from C#, VB, J#, or any third-party language that is compatible with the .NET Framework.

Productive development environment: If you use Visual Studio 2005 to develop your custom assemblies, you get the full power of its editing and debugging features.

Security control: You can exercise fine-grained control over what your assembly can do using security policies.

To use a custom assembly from within your report, you need to create a class library to hold the code, add the methods and properties you want to use from the report to your class, and then compile it into an assembly. To use it from within the Report Designer, you can add a class library project to the solution in Visual Studio, allowing you easy access to both the report and the code you will use in it. Note that you must be using Visual Studio 2005 and not just BIDS for this project. Before you run the included examples, make sure to read the ReadMe.htm file in the solution's Solution Items folder to see whether any steps are required before running the examples for your particular configuration.

Adding a Class Library Project to Your Reporting Solution

To use a custom assembly with your report, you will first need to write your custom code in the form of a .NET class. You can do this by adding a class library project to your existing solution so that you can work on the report and custom code at the same time.

For this example, you want to display the amount an employee is paid for a visit to a patient. The class will get this information from an XML file that is periodically exported from the human resources (HR) system.

■**Note** If possible, you would want to get this information directly from the HR system, possibly through a Web service. The sample code included with this chapter includes a sample Web service and a method to call it.

Using the XML file EmployeePay.xml (supplied as part of the code download for this chapter) in this example allows you not only to write a custom assembly but also to see the steps necessary to access a protected resource such as a local file. To get the information from the XML file and make it available to your report, create a class with a method that takes EmployeeID and a date as a parameter and that will read the employee pay per visit rates from the XML file and then return the pay rate. Although we will not cover it step by step in this chapter, the sample code included also contains an example of doing the same thing using a Web service. This allows you to simulate being able to interact with the HR system via a Web service instead of an exported file.

You can then reference the assembly from an expression in the report and use it to calculate the total visiting costs per patient.

To start, select File ➤ Add Project ➤ New Project from the menu. Pick Visual Basic Projects or Visual C# Projects, depending on your preference. Select Class Library, and enter **Employee** for the name of the project. In this example, we will show you how to use a Visual C# class library project, as shown in Figure 5-9.

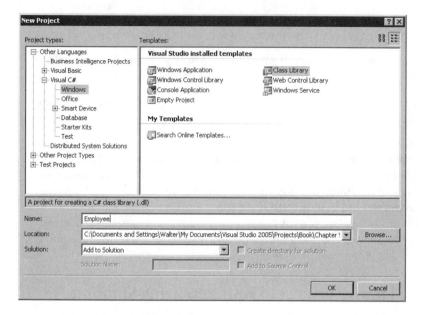

Figure 5-9. *New Project dialog box*

■**Note** Make sure to select Add to Solution instead of Create New Solution in the Solution drop-down list.

Select Class1.cs, and rename it to something a bit more descriptive, such as Employee, because you will use this class to calculate the cost of a visit provided by the employees. Open the Employee.cs file in the Visual Studio 2005 IDE, change the namespace from Employee to Pro_SSRS, and you will see the code editor, as shown in Figure 5-10.

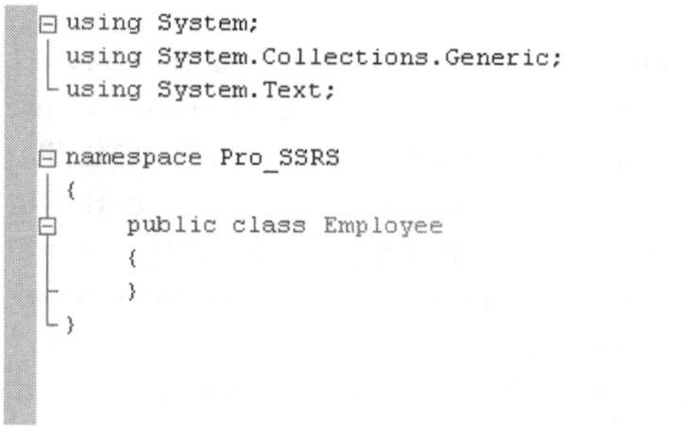

```
using System;
using System.Collections.Generic;
using System.Text;

namespace Pro_SSRS
{
    public class Employee
    {
    }
}
```

Figure 5-10. *The Visual Studio 2005 code editor*

For this example, you'll add a few using statements to import types defined in other namespaces. Specifically, you'll add the System.Data and System.Security.Permissions namespaces so you can reference the DataSet and SecurityAction methods without typing in the full namespace in the Employee assembly, as shown in Listing 5-3.

Listing 5-3. *The Employee Assembly*

```
using System;
using System.Collections.Generic;
using System.Text;
using System.Security.Permissions;
using System.Data;

namespace Pro_SSRS
{
    public class Employee
    {
        public Employee()
        {
        }
        [PermissionSetAttribute(SecurityAction.Assert, Unrestricted = true)]
        public static decimal CostPerVisitXML(string employeeID, DateTime visitDate)
        {

            DataSet empDS = new DataSet();
            empDS.ReadXmlSchema(@"C:\Temp\EmployeePay.xsd");
            empDS.ReadXml(@"C:\Temp\EmployeePay.xml");
            DataRow[] empRows =
                empDS.Tables["EmployeePay"].Select("EmployeeID = '" +
                employeeID + "'");
            Decimal empAmt;
            if (empRows.Length > 0)
            {
                empAmt = Convert.ToDecimal(empRows[0]["Amount"]);
                return empAmt;
            }
            else
                return 0M;

        }
    }
}
```

Any assemblies used by the custom assembly must be available both on the computer being used to design the report and on the SSRS 2005 server itself. Since you are just using common .NET Framework assemblies, this should not be a problem because the .NET Framework is installed on your local computer as well as on the SSRS 2005 server. If you reference other custom or third-party assemblies in your custom assembly, you need to make sure they are available on the SSRS 2005 server where you will be running your report.

> ■**Note** Because this book's focus is on SSRS 2005 and not on writing code, we won't explain the code samples line by line. If you are interested in programming, Apress offers many excellent books for the various programming languages that can help you write custom code for SSRS 2005. Refer to http://www.apress.com.

To use the Employee assembly in your report, you need to deploy it to the appropriate location first. In the next section, you will learn how to deploy custom assemblies and set up the necessary permissions required. Once you have done that, you will return to the report and use the custom assembly you have created and deployed in the Employee Service Cost report.

> ■**Note** Remember that each time you make a change to your custom assembly, you must redeploy the assembly. Also, if you added code that requires additional permissions, you may have to grant them.

Deploying a Custom Assembly

Custom assemblies are more difficult to deploy than code embedded in your report through the Code element. This is because of the following:

- Custom assemblies are not part of the report itself and must be deployed separately.

- Custom assemblies are not deployed to the same folder as the reports.

- The built-in project deployment method in Visual Studio 2005 will not automatically deploy your custom assemblies.

- Custom assemblies are granted only Execution permissions by default. Execution permission allows code to run but not to use protected resources.

To use your custom assemblies with SSRS 2005, you need to take the following steps to place them in a location where SSRS 2005 can find them and to edit the files that control security policy when necessary. The location of the files depends on whether you want to use them in the Report Designer within BIDS, within Visual Studio, or on the report server.

1. You need to deploy your custom assemblies to the Report Designer and/or SSRS 2005 applications folder.

   - For the Report Designer, the default is C:\Program Files\Microsoft Visual Studio 8\ Common7\IDE\PrivateAssemblies.

   - For SSRS 2005, the default is C:\Program Files\Microsoft SQL Server\MSSQL.n\ Reporting Services\ReportServer\bin.

■**Note** You need to have the necessary permissions to access these folders. By default, members of the standard Users group won't have the necessary write/modify permissions on these folders. Logged in as a user with the appropriate security permissions, such as the administrator, you can set the permissions on the folders to allow the necessary access to the folders when you are logged in under a less privileged account. Alternately, you could move the files to the appropriate folders when logged in or running as a user who has the necessary permissions.

   2. Next, you need to edit the SSRS 2005 security policy configuration files if your custom assembly requires permissions in addition to the Execution permission. (For SSRS 2005, the default location is C:\Program Files\Microsoft SQL Server\MSSQL.n\ Reporting Services\ReportServer\rssrvpolicy.config.)

■**Note** The Report Designer runs custom assemblies with FullTrust security, so you may not encounter security-related issues when you are previewing the reports. However, should changes be required, the default location of the preview security configuration file is C:\Program Files\Microsoft Visual Studio 8\ Common7\IDE\PrivateAssemblies\RSPreviewPolicy.config.

■**Note** The MSSQL.n folder will vary depending on the particular installation options you selected when installing SQL Server 2005. It may be in a folder with a period and number appended to the end of *MSSQL.n* such as MSSQL.3. The MSSQL folder for the custom assembly and the security policy file will be the same.

For example, if you were writing a custom assembly to calculate an employee's cost per visit, you might need to read the pay rates from a file. To retrieve the rate information, you would need to grant additional security permissions to your custom assembly. To give your custom assembly FullTrust permission, you can add the XML text shown in Listing 5-4 to the appropriate CodeGroup section of the rssrvpolicy.config file.

Listing 5-4. *Granting* FullTrust *Permission to the Custom Assembly*

```
<CodeGroup class="UnionCodeGroup"
    version="1"
    PermissionSetName="FullTrust"
    Name="EmployeePayCodeGroup"
    Description="Employee Cost Per Visit">
    <IMembershipCondition
        class="UrlMembershipCondition"
        version="1"
        Url="C:\Program Files\Microsoft SQL Server\MSSQL.n\ ➥
```

```
              Reporting Services\ReportServer\bin\Employee.dll"
        />
</CodeGroup>
```

■**Note** If you run your report and you see #Error text in a textbox instead of the expected result, it is more than likely a permission problem of some kind.

Because it's generally not a good idea to grant your assemblies FullTrust unless absolutely necessary, you can use named permission sets to grant your custom assembly just the permissions it needs rather than FullTrust.

To grant the custom assembly just enough permission to read the data files called C:\Temp\EmployeePay.xml and C:\Temp\EmployeePay.xsd, you first need to add a named permission set in the policy configuration file rssrvpolicy.config that grants read permission to the files. You can then apply the specific permission sets to the custom assembly, as shown in Listing 5-5.

Listing 5-5. *Named Permission Sets for Reading Files*

```
<PermissionSet
    class="NamedPermissionSet"
    version="1"
    Name="EmployeePayFilePermissionSet"
    Description="Permission set that grants read access to my employee cost file.">
    <IPermission
        class="FileIOPermission"
        version="1"
        Read="C:\Temp\EmployeePay.xml"
    />
    <IPermission
        class="FileIOPermission"
        version="1"
        Read="C:\Temp\EmployeePay.xsd"
    />
    <IPermission
        class="SecurityPermission"
        version="1"
        Flags="Execution, Assertion"
    />
</PermissionSet>
```

Next, as shown in Listing 5-6, you add a code group that grants the assembly the additional permissions to the CodeGroup section of the policy configuration file rssrvpolicy.config.

Listing 5-6. *Granting File I/O Permission on the* Employee *Assembly*

```
<CodeGroup class="UnionCodeGroup"
    version="1"
    PermissionSetName=" EmployeePayFilePermissionSet "
    Name="EmployeePayCodeGroup"
    Description="Employee Cost Per Visit">
    <IMembershipCondition class="UrlMembershipCondition"
        version="1"
        Url="C:\Program Files\Microsoft SQL Server\MSSQL.n\Reporting ➥
Services\ReportServer\bin\Employee.dll"/>
</CodeGroup>
```

Note The name of the assembly that you add to the configuration file must match the name that is added to the RDL under the `CodeModules` element. This is the name you set for the custom assembly under the Report Properties ➤ References menu, which was introduced in the "Accessing .NET Assemblies from Embedded Code" section; it is discussed in detail in the "Adding an Assembly Reference to a Report" section.

To apply custom permissions, you must also assert the permission within your code. For example, if you want to add read-only access to the XML files `C:\Temp\EmployeePay.xsd` and `C:\Temp\EmployeePay.xml`, you must add code similar to that shown in Listing 5-7 to your method.

Listing 5-7. *Asserting Permission with Code*

```
// C#
FileIOPermission permissionXSD = new
    FileIOPermission(FileIOPermissionAccess.Read,
    @" C:\Temp\EmployeePay.xml");
    permissionXSD.Assert();
    // Load the schema file
    empDS.ReadXmlSchema(@"C:\Temp\EmployeePay.xsd");

FileIOPermission permissionXML = new
    FileIOPermission(FileIOPermissionAccess.Read,
    @" C:\Temp\EmployeePay.xml");
    permissionXML.Assert();
    empDS.ReadXml(@"C:\Temp\EmployeePay.xml");
```

You can also add the assertion as a method attribute, as shown in Listing 5-8. This is the method shown in this chapter's examples.

Listing 5-8. *Asserting Permission with a Method Attribute*

```
[FileIOPermissionAttribute(SecurityAction.Assert,
    Read=@" C:\Temp\EmployeePay.xsd")]
[FileIOPermissionAttribute(SecurityAction.Assert,
    Read=@" C:\Temp\EmployeePay.xml")]
```

■**Tip** For more information about code access security and reporting services, see "Understanding Code Access Security in Reporting Services" in the SSRS 2005 Books Online (BOL). For more information about security, see ".NET Framework Security" in the *.NET Framework Developer's Guide*, available on the Microsoft Developer Network (MSDN) Web site at http://msdn.microsoft.com. You will also want to read about using the Global Assembly Cache (GAC) to store your custom assembly.

Adding an Assembly Reference to a Report

With the EmployeeServiceCost-NoCode report selected and on the Layout tab, select Report ➤ Report Properties; alternatively, right-click within the report design area, and select Properties. Then do the following:

1. In References, click the ellipsis button.

2. Select the Browse tab, and browse to the Employee.dll assembly from the Add Reference dialog box. When you are done, the Report Properties dialog box should look like Figure 5-11.

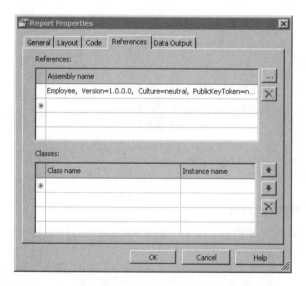

Figure 5-11. *References tab*

> **■Note** The class list on the References tab of the Report Properties dialog box is used only by instance-based members, not static members.

To use the custom code in your assembly in a report expression, you must call a member of a class within the assembly. You can do this in different ways depending on how you declared the method.

If the method is defined as static, it is available globally within the report. You access it in an expression by the namespace, class, and method name. The following example calls the static CostPerVisit method in the Employee class, which is in the Pro_SSRS namespace, passing in an EmployeeID value and the visit date. The method will return the cost per visit for the specified employee.

```
=Pro_SSRS.Employee.CostPerVisitXML(empID, visitDate)
```

If the custom assembly contains instance methods, you must add the class and instance name information to the report references. You do not need to add this information for static methods.

Instance-based methods are available through the globally defined Code member. You access these methods by referring to the Code member and then the instance and method name. The following shows how you would call the CostPerVisitXML method if it had been declared as an instance method instead of a static method:

```
=Code.Employee.CostPerVisitXML(empID, visitDate)
```

> **■Tip** Use static methods whenever possible because they offer higher performance than instance methods. However, be careful if you use static fields and properties, because they expose their data to all instances of the same report, making it possible that the data used by one user running a report is exposed to another user running the same report.

After adding the reference to the Employee custom assembly, you will use it by calling the CostPerVisitXML method as a part of an expression in the report. Highlight the Employee_Cost textbox in the report, as shown in Figure 5-12.

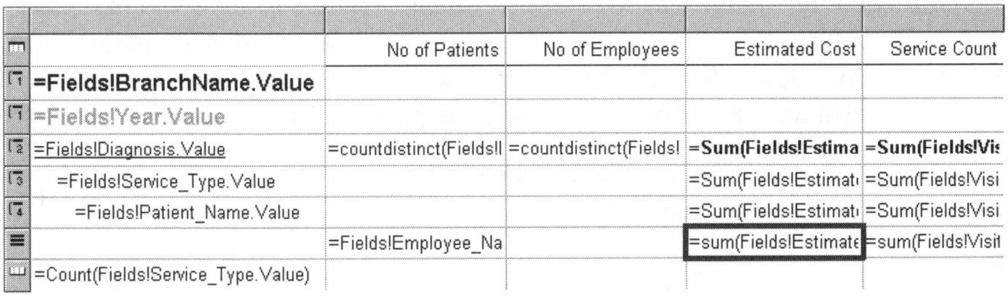

	No of Patients	No of Employees	Estimated Cost	Service Count
=Fields!BranchName.Value				
=Fields!Year.Value				
=Fields!Diagnosis.Value	=countdistinct(Fields!l	=countdistinct(Fields!	=Sum(Fields!Estima	=Sum(Fields!Vis
=Fields!Service_Type.Value			=Sum(Fields!Estimat|	=Sum(Fields!Visi
=Fields!Patient_Name.Value			=Sum(Fields!Estimat|	=Sum(Fields!Visi
	=Fields!Employee_Na		=sum(Fields!Estimate	=sum(Fields!Visit
=Count(Fields!Service_Type.Value)				

Figure 5-12. Employee_Cost *textbox*

Right-click, select Expression, and in the Edit Expression dialog box enter the code shown in Listing 5-9.

Listing 5-9. *Using the* CostPerVisitXML *Method in an Expression*

```
=Pro_SSRS.Employee.CostPerVisitXML(Fields!EmployeeID.Value,
"01/01/2004") * sum(Fields!Visit_Count.Value)
```

Now if you preview the report or build and deploy it, you should see a report similar to Figure 5-13.

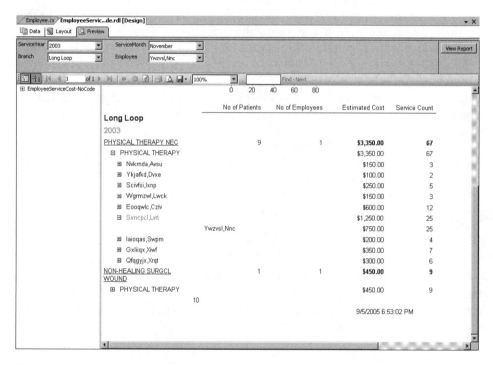

Figure 5-13. *Final report*

In the sample code included for Chapter 5, we have also included a Web service that can be called from the custom code to access the employee pay information. This simulates accessing information from another system via a Web service and is designed to allow you to replace the exported XML file with a call to a Web service. The Employee class included in the sample code already contains a method called CostPerVisitWS that uses the Web service rather than the XML file as its source of data. By simply changing the expression from this:

```
=Pro_SSRS.Employee.CostPerVisitXML(Fields!EmployeeID.Value,
"01/01/2004") * sum(Fields!Visit_Count.Value)
```

to the following:

```
=Pro_SSRS.Employee.CostPerVisitWS(Fields!EmployeeID.Value,
"01/01/2004") * sum(Fields!Visit_Count.Value)
```

you can make the report use the Web service instead of the XML file. To try this, just open the sample solution for this chapter, and edit the expression in the `Employee_Cost` field in the `EmployeeServiceCost.rdl` file. To try the Employee Web Service, you also must publish the Web site by selecting the Employee Web Service project, right-clicking, and then selecting Publish Web Site.

We have also included a sample test application that allows you to call the `CostPerVisitXML` and `CostPerVisitWS` methods of the `Employee` class using a Windows Forms application. This allows you to exercise the class and step through the code in the Windows Forms environment, which is easier to test and debug.

■**Tip** Writing a test application is a great way to make sure your custom code is properly performing the expected functions prior to using the code within your SSRS 2005 report. Not only can you create a custom Windows Forms application as we did, but with the proper version of Visual Studio 2005 you can create specialized test code and automated test routines.

Debugging Custom Assemblies

For ease of debugging, the recommended way to design, develop, and test custom assemblies is to create a solution that contains both your test reports and your custom assembly. This will allow you easy access to both the report and the code you will use in it at the same time from within Visual Studio.

■**Note** The Report Preview that is used during debugging does not grant `FullTrust` security to your custom assembly and may require that you set up appropriate permissions to run your custom assembly. In your development environment, you may want to grant it `FullTrust`, which you can do by editing the `RSPreviewPolicy.config` file. The default location of the preview security configuration file is `C:\Program Files\Microsoft Visual Studio 8\Common7\IDE\PrivateAssemblies\RSPreviewPolicy.config`. You can use the code shown in Listing 5-4 to grant `FullTrust` if you just change the URL element to point to the `Employee.dll` in the `PrivateAssemblies` folder.

We'll now show how to set up Visual Studio to allow you to debug the `Employee` assembly you have just written:

1. In the Solution Explorer, right-click the solution, and select Configuration Manager. This will allow you to set the build and deploy options for debugging.

2. Select `DebugLocal` as the Active Solution Configuration option.

3. Make sure the report project in your solution is set to `DebugLocal` and that `Deploy` is unchecked. `DebugLocal` debugs reports on your local system, rendering the report in the Preview pane within Visual Studio. If `Deploy` is checked, it will publish the reports to the report server instead of running them locally, and you will not be able to debug them.

4. Right-click the project containing your reports.

5. Set the Reports project as the startup project. This will make sure the report runs first when you start debugging. You will set the specific report that will call the custom assembly in a subsequent step.

6. Right-click again, and select Project Dependencies.

7. In the Project Dependencies dialog box, select the Employee project as the dependent project, as shown in Figure 5-14. This will tell Visual Studio that your report depends on the custom assembly you have written.

Figure 5-14. *Project Dependencies dialog box*

8. Click OK to save the changes, and close the Project Dependencies dialog box.

9. Right-click the Reports project again, and select Project Properties.

10. Select StartItem, and set it to the report you want to debug. In this case, select EmployeeServiceCost.rdl. The StartItem option tells Visual Studio specifically which report to run when you run with debugging.

11. In Solution Explorer, select the Employee custom assembly project.

12. Right-click, and select Properties.

13. Expand Configuration Properties, and click Build.

14. On the Build page, enter the path to the Report Designer folder in the Output Path textbox. (By default, this path is C:\Program Files\Microsoft Visual Studio 8\Common7\ IDE\PrivateAssemblies.)

■**Note** You will need to have the necessary permissions to this folder in order to use it for the output path. By default, members of the standard Users group won't have the necessary write/modify permissions on this folder. When you're logged in as a user with appropriate security permissions, such as the administrator, make sure to set the permissions on the `PrivateAssemblies` folder to allow the necessary access when you are logged in under a less privileged account.

■**Note** Debugging requires that you set the permissions.

■**Tip** You could leave the default output path, but changing it saves you some work. With the default path, you'd have to build and then manually copy your custom assembly in order for the Report Designer running within Visual Studio to find it and run it. If you update the `Employee` class, you may find that Visual Studio report preview has a copy of the old version in memory that will prevent your solution from being deployed. If this occurs, exit Visual Studio and start it again.

15. Now set breakpoints in your custom assembly code.

16. Make sure to set Report as the startup project, and then press F5 to start the solution in debug mode. When the report uses the custom code in your expression, the debugger will stop at any breakpoints you have set when they are executed. Now you can use all the powerful debugging features of Visual Studio to debug your code.

■**Note** It is also possible to use multiple copies of Visual Studio to debug your custom assembly. See the SSRS 2005 BOL for details.

Troubleshooting Your Project

If you modify a custom assembly and rebuild it, you must redeploy it, because the Report Designer looks for it only in the Report Designer application folder. If you followed our suggestion in the "Debugging Custom Assemblies" section to change the output path, it should be in the correct location each time you rebuild it while debugging. If not, you will need to follow the instructions in the "Deploying a Custom Assembly" section to move it to the Report Designer application folder. Remember, Visual Studio will not deploy your custom assembly to your SSRS 2005 server machine; you must copy it manually.

You may find that you have to exit the Visual Studio IDE in order to replace the files, as they may otherwise be in use.

Finally, you may want to keep the version of any custom assembly the same, at least while you are developing it. Every time you change the version of a custom assembly, the reference to it must change on the References tab of the Report Properties dialog box, as discussed earlier in this chapter. Once your reports are in production where you want to keep track of version information, you can use the GAC, which can hold multiple versions; this means you have to redeploy only those reports that use the new features of the new version. If you want all the reports to use the new version, you can set the binding redirect so that all requests for the old assembly are sent to the new assembly. You would need to modify the report server's `Web.config` file and `ReportService.exe.config` file.

If you are using a custom assembly and the output on your report shows `#Error`, you likely have encountered a permissions issue. See the "Deploying a Custom Assembly" section in this chapter for information on how to properly set up the permissions.

Summary

In this chapter, you learned how to use custom code with your reports, and we discussed some of the other programmatic aspects of dealing with SSRS 2005. Chapters 6, 7, and 8 will build on this as we show you how to write custom applications to render reports, deploy them to the report server, and schedule them to run using subscriptions.

CHAPTER 6

■■■

Rendering Reports from .NET Applications

Report rendering is the process of outputting the results of a report into a specific format. You pass the appropriate parameters to SSRS 2005, telling it what report you want to run and optionally what format you want the output in, any user credentials, and the actual report parameters. SSRS 2005 then renders the report and returns the results.

The manner in which you pass these parameters and how the results are returned depends on the SSRS 2005 method you're using to render the report. Once SSRS 2005 has the information it needs, based on the particular report you're running, it queries the appropriate data sources. SSRS 2005 uses the passed credentials and parameters if appropriate, renders the report into an intermediate format, and then renders and filters this intermediate format into the final display format requested.

With SSRS 2005, you can render reports in three ways from a .NET application:

Using a URL: You can build a URL that allows the client to access the report on the report server and supply any appropriate parameters, including rendering format, login information, report criteria, and report filters. This method is one of the most flexible because it will work with almost any language and platform that can host or use a Web browser or a Web browser control. In fact, it works with any language that can create a properly formatted URL and that can launch a Web browser using that URL. This method was used a lot with Visual Studio 2003, but it gets a lot simpler with Visual Studio 2005 because you can now use the built-in WebBrowser control rather than using COM Interop with the Internet Explorer Web browser control.

Using the SOAP API: You can use the SOAP API, also known as the Report Server Web service, to render the report. This returns the rendered data as a stream that you then display. This is a more difficult method of rendering. That's because the information you get back from the server is essentially a binary stream of data, and you don't have the benefit of having the server-browser combination to do the actual work of displaying the data. However, you can use the Report Server Web service for more than just rendering; you can use it to access the report server's complete functionality. We'll show how you can use the Report Server Web service in your solution to provide information about the reports you're rendering, such as the report parameters the reports use.

Using a ReportViewer control: You can use the ReportViewer control. This is a new option for SSRS 2005 that provides a simple-to-use Windows Forms application or ASP.NET user control that allows you to simply drag and drop the control onto a Windows or Web Form, set some properties, and render a report. One of the main benefits of the ReportViewer control is that it allows you to render reports that are on an SSRS 2005 report server as well as render reports locally, without the need for a report server.

■**Note** The ReportViewer controls are included with all versions of SQL Server and Visual Studio 2005. You must install SQL Server 2005 Workgroup, Standard, Enterprise or Developer Edition to access the BI projects that create server-side reports.

While the ReportViewer controls are the method that most Visual Studio 2005 users will probably employ to render reports, the most universally usable rendering method is via URL access. In this case, SSRS 2005 provides some defaults for most reporting options. For example, SSRS 2005 provides a default user interface for entering parameter and filter information. It prompts you for login information if necessary, and it defaults to rendering in HTML format. You get all this simply by passing the URL of the report from the browser. This is most useful if you're rendering your reports using just your Web browser, with no other controlling application.

You can optionally pass parameters along with the URL to change these default behaviors, provide login information, change the default rendering, hide the parameter toolbar, and so on. This is useful if you have a custom application and want to control these options yourself rather than provide the default user interface.

You can perform many of the same actions using the Report Server Web service, but there are no real defaults and the actual display of the returned data to the user is left up to the application developer. By using the Web browser in an ASP.NET application, or embedded in a Windows Forms application, you get the benefits of the URL rendering method, but you can exercise control over it. This provides users with a more integrated experience. The methods covered in this chapter apply largely to both Windows Forms and Web Forms applications. The project we'll show how to build is a Windows Forms–based report viewer that allows you to use SSRS 2005 as the reporting solution for your application.

In this chapter, you'll do the following:

URL rendering access: Learn how to build a URL through which a client application can access a report on the report server. You'll use the Employee Service Cost report in the example (available with the code download for this chapter in the Source Code section of the Apress Web site at http://www.apress.com).

URL reporting parameters: Explore the reporting parameters that, when specified in the URL, control how the report is rendered. You can specify the actual format (for example, HTML or PDF). You can specify that a specific page in a report be rendered, or you can search for a particular word and start rendering on that page.

URL viewer application: Build a simple .NET Windows Forms application that accesses and renders a report, via a WebBrowser control that you'll embed in a form.

Report Server Web service calls: Use calls to the Report Server Web service to query for the report criteria and filter parameters, which allows you to display them on your Windows

Forms application. You'll then use the SOAP API again to see whether the parameters have a list of values from which the user can select. If so, you'll use those values to populate combo boxes for each parameter. You'll also give the user a combo box to select a rendering format. You'll then display all the selections to the users and use their selected values to create a URL that contains all the information necessary to run the report. Finally, you'll use this URL with the embedded Web browser to render the report with user-entered report parameters and rendering commands.

Report viewer control, server-side mode: Use the new ReportViewer control to render the same report using the control's server-side mode.

Report viewer control, local rendering: Use the new ReportViewer control and a locally populated dataset to render a report locally without an SSRS 2005 report server.

Before you run the included examples, make sure to read the ReadMe.htm. It is located in a file in the samples root folder. If you have the code open in Visual Studio, it will be under the Solution Items folder. It contains setup and configuration steps that are required before running the examples.

Implementing URL Access

In this section, we'll show you how to build a URL that accesses the desired reports on the report server and passes the appropriate parameters to the report.

The syntax for the entire URL breaks down into two parts. The first part specifies the path to the report file, and the second specifies the parameters. The full URL syntax is as follows:

```
http://server/virtualroot?[/pathinfo]&prefix:param=value [&prefix:param=value]...n]
```

Table 6-1 describes each component of the URL.

Table 6-1. *URL Access Parameters*

Parameter	Description	Supported Values
server	Specifies the name of the SSRS 2005 Web server	None
virtualroot	Specifies the virtual root of the SSRS 2005 Web service	None
?	Separates the application virtual root from the parameters	None
[/pathinfo]	Specifies the optional path to a folder containing the report	None
&	Separates individual parameters	None
Prefix	When used, indicates that the following parameter is a command to the server itself versus a report parameter	rc: Rendering control rs: Report server command dsu: User dsp: Password
Param	Specifies the command parameter name when used with a prefix; otherwise, specifies a report parameter name	None
Value	Specifies the value of the parameter	None

We'll now walk you through the steps of building a URL to access the Employee Service Cost report.

URL Report Access Path Format

As indicated in the previous section, the path to access the appropriate report starts with the name of the report server itself, in this case `http://localhost`. Following that is the name of the SSRS 2005 virtual root folder, such as `/reportserver` (which is the default folder during installation).

■**Note** The `/reports` virtual root folder is mapped to the Report Manager application that ships with SSRS 2005. If you navigate to this URL, you'll find that it lists the folders and the reports within the folders that are on your report server through Report Manager.

You then add ? to the path to let SSRS 2005 know that everything following the URL is a parameter. Next is the optional path information where you can specify any subfolder within the base folder that you use to organize your reports, such as `/Pro_SSRS/Chapter_6`. Finally, you have the name of the actual report, such as `EmployeeServiceCost`.

So, in this example, the full path to access the Employee Service Cost report is as follows:

`http://localhost/reportserver?/Pro_SSRS/Chapter_6/EmployeeServiceCost`

We'll now cover the section of the URL where you specify any necessary parameters.

URL Parameters and Prefixes

You now need to pass the appropriate parameters to the report. You're interested in several categories of parameters:

Report parameters (no prefix): These parameters are supplied to the report's underlying queries and are used as filters for the information as it's rendered. Thus, they control exactly what data the report displays.

HTML viewer parameters (`rc:`): These parameters control which features of the Web-based report viewer are active and at which page the report viewer starts displaying the report. For example, you can use the `FindString` parameter to have the viewer start displaying a report on the first page on which a specific word is found.

Report server command parameters (`rs:`): These parameters control the type of request being made and the format of the returned report. For example, we'll show how to use the `rs:Command=Render&rs:Format=HTML4.0` parameter to render your report in HTML format in your report viewer.

Credential parameters: You use these parameters to pass in data source credentials such as User (`dsu:`) and Password (`dsp:`). You use them to provide credentials when a data source connection is set to `prompt`. If you plan to pass credentials in the URL, you will want to make sure to use an SSL connection to your SSRS 2005 server to protect the username and password information.

Report Parameters

Report parameters are the actual parameters passed to the underlying report, instead of instructions being sent to the report server. That is, you use them to pass criteria to your report such as start and end dates, employee IDs, and so on. You can pass these parameters to the report's query, and they're created when you specify parameters for the data source. You can also use parameters as variables in the report and as values for filters.

HTML Viewer Commands

You use HTML Viewer commands to tell SSRS 2005 how to render the report. You can use the commands in Table 6-2 to control how the viewer appears to the user, as well as to control certain aspects of how the report appears in the viewer.

Table 6-2. *HTML Viewer Commands*

Parameter	Description	Default
Toolbar	Shows or hides the toolbar.	true
Parameters	Shows or hides the parameters area of the toolbar.	true
DocMap	Shows or hides the report document map. For information on what a document map is, see Chapter 4.	true
DocMapID	Specifies the document map ID to which to scroll.	Not applicable
Zoom	Sets the zoom value. You can use a number representing a percentage or a string with standard values such as Page Width and Whole Page.	100
Section	Specifies the page number of the report to display.	1
FindString	Specifies the text to search for in the report.	Not applicable
StartFind	Specifies the page number to start the search on, specified by FindString.	Last page of the report
EndFind	Specifies the page number to end the search on, specified by FindString.	Current page
FallbackPage	Specifies the page number to display if a FindString or DocMapID fails.	Not applicable
GetImage	Gets a particular icon for the HTML Viewer interface.	Not applicable
Icon	Gets the icon for a rendering extension.	Not applicable
Stylesheet	Specifies a style sheet to be applied to the HTML Viewer.	Not applicable

Report Server Command Parameters

Report server command parameters, which are prefixed with rs:, tell the report server the type of request being made (see Table 6-3). You use them to retrieve report and data source information in XML and HTML format and to retrieve child elements such as the current folder's report names. You also use command parameters to tell the server you want to render a report and in what format and whether you want to render that report based on a preexisting snapshot.

Table 6-3. *URL Command Parameters*

Parameter	Description	Supported Values
Command	Specifies the type of request being made	GetDataSourceContents GetResourceContents ListChildren Render
Format	Specifies the format to render the report in	HTML4.0 MHTML IMAGE EXCEL CSV PDF XML NULL
Snapshot	Renders a report based on a snapshot	Valid ID of a snapshot

Credential Parameters

You can use the credential parameters in Table 6-4 to supply the username and password that the report server uses in order to connect to the data source to retrieve data for the report. SSRS 2005 uses credential parameters only if the credential settings for the data source in the report are set to prompt; otherwise, they're ignored. If the report has multiple data sources, you can use the credential parameters to supply credentials for each one.

Table 6-4. *URL Credential Parameters*

Parameter	Description	Example
dsu	Username to access the data source	dsu:employee=walter
dsp	Password to access the data source	dsp:employee=password

Example URLs

Now that you've examined every component part of the URL, it's useful to look at a few complete sample URLs. The following URL renders the report in HTML 4 and hides the HTML Viewer toolbar by setting the rc:Toolbar parameter value to false:

```
http://localhost/reportserver?/Pro_SSRS/Chapter_6/EmployeeServiceCost&rs:Command=➥
Render&rs:Format=HTML4.0&rc:Toolbar=false
```

The next example passes a report parameter for ServiceYear and hides the input display of user-supplied parameters:

```
http://localhost/reportserver?/Pro_SSRS/Chapter_6/EmployeeServiceCost&rs:Command=➥
Render&rs:Format=HTML4.0&rc:Parameters=false&ServiceYear=2003
```

The next one uses the rs:Format parameter to set the default output format to PDF:

```
http://localhost/reportserver?/Pro_SSRS/Chapter_6/EmployeeServiceCost&rs:Command=➥
Render&rs:Format=PDF
```

The final example hides the report document map:

```
http://localhost/reportserver?/Pro_SSRS/Chapter_6/EmployeeServiceCost&rs:Command=➥
  Render&rc:DocMap=false
```

You've taken a brief look at the commands you need to render a report through a URL. In the remainder of this chapter, we'll show how to create your own report viewer. The viewer will use URL commands to integrate an SSRS 2005 report into a .NET Windows Forms–based application.

Integrating SSRS 2005 with .NET Applications

Now that you have some understanding of how URL access works, you'll learn how you can render reports. You'll start by looking at how to render a report by building a Windows Forms SSRS 2005 viewer application that uses the new .NET 2.0 WebBrowser control and URL access to render reports for your application.

Building the Report Viewer Using a WebBrowser Control

We'll show how to create a simple Windows Forms application that contains the embedded browser, which you'll use to view a report.

Creating the Viewer Form

In this example, you will use C# to create the viewer application. Follow these steps:

1. Open Visual Studio 2005.

2. Create a new project.

3. On the New Project dialog box, select Visual C# ➤ Windows ➤ Windows Application. Name it SSRS Viewer WBC. Under Solution, select Create New Solution, and name it Chapter 6. Click OK to create your project.

Now that you have created the project, you'll work with the form you will use to create the report viewer:

1. Visual Studio 2005 will add a single form to the project called Form1.cs. Rename the form to ViewerWBC.cs.

2. Resize the blank form to 800×600.

3. Add the WebBrowser control from the Toolbox's Common Controls section to the form. Name it webBrowser, and anchor the control to the form's top, bottom, left, and right. The WebBrowser control is new to Visual Studio 2005 and simplifies working with the Web browser in your Windows Forms application. You no longer have to add or use COM Interop with the Internet Explorer COM browser control.

4. Now add a textbox, and name it reportURL. Just after the textbox, add a button named reportRun, and set the button text to Run.

You should now have a form that looks like Figure 6-1.

Figure 6-1. *The* ViewerWBC.cs *form*

> ■**Note** One of the great things about using the new WebBrowser control versus the old COM Interop method is that you no longer have to initialize the browser before you can use it. With the COM-based control, you had to navigate to a page before accessing the control. This was often done by adding code to the Form_Load event to navigate to about:blank when the form containing the control was loaded.

Coding the Viewer Form

To code the viewer form, you'll add the code necessary to use this custom report viewer to render the SSRS 2005 reports. You need to add some code to the button's click event to make sure you can browse to and view an existing report. Make sure the ViewerWBC.cs form is open in design view, and double-click the Run button. This will create an empty method to handle the button's click event. Add the code in Listing 6-1 to the method.

Listing 6-1. reportRun click *Event: Browsing to URL*

```
private void reportRun_Click(object sender, EventArgs e)
{
    webBrowser.Navigate(reportURL.Text);
}
```

Now run the project in debug mode. When the form displays, enter the following URL into the textbox:

```
http://localhost/reportserver/?➥
/Pro_SSRS/Chapter_6/EmployeeServiceCost&rs:Command=Render
```

Now click Run. This renders the Employee Service Cost report. Of course, you need to use the name of your report server where you see `localhost` in the preceding URL. At this point, you should see something like Figure 6-2.

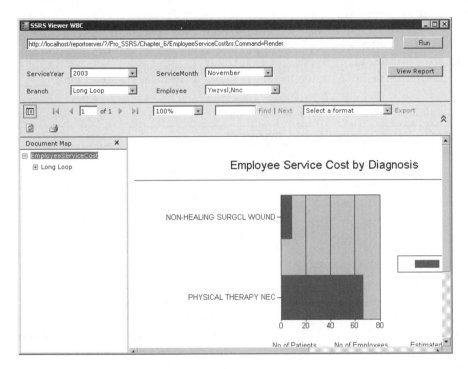

Figure 6-2. *SSRS Viewer WBC application running the Employee Service Cost report*

Next, change the constructor to set up a default report so you don't have to type it in each time. For example:

```
public ViewerWBC()
{
InitializeComponent();
// Setting the initial URL for convenience in the example
reportURL.Text = "http://localhost/reportserver/?➥
/Pro_SSRS/Chapter_6/EmployeeServiceCost&rs:Command=Render";
}
```

Building the Report Viewer Using a Report Viewer Control

Now you'll learn how you can use the new ReportViewer control to render the same Employee Service Cost report. The ReportViewer control is new to Visual Studio 2005 and simplifies working with reports in your .NET application when using Visual Studio 2005 and SSRS 2005.

Not only is it likely to be the most popular method for rendering server-based reports, but it also includes the ability to render reports based on the RDL locally without a report server. This was something that was not possible before.

You can use two new ReportViewer controls, one for Windows Forms applications and one for ASP.NET applications. These new controls allow you to add rich reporting features to your Windows or ASP.NET applications more easily than is possible using any other method. The controls offer the power of the URL rendering method but make it easier to implement in your code because most options are now set as properties on the ReportViewer control. In other words, you don't need to include them in the string that you pass in as the URL. Another main advantage of working with the controls is that you get full IntelliSense support for all the options within the Visual Studio 2005 IDE.

Table 6-5 lists some of the key properties and methods of the ReportViewer controls.

Table 6-5. *Sample ReportViewer Properties and Methods*

Property/Method	Description
ProcessingMode	Determines whether the report is processed locally or by an SSRS 2005 server.
ServerReport.ReportServerUrl	Specifies the URL of the reporting server it will use to render a report when in remote mode.
ServerReport.ReportPath	Specifies the path to the specific report you want to render. Do not include the report server URL as part of the path since it is defined by ReportServerUrl.
LocalReport.ReportEmbeddedResource	Specifies the name of the report to use. By default when you add a local report (rdlc) to a project, Visual Studio 2005 sets the report as an embedded resource. Other properties allow you to point to a path on disk or even a stream for the report definition.
LocalReport.DataSources.Add	Specifies the method used to add a data source to the report.
RefreshReport	Causes the report to be rendered.

■**Note** See the Visual Studio 2005 help for more information about the members of the ReportViewer control as well as for information about a number of other properties, methods, and events that come with the new ReportViewer controls.

In this example, we will cover how to use the Windows Forms version of the ReportViewer controls.

■**Note** In the "Using the Report Server Web Service" section, we will show how to extend the application so that it uses Report Server Web service calls to query the report server for the parameters the report can accept and the values that are possible for each. We'll show how to use these parameters to create drop-down lists for the users of the Windows Forms application.

Creating the Viewer Form

To create the viewer form in C#, you'll start by adding a new project to your solution by taking the following steps:

1. Select File ➤ Add Project ➤ New Project from the menu.

2. In the New Project dialog box, select Visual C# ➤ Windows ➤ Windows Application. Name it SSRS Viewer RVC.

Now that you have created the project, you'll work with the form that will create your report viewer:

1. Name the form ViewerRVC.cs.

2. Resize the blank form to around 800×600.

3. Add the ReportViewer control from the Toolbox's Data section to the form. Name the control reportViewer, and anchor it to the form's top, bottom, left, and right. The ReportViewer control is new to Visual Studio and SSRS 2005; it is not available in earlier versions of Visual Studio or SSRS.

4. Now add a textbox, name it reportURL, and just after the textbox add three buttons named runServer, runLocal, and getParameters. Set their Text properties to Run Server, Run Local, and Parameters, respectively.

You should now have a form that looks like Figure 6-3.

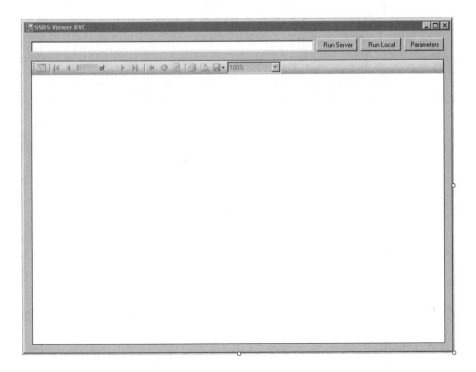

Figure 6-3. The ViewerRVC.cs form

You'll now start adding the code necessary to use the new ReportViewer control to render the SSRS 2005 reports.

Coding the Viewer Form

First, add a using statement for the new namespace, Microsoft.Reporting.WinForms, to the top of the class with the other namespace declarations. Doing this will allow you to access the members of the namespace without typing the full namespace each time you use a method or property from that namespace.

```
using Microsoft.Reporting.WinForms;
```

Second, add the code shown in Listing 6-2 to the Run Server button's click event. Make sure the ViewerRVC.cs form is open in design view, and double-click the Run Server button. This will create an empty method to handle the button's click event.

Listing 6-2. runServer click *Event: Running Report in Remote Mode*

```
private void runServer_Click(object sender, EventArgs e)
{
    reportURL.Text = "/Pro_SSRS/Chapter_6/EmployeeServiceCost";
    reportViewer.ProcessingMode =
        Microsoft.Reporting.WinForms.ProcessingMode.Remote;
    reportViewer.ServerReport.ReportServerUrl =
        new Uri(@"http://localhost/reportserver/");
    reportViewer.ServerReport.ReportPath = reportURL.Text;
    reportViewer.RefreshReport();
}
```

Now run the project in debug mode. Then click Run Server. This renders the Employee Service Cost report. Of course, you need to use the name of your report server where you see localhost in Listing 6-2. At this point, you should see something that looks like Figure 6-4.

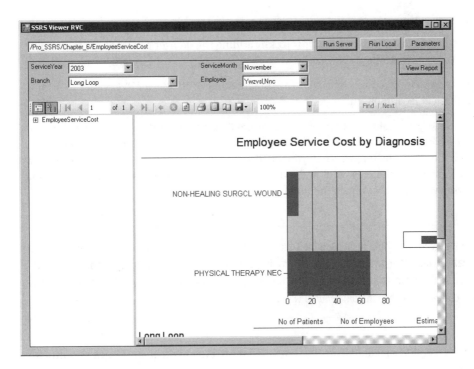

Figure 6-4. *SSRS Viewer RVC running a server report*

That's all there is to rendering a report on an SSRS 2005 server using the new ReportViewer control.

Rendering the Report Locally

We'll now cover how to render the report locally without using an SSRS 2005 server. It is a bit more complicated because you're responsible for filling the data sources with the data that your reports require. However, it does provide tremendous flexibility to the developer because you can use SSRS 2005 reporting features without a server.

■**Caution** The server and local report definition files are not 100 percent compatible. This means it is not possible to use the same RDL source file for both local and remote use. In fact, you will note that by default reports for server-side or remote processing are created with the `.rdl` extension and reports for client-side or local processing are created with the `.rdlc` extension. While they are not 100 percent interchangeable, you can use one for the other with some changes to the underlying RDL.

Creating the Report's Data Source

First you will add a data source to your project by adding the dataset you created previously. To add the data source, follow these steps:

1. In the Project Explorer, right-click the project name SSRS Viewer RVC, point to Add, and select Existing Item.

2. Navigate to the folder containing the Chapter 6 examples, and select EmployeePay.xsd in the SRSS Viewer RVC folder. This is the XML schema file you'll use to define your data source for the report. When you add the .xsd file to your project, it will also appear under the Data Sources window. If you don't see the Data Sources window, select Data ➤ Show Data Sources from the menu.

■**Note** Alternatively, you could have used the Data Source Configuration Wizard found by selecting Data ➤ Add New Data Source. With it you can create several types of data sources including those sourcing from a database, a Web service, or even an object. Just remember that much like this example, it is up to you to retrieve the data and populate the data source with it.

Next you'll create a local RDL (.rdlc) that you'll render using the ReportViewer control in local processing mode.

Designing the Report

To design the report, follow these steps:

1. To add a report to the project, right-click the project name—SSRS Viewer RVC—in the Solution Explorer.

2. On the shortcut menu, select Add ➤ New Item. This opens the Add New Item dialog box.

3. Click the Report icon, enter **EmployeePay.rdlc** for the file name, and then click Add. This launches the Report Designer. The .rdlc extension signifies that it is a report for client or local rendering.

4. Make sure the report is selected. Open the Toolbox. From the Toolbox, drag a Table report item onto the report.

5. From the Data Sources window, drag the EmployeeID field onto the middle row of the first column in the table. The middle row is the Detail row. Notice that the Header row automatically fills in for you when you specify the Detail row.

6. Drag the StartDate field onto the Detail row of the second column so that it is next to the EmployeeID field.

7. Drag the Amount field onto the Detail row of the third column so that it is next to the StartDate field.

You should now have a report that looks like Figure 6-5.

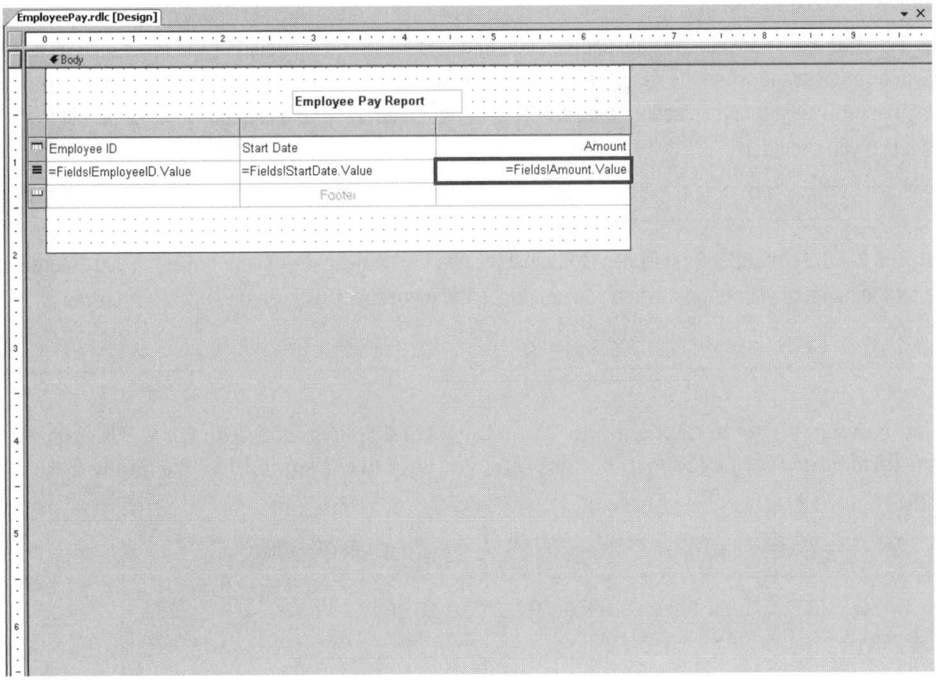

Figure 6-5. *Local report in the designer*

Now you have a report that uses the dataset you created as a data source. Now add the code shown in Listing 6-3 to the runLocal button's click event to populate the dataset and display the values in the ReportViewer control using the .rdlc file you have created. Make sure the ViewerRVC.cs form is open in design view, and double-click the Run Local button. This will create an empty method to handle the button's click event.

Listing 6-3. runLocal click *Event: Running Report in Local Mode*

```
private void runLocal_Click(object sender, EventArgs e)
{
    Employees empDS = new Employees();
    empDS.ReadXml(@"C:\Temp\EmployeePay.xml");
    reportViewer.ProcessingMode =
        Microsoft.Reporting.WinForms.ProcessingMode.Local;
    reportViewer.LocalReport.ReportEmbeddedResource =
        "SSRS_Viewer_RVC.EmployeePay.rdlc";
    reportViewer.LocalReport.DataSources.Add(
        new Microsoft.Reporting.WinForms.ReportDataSource(
            "Employees_EmployeePay", empDS.Tables["EmployeePay"]));
    reportViewer.RefreshReport();
}
```

■Note Make sure the name in the data source code matches the name expected by the report, or you will receive an error message when the report runs. You can determine the exact name by opening the .rdlc file using Report Designer and selecting Report ➤ Report Data Sources. The dialog box that opens will tell you the name you should use.

■Note The ReportEmbeddedResource value must include the namespace of your project. If you entered spaces for the name of your project when you created it, the namespace will use underscores in place of each space.

Now run the project in debug mode. When the form displays, click Run Local. This renders the local Employee Pay report. At this point, you should see something like Figure 6-6.

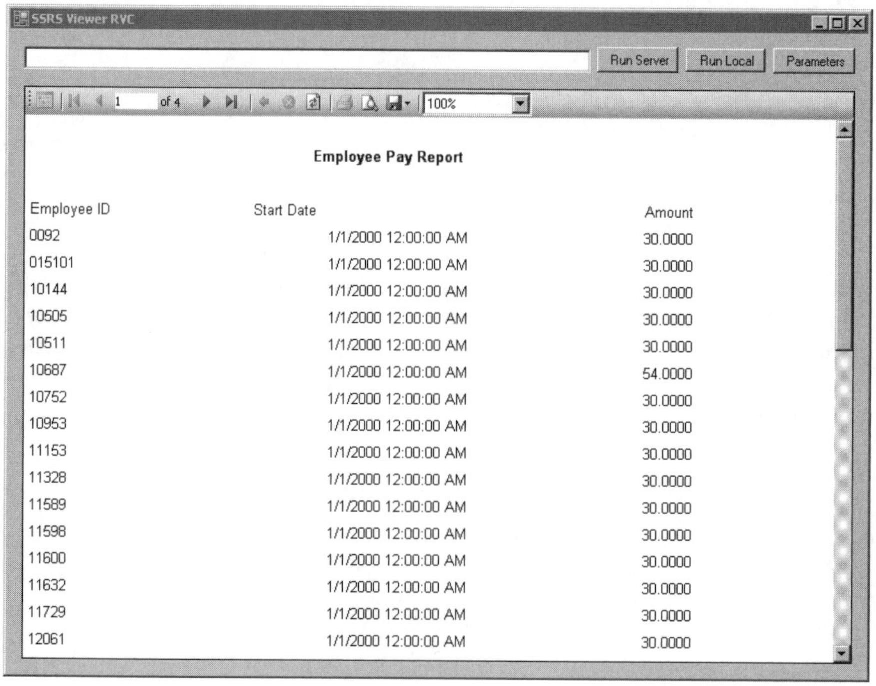

Figure 6-6. *SSRS Viewer RVC running a locally rendered report*

You've now created a report viewer in a Windows Forms application by using the Web-Browser control and URL rendering and by using the new ReportViewer control. You could stop at this point and just use these methods to render the reports and to display the report parameters, toolbar, and report. However, in this example, you want to use the SSRS 2005 Report Server Web service to get a list of parameters for the selected report and to display them to the user in a Windows Forms application. To get this list of parameters, you need to call the GetReportParameters method on the SSRS 2005 Report Server Web service.

Using the Report Server Web Service

The SSRS 2005 Web service is an XML-based Web service. It uses the SOAP API to allow you to call a variety of methods on the report server and interact with them using a rich set of objects provided by the service.

Web Services Method Categories

The Report Server Web service can control every aspect of the report server and consists of several categories of methods, as listed in Table 6-6.

Table 6-6. *Categories of the Report Server Web Services Methods*

Category	Manages
Namespace management	Folders and items on the server and their properties
Authorization	Tasks, roles, and policies
Data source connections	Data source connections and credentials
Report parameters	Setting the retrieval parameters for reports
Rendering and execution	Report execution, rendering, and caching
Report history	Snapshot creation and history
Scheduling	Shared schedule creation and modification
Subscription and delivery	Subscription creation and modification
Linked reports	Linked report creation and management

The Report Server Web service uses many of these methods to control aspects of SSRS 2005 that aren't directly related to rendering reports, so we won't cover them in this chapter. However, you should be aware of the level of control your custom application can have over SSRS 2005 and the types of functions that can be performed, because you might want to provide a user interface to them from your application. Keep in mind that Microsoft built the main SSRS 2005 report server application using ASP.NET and these Web services.

For the SSRS Viewer RVC, you are using the ReportViewer control to render the report, but you want to provide a custom Windows Forms–based user interface to allow users to enter their report parameters. The rest of this chapter concentrates on using methods from the report parameters category listed in Table 6-6. You'll use these methods to obtain a list of the parameters that the report expects and also to find the possible values for those parameters. You'll use this information to create and populate combo boxes that allow the users to enter their choices from a Windows Forms dialog box.

Creating the GetParameters Form

You already have a form (`ViewerRVC.cs`) to render and display the report in the embedded ReportViewer control. You'll now add a second form to the project that you'll use to display the report and rendering parameters and to allow the users to make their selections.

So, add a `GetParameters` form to your project by selecting Project ➤ Add Windows Form. Name the form `GetParameters.cs`. Onto this form, add two controls from the Toolbox; add a `FlowLayoutPanel` control named `parameterPanel`, and add one button control named `buttonOK`. Then set the text for the button to `OK`. When you're done, the form should look like Figure 6-7.

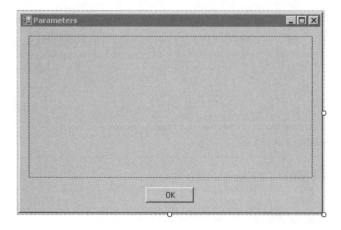

Figure 6-7. *SSRS Viewer RVC* GetParameters *form*

You now need to add a reference to the SSRS 2005 Web service to your project. You do this by selecting Project ➤ Add Web Reference or by right-clicking the references in the Solution Explorer and selecting Add Web Reference. When the dialog box appears, enter the following URL:

http://localhost/reportserver/reportservice2005.asmx

Substitute the name of your server for localhost. Then click the Go button. You'll see a dialog box similar to Figure 6-8.

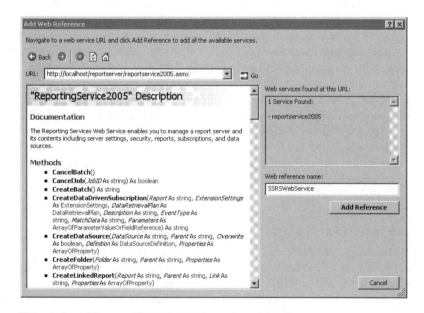

Figure 6-8. *Adding an SSRS 2005 Web service reference*

In the Web Reference Name textbox, enter **SSRSWebService**, which is the name by which you'll refer to your Web service in your code.

Once this dialog box is closed, you will add the following `using` statement to the top of your code in the `GetParameters` class. Note that if your project name is different from SSRS Viewer RVC, you should change the reference to reflect the name of your project.

```
using SSRS_Viewer_RVC.SSRSWebService;
```

Now you can reference the methods and properties exposed by the Web service much more easily because you won't have to enter the fully qualified namespace. Also, add the following directives:

```
using System.Web.Services.Protocols;
using System.Collections;
```

Doing this will allow you to access the members of these namespaces without needing to type the full namespace each time you use a method or property from that namespace.

Because you'll use this form as a dialog box to display the report parameters and their possible values, and allow the user to select them, you need a way to communicate between the two forms.

Coding the Report Parameters Form

When you instantiate the report parameters form (`GetParameters`), you do so by passing in the URL of the report the user has entered in the viewer form (`ViewerRVC.cs`). You use this URL to determine the report server name and the specific report the user wants to run. You need to know both of these for the calls to the report server Web service. Because you'll use this information throughout the rest of the code, in this class you store them in some class-level private variables, as shown in Listing 6-4.

Listing 6-4. *Class-Level Private Variables*

```
private string url;
private string server;
private string report;
private Microsoft.Reporting.WinForms.ReportParameter[] parameters;
ReportingService2005 rs;
```

In the form constructor, break the report server and report name into two separate fields. To break down the URL into the server and report name, use the string `split` method and create a constructor that looks like Listing 6-5.

Listing 6-5. *Report Parameters Form Constructor*

```
public GetParameters (string URL)
{
    InitializeComponent();
    url = URL;
    string[] reportInfo = url.Split('?');
    server = reportInfo[0];
    report = reportInfo[1];
}
```

The GetParameters_Load Event

Now you get to where the real work for this dialog box takes place: the Form_Load event. First, create a ReportingService object so that you can access SSRS 2005 through the Web service that you added as a reference earlier. Next, set your Windows credentials as the credentials to be used for calling the Web service, like so:

```
rs = new ReportingService2005();
rs.Credentials = System.Net.CredentialCache.DefaultCredentials;
```

■**Note** You can also use Basic authentication using rs.Credentials = new System.Net. Network-Credential("username", "password", "domain");. The method you use depends on the security settings for the report server virtual directory. By default, it's configured to use Windows authentication.

Calling the Web Services GetReportParameters Method

The GetReportParameters method takes five parameters:

- Report: The full path name of the report.

- ForRendering: A Boolean value that indicates how the parameter values should be used. You must set it to true to get a list of the possible values for each parameter.

- HistoryID: The ID of the report history snapshot. You set it to null because you aren't running the report from a snapshot.

- ParameterValues: The parameter values (ParameterValue[] objects) that can be validated against the parameters of the report that are managed by the report server. Set this to null for this example.

- Credentials: The data source credentials (DataSourceCredential[] objects) that can be used to validate query parameters. Set this to null for this example.

The GetReportParameters method returns an array of ReportParameter[] objects that contain the parameters for the report. You use this information to render combo boxes that allow the users to select the parameter values they want to use when running the report.

The following code sets up the variables you need to use and then calls the GetReportParameters method to retrieve a list of reports that the report expects, as shown in Listing 6-6.

Listing 6-6. *Call to* GetReportParameters

```
bool forRendering = true;
string historyID = null;
ParameterValue[] values = null;
DataSourceCredentials[] credentials = null;
ReportParameter[] parametersSSRS = null;
parametersSSRS = rs.GetReportParameters(report, historyID,
    forRendering, values, credentials);
```

Once you have the list of parameters from SSRS 2005, you loop through them using the values to create labels as you create your combo box for each parameter, like so:

```
foreach (ReportParameter rp in parametersSSRS)
```

Each ReportParameter object has a read-only property called ValidValues. You can use the ValidValues property, which returns an array of ValidValue objects to populate the items in each combo box, as shown in Listing 6-7.

Listing 6-7. *Iterating Through the* ValidValue *Objects*

```
if (rp.ValidValues != null)
{
    //Build list items
    ArrayList aList = new ArrayList();
    pvs = rp.ValidValues;
    foreach (ValidValue pv in pvs)
    {
        aList.Add(new ComboItem(pv.Label,pv.Value));
    }
    //Bind list items to combo box
    a.DataSource = aList;
    a.DisplayMember="Display";
    a.ValueMember="Value";
}
```

So, for each ReportParameter, you see whether any ValidValues properties exist. If so, you loop through them, adding each item to the combo box. Because you want to retrieve the display name and the actual value for each item in the combo box, you have to create a combo box item class and bind the objects to the combo box. Listing 6-8 shows the GetParameters_Load event, and Listing 6-9 shows the ComboItem class.

Listing 6-8. *Get Report Parameters and Possible Values, and Display Them in Combo Boxes*

```
private void GetParameters_Load(object sender, System.EventArgs e)
{
    rs = new ReportingService2005 ();
    rs.Credentials = System.Net.CredentialCache.DefaultCredentials;

    bool forRendering = true;
    string historyID = null;
    ParameterValue[] values = null;
    DataSourceCredentials[] credentials = null;
    ReportParameter[] parametersSSRS = null;
    ValidValue[] pvs = null;

    int x=5;
    int y=30;
```

```
try
{
    parametersSSRS = rs.GetReportParameters(report, historyID,
        forRendering, values, credentials);

    if (parametersSSRS != null)
    {
        foreach (ReportParameter rp in parametersSSRS)
        {
            this.SuspendLayout();
            this.parameterPanel.SuspendLayout();
            this.parameterPanel.SendToBack();
            // now create a label for the combo box below
            Label lbl = new Label();
            lbl.Anchor = (System.Windows.Forms.AnchorStyles.Top |
                System.Windows.Forms.AnchorStyles.Left);
            lbl.Location = new System.Drawing.Point(x, y);
            lbl.Name = rp.Name;
            lbl.Text = rp.Name;
            lbl.Size = new System.Drawing.Size(150, 20);
            this.parameterPanel.Controls.Add(lbl);
            x = x + 150;
            // now make a combo box and fill it
            ComboBox a = new ComboBox();
            a.Anchor = (System.Windows.Forms.AnchorStyles.Top |
                System.Windows.Forms.AnchorStyles.Right);
            a.Location = new System.Drawing.Point(x, y);
            a.Name = rp.Name;
            a.Size = new System.Drawing.Size(200, 20);
            x = 5;
            y = y + 30;
            this.parameterPanel.Controls.Add(a);
            this.parameterPanel.ResumeLayout(false);
            this.ResumeLayout(false);

            if (rp.ValidValues != null)
            {
                //Build listitems
                ArrayList aList = new ArrayList();
                pvs = rp.ValidValues;
                foreach (ValidValue pv in pvs)
                {
                    aList.Add(new ComboItem(pv.Label, pv.Value));
                }
                //Bind listitmes to combobox
                a.DataSource = aList;
                a.DisplayMember = "Display";
                a.ValueMember = "Value";
```

```
                }
            }
        }
    }

    catch (SoapException ex)
    {
        MessageBox.Show(ex.Detail.InnerXml.ToString());
    }
}
```

Listing 6-9. *Combo Item Class*

```csharp
public class ComboItem
{
    public ComboItem(string disp, string myvalue)
    {
        if (disp != null)
            display=disp;
        else
            display = "";
        if (myvalue != null)
            val=myvalue;
        else
            val = "";
    }

    private string val;
    public string Value
    {
        get{ return val;}
        set{ val=value;}
    }
    private string display;
    public string Display
    {
        get{ return display;}
        set{ display=value;}
    }

    public override string ToString()
    {
        return display;
    }
}
```

Upon loading, you'll see a form like Figure 6-9 that displays a series of combo boxes, each containing the valid values for the report parameters.

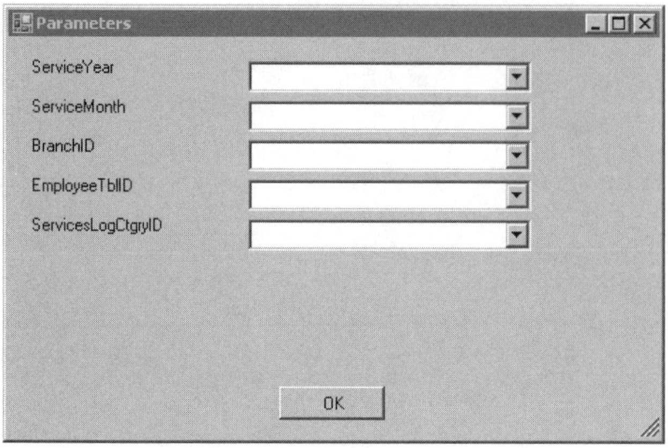

Figure 6-9. *The Parameters dialog box*

Rendering the Final Report

To finish your SSRS 2005 Windows Forms viewer application, you need to set the `parameters'` local variable to the parameter values the user has selected so you can retrieve them from the `ViewerRVC.cs` form using a property you will create in the `GetParameters` class called `Parameters`. You will populate the `parameters` variable by creating a method called `ViewerParameters`.

Make sure the `GetParameters` form is displayed in Designer mode, and double-click the OK button. To the `buttonOK` click event handler, add the code shown in Listing 6-10.

Listing 6-10. `buttonOK` click *Event Handler for the OK Button*

```
private void buttonOK_Click(object sender, EventArgs e)
{
    parameters = ViewerParameters();
    this.DialogResult = DialogResult.OK;
    Close();
}
```

The method that it calls, `ViewerParameters`, simply iterates through the combo boxes and creates an array of `ReportParameters`, which are essentially name-value pairs used by the ReportViewer control, as shown in Listing 6-11.

Listing 6-11. *Get Parameters Entered by User*

```
private Microsoft.Reporting.WinForms.ReportParameter[] ViewerParameters()
{
    int numCtrls = (this.parameterPanel.Controls.Count / 2);
    Microsoft.Reporting.WinForms.ReportParameter[] rp =
        New Microsoft.Reporting.WinForms.ReportParameter[numCtrls];
    int i = 0;
```

```
    foreach (Control ctrl in this.parameterPanel.Controls)
    {
        if (ctrl.GetType() == typeof(ComboBox))
        {
            ComboBox a = (ComboBox)ctrl;
            rp[i] =
                new Microsoft.Reporting.WinForms.ReportParameter();
            rp[i].Name = a.Name;
            if (a.SelectedValue != null &&
                a.SelectedValue.ToString() != String.Empty)
            {
                rp[i].Values.Add(a.SelectedValue.ToString());
            }
            else
            {
                rp[i].Values.Add(null);
            }
                i++;
        }
    }
    return rp;
}
```

To finish your GetParameters form, you need to add some code to allow you to pass the report parameters and their values to the viewer form (ViewerRVC.cs), as shown in Listing 6-12.

Listing 6-12. *Property Used to Get Parameters from the* ViewerRVC.cs *Form*

```
public Microsoft.Reporting.WinForms.ReportParameter[] Parameters
{
    get
    {
        return parameters;
    }
}
```

To bring it all together, you need to add a button and related code to its click event in the ViewerRVC.cs form to use the new Parameters dialog box, passing in the URL of the report you want to run. Then you read the ReportParameter array through the GetParameters forms Parameters property and use it to set the report parameters for the ReportViewer control, as shown in Listing 6-13.

Listing 6-13. getParameters click *Event: Retrieving the Parameters and Running the Report*

```
private void getParameters_Click(object sender, EventArgs e)
{
reportURL.Text = "http://localhost/reportserver?➥
    /Pro_SSRS/Chapter_6/EmployeeServiceCost";
GetParameters reportParameters = new GetParameters(reportURL.Text);
if (reportParameters.ShowDialog() == DialogResult.OK)
```

```
{
    reportViewer.ProcessingMode =
        Microsoft.Reporting.WinForms.ProcessingMode.Remote;
    reportViewer.ServerReport.ReportServerUrl =
        new Uri(@"http://localhost/reportserver/");
    reportViewer.ServerReport.ReportPath =
        "/Pro_SSRS/Chapter_6/EmployeeServiceCost";
    reportViewer.ServerReport.SetParameters(reportParameters.Parameters);
    reportViewer.ShowParameterPrompts = false;
    reportViewer.RefreshReport();
}
}
```

Now run the project in debug mode. When the form displays, click Parameters. The Parameters dialog form will be displayed. Select 2003 for the ServiceYear option, leave the other drop-down lists blank, and click OK. This renders the local Employee Service Cost report, which is located on the SSRS 2005 server using the parameters you have supplied. At this point, you should see something that looks like Figure 6-10.

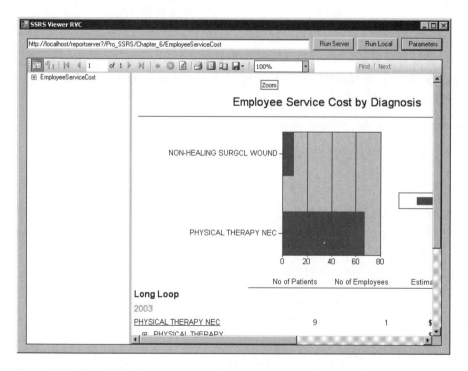

Figure 6-10. *The finished report using your parameters*

Now you have a foundation for a report viewer to use with Windows Forms. This example has implemented URL access as well as used the new ReportViewer controls for rendering the reports, providing you with multiple choices for integrating reporting into your Windows

Forms applications. You've made your viewer a lot more user-friendly by using SSRS 2005's SOAP-based API to access the rich functionality of SSRS 2005 to retrieve the available report parameters and possible values. This allows you to create a more familiar and responsive Windows-based user interface for your users.

You can also render reports using the Report Server Web service directly. However, you lose the functionality of features such as the report toolbar with its built-in navigation and export functionality. This means you have to create these on your own if you use the SOAP API for rendering.

Summary

In this chapter, we showed how to use the URL access capabilities of SSRS 2005 and the new ReportViewer controls to embed reports quickly into applications. Beyond the WebBrowser and ReportViewer controls used in this chapter, you can use other applications to render reports. For example, SSRS 2005 includes a new Report Viewer Web Part for Windows Share-Point Services and SharePoint Portal Server as well as a Report Explorer Web Part. We'll discuss using these in greater detail in Chapter 10. By combining SharePoint and SSRS 2005, you can quickly build a portal that displays your reports without much code at all.

In this chapter, you also learned how to make Report Server Web service calls to augment your Windows Forms viewer application. The application you created allows you to type the URL of a server-based report you want to view. It then uses SSRS 2005's `GetReportParameters` method to retrieve a list of report parameters and the `ValidValues` method to retrieve possible values. It then reads the values selected by the user and populates an array of `ReportParamters`, which is then used by the Report Viewer control to render your report with the selected parameters. In Chapter 8, we'll expand on this example by using the Report Server Web service to allow the user to set the report to run on a schedule with the supplied parameters instead of rendering it immediately.

CHAPTER 7

■■■

Deploying Reports

Throughout the lifecycle of a report—from creation to maintenance—administrators, developers, and now even end users using Report Builder need to deploy reports continually to the SSRS 2005 server. Deploying a report simply means uploading the RDL file onto the SSRS 2005 server so that your users can use it. (For more information on the specifics of the RDL format of these reports, see Chapter 3.)

Fortunately, SSRS 2005 provides several means for deploying reports:

Using the Report Manager interface through your Web browser: This simple method allows anyone with an RDL file to upload it to the SSRS 2005 server. This can be especially useful if you're developing your report's RDL files in an application that doesn't provide you with a method to upload them to the server. It's also useful if you want to make a quick edit of the RDL file—say to change a misspelled word—using an application such as Notepad, which doesn't offer a built in way to upload the report. We cover this scenario in Chapter 8, where Notepad is used to modify a report.

Using the Import option in SSMS: SSMS is now a centralized management tool for all services provided by SQL Server 2005 including Reporting Services. You can use SSMS to import reports and add data sources.

Using the Deploy option in SQL Server BIDS: This method allows you to deploy your reports to the SSRS 2005 server from directly within your development environment. If you're using BIDS and have direct access to the report server to which you want to deploy your reports, this is by far one of the easiest options.

Using the Deploy option in Visual Studio 2005: This method is essentially identical to deploying a report with BIDS, thanks to the high level of integration between SQL Server 2005 and Visual Studio 2005.

Using the Save option in Report Builder: Using the Save option in Report Builder offers a quick and simple way to deploy your custom reports built with Report Builder. We cover this method in Chapter 11, when building and deploying a custom report.

Using the `rs` command-line utility: The rs command-line utility is a runtime environment used to execute VB .NET code in the form of specially formatted script files. You deploy the report in the same way as the method in the next item of this list. You can find out more about the `rs` command-line utility in Reporting Services Books Online.

Programmatically, using the SOAP API: This method gives you complete control over the deployment process with the added advantage of creating any type of UI you want. Unlike the rs command-line utility, you have your choice of languages and the full power of Visual Studio 2005 to help you develop your custom interface. In Chapter 6, we used the SOAP API, otherwise known as the Report Server Web service, to retrieve report parameter information about reports from the SSRS 2005 server, and then used that information to generate a Windows Forms UI for parameter selection. In this chapter, you'll use the Report Server Web service to publish reports to the SSRS 2005 server. This type of interface is useful when you need to integrate the deployment of reports into your setup, installation, or runtime environment for your custom application.

Using Report Manager

To deploy reports using the Report Manager interface, simply open your browser and navigate to your SSRS 2005 server using an address such as http://localhost/reports/. You see a screen similar to the one in Figure 7-1.

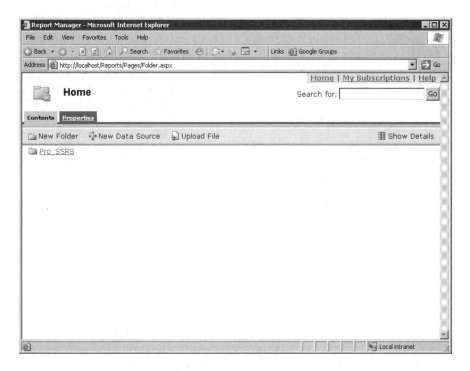

Figure 7-1. *Report Manager*

As you can see, an Upload File option is on the Report Manager toolbar. Selecting Upload File opens a standard browser-based upload-style dialog box such as the one shown in Figure 7-2.

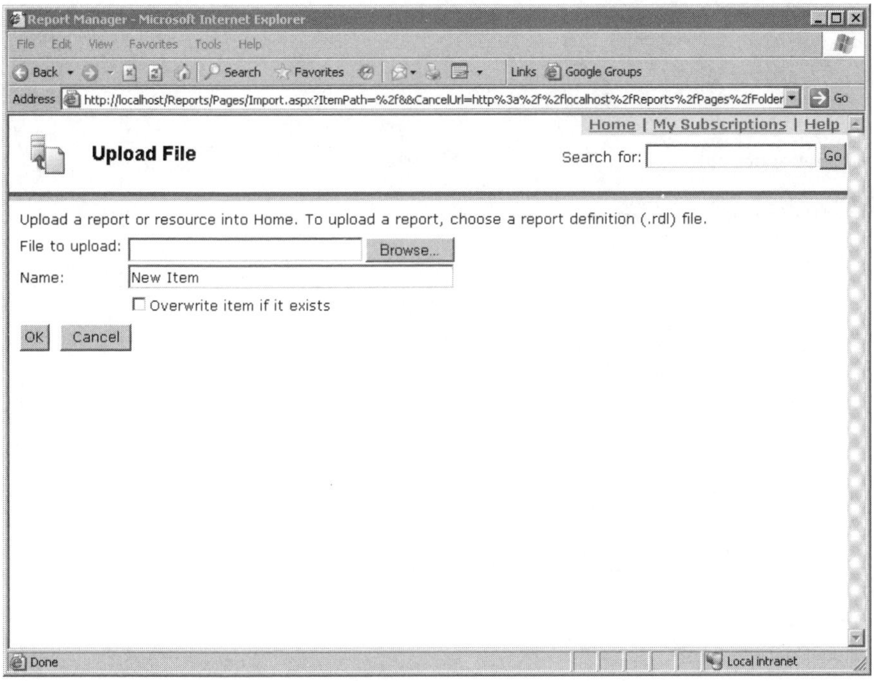

Figure 7-2. *Report Manager Upload File dialog box*

Using this dialog box, you can browse to the RDL file that you want to upload and then upload it. Report Manager places the file into the current folder (the one from which you initiated the upload process).

After the report is uploaded, you can use the Report Properties page of Report Manager to modify the properties of the report, such as the name and description, as shown in Figure 7-3.

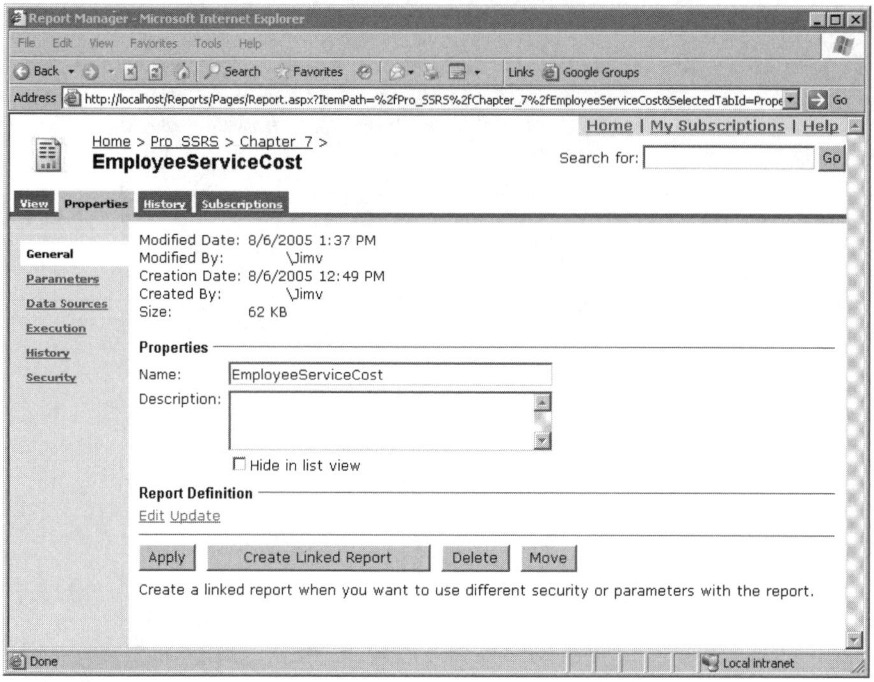

Figure 7-3. *Report Properties page*

This page also enables you to do the following:

Hide the report in the list view: This can be useful if you don't want users with access to the SSRS 2005 server to know that certain reports exist or if you don't want them to see the detailed information about the report. Remember that this only hides the report in the summary view and not the detail view. You can combine the capability to hide reports with security when you need to prevent a user from running a report.

Edit the RDL and update it by uploading a new copy of the RDL file: This can be useful when you want to make a minor modification to a report, such as changing the spelling of a word or modifying an expression. Keep in mind that this method only provides you access to the RDL file; you still have to use another program to edit the file, and then you have to upload the modified file.

Delete the report and/or move it to another location on your report server: This gives you the ability to remove reports that are no longer needed and to organize the reports into folders for organizational and security purposes.

■**Note** You can perform many of these same operations in detail view by clicking the Show Details icon on the Report Manager toolbar.

Using SQL Server Management Studio (SSMS)

To deploy reports using the SSMS, simply open SSMS and connect to your SSRS 2005 server. When the Connect to Server dialog box appears, select Reporting Server in the Server Type list-box. The Server Name selection defaults to the local server's actual name, which you can use if appropriate. If running locally, you can also use `localhost`. If your SSRS 2005 services are running on a different server, simply enter the name here. Choose the appropriate Authentication type; this is usually the default Windows Authentication. You should see a screen similar to the one in Figure 7-4.

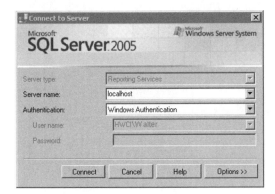

Figure 7-4. *SSMS Connect to Server dialog box*

After you've connected to your SSRS 2005 server, you'll see it listed in the Object Explorer and in the main Summary tab, as shown in Figure 7-5.

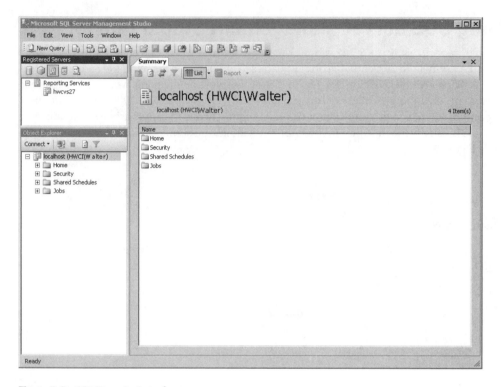

Figure 7-5. *SSMS main interface*

The Home folder that you see in Figure 7-5 represents the root folder where your reports are stored on the SSRS 2005 server. You can click on the Home folder to navigate to other folders on your SSRS 2005 server, or you can right-click and create new ones. You can also set up new data sources and import report files. To import a report's rdl file, right-click on the folder you want to import the file to and the shortcut menu shown in Figure 7-6 appears.

Figure 7-6. *Shortcut menu from a folder*

Select Import File as shown in Figure 7-6. On the Import File form, click the ellipsis button to browse to the RDL file you want to upload. You can then set the name of the file as it will appear on the report server and select to overwrite the file if it already exists. After you have selected the file and named it, it will appear similar to Figure 7-7. Click OK and the report you selected is imported to your SSRS 2005 server.

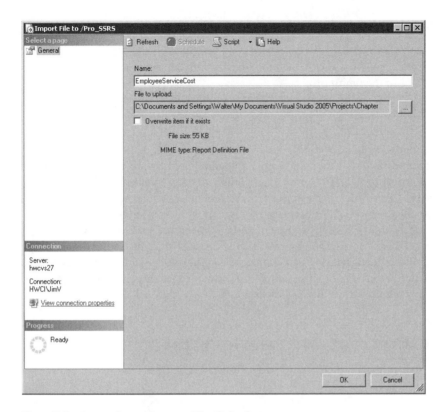

Figure 7-7. *Report Server Import File dialog box*

Using BIDS and Visual Studio 2005

You also can deploy reports using the Deploy option in BIDS and Visual Studio 2005. This is convenient, because probably you'll be using one of these to develop your reports in many cases. In the examples in this chapter, we are looking specifically at Visual Studio 2005; however, using BIDS is nearly identical because they are both now based on the same IDE.

Configuring Report Deployment Options

BIDS and Visual Studio 2005 allow you to configure a different set of properties for each project in your solution. You also can set these properties for each configuration available for your project, such as Debug, DebugLocal, and Release. For each configuration of a report project, you can define values uniquely for the following properties:

- *StartItem*: The name of the report to be displayed in the preview window or in a browser window when the report project is run.

- *OverwriteDataSources*: A Boolean value indicating whether or not to overwrite an existing data source on the server. Set it to true to overwrite, which redeploys any data sources you have defined in your project each time you select Deploy. Set it to false if you don't want existing data sources overwritten.

- *TargetDataSourceFolder*: The name of the folder in which to place your shared data sources.

- *TargetReportFolder*: The name of the folder in which to place your reports. By default, this is the name of the report project.

- *TargetServerURL*: The URL of the target report server, such as http://localhost/reportserver.

The different configurations are convenient for the report developer because you can set up different servers and/or folders for testing and deployment in the same project. By default, when you create a report project, BIDS and Visual Studio 2005 create three different configurations for you: Debug, DebugLocal, and Production. You can access the properties for these configurations through the project's Property Pages. To get to the configuration Property Pages, in the Solution Explorer, right-click the project containing the reports and then click Properties. To see the property settings for each configuration option, select from the Configuration dropdown list at the top of the dialog box. Figure 7-8 shows the Property Pages for the Reports project in the Chapter 7 Solution that is part of the sample code provided for this chapter in the Source Code area of the Apress Web site (http://www.apress.com).

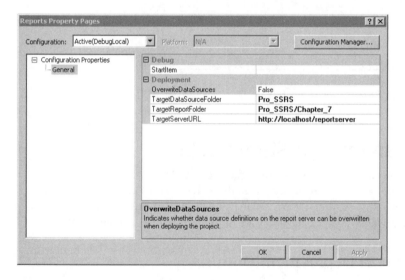

Figure 7-8. *Project Property Pages*

After the configuration information is set up correctly in Visual Studio 2005, you can deploy reports to your server by using the Build and Deploy options in the Configuration Manager or by using the Solution Explorer.

Deploying Reports Using the Configuration Manager

The Build and Deploy options in the Configuration Manager determine whether reports are built, deployed, or both when you start the project in Visual Studio 2005.

To open the Configuration Manager, in the Solution Explorer, right-click the project containing the reports and then click Properties. From there, click Configuration Manager to open the dialog box shown in Figure 7-9.

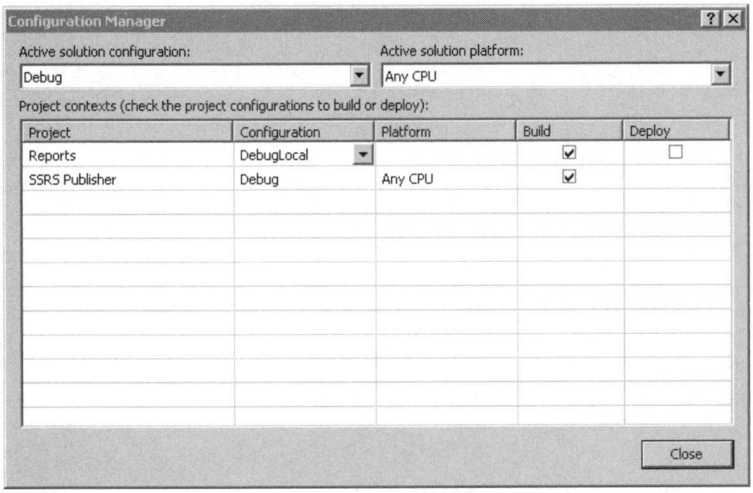

Figure 7-9. *Visual Studio 2005 Configuration Manager*

By default, you see the setup for the currently active configuration. You can select other configurations by choosing from the Active solution configuration drop-down list. As you can see, for each project in your solution, checkboxes are in the Build and the Deploy columns.

Each time you start the project, you want to build it so that you will always run the latest version of your report. If the Deploy checkbox is also checked, then whenever you start the project in that configuration, Visual Studio 2005 deploys the reports to the specified server. However, for certain configurations, such as when you're debugging locally, you won't necessarily want to deploy your report to the server.

Deploying Reports Through Solution Explorer

You can also deploy reports from the Solution Explorer. A list of options follows for deploying from the Solution Explorer. You deploy your reports by right-clicking each of the following items and selecting Deploy:

- *The solution*: Deploys the reports in all the Report Server Projects in your solution to the server that has been set up in each project's properties.

- *The project*: Deploys the reports in the specific project in your solution to the server that has been set up in the specified project's properties. This option is only available for Report Server projects.

- *The report*: Deploys an individual report from a project in your solution to the server that has been set up in the project properties containing the report you're deploying.

Figure 7-10 shows an example of deploying all the reports in a project.

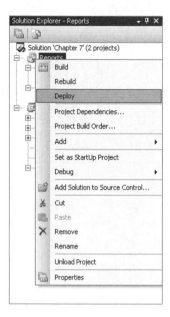

Figure 7-10. *Deploying a solution through the Solution Explorer*

Using the Report Server Web Service

The method provided by SSRS 2005 for deploying reports programmatically is through using the Report Server Web service also known as the SOAP API (introduced in Chapter 6 when we wrote our report viewer). In this section, we'll look at deploying reports to SSRS 2005 by using a Windows Forms application that simulates what customers need to do after they have an RDL file ready for deployment:

- Select a report server to publish their report to.

- Select from a displayed list of folders on that server to determine which folder on the server to publish the report to.

- Browse to the RDL file that is to be uploaded to their report server.

You will use the Report Server Web service to get a list of folders on the server and then upload the report to the server. In this example, you'll upload some of the reports created for the health-care provider. In the healthcare setting, it's important to maintain strict control over the report folders and their permissions on the server, so you won't allow the users to create a new folder, only to upload to the existing folders that they already have permission to use.

The CreateReport method of the Report Server Web service allows you to deploy the report to the report server by creating a copy of the report on the server from an RDL file that you provide, using the following parameters:

- *Report*: A string that is the name of the new report. SSRS 2005 uses this name, and it appears in the SSRS 2005 Report Manager.

- *Parent*: A string that is the full path name of the parent folder to add the report to.

- *Overwrite*: A Boolean expression that indicates whether an existing report with the same name in the location specified should be overwritten.

- *Definition*: Byte array containing the report definition to publish to the report server. This is an in-memory representation of the report that's created by reading the RDL file from disk.

- *Properties*: An array of Property[ ] objects that contains the property names and values to set for the report. Property[ ] objects are simply name-value pairs that hold the report's properties. You can use them to set the description of your report, for example, by using the Description property.

■**Note** The CreateReport method might pass sensitive data, including user credentials, over the network. You should use SSL encryption whenever possible when making Web service calls with this method.

First you'll create a new C# Windows Forms solution with Visual Studio 2005. Call this project SSRS_Publisher.

Accessing the Web Service

You need to add a reference to the SSRS 2005 Report Server Web service, which is the same as you did in Chapter 6 for the report viewer. You do this by selecting Project ➤ Add Web Reference or by right-clicking the references in the Solution Explorer and selecting Add Web Reference. When the dialog box appears, enter the following URL:

http://localhost/reportserver/reportservice2005.asmx

Substitute the name of your server for localhost in the preceding URL, and then click the Go button. You see a dialog box similar to the one in Figure 7-11.

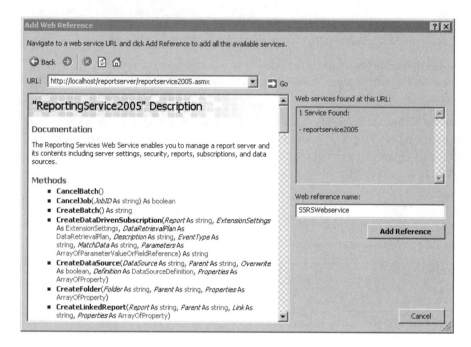

Figure 7-11. *Add Web Reference dialog box*

In the Web reference name textbox, enter **SSRSWebService**, which is how the Web service is referenced in the code.

After this dialog box is closed, add the following `using` directives to the code:

```
using SSRS_Publisher.SSRSWebService;
```

Now you can reference the Web service much more easily because you don't have to enter the fully qualified namespace. You'll also add three other `using` directives that allow you to access the Web services and I/O-specific functions more easily in your code, as shown in Listing 7-1.

Listing 7-1. *Using Directives*

```
using System.IO;
using System.Text.RegularExpressions;
using System.Web.Services.Protocols;
```

Laying Out the Form

From the Toolbox, add one label, one textbox, and one button near the top of the form, set the label text to **Report server**, and name the textbox `reportServer`. Name the button `getFolders` and set its text to **Go**. You'll use the `reportServer` textbox to allow the user to enter in the report server URL that they want to deploy to.

Next, add a TreeView control to the center of the form and name it **ssrsFolders**. You'll use it to display a list of available folders on the server where you can upload your report when the user enters in a server name and clicks Go.

Add one label, one textbox, and one button near the bottom of the form; set the label text to **Report file**; name the textbox reportFile; name the button browseFile; and set the text to **Browse**. You'll use the reportFile textbox to accept or display the path name and file name of the report file you want to upload to the specified SSRS 2005 server. You'll use the Browse buttons to choose the form that accepts the users' input.

After you've added all these controls, the form should look something like Figure 7-12.

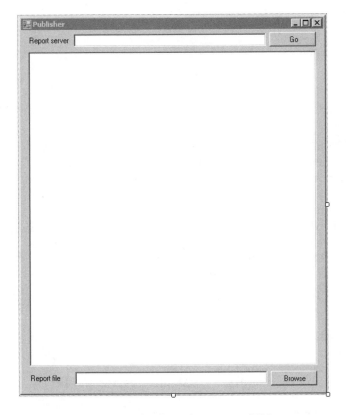

Figure 7-12. *Publisher, the example report publisher*

Coding the Form

Now that you have the form laid out, you'll add code to handle the functions necessary to allow users to do the following:

1. Enter in a server name.

2. Get a list of the folders available on that server.

3. Select the folder to upload to.

4. Select an RDL file to upload.

Identifying the SSRS 2005 Server

When a user types in a server name on the form, the code needs to build the URL that fully identifies the SSRS 2005 server to deploy the RDL file to.

First, you create a class-level variable to hold the reference to the report server, much as you did in the SSRS viewers in Chapter 6. You do this by adding the variable definition `private ReportingService2005 rs;` to the class, as shown in Listing 7-2.

Listing 7-2. *Class-level Variable in Context*

```
public partial class Publisher : Form
{

    private ReportingService2005 rs;

    public Publisher()
```

To build the URL that identifies the server based on the user input, you first instantiate the Report Server Web service and then set the URL property to reflect the name of the server that the user entered into the `reportServer` textbox.

To do this, first create a short function to check the server name that the user enters and then append the rest of the path name to the Reporting Services Web service to make up the complete URL necessary to reference the Reporting Services Web service on the desired server. By constructing the URL based on the user's input, you can use the report deployment application to deploy the reports on any SSRS 2005 server where the user has permission to do so. Start by adding the code shown in Listing 7-3 into the `Publisher` class.

Listing 7-3. *Get Report Server URL*

```
private string GetRSURL()
{
    if (reportServer.Text.StartsWith("http://"))
        return reportServer.Text + "/reportserver/ReportService2005.asmx";
    else
        return "http://" + reportServer.Text
            + "/reportserver/ReportService2005.asmx";
}
```

Populating the TreeView Control

Now you'll use the Reporting Services Web service to retrieve a list of objects from the server and use them to populate the `ssrsFolders` TreeView control. We'll do this by placing a call to the `ListChildren` method of the Report Server Web service.

The `ListChildren` method takes two parameters:

- *Item*: The full path name of the parent folder.

- *Recursive*: A Boolean expression that indicates whether to return the entire tree of child items below the specified item. The default value is `false`.

■**Note** The `ListChildren` method returns all objects on the report server, including data sources and reports, not just folders. In this example, you'll filter out everything but the folders because you're only interested in the folders. You do this by using the `ItemTypeEnum` enumeration object and then testing it against the `Type` property of the `CatalogItem`.

Make sure the `Publisher.cs` form is open in design view and double-click the Go button. This creates an empty method to handle the button's `click` event. Add the code in Listing 7-4 to the method.

Listing 7-4. *Code to Populate the TreeView Control*

```
private void getFolders_Click(object sender, EventArgs e)
{
    ssrsFolders.Nodes.Clear();
    rs = new ReportingService2005();
    rs.Credentials = System.Net.CredentialCache.DefaultCredentials;
    CatalogItem[] items = null;
    rs.Url = GetRSURL();

    TreeNode root = new TreeNode();
    root.Text = "Root";
    ssrsFolders.Nodes.Add(root);
    ssrsFolders.SelectedNode = ssrsFolders.TopNode;

    // Retrieve a list of items from the server
    try
    {
        items = rs.ListChildren("/", true);

        int j = 1;

        // Iterate through the list of items and find all of the folders
        // and display them to the user
        foreach (CatalogItem ci in items)
        {
            if (ci.Type == ItemTypeEnum.Folder)
            {
                Regex rx = new Regex("/");
                int matchCnt = rx.Matches(ci.Path).Count;
                if (matchCnt > j)
                {
                    ssrsFolders.SelectedNode =
                        ssrsFolders.SelectedNode.LastNode;
                    j = matchCnt;
                }
```

```
                else if (matchCnt < j)
                {
                    ssrsFolders.SelectedNode = ssrsFolders.SelectedNode.Parent;
                    j = matchCnt;
                }
                AddNode(ci.Name);
            }
        }
    }

    catch (SoapException ex)
    {
        MessageBox.Show(ex.Detail.InnerXml.ToString());
    }
    catch (Exception ex)
    {
        MessageBox.Show(ex.Message);
    }

    // Make sure the user can see that the root folder is selected by default
    ssrsFolders.HideSelection = false;

}
```

Right below the method for the Go button's click event, add the following method as shown in Listing 7-5.

Listing 7-5. *AddNode Method*

```
private void AddNode(string name)
{
    TreeNode newNode = new TreeNode(name);
    ssrsFolders.SelectedNode.Nodes.Add(newNode);
}
```

You tell the ListChildren method to start at the root folder by passing in a "/" as the starting point, and also set the recursive option to true, which causes the ListChildren method to iterate through all the folders and subfolders on the SSRS 2005 server. You use this information to create nodes in the TreeView control to display each folder in a hierarchy that represents the hierarchy of the folders on the server. Use a regular expression to look for the number of "/" characters in the path of each CatalogItem to determine how deep you are in the hierarchy (one level, two levels, and so on).

Opening the RDL File and Uploading It to the Server

Now you need to add some code to allow users to browse for the file that they want to upload. You'll want to limit the users to browsing for files ending in "rdl" by default, because this is the native extension for SSRS 2005 report definition files. You also want to read the selected node in the ssrsFolders TreeView so that you know what folder users have selected to deploy the report to on the SSRS 2005 server.

Start by reading the path of the selected node from the TreeView control and turning it into a path name you can use with SSRS 2005's CreateReport method.

Make sure the Publisher.cs form is open in design view and double-click the Browse button. This creates an empty method to handle the button's click event. Add the code in Listing 7-6 to the method.

Listing 7-6. *Code to Browse for an RDL File*

```
private void browseFile_Click(object sender, EventArgs e)
{
    // Get the full path name from the TreeView control
    string pathName = ssrsFolders.SelectedNode.FullPath;

    if (pathName == "Root")
        pathName = "/";
    else
    {
        // Strip off the Root name from the path and
        // correct the path separators for use with SSRS
        pathName = pathName.Substring(4, pathName.Length - 4);
        pathName = pathName.Replace(@"\", "/");
    }

    byte[] definition = null;
    Warning[] warnings = null;
    string warningMsg = String.Empty;

    OpenFileDialog openFileDialog = new OpenFileDialog();
    openFileDialog.Filter = "RDL files (*.rdl)|*.rdl|All files (*.*)|*.*";
    openFileDialog.FilterIndex = 1;
    if (openFileDialog.ShowDialog() == DialogResult.OK)
    {
        try
        {
            // Read the file and put it into a byte array to pass to SRS
            FileStream stream = File.OpenRead(openFileDialog.FileName);
            definition = new byte[stream.Length];
            stream.Read(definition, 0, (int)(stream.Length));
            stream.Close();
        }
        catch (Exception ex)
        {
            MessageBox.Show(ex.Message);
        }
```

```csharp
        // We are going to use the name of the RDL file as the name of our report
        string reportName =
            Path.GetFileNameWithoutExtension(openFileDialog.FileName);
        reportFile.Text = reportName;

        // Now let's use this information to publish the report
        try
        {
            warnings = rs.CreateReport(reportName, pathName, true, definition, null);
            if (warnings != null)
            {
                foreach (Warning warning in warnings)
                {
                    warningMsg += warning.Message + "\n";
                }
                MessageBox.Show ➥
                    ("Report creation failed with the following warnings:\n" + ➥
                        warningMsg);
            }
            else
                MessageBox.Show ➥
                    (String.Format ➥
                        ("Report: {0} created successfully with no warnings", ➥
                            reportName));
        }
        catch (SoapException ex)
        {
            MessageBox.Show(ex.Detail.InnerXml.ToString());
        }


    }
}
```

The code starts by getting the full path on the SSRS 2005 server where the user has selected to place the report from the ssrsFolders TreeView control, strips the word *Root* off the front of the path, and then replaces all occurrences of a backslash in the string with the forward slash needed for SSRS 2005.

You then set the options for the openFileDialog control so that it browses by default for files with the RDL extension and then displays the dialog box to the user. If the user makes a selection, the file is opened using a FileStream object and read from the stream into a byte array. That's because the SSRS 2005 CreateReport method expects the contents of the RDL file to be passed in as a byte array.

Next the file name that the user selected is read and used as the title for the report in SSRS 2005. After you have a title, you have everything necessary to upload the report, which you do by calling the CreateReport method with the values you've created. You can see at the end of Listing 7-6 where the necessary code has been added into the complete listing.

Running the Application

Now let's run the example. Start the project and when the form displays, enter the name of your report server in the Server textbox and click Go. localhost was used in the example; use the name of your server if it is different. Your form now looks similar to Figure 7-13, with the folders on your SSRS 2005 server displayed and the Root folder highlighted.

Note You need to deploy the Shared Data Source from the Chapter 7 sample code prior to uploading the sample report included in Chapter 7. The report uses this shared data source and will tell you that it could not publish the report because it can't find the shared data source on the SSRS 2005 server. Also note that the shared data source in this chapter is in the local Chapter 7 folder instead of the Pro_SSRS folder we have been using. We did this because when uploading the report using the SSRS Publisher, it will make the connection to the shared data source Pro_SSRS only if it resides in the same folder as you deploy the report to.

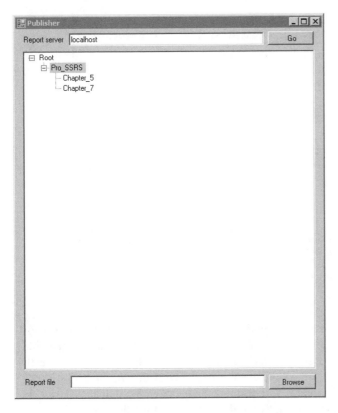

Figure 7-13. *Complete report publisher showing folders on the SSRS 2005 server*

By default, the Root folder on your server has been selected. Drill down and select the Chapter 7 node in the TreeView. After you've selected the folder to use, click Open and select the report included in the EmployeeServiceCost.rdl file included in the Chapter 7 sample code. When you click Open, your report publishing application uses the Report Server Web services CreateReport method and publishes the report to the selected server.

In this case, the Pro_SSRS/Chapter_7 folder on the localhost server has been selected, and we're uploading a report called EmployeeServiceCost.rdl. If you navigate to that folder with your Web browser, you'll see something similar to the screen shown in Figure 7-14 (note that Report Manager marks it as "!NEW" to indicate that it has just been deployed).

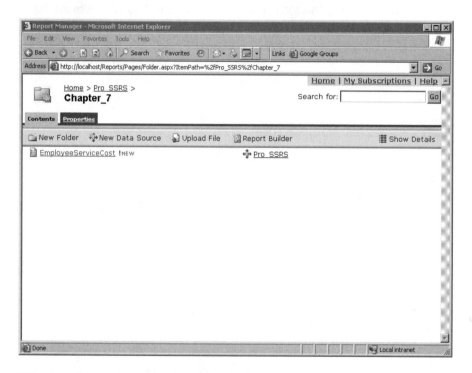

Figure 7-14. *Report Manager showing uploaded report*

You now have a Windows Forms application that allows files to be uploaded to your report server. This can be a handy way to add the capability to upload or update reports from within an application without needing the user to interact with the SSRS 2005 Report Manager directly.

This can be especially useful if you want users to interact with all aspects of SSRS 2005 from within your application. In Chapter 6, you developed an application that allows users to display reports from within the application. By combining that application with this report publisher, you can handle a number of nonadministrative tasks directly from your application. You also could expand on this example by providing the user with some additional options:

- You could allow the user to create shared data sources.

- You could allow the user to enter the name of the report to publish instead of taking the name from the RDL file itself. For example, you could add another textbox to the form and read it for the report title. So, instead of the following code:

```
// We are going to use the name of the RDL file
// as the name of our report
string reportName =
    Path.GetFileNameWithoutExtension(openFileDialog.FileName);
```

  you could do the following:

```
// We are going to read the contents of textbox reportTitle
// as the name of our report
string reportName = reportTitle.text
```

- You could allow the user to set other properties of the report, such as adding a description that will be displayed in Report Manager in the detailed list view. For example, you could add a `Description` property:

```
Property[] itemProps = new Property[1];
Property itemProp = new Property();
itemProp.Name = "Description";
itemProp.Value = "Employee Service Cost by Patient";
itemProps[0] = itemProp;
```

- You could then change your call to `CreateReport` from the following code:

```
warnings = rs.CreateReport(reportName, pathName,
    true, definition, null);
```

  to the following code instead:

```
warnings = rs.CreateReport(reportName, pathName,
    true, definition, itemProps);
```

With Report Server Web service, there isn't much you can't do. For more details on additional properties that you can set on reports or to find out more about the SOAP API, see the SQL Server 2005 Books Online.

Summary

In this chapter, you used the SOAP APIs through the Report Server Web service to list the folders on the selected server and then allowed the user to select an RDL file and upload it to the user-specified folder on the selected report server. We also examined some of the additional features you could provide the application by using a few of the many methods and properties exposed by SSRS 2005.

CHAPTER 8

■■■

Managing Reports

In many reporting solutions prior to SSRS, report management required little more than delivering the completed report file to the end user via a file share or embedded in a third-party application. SSRS is a full reporting environment with features such as scheduled report execution, report subscription services, snapshots, content caching, and on-demand Web access.

With these added benefits comes an additional level of management responsibility. Depending on the size of the organization, some management tasks can be delegated to other users, such as departmental managers, who might maintain report folders for their departments, as well as to system administrators and DBAs. Fortunately, SSRS provides several means of managing the report server at all levels. In this chapter, you'll continue to work with built-in tools such as Report Manager and command-line utilities, as well as with custom .NET management tools that take advantage of the SSRS programming models to administer an SSRS deployment. We'll also demonstrate SSRS's new Report Server Configuration Manager. When connecting to an SSRS instance, it provides much, if not all, of the functionality that is provided by Report Manager and the command-line utilities. We'll show the tasks that can be completed with the well-designed SSMS tool. However, we have chosen to use Report Manager for most of the examples here, mainly because it can be accessed from a Web browser, which does not require a local install of the SQL client tools.

Exploring Management Roles in SSRS Deployment

You can subdivide the management roles for an SSRS deployment into three basic categories:

- Content management

- Performance

- Report execution

It is always best practice to perform a test deployment of any application or service before placing it in a production environment. Because our company provides services via the Internet to a wide range of users, special management considerations—such as how to provide report subscriptions to the same report for different companies—were imperative, and we needed to test various scenarios to ensure proper functionality in each case. Let's begin by looking at the three management categories and how we implemented and tested them to make sure that when deployed to production, we would have few (if any) unexpected consequences. We will show how to perform all these tasks using the built-in administration tools with SSRS and SQL Server 2005. Later in the chapter, we'll show how to build a management application interface with .NET that provides the ability to schedule reports.

Managing Content

To effectively manage content on the SSRS report server, you need to be familiar with the management tasks available. Several aspects of report management are available only after the report has been deployed. We'll cover each aspect in detail as we show how to deploy the health-care reports for selected users:

- Shared schedules

- Report parameters and data sources

- Report snapshots, history, and caching

- Subscriptions

For each content management task, we'll provide specific real-world scenarios, continuing with the health-care agencies as an example. Up to this point, you have deployed several reports, data sources, and other report items, such as graphic images and code, which you have developed throughout the book. Now it's time to put on your administrator's cap and take advantage of all the features that make SSRS a unique and powerful report-delivery system in addition to providing a rich report-authoring environment.

Setting Up Shared Schedules

Generally speaking, a shared schedule is like a shared data source in that it is available systemwide to users who have permission to access it. You can create a shared schedule specifically for a certain job type. It is possible to configure a recurring shared schedule to execute by the hour, day, month, and week or to run only once. In this example, the financial reports will execute at the end of each month. It is important that a history be maintained for these reports so that you can freeze the values at any point in time or use them for auditing capabilities, such as understanding which users viewed a report and what they saw in the report.

You'll create a shared schedule that will be used to run the financial reports on the last day of each month to provide the following benefits:

- You can schedule the reports to execute at a predetermined time.

- You can store a snapshot of each report to maintain an historical perspective of the data.

Note Report snapshots are reports that are executed at a specific time, either when initiated by a user or as part of a schedule, and that collectively make up the report history. We'll cover snapshots in more detail later.

One financial report that customers might run at the end of the month is an AR Reconciliation report. This report lists financial transactions that occurred during the current accounting period, such as 10-2005 for October 2005. This report may be one of several that need to execute on the same schedule. Other financial reports might include an Aged Trial Balance report and an AR Aging report. We'll use the AR Reconciliation report in the following section to show the management tasks associated with setting up shared schedules and creating report snapshots. We've included the AR Reconciliation report in the Pro_SSRS report project download, available in the Source Code section of the Apress Web site (http://www.apress.com). The report definition file is AR Reconciliation.rdl. In this section, we'll show how to use a deployed version of the AR Reconciliation report to configure its parameter values to coincide with the scheduled times that it will execute each month.

To deploy the AR Reconciliation report, open the Pro_SSRS project in BIDS and then open the Solution Explorer. Before deploying this report, however, you need to change the project property that controls which folder the report will be deployed in on the report server. In the AR Reconciliation example, you will deploy the report to a folder called End of Month Financials. In the Solution Explorer, right-click the Pro_SSRS report project, and select Properties. Change the TargetReportFolder value from Pro_SSRS to End of Month Financials, and click OK. Now, when you right-click the AR Reconciliation report in the Solution Explorer and select Deploy, the new folder is created on your report server that contains the AR Reconciliation report.

Creating a Shared Schedule

To create the shared schedule in Report Manager, click Site Settings, and then select Manage Shared Schedules at the bottom of the page. Click New Schedule, and name the schedule End of Month Financials. In the Schedule Details section, you are presented with the standard scheduling options: Hour, Day, Week, Month, or Once. For this report, choose Month.

The first challenge when configuring a shared schedule to run on the last day of each month is to overcome the built-in data validation on the Shared Schedule form. Although it is possible to tell SSRS to execute the report on the last Sunday of every month, it is not possible to select the last day of each month because the last day is variable (that is, it could be 28, 29, 30, or 31, depending on the month). Well, it should be possible to create a single schedule to encompass all four dates, right? Not exactly. Choosing 31 causes an error when all the days of the month are selected, as shown in Figure 8-1, because not all months have 31 days.

■**Note** You must be logged in as a user who is a member of the SSRS 2005 System Administrators role to add new schedules.

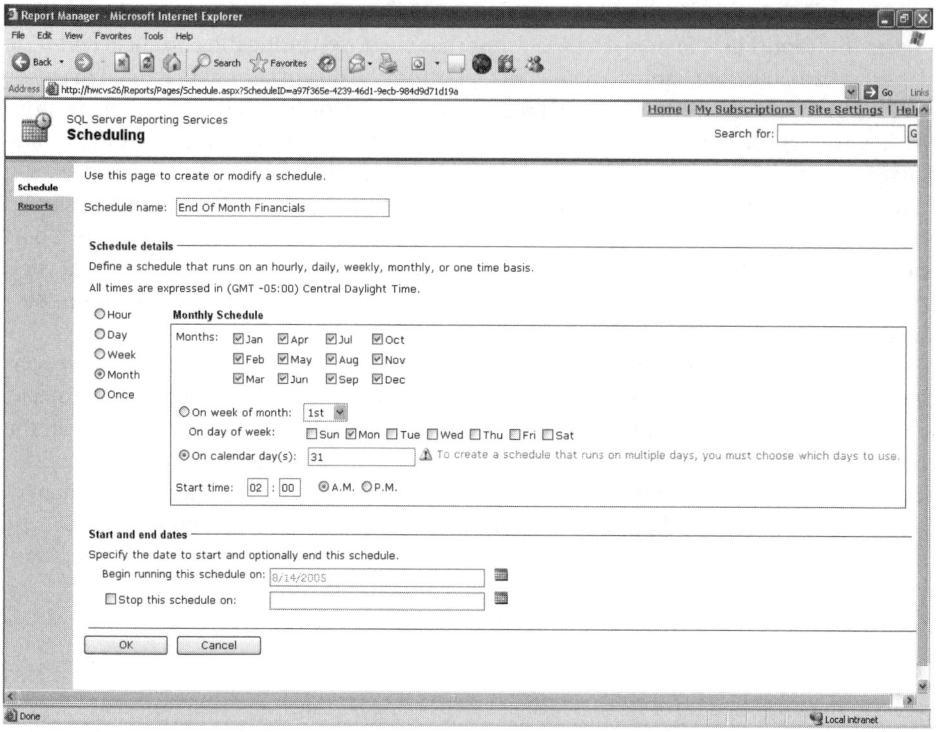

Figure 8-1. *Choosing the last day of the month*

The solution in this example—because we know that no activity will occur after 12:00 AM on the last day of the month—is to set the schedule to run on the first day of the month at 12:01 AM. This essentially gives you the last day for every month.

Next, select an appropriate start date and end date for the schedule (in this case, don't specify an end date), and then click the OK button. Now you can move on and prepare the report itself to use the new schedule. As a note, schedules in SSRS rely on the SQL Server Agent service, and as such, the service must be running before you can successfully create a schedule.

■**Note** Note that when a job, such as a subscription or an execution snapshot, is scheduled to run within SSRS, a SQL Server job is created using the SQL Server Agent. Jobs can be monitored through SSMS or Report Manager.

Configuring a Report to Use a Shared Schedule

The AR Reconciliation report contains report parameters that can limit the data displayed on the report. Two of the parameters, AcctPeriodYear and AcctPeriodMonth, are used in the driving stored procedure to limit financial data to an accounting period. When the AR Reconciliation report is executed from a shared schedule, it is important that all the parameters for the report have default values. To begin with, all eight parameters in the AR Reconciliation report are set to allow NULL values, as shown in Figure 8-2, which causes the default value of the parameter to be set to NULL when executed. This is OK because the logic in the main stored procedure that uses the parameters knows to return all data when a NULL value is passed to it.

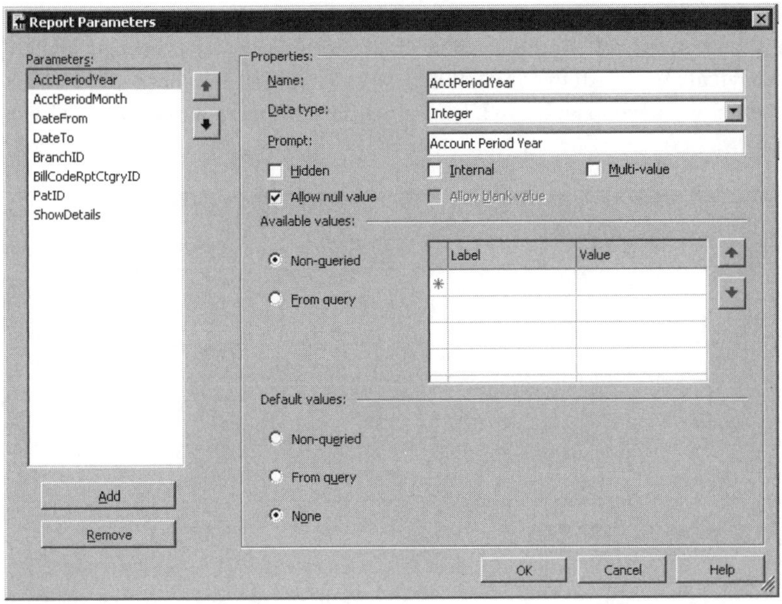

Figure 8-2. *AR Reconciliation report parameters*

For the parameters AcctPeriodYear and AcctPeriodMonth, however, you need to add default non-NULL parameter values so that the returned dataset includes only those records for the current accounting period. To do this, you use two functions:

- DATEPART: Returns an integer representing one of the component parts of a date, such as year, quarter, month, or day

- TODAY: Returns the current date

Used together in an expression, these functions allow you to set the desired default values for your two parameters. For AcctPeriodYear, you simply set the default value to the current year, as follows:

```
=DATEPART("yyyy",TODAY())
```

For AcctPeriodMonth, you essentially do the same thing, but you need to subtract 1 from the expression value to return the data for the correct month. For example, the expression =DATEPART("m",TODAY()), when run at 12:01 AM on November 1, would return a value of 11, when the current accounting period is 10-October. To account for January, you add an IIF function to evaluate the DATEPART so that when 1 is returned for January, a 12 is returned, letting the report know to process the December accounting period. So the correct expression is as follows:

```
=IIF(DATEPART("m",TODAY()) = 1, 12,DATEPART("m",TODAY()) -1)
```

Updating and Uploading the RDL File Using Report Manager

For this section, you will navigate to the AR Reconciliation report in Report Manager and modify the RDL manually to add the `AcctPeriodMonth` and `AcctPeriodYear` default parameter values via Notepad instead of using BIDS or SSMS. This will demonstrate that you can make simple modifications to published reports without the need for a full-blown design environment. Open Report Manager, and navigate to the AR Reconciliation report in the `End of Month Financials` folder on your report server, as shown in Figure 8-3. The names have been intentionally scrambled.

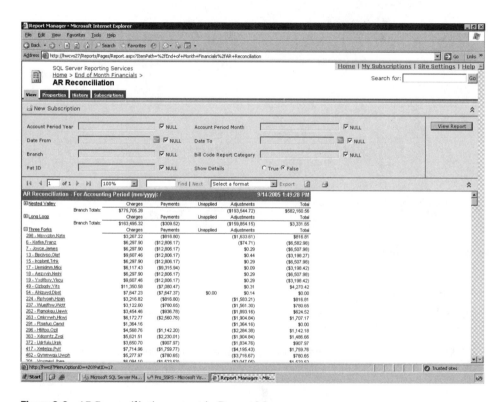

Figure 8-3. *AR Reconciliation report in Report Manager*

On the properties page for the AR Reconciliation report are two links under the Report Definition section, Edit and Update, that administrators can use to modify the RDL directly without having to redeploy reports through other means (such as through use of custom code, the authoring environment, or the `rs` command-line utility). Click the Edit link to open the RDL file in the default text editor, which is typically Notepad if Visual Studio is not installed. Figure 8-4 shows the RDL file for the AR Reconciliation report. Notice the `AcctPeriodYear` and `AcctPeriodMonth` parameters in the RDL code.

```
<ReportParameters>
  <ReportParameter Name="AcctPeriodYear">
    <DataType>Integer</DataType>
    <Nullable>true</Nullable>
    <Prompt>Account Period Year</Prompt>
  </ReportParameter>
  <ReportParameter Name="AcctPeriodMonth">      ◄------  Report parameters where default
    <DataType>Integer</DataType>                                 values will be added
    <Nullable>true</Nullable>
    <Prompt>Account Period Month</Prompt>
  </ReportParameter>
  <ReportParameter Name="DateFrom">
    <DataType>DateTime</DataType>
    <Nullable>true</Nullable>
    <Prompt>Date From</Prompt>
  </ReportParameter>
  <ReportParameter Name="DateTo">
    <DataType>DateTime</DataType>
    <Nullable>true</Nullable>
    <Prompt>Date To</Prompt>
  </ReportParameter>
  <ReportParameter Name="SrvProvID">
    <DataType>Integer</DataType>
    <Nullable>true</Nullable>
    <Prompt>Service Provider</Prompt>
  </ReportParameter>
  <ReportParameter Name="BranchID">
    <DataType>Integer</DataType>
    <Nullable>true</Nullable>
    <Prompt>Branch </Prompt>
  </ReportParameter>
  <ReportParameter Name="ProgramTblID">
    <DataType>Integer</DataType>
```

Figure 8-4. *RDL file edited in Notepad*

To update the report to include the default parameter values that you created in the previous section, you can place RDL code directly in the file and save it. The section of the RDL that generates the default values for each parameter is only five lines long, as you can see in Listing 8-1, which shows the default value section for the AcctPeriodYear parameter.

Listing 8-1. *RDL Default Value Section*

```
<DefaultValue>
    <Values>
        <Value>=datepart("yyyy",TODAY())</Value>
    </Values>
</DefaultValue>
```

Figure 8-5 shows the RDL file after the default value code was inserted for both parameters.

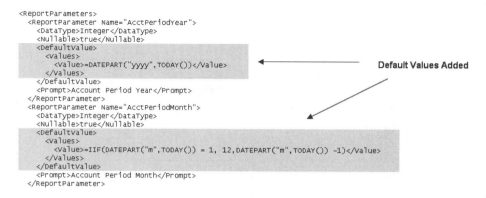

```
<ReportParameters>
  <ReportParameter Name="AcctPeriodYear">
    <DataType>Integer</DataType>
    <Nullable>true</Nullable>
    <DefaultValue>
      <Values>
        <Value>=DATEPART("yyyy",TODAY())</Value>          ◄──────────    Default Values Added
      </Values>
    </DefaultValue>
    <Prompt>Account Period Year</Prompt>
  </ReportParameter>
  <ReportParameter Name="AcctPeriodMonth">
    <DataType>Integer</DataType>
    <Nullable>true</Nullable>
    <DefaultValue>
      <Values>
        <Value>=IIF(DATEPART("m",TODAY()) = 1, 12,DATEPART("m",TODAY()) -1)</Value>
      </Values>
    </DefaultValue>
    <Prompt>Account Period Month</Prompt>
  </ReportParameter>
```

Figure 8-5. *RDL file with default parameters*

Now you have to save a copy of the RDL file to disk, because you can't save directly back to the SSRS server from Notepad. Any accessible location is fine, such as a network share. After the file is saved, you can click the Update link, locate your updated RDL file on disk, and click OK to update the existing report. If you executed the report now, you would see the report with correct default values, as shown in Figure 8-6.

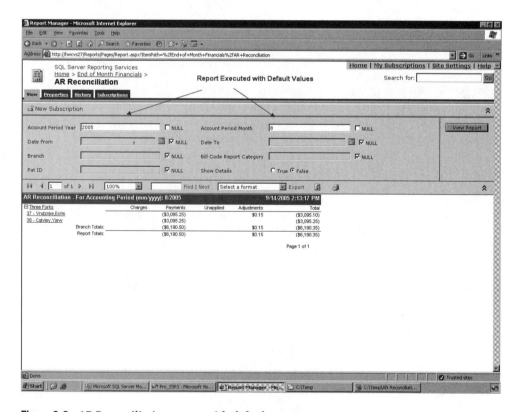

Figure 8-6. *AR Reconciliation report with default parameters*

Updating the report through Report Manager doesn't overwrite other properties of the report such as history, schedules, and execution methods.

■**Caution** When you use default values based on variable data such as values in a database, it's important to note that the returned value must coincide with available values. In this example, if a value of 5 is returned for May, but no values for May can be selected, the report will force the user to make a selection, as opposed to executing and returning no data. We chose to limit the data to values actually stored in the database.

Setting Up a Data Source for the Report

The AR Reconciliation report will be set up to generate a history that allows users to view the report as it was when it was executed. Also, because the report will be run at a prescheduled time, SSRS needs to know what credentials to use to access the data for the report. You need to create a new data source to accommodate this.

First navigate to the folder that contains the report, End of Month Financials, and then select New Data Source. Name the data source EOM Financials. Because this is a SQL Server–based connection, you supply the appropriate connection string, which includes the server name and database or catalog for the connection. Next, choose to store the credentials securely on the server, and supply a name and password—in this case, SQL authentication credentials. Finally, choose to hide the data source in list view so that you can prevent users from accidentally selecting it when browsing. Your configuration should look similar to Figure 8-7. After you click the Apply button to create the data source, all you need to do is associate the report to the new shared data source, which you'll do in the following sections.

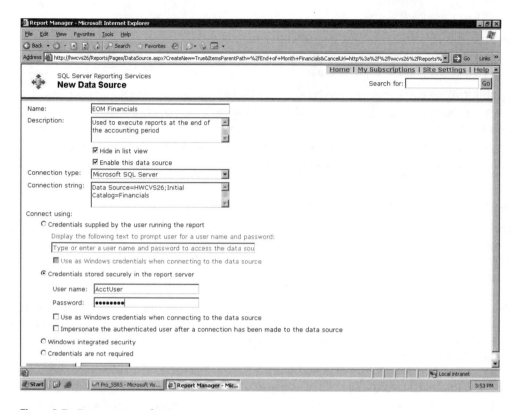

Figure 8-7. *Data source selections*

Note Microsoft recommends using Windows authentication when connecting to SQL Server. We chose SQL authentication in this example simply because our health-care application was originally developed with SQL authentication.

Creating Snapshots for the Report History

The goal for the AR Reconciliation report is to allow it to execute at a specified time of month, during off-peak hours for performance benefits, and to maintain an historical picture of each month's processing. To this end, the shared schedule, End of Month Financials, has been created. Now it's time to use a beneficial feature of SSRS, which is the capability to process a report as a snapshot.

A snapshot is a static "point-in-time" copy of a report. Two types of snapshots are used in SSRS: those generated as execution snapshots, which render a single report from a preexecuted point in time, and those generated to be stored in report history, which can contain multiple copies of a report at given points in time. In this section, we are concerned with showing how to configure the AR Reconciliation report to generate snapshots for the report history so that we can generate a series of historical financial reports.

You'll use Report Manager to configure the report history properties for the AR Reconciliation report so that a snapshot of the report is generated each time the report is processed, according to the End of Month Financials schedule.

Let's begin by looking at the available settings for the report history. As you can see in Figure 8-8, several settings affect not only the creation of snapshots but also how the snapshots are stored in the report history. You can navigate to the report history properties for any report by clicking the Properties tab in Report Manager while viewing the report and then selecting History in the left frame.

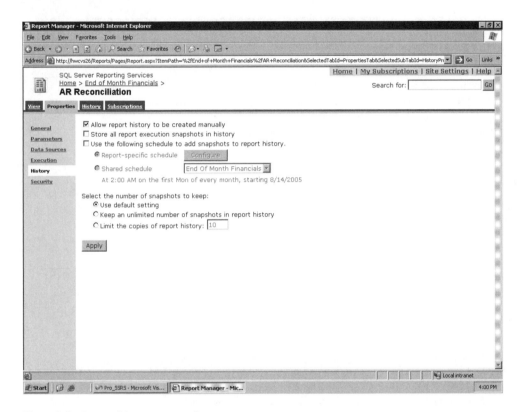

Figure 8-8. *Report history properties*

For the AR Reconciliation report, set the history properties so that

- Users will not be able to create snapshots for the report history. Set this entry so that only reports that are run by the schedule will appear in the report history.

- Report execution snapshots are not stored in the report history. This option is related to report Execution properties, which is covered in the next section.

- The End of Month Financials shared schedule is used.

- The Default setting is used for the number of snapshots to keep in the report history. The Default setting keeps an unlimited number of reports, but you can change this via Site Settings in Report Manager. If a specific number of snapshots is selected to be kept, such as 10, then older snapshots are removed first to make room.

After making the selections as shown in Figure 8-9, click Apply.

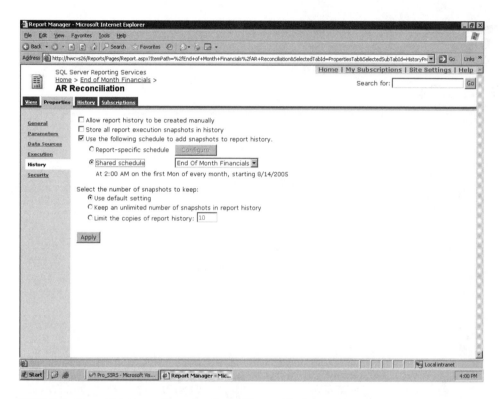

Figure 8-9. *Report history settings for the AR Reconciliation report*

Over time, the snapshots will be created in the report history. Users who have access to the report history can access the snapshots through Report Manager by navigating to the History tab for the report. The History tab for the AR Reconciliation report, as shown in Figure 8-10, indicates that over a two-month period, two snapshots have been generated, as expected.

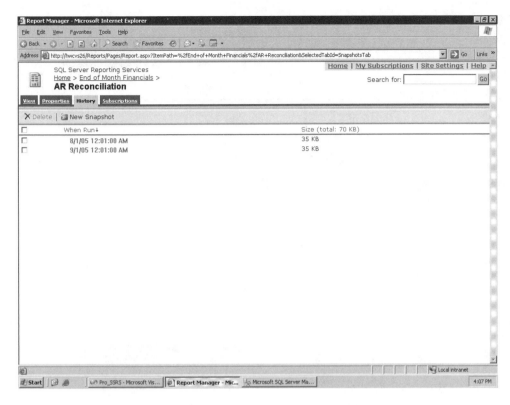

Figure 8-10. *AR Reconciliation report snapshots created on schedule*

It is beneficial for performance to render a report from the history, first because the report has been preprocessed and second because there is no need to query the data source for the report, as both the data and layout information are stored in the snapshot. When generating large reports, such as financial reports with hundreds of pages, we highly recommend using snapshots, as well as other performance-enhancing features of SSRS such as report caching, which we will cover next.

Executing Reports and Performing Caching

The AR Reconciliation report is now set up to be delivered from a schedule, rendered from a snapshot, and saved in the report history. Employees will also run this report on-demand, meaning that users can view the report with the most recent data. Because this is potentially a resource-intensive financial report, you should ensure that performance isn't affected when the report is rendered for multiple users simultaneously. You'll use Report Manager to configure the settings that control how the report is executed.

The first step is to navigate to the Properties tab for the AR Reconciliation report and then select Execution in the left frame. Figure 8-11 shows the available settings for report execution.

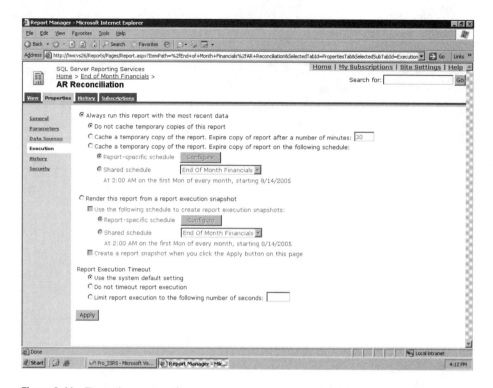

Figure 8-11. *Execution properties*

The first execution selection, Always Run This Report from the Most Recent Data, has several options that control report caching.

Caching is an SSRS feature that allows temporary copies of a report to be stored and rendered to a user. The main advantage for creating a cached copy of a report is increased performance. Users who access a report that is set to be cached generate the first cached instance. Every subsequent user receives the cached copy if certain conditions are met. The conditions for a user to receive the cached copy are as follows:

- The subsequent user must access the report within the time interval before the cached report is set to expire. When the cached report expires, the next user must create a new copy.

- If the cached report has parameters that change during subsequent executions, and each user receives a new report based on that parameter, each report that's generated becomes a cached copy specific to the parameter value.

- The report's data source isn't set to Windows authentication or to prompt the user for login credentials.

For our report, instruct SSRS to cache a temporary copy of the report and expire the cached copy after ten minutes. Ten minutes is generally a good length of time to maintain cached reports, although it really depends on the time sensitivity of your data. The data in a cached report will, of course, reflect the time at which the report was rendered rather than the current time, and short of printing the execution time on the report, users have no way to know if they're viewing a cached or live report.

The second selection, Render This Report from a Report Execution Snapshot, shouldn't be confused with a snapshot that creates a report history. An execution snapshot, unlike a history snapshot, is viewed from a `Report` folder in Report Manager just like on-demand reports would be viewed. History snapshots, on the other hand, are viewed from the History tab of the report and can accumulate many copies.

Execution snapshots don't expire like cached reports; rather, they're refreshed at a specified interval. If you choose to generate an execution snapshot for a report, then that report can't be cached. In this example, don't select this option.

The final report execution option sets the timeout interval for the report, either at a default setting, which is typically 1,800 seconds (30 minutes), or at a specified value. This is an important setting because long-running reports use valuable system resources. You'll use the default value for the AR Reconciliation report.

We mentioned the trade-off involved in using caching for reports with time-sensitive data. Another important consideration when choosing to use either snapshots or cached reports is disk space. Over time, history and cached reports set with lengthy expiration times can accumulate. The cost of disk storage compared to the performance and subsequent productivity increase is negligible, however, and shouldn't stop anyone from taking advantage of these beneficial features of SSRS.

Managing Subscriptions

Subscription services for SSRS provides a means for delivering preexecuted reports to specified locations, to a user via e-mail, to a network file share, or even directly to a printer. Using subscriptions has several key benefits. Internally in an organization, employees need key information at certain times, such as daily or at the end of a month. Externally, customers may want to receive newsletters or financial statements on a predetermined schedule. Subscriptions can accommodate both of these needs easily.

Setting up subscriptions has the added benefit of allowing you to schedule the processing of resource-intensive reports at off-peak hours, thus ensuring little or no degradation to performance during periods of heavy usage. You'll be working with two types of subscriptions in this section:

- *Standard subscriptions*: Statically set up for one or more users.

- *Data-driven subscriptions*: Subscriber lists can be derived from multiple data source locations and can be generated from a custom query.

■**Note** Data-driven subscriptions are by far the most powerful form of subscriptions. They're available only in the Enterprise edition of SSRS.

Managing Standard Subscriptions

You'll begin by setting up a standard e-mail subscription for employees in a health-care organization that provides home-care services to patients. The report, called Patient Recertification Listing, was designed for employees who are responsible for tracking patient documentation. You can create standard e-mail subscriptions with any report. In our business, it is a requirement that the patient's documentation, in this case an HCFA 485, be completed and signed by the attending physician. The report is essentially a daily work list for these employees, where any documentation that is unsigned becomes a work item.

You can find the Patient Recertification Listing report in the Pro_SSRS report project provided in the Source Code area on the Apress Web site (http://www.apress.com). You can deploy the report to your report server using BIDS. Open the Pro_SSRS project, and change the TargetReportFolder for the project to Patient Documentation. Next, right-click the Patient Recertification Listing report, select Deploy to create the Patient Documentation folder, and publish the report and data source to your report server. It is important to note that the Pro_SSRS data source that is provided in the Pro_SSRS project uses Windows authentication, and for subscriptions to work successfully, the credentials will need to be stored securely in the database. To change the deployed Pro_SSRS data source from Windows authentication to stored credentials, navigate in Report Manager to select the Pro_SSRS data source in the Patient Documentation folder. Change the Connect Using option to Credentials stored securely in the report server, and supply the appropriate credentials.

Because this report needed to be generic enough for on-demand viewing in addition to being used for subscriptions, we added a report parameter called Unsigned that works with a report filter to show patients with both signed and unsigned documentation. This report has other parameters as well, as shown in Figure 8-12. As you'll see, you will use the parameters when you generate the subscription.

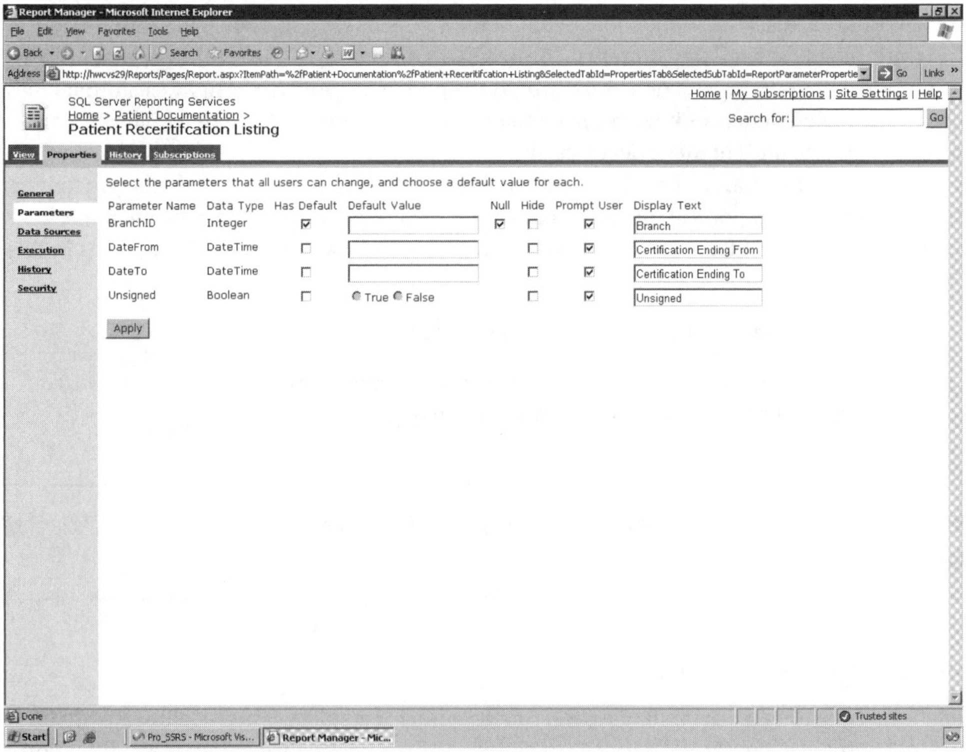

Figure 8-12. *Patient Recertification Listing report parameters*

Creating a Standard Subscription

The first step in manually creating a subscription is to run Report Manager and navigate to the report for which you want to create the subscription. You can also create and manage subscriptions using SSMS. Later in this chapter, you'll learn how to manage the subscription that you create here for the Patient Recertification Listing report using SSMS in the "SSMS and SSRS" section.

For the example, navigate to the Patient Certification Listing report, which is in the Patient Documentation folder on the report server. Each report has a number of configurable values under four different pages: View, Properties, History, and Subscriptions.

Select the Subscriptions page, and then click New Subscription for the report. If you have configured your SMTP server correctly during installation, you will see an option, after clicking the Subscription page, to select Report Server E-mail. If this option is not available, you can use the Report Server Configuration Manager to set up e-mail, as shown in Figure 8-13. The Report Server Configuration Manager can set many of the same properties that control the report server as the command-line tools or SSMS. The Report Server Configuration Manager is a good tool to use to set the properties of the report server that may need to be configured post-installation, such as the report server virtual directory or the account used to execute unattended reports. You'll use the Report Server Configuration Manager again to join the instance of SSRS to another report server, which creates a Web farm of report servers to gauge performance. For now, check to ensure that the SMTP settings are correct.

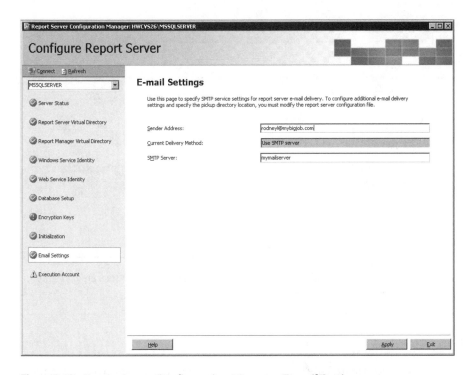

Figure 8-13. *Report Server Configuration Manager, E-mail Settings*

A subscription that is delivered via e-mail provides standard delivery options for Cc, Bcc, Reply-To, Subject, Priority, and Comment, which will be the body of the e-mail message. You can also send the entire report in the e-mail, a link to the report, or both. Because the user who will be receiving this subscription will have network access to the report server, you can send just a link to the report. Sending the report itself via e-mail does have benefits, however, especially when working with users who need the report offline, such as traveling staff. We will demonstrate this in the next section when you set up a data-driven subscription. Figure 8-14 shows the e-mail options available for a report subscription.

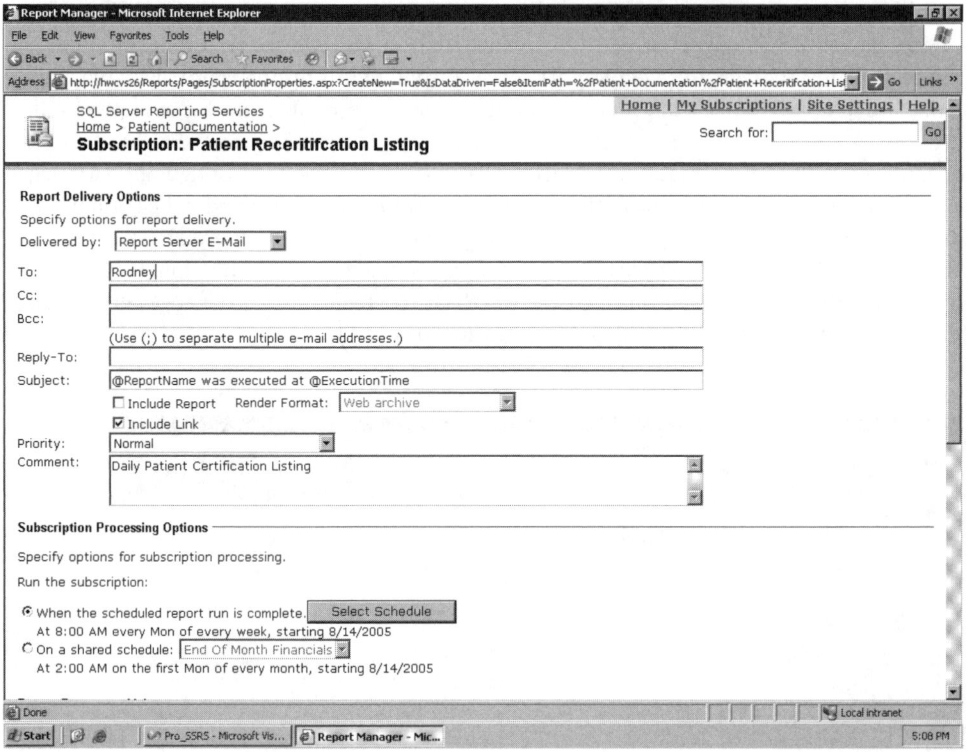

Figure 8-14. *E-mail options for subscriptions*

■**Note** During the default installation of SSRS, an SMTP server and default e-mail address are configured, which SSRS uses to send e-mail based subscriptions.

Configuring the Subscription

Subscriptions are configured to execute at a scheduled time. You can customize the schedule for individual reports or based on a shared schedule. This report needs to be delivered to staff members in the morning, and it can be run anytime after 5:00 PM on the previous day as long as it is delivered by the next business day. For our needs, a schedule of 9:30 PM every day except Saturday is sufficient, as shown in Figure 8-15, which is set by clicking the Select Schedule button under Subscription Processing Options.

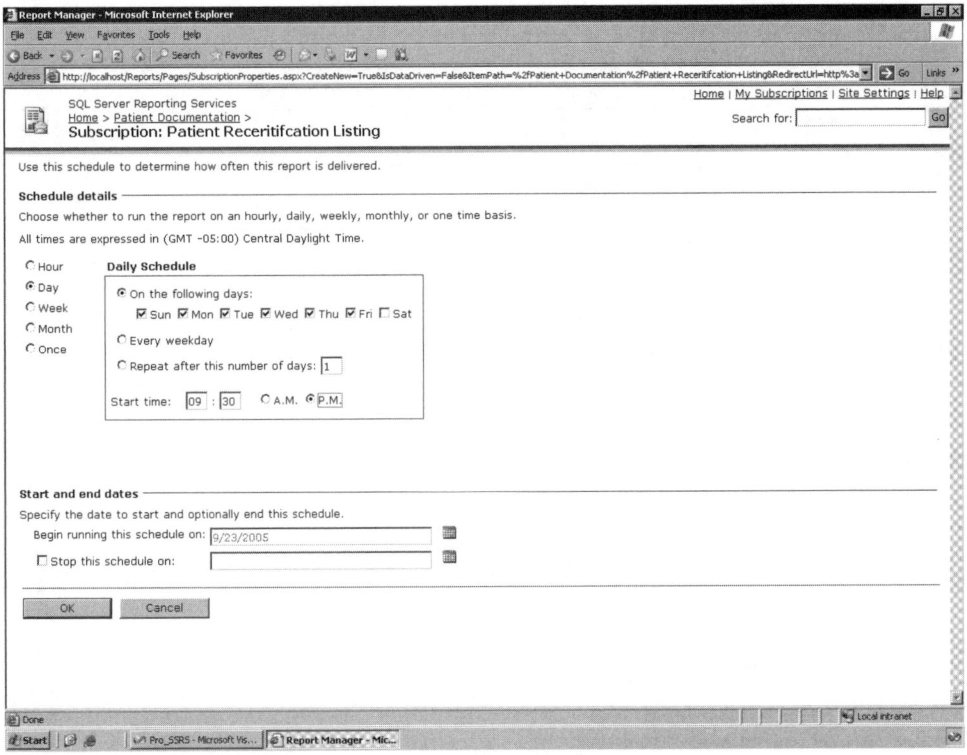

Figure 8-15. *Daily schedule for Patient Certification Listing report*

Next, you configure the parameters for the report. As mentioned earlier, this particular report has a parameter called Unsigned, which is a Boolean datatype (either True or False) that shows both signed and unsigned documentation. When this report is rendered, by default it includes all patients, whether signed or unsigned documentation exists. The subscribers of this report, however, will be interested in seeing only unsigned documentation, so set the parameter for Unsigned to be True. Because this report has been designed to provide populated drop-downs for the parameter values that are based on individual datasets, these values are available here, such as populated Branch selections, as shown in Figure 8-16. For now, leave all the parameters, except Unsigned, with their default values.

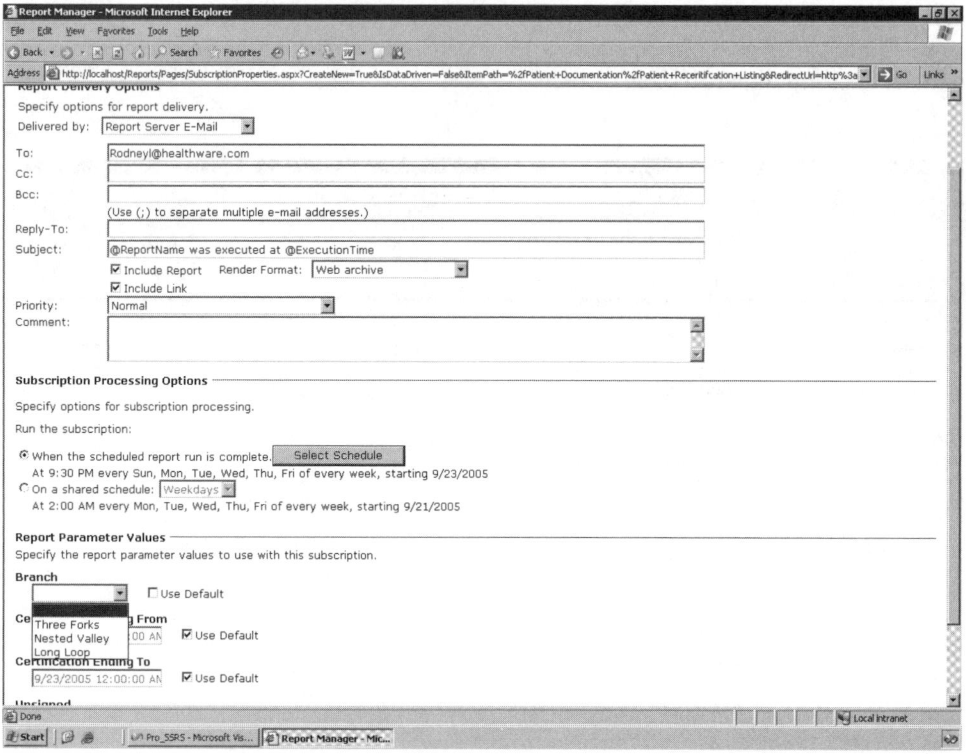

Figure 8-16. *Subscription parameter drop-downs*

To verify that the subscription is working as anticipated, we made rodneyl@healthware.com the sole recipient of the mail for testing. In Figure 8-17, you can see standard e-mail options for To, Cc, Bcc, and Reply-To. In the To field, you add the recipient's e-mail address and then click OK to add the subscription. After you verify the subscription's success, modify the attributes of the subscription to add the real subscribers by navigating to the report in Report Manager, selecting Subscriptions, and then selecting Edit.

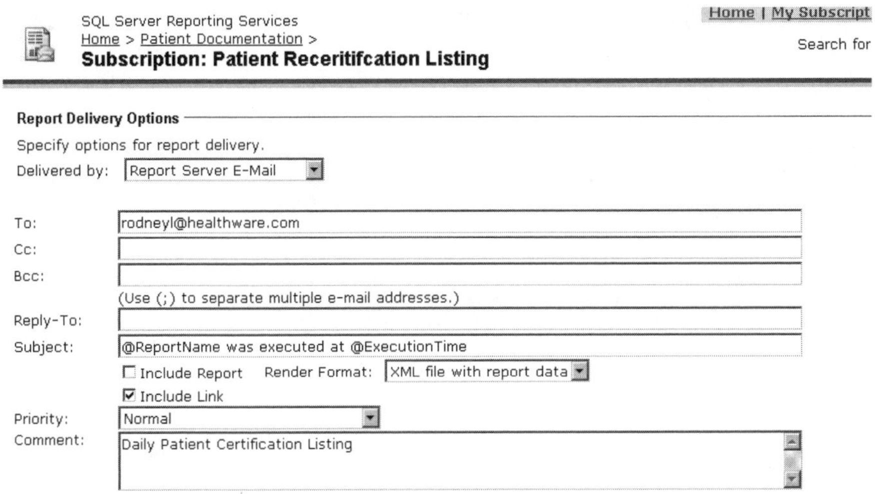

SQL Server Reporting Services

Home > Patient Documentation >

Subscription: Patient Receritifcation Listing

Search for

Report Delivery Options

Specify options for report delivery.

Delivered by: Report Server E-Mail

To:	rodneyl@healthware.com
Cc:	
Bcc:	
	(Use (;) to separate multiple e-mail addresses.)
Reply-To:	
Subject:	@ReportName was executed at @ExecutionTime

☐ Include Report   Render Format: XML file with report data

☑ Include Link

Priority: Normal

Comment: Daily Patient Certification Listing

Figure 8-17. *Assigning recipients to subscriptions*

Managing Data-Driven Subscriptions

Standard subscriptions address the needs of many companies that want to set up custom subscriptions for both their employees and their customers. However, you can use another, much more flexible method for delivering reports: the data-driven subscription. Data-driven subscriptions allow administrators or content managers to query a data source—a SQL Server table, for example—to return a list of subscribers that meet a specific set of criteria. This is the ideal way to deliver reports to a wide-ranging list of subscribers. Plus, you have to manage only one subscription for all subscribers, and those subscribers could have different parameters that are used to generate personalized reports.

We knew we would want to let our customers and their employees take advantage of data-driven subscriptions, and fortunately we had long ago structured our application database to include employee information that would be useful for just this purpose. By storing the employees' e-mail addresses as well as other data, such as geographical locations and certifications, we had all we needed to provide a flexible delivery system, via e-mail, to traveling staff. The employees we initially targeted were clinicians who had a daily schedule of patients to see. Most of the clinicians operated laptops or PDAs as part of their daily routines.

Designing the Subscription Query

The first step was to redesign a report in SSRS so that it would provide clinical employees with their daily schedules and parameterize it so that it would be employee-specific each time it was executed. As part of the data-driven subscription, the report would be processed and delivered to employees as both an embedded, printable format, and as a link to connect to the SSRS report server if they were online. Figure 8-18 shows the report we created, Daily Activity.

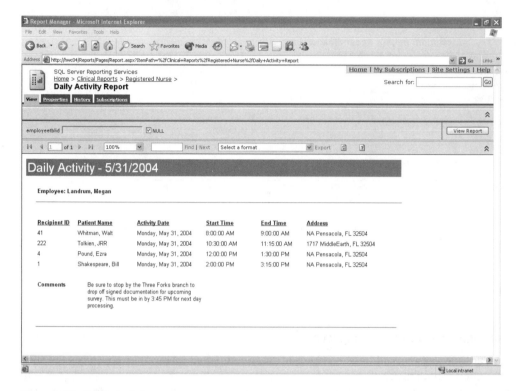

Figure 8-18. *Daily Activity report*

Because data-driven subscriptions are based on just that, data, a query to drive the subscription is essential. It is important to design the query to have selective criteria, because SSRS delivers a copy of the report for every record that is returned from the data source.

For our recipient list, we use the query in Listing 8-2. Essentially, the query returns all employees who have an e-mail address and who also have scheduled activities for the day following the date of report execution. The report is processed and delivered after hours. It is unusual in our environment that an employee's schedule will change after 9:00 PM, so we set up the report to execute at that time.

Listing 8-2. *T-SQL Query to Return the Subscriber List*

```
SELECT
      DISTINCT EmployeeTblID,Email,HWUserLogin,ActivityDate
FROM
      Employee INNER JOIN
      Activity ON Employee.EmployeeTblID = Activity.ProviderID
WHERE
      Email IS NOT NULL AND
      ActivityDate BETWEEN GETDATE() AND GETDATE () + 1
```

When this query is executed, the output of the query yields six rows of data, as you can see in Table 8-1, indicating that six clinicians have activities for the next day. You have many ways to format and compare datetime values. However, in this case, using the GETDATE function to compare the current date with the ActivityDate field value was the best choice. It was necessary to use BETWEEN with GETDATE because the ActivityDate value defaults to 00:00:00 for the time value, whereas GETDATE returns the current time. The comparison values wouldn't match in a one-to-one comparison.

Table 8-1. *Output of a Data-Driven Query*

EmployeeTblID	Email	UserLogin	ActivityDate
15	NurseC@healthware.com	hwci\Nursec	2005-08-15
34	Lottah@healthware.com	hwci\Lottah	2005-08-15
44	MaryElizah@healthware.com	hwci\MaryElizah	2005-08-15
147	Fayel@healthware.com	hwci\Fayel	2005-08-15
155	Brendanl@healthware.com	hwci\brendanl	2005-08-15
159	Ethanl@healthware.com	hwci\Ethanl	2005-08-15

Creating the Data-Driven Subscription

Now we will show the procedure for creating the data-driven subscription in Report Manager. The Daily Activity report is included in the Pro_SSRS report project available in the Source Code area of the Apress Web site. You can deploy the report to any folder on your report server for testing the subscription. Make sure when you deploy the report that you modify the Pro_SSRS data source that is deployed with the report so that it stores the credentials on the report server, which is required for the subscription to be created. Open the browser, and navigate to the Daily Activity Report, and from there select Subscriptions. On the toolbar, select New Data-Driven Subscription. Follow these steps to complete the data-driven subscription:

1. Choose a name, delivery method, and data source type.

2. Choose the data source location or define a new data source.

3. Choose the command or query to return a list of recipients.

4. Choose the settings for the Report Server Delivery E-mail delivery extension.

5. Choose the report parameters.

6. Choose when the subscription will be processed.

7. Set up a schedule for the report.

The most important of these steps is step 4, in which you specify the settings for the delivery extension. This is where you'll use the data from the driving query to instruct SSRS how to send the subscription. Every selection in step 4 has the option to retrieve the value derived from the query used in step 3, which is much more versatile than a standard subscription.

You paste the query into the query box in step 3, as you can see in Figure 8-19, and verify it by clicking the Validate button. From this point, the fields you selected in the query, namely EmployeeTblid, Email, HWUserLogin, and ActivityDate, can all be used as criteria in the remaining steps.

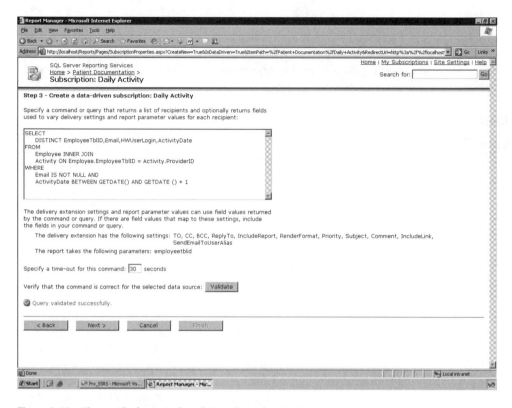

Figure 8-19. *The verified query that drives the subscription*

In step 4, several settings control how the report will be sent to subscribers: To, Cc, Bcc, ReplyTo, IncludeReport, RenderFormat, Priority, Subject, Comment, and IncludeLink. For each setting, except for To, you can choose a static value, a database value, or no value, as shown in Figure 8-20. You assign the To field to the Email field from the subscription query. Leave the values for all the other fields at their default settings. By leaving the defaults, the subscription automatically includes the report itself and the link to the report in the e-mail to the subscribers.

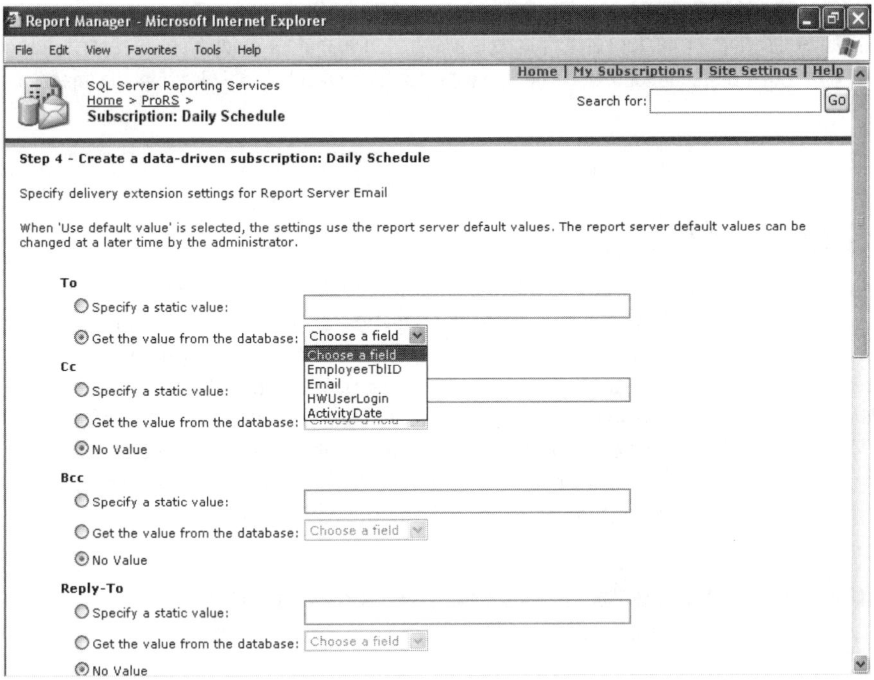

Figure 8-20. *Subscription settings*

■**Tip** All the report-rendering formats are available for subscriptions, except for HTML Office Web Components. With data-driven subscriptions, unlike with standard subscriptions, you can control the rendering format per subscriber because it too is a data-driven setting. If you need to control the rendering format per user, you can add a field to store this value in the Employee table and select this value in the query.

The EmployeeTblid field is used for the one parameter in the report. Because you've selected this field in the query and passed this as a parameter input, each report is automatically generated with data specific to the employee who subscribed to the report. The other field, HWUserLogin, is put in the driving query, which you'll ultimately compare to the Windows login name of the user executing the report. You can accomplish this, as you'll see in Chapter 9, by using the User global collection.

For the final step, you create a schedule that processes the report each weeknight at 9:30 PM, as described earlier. You can create another shared schedule to process the subscription and test it to verify that the e-mail is being delivered successfully. After that is complete, you're finished with the subscription configuration.

> **■Note** The default rendering format for subscriptions is a Web archive, but for many types of reports, this isn't the ideal choice. Other printable reports are better suited for Adobe Acrobat PDF files or static image files such as TIFF.

Using SSMS and SSRS

Most of the management tasks that are available with other SSRS tools, such as Report Manager and `rsconfig`, are available in SSMS, and often SSMS is the best application for the job because its tasks are contained within a single, familiar environment that does not require the cumbersome page refreshes and maneuvering through the browser-based Report Manager. Let's take a quick look at SSMS, which by now you know is new to SQL Server 2005. You can configure all the report objects and their properties, including data sources, subscriptions, execution, history, and shared schedules, that you have completed with Report Manager just as easily using SSMS. Figure 8-21 shows SSMS and the configuration tasks available within the IDE.

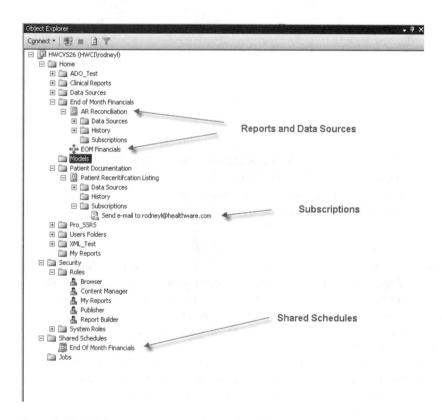

Figure 8-21. *SSMS report server configuration objects*

We mentioned earlier in the chapter, when creating a schedule for the Patient Certification Listing report, that we would show how to configure it in SSMS. Let's do that now by opening SSMS and connecting to the Reporting Services Server type connection. For your server, enter *localhost* or the name of the computer where you are hosting SSRS. Next, navigate to the Patient Certification Listing report, as shown in Figure 8-22, that you deployed to the Patient Documentation folder. Notice that under the report are three folders, Data Sources, History, and Subscriptions. When you expand the Subscriptions folder, you should see the e-mail subscription.

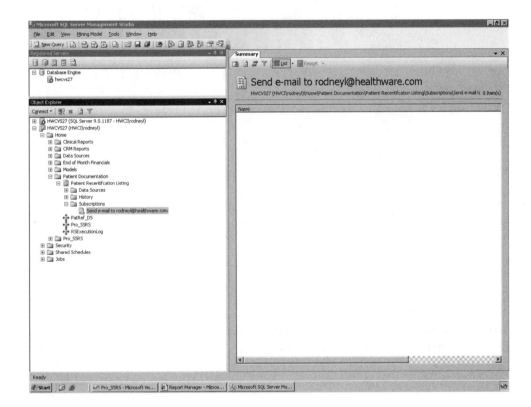

Figure 8-22. *Navigating to the subscription in SSMS*

Double-clicking the subscription opens its Properties window, which at first glance contains all the values that you could configure in Report Manager when you first created it. The General page shows the e-mail properties, such as To, Cc, and whether to include the report or a link. In this case, let's say you had a request to change the time for the report schedule, from 9:30 PM, as it was originally set, to 10:30 PM. To do this, select the Scheduling page, as shown in Figure 8-23. You can see that the schedule set up in Report Manager is available and can be modified by clicking Set Schedule.

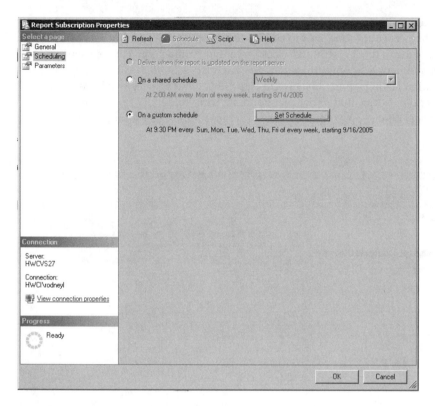

Figure 8-23. *Scheduling page in SSMS Report Subscription properties*

When you click Set Schedule, a Create Custom Schedule form appears, as shown in Figure 8-24. Simply change the 9:30 start time to 10:30, and click OK. If you need to change the default parameters for the subscription, you can do that as well by selecting the Parameters page.

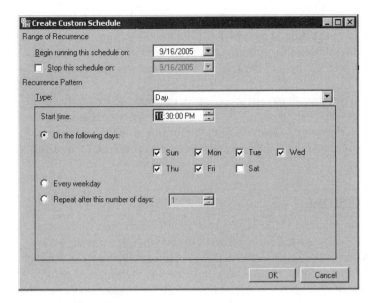

Figure 8-24. *Changing the subscription start time*

One of the main drawbacks to using SSMS is that it has to be installed on your workstation, unlike the browser-based Report Manager that is accessible from anywhere. If you are doing a lot of management work at one time such as setting security for a large number of users, however, SSMS is definitely a much faster front-end application.

Performing Execution Auditing and Performance Analysis

As you deploy SSRS in both test and production environments, gauging performance involves a variety of benchmarking and analysis tools. Based on the performance analysis, administrators are armed with the knowledge of what stress levels their servers can endure, and they'll be able to configure the environment accordingly. We'll show how to put the components of your SSRS deployment to the test and show how to analyze the output using standard tools.

Many agencies need to monitor and archive the details of user activity. This is especially important if you suspect there's undesired access to data. SSRS provides a built-in logging feature that captures several key pieces of information. This information is useful in two ways:

- You can capture performance information about the reports, such as the processing duration and record count.

- You can capture security information, such as who executed the report and whether or not they were successful.

The first goal in the following sections is to set up and extend the built-in logging functionality of SSRS using tools provided in the SSRS installation. You'll need to log all activity so that you can pinpoint the reports and users who are most impacting the server. We have created a custom SSRS report, Report Execution Log, which will deliver the logging statistics to administrators and contain dynamic column groupings based on a report parameter and be rendered in HTMLOWC for PivotTable analysis. We'll show how you can use this report for your SSRS deployment.

The second goal in the following sections is to show how to perform benchmarking tests on the SSRS servers in our test Web farm to ensure there won't be any unexpected performance problems when SSRS is deployed to a production environment. We'll show how to work with a Web application stress-test utility called Application Center Test (ACT) to gauge performance.

Configuring SSRS Logging

Getting to the execution log information in SSRS is a fairly straightforward procedure. It consists of a main table in the SSRS database called, appropriately enough, `ExecutionLog`. When SSRS is installed by default, execution logging is enabled. However, the data in the table, although useful by itself, isn't ideally formatted for direct querying. Because one of the aims is to build a custom SSRS report to deliver report execution information to administrators, you'll need to be able to query the log data. Fortunately, SSRS provides a means of transforming the data in the `ExecutionLog` table into several tables that can be queried more easily to produce valuable output.

Transforming the ExecutionLog Table

Setting up SSRS to transform the logging data is a simple step-by-step procedure. We will show how to step through the process in our environment here. You can find all the files you'll need to create and transform the SSRS logging data in the SQL Server 2005 installation folder in the following sub-folder: `Samples\Reporting Services\Report Samples\ Server Management Sample Reports\Execution Log Sample Reports`. Which in a default installation is: `C:\Program Files\Microsoft SQL Server\90\Samples\Reporting Services\ Report Samples\Server Management Sample Reports\Execution Log Sample Reports`. The first step is to create the database where the execution log data will be stored. The database may reside on the same SQL Server as SSRS, but you can create it on another database server if desired. In SSMS, connect to the SQL Server where the `ReportServer` database is stored. Next, right-click the `Databases` folder in SSMS, and select New Database. Name the database RSExecutionLog, and click OK. Still in SSMS, highlight the newly created database, and then click New Query on the toolbar. The script to create the required tables in the `RSExecutionLog` database is called `CreateTables.sql`. You can load the script and execute it in the query window in SSMS.

After creating the database that will store the log data, you load and execute the SSIS package called `RSExecutionLog_Update.dtsx`, which populates the tables in the newly created database, as shown in Figure 8-25.

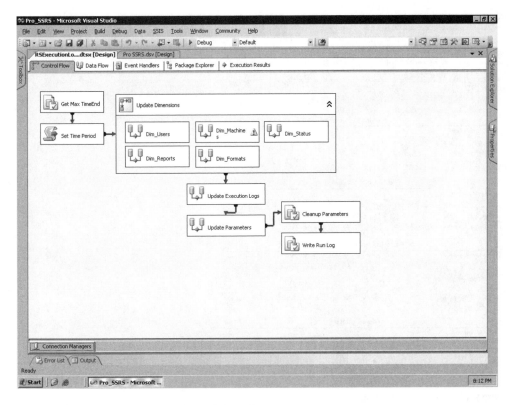

Figure 8-25. RSExecutionLog_Update *SSIS package*

This package uses an initialization file that specifies the source and destination databases and their locations—typically ReportServer and RSExecutionLog, respectively—on the local server. You can modify these values if the default names and locations were not used to create the execution log database.

■**Tip** Note that the package needs to be executed regularly to keep the transformed log data current. In our situation, we created a scheduled job for this purpose that runs the SSIS package every evening.

Microsoft provides a set of sample reports that you can use with the ExecutionLog database. These reports are included in the SQL Server 2005 installation in the following location: Samples\Reporting Services\Report Samples\Server Management Sample Reports\ Execution Log Sample Reports. The sample reports are useful for giving administrators information, such as report execution by user and report size, among other things. You will find three SSRS execution log sample reports in all, one of which, Execution Summary, is shown in Figure 8-26.

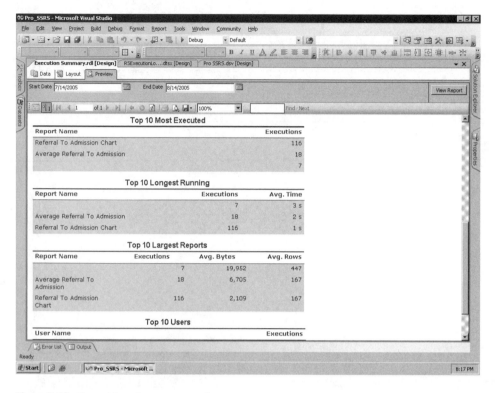

Figure 8-26. Execution Summary *sample report*

Designing the Log Report

We knew we would need a single report that contained all the execution log information and was easy for administrators to analyze. Thus, we created a matrix-style report, called Report Execution Log, using data from a single query. We needed to use the OWC rendering format to take advantage of the user interactivity and drag-and-drop capabilities of the PivotTable control.

To measure performance from information contained in the execution log, you need several statistics:

- *Total time to retrieve the data*: How long did it take to retrieve data?

- *Total time to process*: How long did the report take to process?

- *Total time to render*: How long did the report take to render?

- *Byte count*: How many bytes are in the report?

- *Row count*: How many rows of data are in the report?

In addition, knowing when the report was executed is also useful. For the row groupings in the matrix, we want to see what report was executed, who ran the report, and from which client machine the report was run. For the column group, we want to have two possible selections: either rendering format, such as HTML 4.0, HTMLOWC, or PDF, or source types, meaning how SSRS generated the report (live, cache, or snapshot, for example). Source_Type is an important field to monitor because how SSRS generates reports directly impacts performance. Generating reports from a cached copy or a snapshot, which are both preprocessed copies of reports, is a performance benefit. If SSRS is always generating live or on-demand reports for users, performance may suffer.

To accomplish the dynamic column groupings in the matrix, you'll use a parameter called `Column_Group` that takes the values of the field names in the query, `Format` or `Source_Type`. You'll use a default value of `Format` so that the report is automatically rendered when previewed. Both the column grouping and heading values will use the following expression to make the column dynamic based on the parameter:

```
=Fields(Parameter!Column_Group).Value
```

When the report is rendered, as you can see in Figure 8-27, it will default to the `Format` field, but you can change it dynamically by changing the parameter drop-down selection to `Source_Type`.

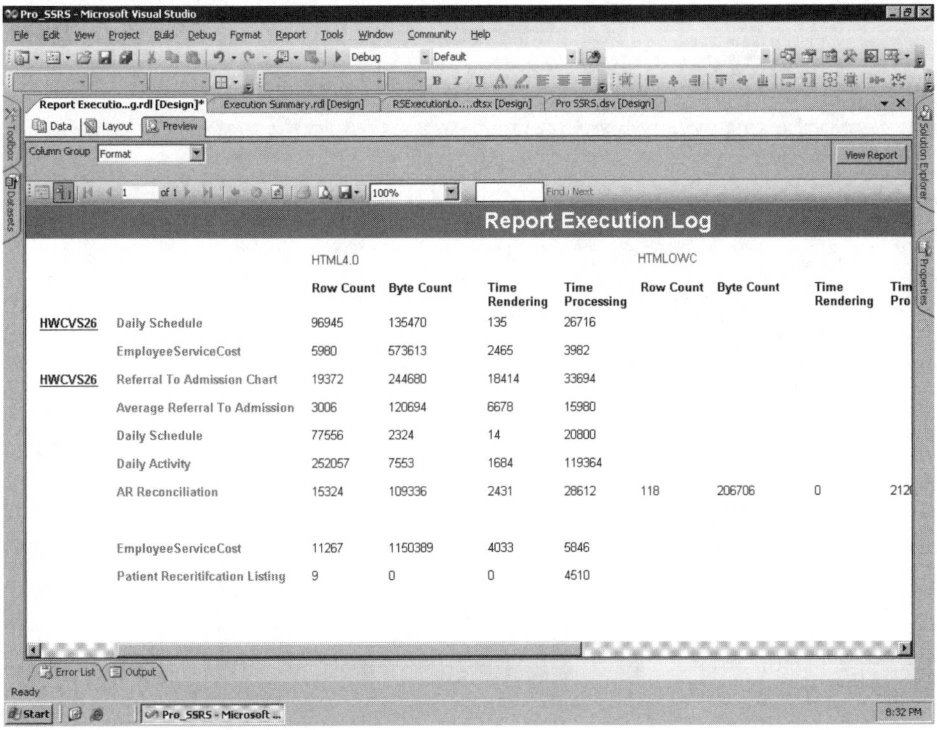

Figure 8-27. *Report Execution Log report*

One problem remains: automatically rendering the report in OWC instead of the default HTML 4.0. To accomplish this goal, you can simply navigate to Report Manager and export the base Report Execution Log to the HTML with Office Web Components format. The URL will look similar to the following: `http://hwcvs26/Reports/Reserved.ReportViewerWebControl.axd?ReportSession=4k45vk55nkth5dnpes5nvq55&ControlID=727156ae-c1ea-4457-95b0-45a9f80c47b2&OpType=Export&Format=HTMLOWC`.

When administrators execute the report from this URL, they will be able to dynamically work with the report to gain a clear picture of the longest-running reports overall, as well as the report that contained the most data. Having the ability to group by user and machine will further narrow potential bottlenecks. You could gather additional performance measures to report on if you chose to, such as the parameter value that the user selected. This would be useful when a pattern is discovered, such as that a particular user runs a certain report and always chooses the same parameters that return more than 10,000 records. Thousands of possible combinations of data views exist for the administrator within the PivotTable. Further, if administrators want to save a custom view of the report, they can export the PivotTable from OWC directly to Excel.

Figure 8-28 shows the Report Execution Log report rendered in OWC. We have included this report for download in the Source Code area on the Apress Web site; you will find it in the Pro_SSRS project and can use it directly with your SSRS deployment.

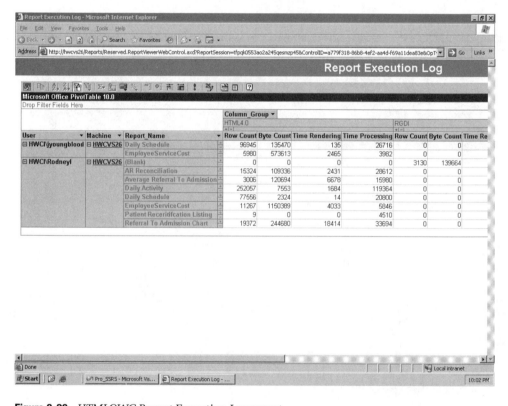

Figure 8-28. *HTMLOWC Report Execution Log report*

Working with OWC for SSRS for SQL Server 2005 has one major caveat: it has been stricken from the base formats by default. You may notice, on your initial installation of SSRS 2005 that the HTML with Office Web Components option is not a selectable option. I (Rodney) was not pleased with this, so I put it back in, and you can too, with a few simple lines added to the reportserver.config file located in your SSRS installation path, typically C:\Program Files \Microsoft SQL Server\MSSQL.n\Reporting Services\ReportServer. Listing 8-3 shows these lines, which you can add to the Render section of the `reportserver.config` file. You can find this code, called `HTMLOWC.txt`, in the `Queries` folder in the Source Code section of the Apress Web site.

Listing 8-3. *Code to Add HTMLOWC Support*

```
<Extension Name="HTMLOWC" Type="Microsoft.ReportingServices.Rendering➥
.HtmlRenderer.HtmlOWCRenderingExtension,Microsoft.ReportingServices.HtmlRendering">
    <Configuration>
      <OWCConfiguration>
        <OWCDownloadLocation language="de">http://office.microsoft.com/germany/➥
downloads/2002/owc10.aspx</OWCDownloadLocation>
        <OWCDownloadLocation language="en">http://office.microsoft.com/➥
downloads/2002/owc10.aspx</OWCDownloadLocation>
        <OWCDownloadLocation language="ja">http://office.microsoft.com/japan/➥
downloads/2002/owc10.aspx</OWCDownloadLocation>
        <OWCDownloadLocation language="zh-chs">http://office.microsoft.com/china/➥
downloads/2002/owc10.aspx</OWCDownloadLocation>
        <OWCDownloadLocation language="zh-cht">http://office.microsoft.com/china/➥
downloads/2002/owc10.aspx</OWCDownloadLocation>
        <OWCDownloadLocation language="es">http://office.microsoft.com/spain/➥
downloads/ 2002/owc10.aspx</OWCDownloadLocation>
        <OWCDownloadLocationlanguage="ko">http://office.microsoft.com/korea/➥
downloads/2002/owc10.aspx</OWCDownloadLocation>
        <OWCDownloadLocation language="fr">http://office.microsoft.com/france/➥
downloads/2002/owc10.aspx</OWCDownloadLocation>
        <OWCDownloadLocation language="it">http://office.microsoft.com/italy/➥
downloads/2002/owc10.aspx</OWCDownloadLocation>
      </OWCConfiguration>
    </Configuration>
</Extension>
```

You also need to make sure that the client machine where the report is being exported to HTMLOWC contains the OWC installed that is the supported version for SSRS, version 10. SSRS will instruct the user where to download the OWC installation file if it's not already installed; otherwise, you can download and preinstall it from `http://office.microsoft.com/downloads/2002/owc10.aspx`. The default installation of Office XP or 2003 also installs these controls.

Monitoring Performance

Of course, no one wants to experience the frustration of building a solid reporting solution in a development environment only to find out that when deployed to the masses, it can't hold up under the strain. Generally, it's a best practice to put a simulated load on your servers to gain a better understanding of how the systems will function. Also, when you roll out a full solution, it's a common practice to roll out several pieces at a time to a limited number of users. That is what we've done in our online models.

The strategy for rolling out should also include a plan for which reports will be available on-demand versus which ones will be provided via report snapshots or subscriptions, as you've done up to this point in the chapter. Combining a strategy of peak and off-peak report processing will greatly improve performance. Another consideration for performance with SSRS lies in splitting the load of SSRS Web services and database services. That is, if the entire SSRS installation resides on the same system, this could negatively impact performance.

In this section, we'll show the results of a stress test that we ran accessing two report server instances on two separate servers, RS05 and HWC04. Many tools, such as SSRS, are available for stress testing Web applications; fortunately, Visual Studio 2005 has a Web stress-test tool built in that we used to perform a simulated load on the two servers.

We'll also show you how to use rsconfig to join an SSRS server to a Web farm to see how offloading resources to another system will enhance performance. The Report Server Configuration Manager can also be used for this purpose.

We began by running a simulated load of 15 users, all executing a single report against RS05. We quickly assessed the performance impact by monitoring the server with Task Manager. Unfortunately, our test pushed the server to 100 percent CPU utilization. Analyzing the individual processes that were taxing the processor, we ascertained that they were SQL Server and the Web service W3WP.exe. Figure 8-29 shows the CPU usage jumping to 100 percent as the test was running.

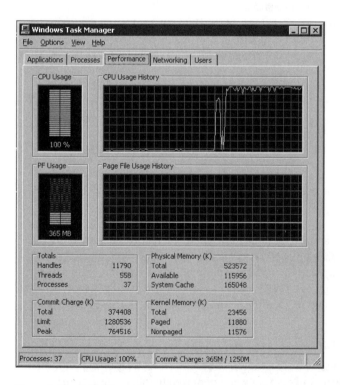

Figure 8-29. *Task Manager at 100 percent*

We knew our test SSRS server was a single processor system with more than 500MB of RAM. In this case, it was the CPU that was the bottleneck. Because our production deployment of SSRS would not mirror the setup of RS05 (in other words, the production server would be a high-end multiprocessor system with at least 2GB of RAM), we could take that into consideration.

However, one other factor would have a substantial impact on the difference in performance between the production and test environments. In the test environment, the SSRS Web service and SQL Server were on the same system, RS05. What if we configured the SSRS Web service to use a remote SQL Server instance for its database? Any performance degradation caused by accessing the ReportServer database over the network instead of a local database would be negligible if the CPU utilization percentage dropped down to a more manageable number.

If you have two SSRS servers, then moving an SSRS server from one instance to another is simple. We had two SSRS servers in the test environment, RS05 and HWC04, so the move was easy enough. To instruct the Web service on RS05 to use the SSRS databases on HWC04, we used the command-line utility rsconfig. The rsconfig command or Report Server Configuration Manager is required when first joining one SSRS Web service to a Web farm that uses the same ReportServer database. The syntax for the rsconfig command is as follows:

```
rsconfig -c -s HWC04 -d ReportServer -a SQL -u username -p password
```

With RS05 using the remote SQL Server database, we initiated another test to see whether the CPU utilization improved. As you can see in Figure 8-30, CPU utilization improved substantially and was now under the 60 percent average.

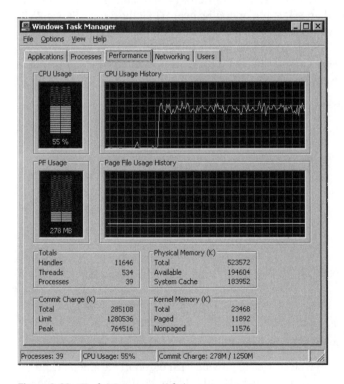

Figure 8-30. *Task Manager with improvements*

■**Note** Specific licensing guidelines are available for the SSRS 2005 deployment and the location of the databases and data sources. For more information, visit http://www.microsoft.com/sql/reporting/.

Controlling SSRS Programmatically

SSRS 2005 offers two main methods of controlling SSRS 2005 through code:

- Web services

- Windows Management Interface (WMI)

In the following sections, we'll give an introductory look at using both of these technologies to manage reports from code. You'll use the SOAP API, otherwise known as the Report Server Web service, to add subscription functionality to the SSRS viewer you created in Chapter 6, and you'll extend it to allow your users to add subscriptions for the reports you've developed and deployed so far. This has two main benefits. First, it allows you to offload some of the processing activity from the SQL Server and SSRS 2005 server during the day, when they are used most heavily. Second, it saves the executives who want to receive the reports from spending time navigating to the report server, entering the parameters, and waiting for the results.

Controlling SSRS with SOAP

The SSRS 2005 Report Server Web service offers a feature-rich way of interacting with and controlling your reporting server. Based on SOAP and operating over HTTP, the Report Server Web service is a simple, yet powerful, way to access the features of the server. In fact, SSRS 2005's Report Manager is built using ASP.NET and the SSRS Report Server Web service.

Using the Report Server Web service, you can create custom applications that control all aspects of the server and cover the entire reporting life cycle:

- Folder and resource management

- Task, role, and policy management

- Data sources and connections

- Report parameters

- Report rendering

- Report history

- Report scheduling

- Report subscriptions

- Linked reports

Adding Subscription Functionality to SSRS Viewer

You've already used the Report Server Web service to provide a list of report parameters and their possible values and to deploy reports in Chapters 6 and 7. In this chapter, you'll learn how to use the Report Server Web service to schedule reports to run automatically each morning before the office opens.

As you saw in the earlier part of this chapter, you can set up subscription services through the user interface of the report server itself. You may, however, want to provide this functionality within your customized Windows Forms (or Web) application. In the example, you'll expand on the previous Windows Forms application to allow users to provide the parameters that they want to run the report with, as well as schedule the time to run the report and indicate the delivery mechanism to use.

In the example, you'll allow the users to pick only a shared schedule that has already been defined by the systems administrator. Because you want centralized control over when scheduled reports will be run, you won't give users the ability to define their own schedules. You'll also allow them to trigger a subscription based on a snapshot. This allows them to receive their subscribed report whenever a snapshot is created for it. See the "Creating Snapshots for the Report History" section earlier in this chapter for details.

Before you run the included examples, make sure to read the ReadMe.htm file. It is located in a file in the samples root folder. If you have the code open in Visual Studio, it will be under the Solution Items folder. It contains setup and configuration steps that are required before running the examples.

Accessing an Existing Shared Schedule

If you are walking through this code, start by opening the project from Chapter 6, as it will serve as the starting point for our additions. After you have the solution, open the SSRS Viewer RVC project, and complete the following steps:

1. Select Project ➤ Add New Item.

2. In the Add New Item dialog box, select Windows Form, and enter **PickSchedule.cs** for the name.

3. With the PickSchedule.cs form open in design mode, resize it to 450×150 through the properties page.

4. Add a label, set its Text property to Schedules, add a combo box named sharedSchedules, and add a button named setSchedule and set its Text property to OK. When you're done, you should have a form that looks like Figure 8-31.

Figure 8-31. *Pick Schedule dialog box*

Now select View Code for the PickSchedule class. For this example, you'll add a few using statements to import types defined in other namespaces so you can avoid typing the full namespaces during the actual coding. Add the namespaces shown in Listing 8-4 to the PickSchedule.cs class file below the other using statements.

Listing 8-4. *Importing Namespaces*

```
using System.Collections;
using System.Diagnostics;
using System.Web.Services.Protocols;
using SSRS_Viewer_RVC.SSRSWebService;
```

Next, add the class variables shown in Listing 8-5 to PickSchedule.cs just below the class declaration. The ReportingService2005 type contains the methods and properties you can use to call the SSRS 2005 Report Server Web service and is made available through the Web reference you added to the SSRS Viewer RVC project in Chapter 6.

Listing 8-5. *Class-Level Private Variables*

```
private string url;
private string server;
private string report;
private ReportingService2005 rs;
```

Next, modify the PickSchedule_Load event to query the SSRS 2005 server for the shared schedules that are available.

■**Note** You'll need to set up these shared schedules in advance using Report Manager on your SSRS 2005 server. You can add and edit shared schedules by navigating to your SSRS 2005 server with your Web browser, selecting Site Settings, and then under Other, selecting Managed Shared Schedules. You can also use SSMS to setup shared schedules. By default, you need to set up these Shared Schedules as a user who is in the SSRS 2005 System Administrator role, and users who access them must be members of the System Users role. Also, subscriptions require that the SQL Server Agent is running and that your data source has stored credentials. See the "Shared Schedules" section earlier in this chapter for details.

Next, take the URL that is passed in when the PickSchedule class is initialized and break it apart to get the report name for which you are setting the schedule. Add the code in Listing 8-6 to the class's constructor.

Listing 8-6. PickSchedule *Constructor*

```
public PickSchedule(string URL)
{
    InitializeComponent();
    url = URL;
    string[] reportInfo = url.Split('?');
    server = reportInfo[0];
    report = reportInfo[1];
}
```

■**Note** The call to `InitializeComponent` is present in the constructor already. It was added automatically when the form was created.

To get a list of available shared schedules from your SSRS 2005 server, you'll use the `ListSchedules` method of the Report Server Web service. The `ListSchedules` method returns an array of `Schedule` objects, so after you call the method, you'll need to loop through the array to populate your combo box. Because you're expanding the existing viewer, you still want the user to be able to run the report immediately. You also want your users to be able to trigger the subscription whenever a snapshot of the report is created. To do this, add a Do Not Schedule choice and a Schedule with Snapshot choice to your combo box.

■**Note** You can set up snapshots through the Report Manager Web interface of your SSRS 2005 server or through SSMS.

The code shown in Listing 8-7 uses the `ComboItem` class that you created in Chapter 6 to add the items to combo boxes. With `PickSchedule.cs` in design mode, double-click the form. This creates an empty method to handle the form's `Load` event. Add the code shown in Listing 8-7 to the `PickSchedule_Load` method.

Listing 8-7. *Getting Shared Schedules*

```
private void PickSchedule_Load(object sender, EventArgs e)
{

    rs = new SSRSWebService.ReportingService2005();
    rs.Credentials = System.Net.CredentialCache.DefaultCredentials;
    Schedule[] schedules = null;

    try
    {
        schedules = rs.ListSchedules();
        if (schedules != null)
        {
            //Build list items
            ArrayList aList = new ArrayList();
            // Now add the Do Not Schedule item
            aList.Add(new ComboItem("Do not schedule", "NS"));
            // And the Snapshot schedule
            aList.Add(new ComboItem("Schedule with Snapshot", "SS"));
            foreach (Schedule s in schedules)
```

```
            {
                aList.Add(new ComboItem(s.Description, s.ScheduleID));
                Debug.WriteLine(String.Format("Desc: {0} - ID: {1}", s.Description,
                    s.ScheduleID));
            }
            //Bind list items to combo box
            sharedSchedules.DataSource = aList;
            sharedSchedules.DisplayMember = "Display";
            sharedSchedules.ValueMember = "Value";
            }
    }
    catch (SoapException ex)
    {
MessageBox.Show(ex.Detail.InnerXml.ToString());
    }

}
```

Scheduling the Report

Now that you have the list of available scheduling options, you need to add some code to handle the case in which the user has selected to schedule the report to be delivered based on one of the shared schedules or on the creation of a snapshot. To do this, you'll use another method of the Report Service Web service, CreateSubscription. The CreateSubscription method of the API takes six parameters:

- Report: The full path name of the report for which to create a subscription.

- ExtensionSettings: Represents a delivery extension and contains a list of settings specific to the extension. SSRS 2005 comes with two built-in extensions, the Email Delivery extension and the File Share Delivery extension.

- Description: A meaningful description displayed to users.

- EventType: The type of event that triggers the subscription. The valid values are TimedSubscription and SnapshotUpdated.

- MatchData: The data that is associated with the specified EventType parameter. This parameter is used by an event to match the subscription with an event that has fired.

- Parameters: An array of ParameterValue[] objects that contains a list of parameters for the report.

In your report scheduler, you'll create a new method, ScheduleReport, which is called whenever the user chooses to have a report scheduled. This method sets these parameters to the appropriate values and then calls the CreateSubscription method of the SSRS 2005 Report Server Web service. Most of the values are just strings and are straightforward to set.

Check to see whether the user selected a subscription and, if so, whether it is based on a shared schedule or a snapshot. You'll use this to set the EventType accordingly. If the user selected Shared Schedule, then set the variable matchData to the ScheduledID. If not, set the variable to null to tell SSRS 2005 to trigger it based on a snapshot.

```
if (sharedSchedules.SelectedValue.ToString() == "SS")
{
    eventType = "SnapshotUpdated";
    matchData = null;
}
else
{
    eventType = "TimedSubscription";
    matchData = sharedSchedules.SelectedValue.ToString();
}
```

To set up a subscription, you have to provide SSRS 2005 with some information about how to deliver the subscription. To do this, set the delivery extensions through an `ExtensionSettings` object, which itself contains `ParameterValue` objects. `ParameterValue` objects are essentially name-value pairs, making the `ExtensionSettings` object essentially an array of name-value pairs.

To use the `ExtensionSettings` object, create `ParameterValue` objects (your name-value pairs) with your delivery settings and then add them to the `ExtensionSettings` object. You'll then call the `CreateSubscription` method and pass in the `ExtensionSettings` object to give SSRS 2005 the subscription specifics. (See Listing 8-8 for details.)

If the user decides on a subscription based on a shared schedule, and the report accepts parameters, then you'll need to collect them from your report viewer interface so that you can set them in the subscription. These are the values that the report will run with whenever it's run by the subscription. To do this, you'll add code to the `PickSchedule` form to call the `GetParameters` form. Because the `GetParameters` class returns values in the form of `Winforms.ReportParameters`, you'll have to convert them into an array of `ParameterValue` objects required by the Report Server Web service. The only other item you need is the report itself, which you already have as a class-level variable that was set in the `Forms` constructor. The final method should look like Listing 8-8; add it to `PickSchedule.cs`.

Listing 8-8. *Report Scheduler*

```
private void ScheduleReport()
{

    // See whether the user wants to schedule this versus run it now
    if (sharedSchedules.SelectedValue.ToString() != "NS")
    {
        string desc = "Send report via email";
        string eventType = String.Empty;
        string matchData = String.Empty;
        // If the user selected SnapShot, then
        // set up the parameters for a snapshot
        if (sharedSchedules.SelectedValue.ToString() == "SS")
        {
            eventType = "SnapshotUpdated";
            matchData = null;
        }
```

```
// otherwise the user is using a subscription
else
{
    eventType = "TimedSubscription";
    matchData = sharedSchedules.SelectedValue.ToString();
}

ParameterValue[] extensionParams = new ParameterValue[8];

extensionParams[0] = new ParameterValue();
extensionParams[0].Name = "TO";
extensionParams[0].Value = "someone@company.com";

extensionParams[1] = new ParameterValue();
extensionParams[1].Name = "ReplyTo";
extensionParams[1].Value = "reporting@company.com";

extensionParams[2] = new ParameterValue();
extensionParams[2].Name = "IncludeReport";
extensionParams[2].Value = "True";

extensionParams[3] = new ParameterValue();
extensionParams[3].Name = "RenderFormat";
extensionParams[3].Value = "PDF";

extensionParams[4] = new ParameterValue();
extensionParams[4].Name = "Subject";
extensionParams[4].Value = "@ReportName was executed at➥
    @ExecutionTime";

extensionParams[5] = new ParameterValue();
extensionParams[5].Name = "Comment";
extensionParams[5].Value = "Here is your @ReportName report.";

extensionParams[6] = new ParameterValue();
extensionParams[6].Name = "IncludeLink";
extensionParams[6].Value = "True";

extensionParams[7] = new ParameterValue();
extensionParams[7].Name = "Priority";
extensionParams[7].Value = "NORMAL";

ParameterValue[] pvs = ReportParameters();

// Configure the extension settings required
// for the CreateSubscription method
ExtensionSettings extSettings = new ExtensionSettings();
```

```csharp
        extSettings.ParameterValues = extensionParams;
        extSettings.Extension = "Report Server Email";

        // Get the report parameters using the GetParameters form
        GetParameters reportParameters = new GetParameters(url);
        reportParameters.ShowDialog();
        Microsoft.Reporting.WinForms.ReportParameter[] rps =
            reportParameters.Parameters;

        // Convert the Winforms.ReportParameter returned
        // from the GetParameters to ParameterValues required for
        // the CreateSubscription method

        int i = 0;
        foreach (Microsoft.Reporting.WinForms.ReportParameter rp
            in rps)
        {
            if (rp.Values.Count != 0)
                i++;
        }
        ParameterValue[] pvs = new ParameterValue[i];
        int j = 0;
        foreach (Microsoft.Reporting.WinForms.ReportParameter rp in rps)
        {
            if (rp.Values.Count != 0)
            {
                pvs[j] = new ParameterValue();
                pvs[j].Name = rp.Name;
                pvs[j].Value = rp.Values[0];
                j++;
            }
        }

        // Now set up the subscription
        try
        {
            rs.CreateSubscription(report, extSettings, desc,
                eventType, matchData, pvs);
        }

        catch (SoapException ex)
        {
            MessageBox.Show(ex.Detail.InnerXml.ToString());
        }
    }
}
```

To complete the PickSchedule form, you need to wire up the setSchedule button's click event so it will call the ScheduleReport method to actually schedule the report with the schedule selected by the user. With the PickSchedule.cs in design mode, double-click the OK button. Add the code shown in Listing 8-9.

Listing 8-9. *Hooking the Schedule Button's* click *event to the* ScheduleReport *Method*

```
private void setSchedule_Click(object sender, EventArgs e)
{
    ScheduleReport();
}
```

Now let's add a button to the ViewerRVC.cs form that you'll code to call the new PickSchedule.cs form. First, you need to add a new button to the ViewerRVC.cs form. Name it pickSchedule, and set its Text property to Schedule. This will allow the user to pick a schedule from the viewer. Second, after you add the button to the form, add the code shown in Listing 8-10 to the button's click event by double-clicking the Schedule button with the ViewerRVC.cs in design mode. Of course, you need to use the name of your report server where you see localhost in the URL.

Listing 8-10. *The* pickSchedule *Button's* click *Event*

```
private void pickSchedule_Click(object sender, EventArgs e)
{
    reportURL.Text = "http://localhost/reportserver?/Pro_SSRS/➥
        Chapter_6/EmployeeServiceCost";
    PickSchedule reportSchedule = new PickSchedule(reportURL.Text);
    reportSchedule.ShowDialog();
}
```

At this point, you can run the program; however, before you can schedule the report, you must set the credentials for the shared data source so the report will have login credentials to use when it is run noninteractively. If you are using SQL authentication, you can do this by opening the Reports project in the solution and double-clicking the Pro_SSRS.rds data source. On the Shared Data Source dialog box, select the Credentials tab, and select Use a Specific User Name and Password. Enter the appropriate username and password to use when running this report. If you are using Windows integrated authentication, such as running reports under your Windows account, you need to use Report Manager or SSMS to edit the data source and select the Use As Windows credentials when connecting to the data source option. For Windows accounts, specify the login name using the format domain\user.

Now run the program, and pick one of your previously configured schedules. For the parameters, enter **ServiceYear 2003**, **ServiceMonth November**, **BranchID Long Loop**, and **EmployeeTblID Ywzcsl,Nnc**.

■**Note** Remember to use SSMS or Report Manager to set up your shared schedules. You must be logged in as a user who is a member of the SSRS 2005 System Administrators role to add new schedules. See the section titled "Creating a Shared Schedule" earlier in this chapter for details.

Delivering the Report

In the example, you've used PDF to deliver the report to the subscription user. You've also hard-coded the e-mail address, which isn't practical in the real world. One other issue of concern, especially in the health-care setting, is complying to HIPAA and protecting patient information.

You could give the user a textbox with which to enter the e-mail address to which the user wants the report delivered. However, the user could possibly type in an incorrect e-mail address and deliver the report to the wrong person. It would be great if the user's e-mail address could be filled in automatically, to make sure it is the correct address. You can do this by pulling the address from a field in a table in the database similar to the data drive subscription example given earlier in the chapter where you pulled the e-mail address from the Employee table. However, in this case, the user pulling the report may not be in the database table, and you want the report delivered automatically to the user scheduling it. Fortunately, the .NET Framework and Active Directory offer an easy way to do this. For many organizations using Microsoft Exchange Server 2000 or 2003, e-mail addresses are integrated with Active Directory. If you aren't using Exchange Server, e-mail addresses aren't integrated with Active Directory, but you can still enter them into Active Directory manually.

Let's create a method that determines the e-mail of the currently logged-in user. Then you can use it to provide the To e-mail address for the subscription. Start by adding a new reference to the project for System.DirectoryServices. Select References under the SSRS Viewer RVC project in your solution, and then select Add Reference. In the Add Reference dialog box under the .NET tab, select System.DirectoryServices from the list of component names. Next, add using statements to simplify your typing, as follows:

```
using System.DirectoryServices;
using System.Security.Principal;
```

To find the current user's e-mail address, use DirectorySearcher, which allows you to perform queries against Active Directory, as shown in Listing 8-11. You'll start at the root level of the directory and look for the user by name. When you find the user's name, you return the first e-mail address you find for the user.

Listing 8-11. *Code to Query Active Directory for E-mail Addresses*

```
private string GetEmailFromAD()
{

    DirectoryEntry rootEntry;
    DirectoryEntry contextEntry;
    DirectorySearcher searcher;
    SearchResult result;

    string currentUserName;
    string contextPath;

    WindowsPrincipal wp =
        new WindowsPrincipal(WindowsIdentity.GetCurrent());
    currentUserName = wp.Identity.Name.Split('\\')[1];
```

```
    rootEntry = new DirectoryEntry("LDAP://RootDSE");
    contextPath =
        rootEntry.Properties["defaultNamingContext"].Value.ToString();

    rootEntry.Dispose();
    contextEntry = new DirectoryEntry("LDAP://" + contextPath);

    searcher = new DirectorySearcher();
    searcher.SearchRoot = contextEntry;
    searcher.Filter =
        String.Format("(&(objectCategory=person)(samAccountName={0}))",
        currentUserName);
    searcher.PropertiesToLoad.Add("mail");
    searcher.PropertiesToLoad.Add("cn");
    searcher.SearchScope = SearchScope.Subtree;

    result = searcher.FindOne();

    return result.Properties["mail"][0].ToString();
}
```

To use this, all you have to do is modify the TO parameter for the delivery extension in the ScheduleReport method you wrote earlier to use the new method you just wrote. So, your previous code for the TO parameter becomes this:

```
extensionParams[0] = new ParameterValue();
extensionParams[0].Name = "TO";
extensionParams[0].Value = GetEmailFromAD();
```

Now run the SSRS Viewer RVC, and choose a schedule from the shared schedules you previously configured. For the parameters, enter **ServiceYear 2003**, **ServiceMonth November**, **BranchID Long Loop**, and **EmployeeTblID Ywzcsl, Nnc.**; this will create a subscription that is e-mailed to you on the schedule you selected. If you navigate to the server now using your browser, select the Employee Service Cost report, and then select the Subscriptions tab, you should see your subscription, as shown in Figure 8-32. If you click Edit, you see that it has provided all the parameters you selected, and it inserted your e-mail address in the To field.

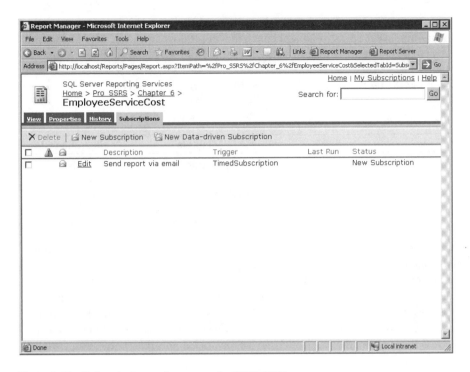

Figure 8-32. *Subscription as it appears in SSRS 2005*

You haven't seen all the possible options that you can use when scheduling reports such as the Employee Service Cost report, but we've given you a good start to schedule and deliver reports and add other functionality. Some possibilities include the following:

- Allowing the user to decide the format the report will be delivered in

- Allowing the user to attach the report or just provide a link

- Allowing the user to create schedules on the fly

You can use the SSRS 2005 Report Server Web service to control many more aspects of the report server and the reports under its control. We have just scratched the surface here of what you can do, but be aware that the basic aspects of dealing with the report server through the Report Server Web service are the same for nearly all the functions.

Controlling SSRS with WMI

Before we finish this chapter, we should also briefly discuss how you can manage SSRS using two WMI classes. These classes are used more for administrative tasks and allow you to programmatically access server settings. WMI is not used for manipulating reports or report settings.

WMI offers a standardized way to monitor and control systems and services running anywhere on your network. Using the WMI provider, you can write code that allows you to query the current settings of an SSRS 2005 server and also to change those settings through properties and methods of the classes providing these services.

Essentially, these providers allow you to change the settings of the configuration files on the server programmatically. So, as you might guess, the properties of these classes correspond almost directly to the elements within the XML files that hold SSRS 2005 configuration information.

Table 8-2 shows the two classes provided by SSRS 2005 for use with WMI.

Table 8-2. *SSRS 2005 Classes for Use with WMI*

Class	Controls	Configuration File
MSReportServer_ConfigurationSetting	Report Server	RSReportServer.config
MSReportServerReportManager_ConfigurationSetting	Report Manager	RSWebApplication.config

You can use the MSReportServer_ConfigurationSetting class to determine and/or configure most of the database settings used by SSRS 2005 itself—that is, for the database that SSRS uses to store the reports, snapshots, and so on. This class doesn't control the data source connection information used in your reports, although you can set the login information that the server uses to run a report in unattended mode. You can also work with things such as the database server name, database name, and login credential information in this class. You can also use this class to configure the SSRS 2005 service instance name, path name, and virtual directory it maps to in IIS.

You can use the MSReportServerReportManager_ConfigurationSetting class to determine the instance name, path name, and virtual root of the SSRS 2005 Report Manager, as well as to read or set the URL of a particular instance.

To access this information through the SSRS 2005 WMI providers, you use the System.Management namespace, which provides access to WMI.

■**Note** If more than one instance of a report server is installed, you'll need to locate the correct instance before reading and setting properties. The PathName property is the key property, and it uniquely identifies a particular instance.

Summary

SSRS 2005 provides many tools for management tasks, and we covered several of them in this chapter. Because SSRS 2005 is a full reporting solution, administrators may find it difficult to manage the entire site single-handedly without some level of automation or divided tasks, especially as the number of reports and other objects such as data sources, models, folders, and subscriptions grows. Maintaining these objects, whether it be to update the report via Report Manager or to mass deploy reports via a custom application, administrators will continually find themselves maintaining their SSRS report servers. Tools such as SSMS, Report Server Configuration Manager, and Report Manager go a long way to centralize the administrative tasks but do not necessarily reduce the potential rote tasks associated with managing a large installation. Fortunately, SSRS provides the flexibility to allow other professionals, department managers, and users to maintain their own reports using tools provided with SSRS 2005 or through your own custom applications. Of course, with this flexibility comes the need for tighter security. We will turn now, in the next chapter, to security and show how to make sure that you can lock down and monitor this flexible model.

CHAPTER 9

■■■

Securing Reports

If a topic is currently on the minds of operating system makers, application developers, and system administrators more than security is, we would be hard-pressed to name it. We all know that security threats come in many flavors and levels of severity—from the innocuous pop-up Web pages to the invasive worms and viruses that wreak havoc on systems and take their toll on productivity by wasting time and resources.

These threats are often anonymous scripts or executables—*automatons*—that their human creator has released into the wild. But what about the security violations from real individuals? These are not just elusive system crackers bent on destruction; they can be the overlooked disgruntled employee who left the company with a notebook full of passwords and the determination to make a point about the insecurity of the company's vital data.

Securing systems takes time and effort and sometimes, unfortunately, has a lower priority than other important daily tasks. However, if your company, like ours and thousands of others, is affected by the regulations imposed by HIPAA, meeting stringent security standards is a requirement, not just a recommended practice. Most companies have policies and procedures in place that will meet HIPAA compliance, which took effect in April 2005. As a roles-based application, SSRS will take advantage of the underlying authentication and network already at work in your organization, especially if you are running a Windows 2000 or 2003 domain. The SSRS security model has three important components:

- Data encryption

- Authentication and user access

- Report audits

The goal in this chapter is to meet the challenge of effectively setting up and testing each of these security components in your SSRS deployment. We will show how to do this through our experience using SSRS to meet HIPAA compliance.

When we first decided to incorporate SSRS into our business, we knew we would have to deploy it in two environments: the first is an internal deployment to a secure intranet site for our employees, and the second is as an application service provider (ASP) to our Internet customers who use our health-care application via a hosted Terminal Services connection. Though each model requires unique security considerations, which we will discuss in the "Exploring Deployment Models" section, fundamentally our three security checkpoints—authentication, encryption, and report auditing—apply to both environments.

When we decided to deploy SSRS to our clients, it was not without much consideration and testing. We had already determined, through the beta test cycles with Microsoft, that the report design aspects of SSRS met our needs. But until we could actually deploy and monitor the access and execution of the reports we would be rewriting for our health-care application, we could not be certain we would be able to deploy for each of our required models.

Further, we knew that at some point we may alter our then-current model, which required all our clients to have their own Windows domain accounts. With SSRS, where the default authentication method is Windows authentication, we realized we could remove this requirement. This would open the possibility of allowing Internet reporting, where users could access reports from their browser or other custom forms we provided. If we had to require every user to have a Windows account, this would be impossible, or at least more difficult to administer. Knowing that SSRS offered an extendable security model, we were aware that we could go forward with our plans to incorporate the default Windows security model into our application, and when and if we decided to, we could create our own authentication.

Encrypting Data

When working with confidential data of any kind, the chief concern is that the only people who can see that data are those who need to see it and who have been specifically granted permission to see it. This is especially true of patient identifiable (PI) data, as defined by HIPAA, with which we as a software development company had to be concerned. We'll start with the first of the three main challenges we defined as crucial to a successful, secure deployment of SSRS: data encryption.

Introducing Encryption

In today's mixed-technology networked environment, data encryption comes in many varieties. However, regardless of the technology, the encryption algorithms must meet a high standard for complexity and reliability. Fortunately, many applications provide built-in levels of encryption. SSRS natively supports encrypting the data it stores in the ReportServer database and configuration files. Companies may have the following other technologies in place that can be used in conjunction with SSRS encryption:

- *Wireless*: Uses Wireless Encryption Protocol (WEP), with shared keys to encrypt data transmitted through wireless access points.

- *IIS*: Uses a server certificate, generally from a trusted authority such as VeriSign, to provide encryption over Secure Sockets Layer (SSL). SSL is used when transmitting data with HTTPS instead of HTTP.

- *Terminal Services*: Uses Remote Desktop Protocol (RDP) for connecting remotely from a client workstation to a terminal server. This provides four levels of data encryption in Windows 2003 with Service Pack 1: Low, Client Compatible, High, and FIPS Compliant.

- *VPNs*: Allows accessibility to internal networks from VPN client systems. Encapsulates and encrypts Point-to-Point Tunneling Protocol (PPTP) and Layer 2 Tunneling Protocol (L2TP).

- *IPSec*: Is the standard security protocol for Transmission Control Protocol/Internet Protocol (TCP/IP) traffic. This adds several layers of security, including data encryption.

In our health-care application's two deployment scenarios for SSRS, we utilize several of the encryption technologies listed here. In the Internet-hosted deployment model, for example, we use both SSL and Terminal Services encryption. For the internal deployment, on an intranet server, we set up a VPN solution, configured a wireless access point to encrypt data packets transmitted to and from wireless devices, and also provided SSL pass-through from a Microsoft Integrated Security and Accelerator (ISA) server.

Securing Network Traffic Using SSL

In the following sections, we will show how to set up the SSRS server to use SSL. By having an SSL server certificate installed on the server, all data transferred between the client application (which can be a browser or custom application) and the report server will be encrypted. This is essential when transmitting confidential data such as PI information over the Internet. Having a certificate from a trusted authority such as VeriSign or Thawte also ensures that the registered domain name used to access the Web server has been validated and can be trusted to be from the legitimate company that it claims to be from.

Before we show how to install the certificate on the SSRS server, we will cover what data is being transmitted at the packet level to your SSRS server through HTTP requests. In this way, when you do actually install the certificate, you will be able to compare the data packets before and after installation to verify that the certificate is working as it should. To begin, we will show how to use a tool that is included with most versions of Windows, Network Monitor.

Analyzing HTTP Traffic

Network Monitor is a packet analysis utility that allows you to capture all the data packets transferred to and from the target server and client. The version of Network Monitor that comes with Windows is unlike other network capture tools, such as the version of the same tool included in Systems Management Server, in that it can listen to traffic that is destined only for the machine on which it is executed. Network Monitor is not installed with Windows by default, though. You can add it post-installation through the Add/Remove Programs applet. In this applet, select Add Remove Windows Components and then Management and Monitoring Tools. Next click Details, and then select Network Monitoring Tools.

On the SSRS server, we will show how to launch Network Monitor from Administrative Tools. If more than one network interface card (NIC) is installed on your machine, as in our case, make sure you select the card on which you will be testing. Figure 9-1 shows the main screen of Network Monitor and the traffic that it is capturing on the network, including broadcasts and local packets. Network Monitor can be daunting to the uninitiated, as it was designed to be used by network administrators who have more than a cursory understanding of network protocols.

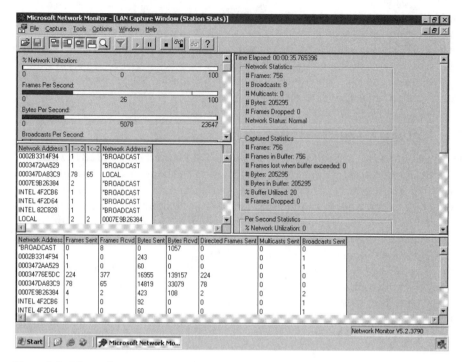

Figure 9-1. *Network Monitor*

You can filter out any unwanted traffic, which we will cover in this section because we will be showing how to capture data through a Remote Desktop session that sends a steady stream of RDP frames on ports 3389 and 3381; for our health-care example, we want to see only HTTP traffic on port 80. We could actually go to the server's console to run Network Monitor, which would preclude capturing unwanted RDP frames, but that would require leaving our office chairs and thus interrupt our sedentary lifestyles that have been exacerbated—or should we say *enhanced*?—by the creation of the remote administration features of Windows. So, we will lazily apply a filter.

You could, for example, define a capture filter that uses a pattern match in the data packet to limit the results of the capture. Alternately, you could capture everything and then configure a display filter to limit the results. In this case, it is worth the effort of setting up a capture filter to exclude RDP traffic. To do this, you must know two important values, the pattern and the offset. The pattern is a hexadecimal value that represents the port numbers, 3389 or 3381. The offset is the location pointer of the pattern in the frame. You can glean both of these values by running a capture with no filters applied. In Figure 9-2, you can see a frame that has a source port of 3389 (OD3D in hex) and the offset location. You can use these values, as well as the values for port 3381, to now exclude all RDP traffic and then open Report Manager from your client machine and navigate to your reports to capture SSRS-specific traffic.

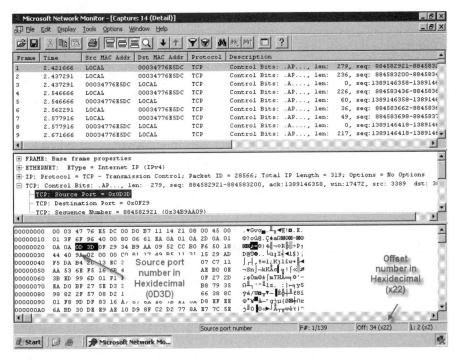

Figure 9-2. *Offset and pattern location*

On the Network Monitor toolbar, click the Edit Capture Filter button. In the Capture Filter dialog box, click Pattern and enter your pattern for port 3389 as a hexadecimal value, **0D3D**. For the offset, enter a value of **22**, and leave From Start of Frame checked. Next, because you want to exclude these frames, select each pattern, click Not to add the exclusion to the tree, and then click OK, as shown in Figure 9-3.

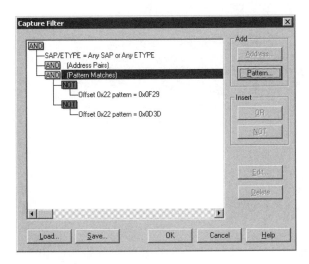

Figure 9-3. *Capture Filter properties*

Now, click the Start Capture button, and let the capture run as you view a report with Report Manager. You will want to make sure you access a report that could have identifiable information in it. The Employee Service Cost report that you have been working with does, so you can use it for this purpose. You are concerned not only with capturing user login information potentially passed in a URL but also with any information that may identity a patient. If this is the case, and you allow access to the report over the Internet, you would have a serious problem and be out of compliance with HIPAA regulations.

After executing the report, analyzing the captured frames reveals the disturbing news. You can see the name of one of the patients (whose true identity has been altered to be Bill Shakespeare) returned directly in an HTTP frame, as clearly shown in Figure 9-4. In this case, you have not analyzed other types of traffic, such as SQL requests on port 1433, to see whether other protocols are potentially sending plain-text information, but you can use the same tool to do that.

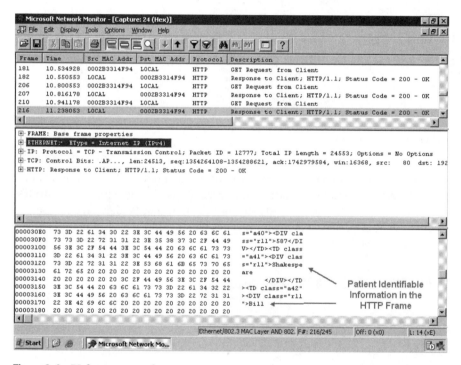

Figure 9-4. *PI data captured*

■**Tip** Though we will not cover the steps to configure SQL Server itself to encrypt network traffic, as we will be doing with IIS, it is important to mention that SQL Server uses SSL as well, and that by having a certificate installed, you can easily configure SQL Server to transmit encrypted data. A minimal performance hit is associated with encryption.

Applying the SSL Certificate

Now it is time to apply a certificate to the SSRS server and rescan the traffic to make sure the viewable data in clear text will be encrypted.

Several companies provide server certificates that can be installed on a Web server and verified directly over the Internet from the trusted site that issued the certificate. By using the certificates issued from these trusted sources, such as VeriSign, the client will automatically trust the site. Other certificates, such as those generated through Certificate Services in Windows, may require that the certificate be installed on the client machine, because the client will not automatically trust the certificate if it cannot reach the certificate authority. Generally, for Internet use, it is more practical to pay the fee to use the commercial certificate. The online deployment uses a server certificate issued from a commercial certificate authority. However, for the temporary test environment, you can use SelfSSL, a handy little utility that comes with the IIS 6.0 Support Tools. You can download SelfSSL from the following location:

```
http://www.microsoft.com/downloads/details.aspx?FamilyID=56fc92ee-a71a-4c73-b628-↵
ade629c89499&displaylang=en
```

SelfSSL will generate and automatically apply a temporary certificate to a Web site. You run SelfSSL from the command line on the server on which you want to add the certificate. Once installed, you can open a command prompt for SelfSSL by clicking Start ➤ All Programs ➤ IIS Resources ➤ SelfSSL. The typical syntax will be in the following format:

```
Selfssl.exe /N:CN=HWCVS26 /V:20 /T
```

The /N:CN=HWCVS26 option indicates that the common name on the certificate will be the name of the server (HWCVS26). The /V:20 portion indicates that the certificate is valid for ten days. The /T option instructs SelfSSL to add the certificate to the Trusted Certificates list so that the local browser will automatically use the certificate when connecting to the site. You can manually install a local copy of the certificate on other client machines that will access this server. Because SelfSSL installs the certificate that it generates, you don't need to go through the process of generating a certificate request, which would normally be sent to a commercial certificate authority. You can view the installed certificate in IIS Manager. To do this, right-click the default Web site, select Properties, and then click the Directory Security tab. Next, select View Certificate. As you can see in Figure 9-5, the certificate is good for twenty days and is issued to the test server, HWCVS26.

Figure 9-5. *SelfSSL-assigned certificate*

Capturing HTTPS Traffic

Now that you have the certificate installed, let's return to Network Monitor and capture running the reports, this time using https in the URL to the report server on HWCVS26, which instructs the browser to connect to the site with SSL on port 443, instead of HTTP on port 80.

The first thing you'll notice when you navigate directly to the report is a warning that the certificate has not passed all the criteria to be trusted because it does not come from a known certificate authority (see Figure 9-6).

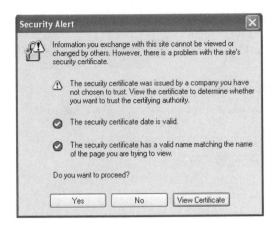

Figure 9-6. *Warning for nontrusted security certificate*

You can select Yes to continue because you do indeed trust the site. You could also install the certificate on the local machine by clicking the lock at the bottom of the browser and selecting Install Certificate so that you will not be prompted with this message again. Installing the certificate in the local client's certificate store causes the browser to automatically trust the site. These steps are not required for known certificate authorities such as VeriSign but are required for this self-assigned certificate.

At this point, because the instance of the report server is still at the default security level, which does not require SSL, you can access Report Manager with either HTTP or HTTPS. You can control the required level of security in a few ways. During installation, for example, if you had a certificate installed already on the default Web site for IIS, you could configure SSRS to use SSL initially. Because you waited to configure your report server's required security connection level until after installation, either you can now use the Report Server Configuration Manager mentioned in the previous chapter, or you can manually set the security level in the rsreportserver.config file.

To configure the security using the Report Server Configuration Manager, select Start ➤ SQL Server 2005 ➤ Configuration Tools. Once connected to the report server instance, select Report Server Virtual Directory, and check the box requiring SSL connections, as shown in Figure 9-7. When the changes are applied, the report server will now require SSL connections to execute reports.

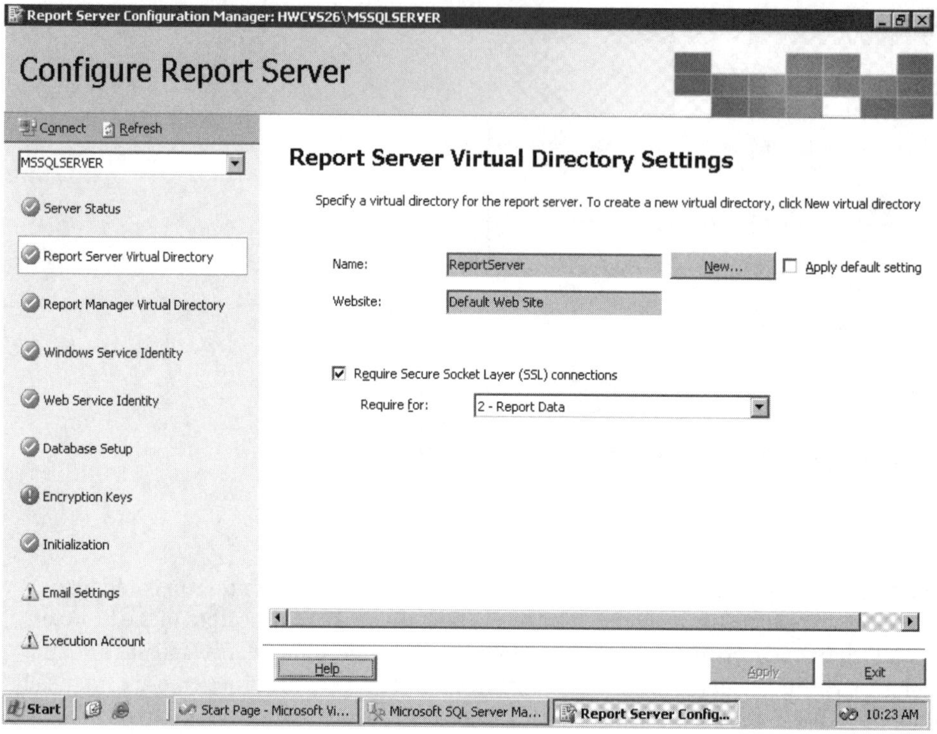

Figure 9-7. *Report Server Configuration Manager*

You can also control the level of security that SSRS will use via the service config file, rsreportserver.config, located in the installed folder, typically *DriveLetter*:\Program Files\ Microsoft SQL Server\MSSQL.3\Reporting Services\ReportServer. Open the file in Notepad, and look for the following entry:

```
<Add Key="SecureConnectionLevel" Value="0"/>
```

Four values control the level of security, 0 through 3. The default for a deployment that does not configure SSRS for SSL during installation is 0, which is the least secure. A value of 3, the most secure, requires every SOAP API call to use SSL. For this example, set the value to 2, which will require encryption of all report data. All calls to the server will now automatically use port 443 and encrypt the data, including the URL string itself, which is important if you are passing any confidential information in the URL. If a user tried to connect to the Report Manager or report server URL using HTTP, the report server would automatically redirect the client to HTTPS to require a secure connection.

When you capture the frames in Network Monitor, you can see that all the previous HTTP frames on port 80 are now using SSL on port 443, as shown in Figure 9-8.

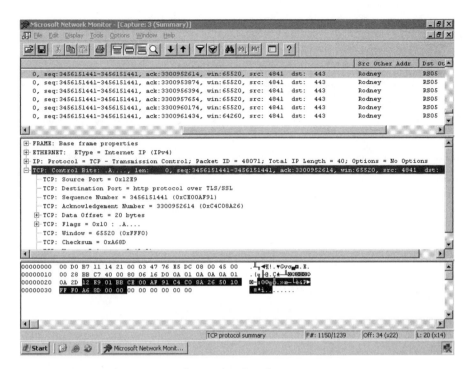

Figure 9-8. *Network Monitor with encrypted packets*

Securing Data Storage in SSRS

While it is important to ensure that network traffic is encrypted, this is only one aspect of maintaining a secure environment. SSRS requires that sensitive data, such as account information used for data access, be stored securely. Since this data is stored in different locations, such as database tables and configuration files, SSRS uses a symmetrical key encryption process to securely store and access this information. What this means is that the authentication information in the database and configuration files is stored in an encrypted format, and SSRS uses the encryption keys it generates to decrypt the information when needed.

As with many SSRS tasks in SQL Server 2005, multiple tools are available to make configuration changes to the report server. You can manage keys with the Report Server Configuration Manager as well as a command-line utility called RSKeyMgmt. You can use either of these tools to back up the keys associated with the report server instance so that if something were to occur that caused the server to have to be rebuilt, you could reapply the keys to the installation. The encryption keys are generated when SSRS is installed or joins a web farm. Figure 9-9 shows the RSReportServer.config file, which contains sensitive authentication credentials required to connect to SSRS server components. Notice that several pieces of data inside the file are encrypted. SSRS uses the keys associated with the report server instance to decrypt the contents of this file as well as the encrypted content stored in the ReportServer database.

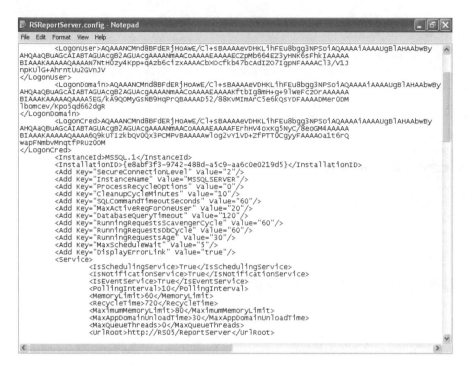

Figure 9-9. `rsreportserver.config` *encrypted values*

We will show how to use both tools, the Report Server Configuration Manager and the RSKeyMgmt utility, to extract the key for the HWCVS26 SSRS installation.

First, open the Report Server Configuration Manager, click Find to locate and connect to your report server instance (called MSSQLSERVER by default), and then click the Encryption Keys icon on the left. You will see four options on the Encryption Key page: Backup, Restore, Change, and Delete. You can back up the encryption key to a key file and supply a password, as shown in Figure 9-10. This file should be stored in a secure location. If the report server ever had to be rebuilt for any reason—because of a hard drive failure, for example (and we're ashamed to admit this happened to an important test machine of ours)—then having this key is crucial to restoring the ReportServer database to its previous state. Without the key file, it is still possible to restore and initialize the ReportServer database from backup. However, all objects that require encryption, such as data sources with stored account information, must be reset manually, which could be an arduous task at best.

Figure 9-10. *Encryption keys in the Report Server Configuration Manager*

To use the command-line tool that will essentially perform the same task of backing up, restoring, and deleting the encryption keys for the report server instance, the syntax is as follows:

```
RSKeyMgmt -e -f E:\Temp\HWCVS26_SSRS_Key -P Password
```

The -e option tells RSKeyMgmt to extract the key to the file HWCVS26_SSRS_Key in the E:\Temp folder. The password option is required. If you needed, you could reapply the key to the server using the same command but changing the -e option to -a. After executing the command, you are timidly instructed to SECURE THE FILE IN A SAFE LOCATION!

Setting Up Authentication and User Access to Data

Access to confidential electronic data, no matter where it resides, begins and ends with user authentication. Having security users or roles properly configured is critical to a secure deployment of SSRS. In a Windows 2000 or 2003 domain environment, SSRS can then take advantage of the authentication provided by Active Directory's security groups and users. The SSRS administrator is responsible for configuring SSRS-specific security roles that link to Active Directory security accounts. In the following sections, we will show how to set up a test Windows account for an employee who will have limited access to the SSRS report server. We will discuss the following:

- *Setting up SSRS roles*: SSRS roles dictate what permissions the users will have when they access the SSRS server. An Active Directory security account, either a group or a user, is assigned either to one of four predefined SSRS roles or to a new role that the SSRS administrator may create.

- *Assigning SSRS roles*: Assignments are the actual SSRS tasks that a user in a specific SSRS role may perform.

- *Configuring and testing permissions for SSRS objects*: Each report folder and its objects maintain individual permissions that can be set at the folder level and propagated to all children objects or that can be set specifically per object. We will show how to set up two folders for the test user account and add report objects that are to be secured.

- *Filtering reports*: It is possible to limit what data is displayed within a report based on the Active Directory login account that is accessing the report server. You do this by associating the value returned from an SSRS global collection, User!UserID, with a field value in the dataset of the report; User!UserID returns the current login account.

- *Authenticating data sources*: In addition to the Windows login account and SSRS role assignments, data sources maintain their own authentication properties, which we will discuss.

- *Setting permissions on the data source database objects*: You may recall from Chapter 2 that you created a stored procedure, Emp_Svc_Cost, to use with the Employee Service Cost report but did not assign user-specific permissions. We will show how to assign the permissions settings in this chapter.

Introducing SSRS Roles

By default, the SSRS Web service installed in IIS uses Windows integrated authentication to access reports and report content. Windows user or group security accounts stored in Active Directory must be associated with an SSRS role before they will have access to the SSRS server. Administrators can assign the Windows accounts to SSRS roles with Report Manager. In the test scenario for our health-care application, we have setup a test Windows account, named jyoungblood, in Active Directory; you will assume jyoungblood is a registered nurse in a health-care organization who makes home visits to patients.

All the clinical staff, including nurses such as jyoungblood, are associated with security groups within Active Directory for the domain. So, you will make jyoungblood a member of the RN security group. In addition to the security group RN, all registered nurses, including jyoungblood, will be contained with an organizational unit (OU) inside Active Directory, as shown in the Active Directory Users and Computers window in Figure 9-11. Though you will not use OUs when assigning a user or group to a role in SSRS, it is important to note that you can use OUs to configure Group Policy settings that apply to security as well, such as locking down the user's desktop or Internet Explorer.

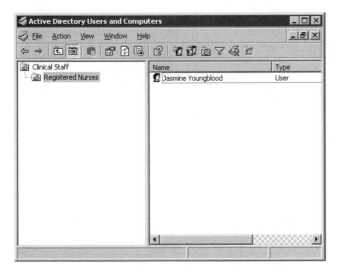

Figure 9-11. *Test Windows account in Active Directory*

Before assigning the test Windows user to an SSRS role and testing the permissions settings, first look at these five predefined roles:

- *Browser*: Users assigned to the Browser role may only view reports, folders, and resources. They may also manage their own subscriptions.

- *Content Manager*: Administrators are assigned to the Content Manager role by default. Users assigned to this role can perform every task available for SSRS objects such as folders, reports, and data sources that they manage.

- *My Reports*: This is the default role automatically assigned to a user when the My Reports feature is enabled on the SSRS server, discussed later in this section.

- *Publisher*: Users assigned to this role have by default enough privileges to publish reports and data sources to the report server. Typically this role is used for report authors who work with Report Designer to create and deploy reports.

- *Report Builder*: The Report Builder role is new to SSRS 2005 and is used primarily for assigning the required permissions to users who will use the Report Builder application, which is covered in Chapter 11.

SSRS roles are defined by the tasks that users assigned to each role may perform. SSRS tasks provide content management permissions and define which SSRS objects are viewable by the user. Users can perform the following tasks:

- Consume reports

- Create linked reports

- Manage all subscriptions

- Manage data sources

- Manage folders

- Manage individual subscriptions

- Manage models

- Manage report history

- Manage reports

- Manage resources

- Set security for individual items

- View data sources

- View folders

- View models

- View reports

- View resources

Each predefined role is configured by default, with a specific combination of allowable tasks. Users assigned to the Publisher role, for example, may manage folders, reports, resources, models, and data sources as well as create linked reports. To view the allowable tasks for each role, you can open Report Manager and navigate to the Site Settings page from the Home folder. On the Site Settings page, click Configure Item-Level Role Definitions. From here you can select any of the five predefined roles and see the tasks available to each. Figure 9-12 shows the default tasks available for the My Reports role.

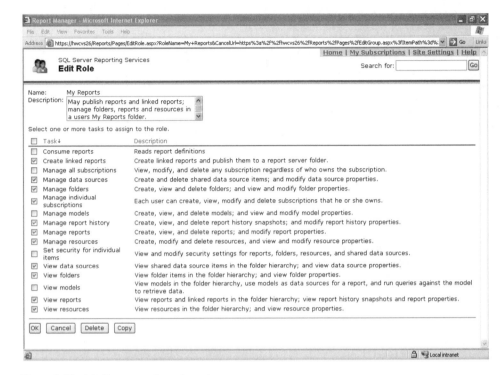

Figure 9-12. *My Reports role task assignments*

The My Reports feature in SSRS creates individual report folders specific to the Windows user. My Reports is useful for companies that need to provide a workspace for employees to create and manage their own reports. The feature is disabled by default but can be enabled in the Site Settings area of Report Manager by checking Enable My Reports to Support User-Owned folders for Publishing and Running Personalized Reports. When it is enabled and a logged-in user clicks the My Reports link, SSRS creates a folder structure based on the user's login name and automatically takes the user to that folder. SSRS also creates a Users Folders folder that the administrator can use to manage the My Reports folders for each user, as shown in Figure 9-13.

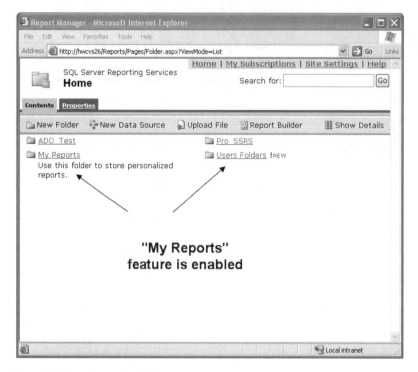

Figure 9-13. My Reports *folder*

As with many tasks for SSRS, multiple tools are available to accomplish the same result. In this case, we showed using Report Manager to view the role assignments and view the My Reports folder. You can view and configure the same role assignments and folders with SSMS. Where applicable, we will show both Report Manager and SSMS in this chapter. To enable the My Reports feature in SSMS, for example, first open SSMS, and then select Reporting Services as the server type in the Connect to Server dialog box. After successfully connecting, right-click the server name, and select Properties. On the General tab, as shown in Figure 9-14, the Enable a My Reports Folder for Each User selection is available. Checking this box will enable the My Reports feature just as in Report Manager.

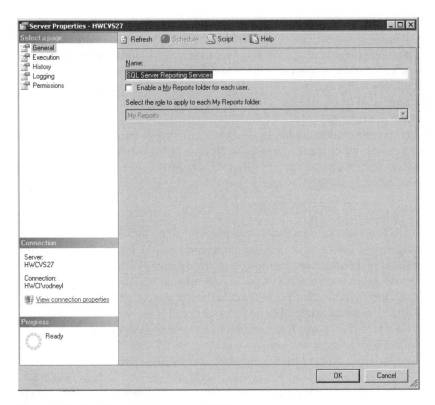

Figure 9-14. *Enabling My Reports in SSMS*

Testing SSRS Role Assignments

In this section, we will go through the process of adding folders and report objects that would be in line with what nurse `jyoungblood` would use. You will want to ensure that she will not have the ability to navigate to other folders and run other reports that may contain confidential information.

The first step in testing `jyoungblood`'s access to the reports that have been defined for her security group, RN, is to publish the reports to a folder on the SSRS server that will contain reports for registered nurses. As the administrator for the test, open Report Manager, and create two new folders, one in the root folder called `Clinical Reports` and then one inside the `Clinical Reports` folder called `Registered Nurse`. To do this, simply click New Folder in Report Manager. Because both of these folders, by default, are inheriting permissions from the parent folder, which currently is configured for administrator access only, you will alter the permissions manually so that the new folder (and the reports and data source you will add to it) will maintain its own security settings.

To publish reports to the `Registered Nurse` folder, you could use any method already covered, but for this test simply upload a report you have already worked with, Daily Schedule, and then create a data source called `RN_DS` for the purposes of testing security. Upload the report file `Daily Schedule.rdl` from either Report Manager or SSMS from where it resides in the `Pro_SSRS` project. In Report Manager, in the `Registered Nurse` folder, simply click Upload File, browse to `Daily Schedule.rdl`, and click OK. In SSMS, after connecting to the report server using the Reporting Services type connection, navigate to and right-click the Registered Nurse folder under Home; then select Import File. You will notice the default selection is for .rdl or report files. Click the ellipsis to navigate to the Daily Schedule.rdl file, and click Open. Though it is possible to upload an .rds file or data source file to the report server via Report Manager and SSMS, neither method will successfully create the actual data source object as such. After the data source is uploaded, it shows as a link and not as an actual data source. So, you will need to create the data source manually.

To create the data source manually with Report Manager, simply click New Data Source in the Registered Nurse folder, name the data source RN_DS, and set the connection string to the following (replacing localhost, if necessary, with your SQL Server 2005 server name where you have created the Pro_SSRS database):

```
Data Source=localhost;Initial Catalog=Pro_SSRS
```

In this case, you will choose to set the data source authentication method to Credentials Stored Securely in the Report Server and supply a name and password that will be used to access the data in the Pro_SSRS database. Assuming that jyoungblood's Windows account was granted access to the data source database, you could have selected the Windows Integrated Security option to pass through the Windows account to the SQL Server 2005 database. You know that you will configure the report to filter out data that is relevant only to the clinician jyoungblood, so you don't need to be overly concerned with the stored credentials.

Figure 9-15 shows the folder structure and setup of the report objects for the initial test you will perform. At this point, you have not granted SSRS role assignments to the Windows account, jyoungblood, or the security group, RN, of which she is a member. The Daily Schedule report, as you may recall from the previous chapter, provides clinicians with a list of their daily activities. In a data-driven subscription, where the report can be mailed to the clinicians after processing, the parameter for the employee's ID was used to create reports with data unique to each individual. In this test now, however, you want to allow access to the same report to be run manually from Report Manager. This poses its own set of concerns, which we will cover as we step you through the process.

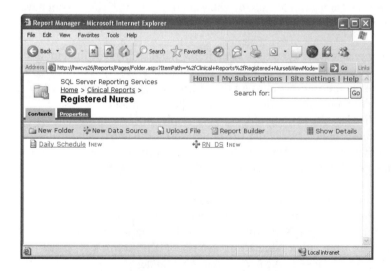

Figure 9-15. *Report objects for registered nurse test*

You'll see the same folder structure in SSMS, which places report server objects, such as reports and data sources, in a more structured and easily expandable view. Figure 9-16 shows the SSMS view of the report and data source objects you created in the Registered Nurse folder.

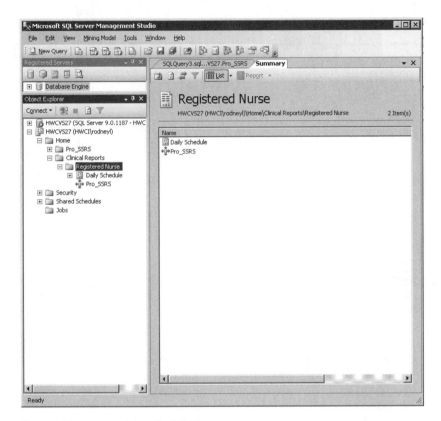

Figure 9-16. *Report objects in SSMS*

To begin the test, log in as jyoungblood, open your Web browser, and paste the link in the address bar to the Registered Nurse folder you created previously, as shown here:

```
http://YourServerName/Reports/Pages/Folder.aspx?ItemPath=%2fClinical+Reports%2➥
fRegistered+Nurse&ViewMode=Detail
```

You have to paste the link into the browser because the permissions for jyoungblood currently do not allow navigation to the report directly through Report Manager. As you can see in Figure 9-17, when you view this link, you receive an error message indicating that the user does not have permissions to view the resources in the folder.

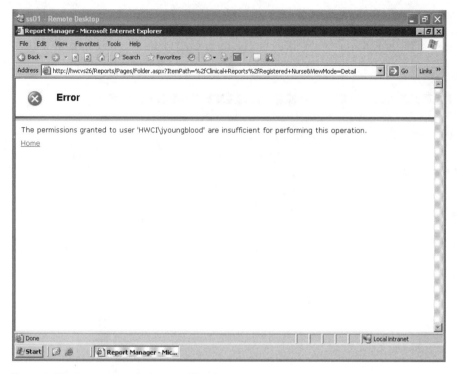

Figure 9-17. *Error message for insufficient permissions*

Running Report Manager as an administrator again, you are now going to set the permissions for the test user. You can control security settings on the Property tab for each folder as well as on individual report items. In this case, you will set permissions at the folder level for the `Registered Nurse` folder. Navigate to this folder, click the Properties icon, and then select Security. As you can see in Figure 9-18, the default security group is `BUILTIN\administrators`, which is assigned to the Content Manager role.

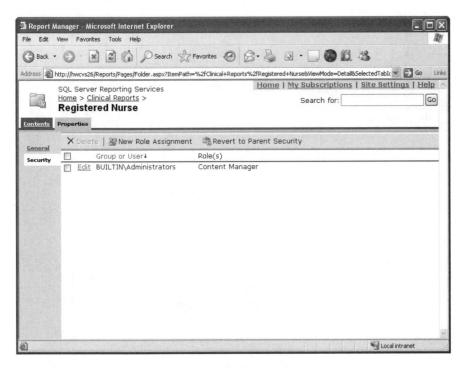

Figure 9-18. Registered Nurse *folder's default permissions*

To set permissions for the RN group, click New Role Assignment, and add the RN security group as the group name on the New Role Assignment form. For the role assignment, choose Browser, which will allow the users assigned to the RN group to view the Registered Nurse folder and all its child nodes, to view reports and resources, and to configure their own subscriptions. You can accomplish the same task via SSMS by right-clicking the Registered Nurse folder in the SSMS report server tree view, selecting Properties, and then clicking the Permissions link to add the RN security group to the folder.

Now when you access the Registered Nurse folder logged in as jyoungblood, all you see are the reports that have been deployed to that folder, not the data source. In addition, all the properties for the objects you can view have limited accessibility and content. If you click the properties of the Daily Schedule report, for example, you will see only the general properties information, such as the Creation Date and Modified Date of the Daily Schedule report. By contrast, an administrator viewing the same properties page would be able to see and modify other report property settings such as Parameters, Data Sources, Execution, History, and Security, as shown in Figure 9-19.

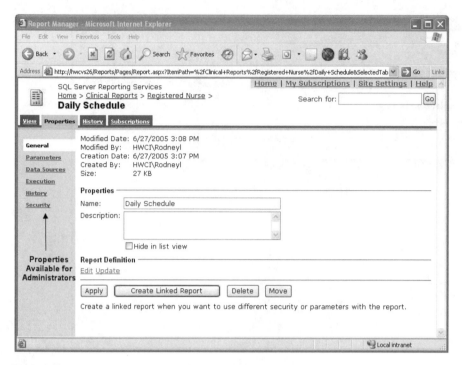

Figure 9-19. *Report properties available for administrator*

To complete the test, you will simply execute the Daily Schedule report as jyoungblood. You have granted permission for the RN Windows security group to inherit the SSRS Browser role, so you should not have a problem executing the report. The report executes successfully. However, Figure 9-20 shows one glaring issue—even though jyoungblood has executed this report, she is seeing other employees' scheduled visits. Though she would be able to enter an EmployeeID parameter value that would limit the data on the report to only her data, she would still be able to see other employees' schedules by entering their IDs, assuming she knew what they were. Though this might be an acceptable practice for many companies, in the next section we will show how to go a step further to ensure that she will be able to view her schedule only.

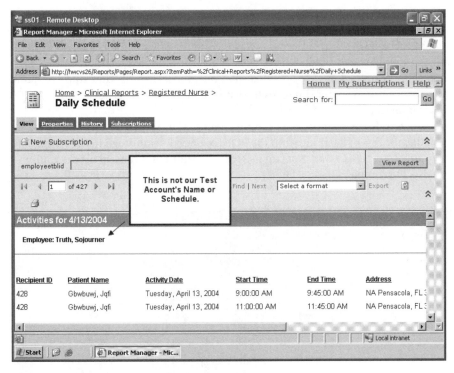

Figure 9-20. *Test account viewing other employees' data*

■**Tip** When building a testing environment, a number of available resources can simplify the process. In our testing, we made extensive use of Remote Desktop Client and the remote administration features of Windows 2003 Server. Since this would be the environment we would ultimately deploy in—in other words, Terminal Services—it was beneficial also to see how SSRS would work in this scenario. Microsoft's Virtual Server is another advantageous tool for testing, as it allows you to run multiple operating systems simultaneously on a single machine.

Filtering Report Content with User!UserID

For the Daily Schedule report, say you have decided that you want the users to be able to view only their own schedules. SSRS allows you to accomplish this by creating a report filter that uses the value of the login account for the user executing the report. The login name value is returned from a global collection in SSRS. You have been using global collections all along—for example, when you use an expression such as =Fields!FieldName.Value, you are actually returning a value from the Fields global collection. The global collection that you will use for the report filter is User, and the value you are interested in is UserID. The expression will therefore be =User!UserID.

To use User!UserID in the filter, you will need a field in the dataset that will equal the UserID value. In the dataset for the Daily Schedule report, you may recall that you have a field called HWUserLogin that you can use for this purpose. When compared by the filter, the two values will be identical—one value delivered with the dataset and the other at execution time of the report. After the filter is applied, the report will display only those records where the username of the employee executing the report matches the value of the HWUserLogin field returned with each record of the dataset.

Unlike parameters, filters cannot be set through Report Manager. To set up a filter, you will need to modify the report itself, either in the RDL file directly or through Report Designer, as shown in Figure 9-21. Notice that you can use the RTRIM function to strip off the trailing spaces; otherwise, the comparison may fail.

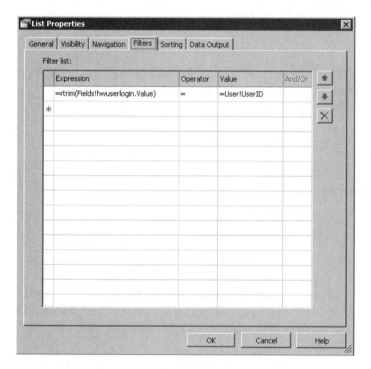

Figure 9-21. UserID *filter for daily schedule report*

Because this report may return several hundred records even though it will filter automatically for each user, it is a good idea to cache the report for ten minutes. Caching, which is discussed in Chapter 8, will help alleviate the performance hit of requerying the data source every time a new user accesses the report. When the user jyoungblood executes the report again, you can see that the schedule now reflects only her schedule, as shown in Figure 9-22. Also notice that you can choose to employ another new feature of SSRS, and that is to hide the employeetblID parameter from the user so users will be unable to select another employee's schedule. You can hide parameters during design time by selecting Hidden in the Report Parameters dialog box or after deployment in Report Manager by selecting Hide on the report properties page under Parameters.

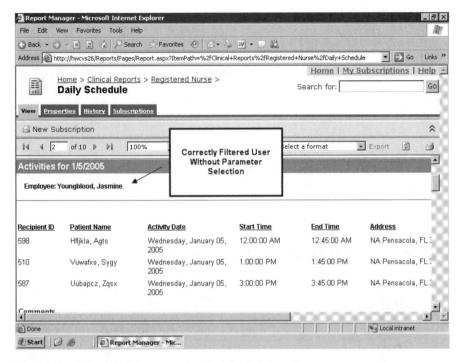

Figure 9-22. *Filtered report execution for test user*

Setting Data Source Security

Once you have deployed the data source to the report server, you can specify its connection properties. This is an important step because the property settings determine how both the user and SSRS will connect to the data source. When executing unattended reports—for example, for a user subscription—SSRS will control passing authentication credentials to the data source and must have access to valid authentication credentials.

Four connection options for the data source are available in Report Manager:

- *The Credentials Supplied by the User Running the Report*: With this option, users are always prompted to log in to the data source when executing the report.

- *Credentials Stored Securely in the Report Server*: SSRS uses authentication credentials stored in the ReportServer database. The sensitive login information is encrypted.

- *Windows Integrated Security*: This option passes the login information for the current user to the data source. Don't choose this option if the data source will be used for unattended installs or if Kerberos is not configured for the Windows domain.

- *Credentials Are Not Required*: This is the least secure option and is used when the data source does not require authentication.

Setting SQL Server Permissions

In Chapter 2, when you created the stored procedure called Emp_Svc_Cost, you set the permissions to allow public execution while designing the report. The environment you were working in was otherwise secure, as it was isolated from other networks and there was no fear of it being compromised.

Now that you are deploying the stored procedure in a production environment, you will need to lock down the stored procedure as well. You can do this through SSMS by right-clicking the stored procedure and selecting Properties. Next, click the Permissions page. Uncheck the Execute checkbox for the public role, and check the Execute checkbox for valid security groups in the domain, including the RN security group, as shown in Figure 9-23. You do not need to explicitly grant Execute rights to the test user jyoungblood, as she is a member of the RN security group.

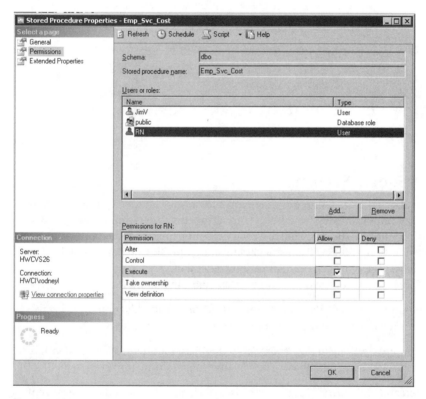

Figure 9-23. *Setting SQL Server stored procedure permissions*

Auditing Reports

Having the ability to know the details of report execution, specifically for undesired access, is an essential piece of the security puzzle. In Chapter 8, we showed how to set up the extended execution-monitoring feature provided with SSRS. Having an audit trail of report execution is essential for gaining insight into user behavior and possible security breaches.

Introducing SSRS Auditing

In this section, we'll show how to use the same execution log database, called RSExecutionLlog, to audit the following in SSRS:

- *Report execution activity*: Which user executed which report and when, and whether a user was denied access to a report because of permissions

- *Parameter inputs for reports*: Which parameters were entered by a user

The latter is important because even though SSRS contains validation for certain types of parameters, such as Integer and DateTime, when a report parameter uses a string, it is susceptible to a SQL injection attack. SQL injection attacks are made possible when a Web page or service takes input from a user or program that could contain injected code that could execute on the SQL Server machine. These types of attacks can be malicious in nature or cause the report or page to deliver more data than was intended.

We will show how to use a modified version of the Report Execution Log Report created in Chapter 8 for performance measuring. In the modified version, you are interested primarily in report execution for a security audit. You need to know which user executed which report and when. The generic report shows the user and report name, as well as the times the report was executed. This report is driven from the same data source, RSExecutionLog, that you have already used.

We have simply made the report a table instead of a matrix, which was more in line with the PivotTable analysis for performance. In this modified report, called Report Execution Audit (which is available in the Pro_SSRS project), you will also include the parameters that the user has selected.

In Figure 9-24, you can see the times that the selected reports were executed as well as the parameter name and value that were entered. The user jyoungbloodyoungblood has naughtily attempted to enter questionable parameter values. In addition to showing how the user interacted with the report via the Parameter field, the Report Execution Audit report also shows from which machine the report was accessed. Having this level of auditing is a valuable ally in the struggle to maintain security for confidential information. With HIPAA, it is also necessary to maintain an audit trail of user access to data. If you are suspicious that someone is accessing information they are not authorized to view, this report can serve as the audit trail, along with other normal auditing procedures such as the Windows event log.

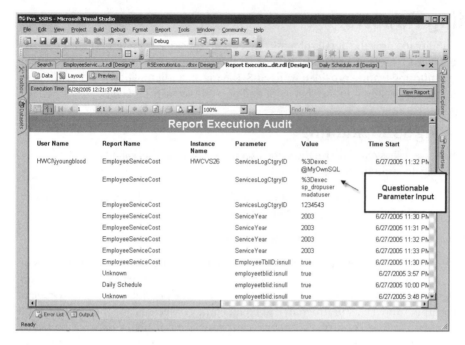

Figure 9-24. *Report Execution Audit report*

Introducing Log File Auditing

In addition to report auditing, SSRS supports two other types of logging: standard Windows event logging and trace file logging. You can use both of these resources to search for errors and warnings as well as other important information, such as security information.

All the trace files are stored in the default installation location *Drive*:\Program Files\ Microsoft SQL Server\MSSQL.3\Reporting Services\LogFiles. Three types of log files exist: ReportServerService, ReportServerWebApp, and ReportServer. Each file is named with a time-stamp, such as ReportServerService_05_31_2004_17_00_30.log, and contains information specific to its individual service. You can gather five levels of trace log information—0 through 4— that are controlled in the ReportingServicesService.config file. Selecting 0 will disable tracing, and selecting 4 will enable verbose mode. Whenever an issue arises with SSRS, the administrator can generally isolate the problem by looking in either the event log or one of the trace files.

Exploring Deployment Models

We will cover two deployment scenarios—one is an application hosted on the Internet combining Terminal Services and SSRS, and the other is an internal deployment of SSRS that serves the reporting needs of employees on an intranet and through VPN. As you will see in both deployment strategies, much of the security benefits are gained by the logical layout of the systems themselves.

You may note as we go through each model that we will not be deploying SSRS so that it is directly exposed to the Internet. The primary reason for this is that the version of SSRS released for SQL Server 2000 as well as for SQL Server 2005 by default directly supports only Integrated or Basic authentication. This means that without modifying the default installation to include other authentication mechanisms, a valid Windows login is required to access reports and objects. Although you can create other authentication methods by building a custom security extension, SSRS does not, for example, provide forms-based authentication natively, which would be ideal for full Internet deployment. It is certainly feasible to create a limited Internet deployment for a select group of users by configuring SSRS to use a fully qualified domain name that is hosted on the public Internet. To ensure that these Internet users have access to only the report data you intend for them to see, you'll need to take security precautions. For example, you could provide report snapshots, which do not query data sources directly, rather than live reports.

In this scenario, using a preexisting infrastructure with Terminal Services hosted on the Internet was the ideal solution for integrating SSRS within our health-care application, and this type of deployment, along with an intranet environment, is what we will cover in the following section.

If you would like more information, including security extensions designed to deploy SSRS using custom authentication for Internet reporting, even though the guidelines were originally written with SSRS for SQL Server 2000 in mind, the following URL is a great resource that covers the topic in detail:

```
http://msdn.microsoft.com/library/default.asp?url=➡
/library/en-us/dnsql2k/html/ufairs.asp
```

Implementing SSRS with Terminal Services

When our company decided several years ago to host our SQL Server–based application on the Internet, the one solution that was most evident at the time was Windows Terminal Services. The reason that this technology was the best choice for us was that our application was not yet Web enabled. We needed a thin-client solution for our fat-client application. Servers were added over the years to support more users, and technology advancements in Windows Server and .NET provided many benefits that were natively supported. Technologies such as Active Directory, network load balancing, and Internet printing allowed us to provide a secure and reliable service to our customers.

When SSRS was released, we were already poised to integrate it within our Internet-hosted application. We will now show a design for Internet access using Terminal Services. As you can see in Figure 9-25, the terminal servers are positioned to reside on the Internet zone as well as a demilitarized zone (DMZ), which is inaccessible to the outside world. In the DMZ are several key components that all work together to provide services to the terminal servers, namely, SQL Server, SSRS, and Active Directory. Users log in to the terminal servers directly, authenticating to one of two domain controllers. Once authenticated, they are allowed to utilize the services of the domain.

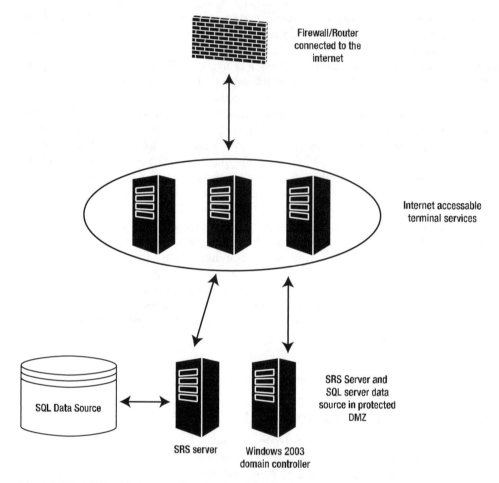

Figure 9-25. *SSRS with Internet-hosted Terminal Services*

Several additional security measures are in place besides Windows authentication. Each Windows 2003 terminal server has its built-in firewall capabilities enabled on the Internet-facing network card to allow network traffic only on a specific port, 3389, for Terminal Services. All other network packets, including PING requests, will be dropped. This setup lessens the likelihood of this server being "discovered" using port-scanning tools. The networking components that provide Windows networking services, such as Client for Microsoft Networks and File and Printer Sharing for Microsoft Networks, have been disabled on the Internet.

On the DMZ-facing network cards, we can be more liberal with our service abilities. In the DMZ, we still need to encrypt data, so we have applied a server certificate to our SSRS server, as demonstrated earlier in the chapter. The only difference is that we are using a commercial certificate from a trusted authority.

Terminal Services in Windows Server 2003 provides two levels of security at the network packet level. The first level is because, by its nature, Terminal Services sends data that constitutes only screen shots, keystrokes, and mouse clicks. To glean confidential information from the RDP stream, which Terminal Services uses, you would need to capture and replay the packets. It is certainly possible but unlikely. Second, Terminal Services provides four levels of encryption, the lowest being 56-bit and the highest being FIPS Compliant, as shown in Figure 9-26. By turning on High encryption, clients that do not support the maximum encryption level of the server will be unable to connect.

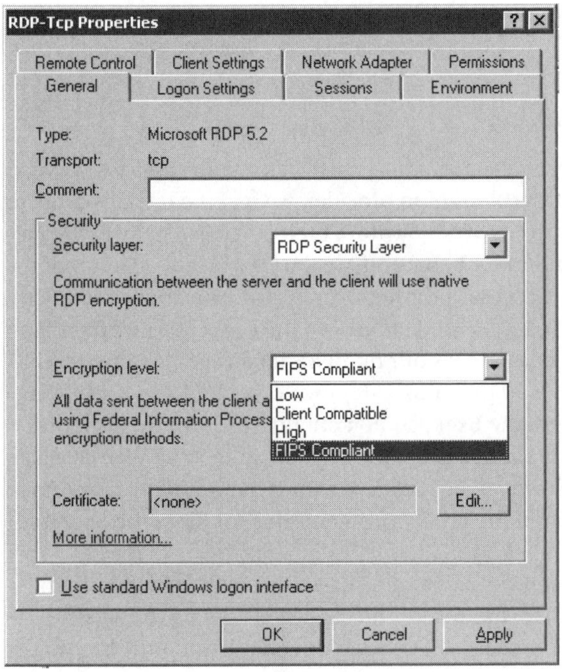

Figure 9-26. *Terminal Services encryption levels*

Finally, we have implemented several other security techniques in the Internet-hosted model by taking advantage of Terminal Services configurations through the use of the Group Policy feature. These are two important settings for controlling client behavior with Terminal Services:

- Forcing each user to connect to only one Terminal Services session at a time.

- Automatically executing an application when the user logs in. In our case, every time the user logs into a session, they will see only our health-care application and not a desktop.

By configuring Terminal Services in this way, we can be assured users cannot share their logins to gain access simultaneously to the server. Equally important, our users will not be allowed to interact with a desktop. All the tasks they will need to perform will be available within the user interface of the health-care application. Further, because we have built our own .NET report viewer that is executed from within our application, users will not need to access Internet Explorer or another browser because they will view the reports from a Web control within a Windows Forms application.

In the future, as SSRS matures into an application that supports additional authentication methods, we will look to provide reports directly on the Internet. Currently, SSRS supports only one type of authentication at a time. In other words, it is not possible to deploy a forms-based custom security extension and still allow Windows authentication. For now, the Terminal Services model is the best solution for us and fits in ideally with a preexisting infrastructure.

Implementing for Internal Access

In this scenario, each agency maintains (through an internal IT staff) its security policies, servers, and applications. We knew that, as a third-party solution provider, we had the responsibility to offer recommendations for secure deployments of SSRS within their agencies that would take advantage of their existing security infrastructure. To that end, we decided to embed our reports inside a custom report viewer that could be accessed through our health-care application. This would serve to provide a browser control that we could lock down through code and pass the authentication that they had used initially to access our main application. This method of deployment was also identical to how we had previously deployed Crystal Reports. Clients could now have control over which reports the users could actually see from their menu choices. This did not address the concern about being able to access the SSRS Web service from a browser and launch the report. However, because we would deploy all our reports to a single known folder, the client maintained the ability to secure this folder at the user and role level, as demonstrated earlier.

An internal deployment of SSRS requires the same roles-based security as in the Internet-hosted model. A Windows domain controller with Active Directory will contain the security grouping to associate with the SSRS roles. The main difference between the two models is that, instead of using Terminal Services entirely, users will have the ability to access the reports through a browser or via custom forms with embedded SSRS controls. In addition, each company may employ traveling or off-site personnel who need access to the reports. This will be accomplished in one of two ways, either through VPN access or via secure redirected HTTPS traffic through a firewall, such as the Microsoft ISA server. With VPN access, clients will connect to the internal network through a VPN client and will then use the native encryption on that connection, such as PPTP or L2TP, to access the SSRS server to view reports. The Microsoft ISA server supports SSL *bridging*, which allows incoming SSL requests to be redirected to any internal Web site, providing, in our SSRS deployment, a means of encrypting the data from users directly on the Internet. The client's Windows credentials for which they will be prompted can be passed through the ISA server. Further, the ISA server can limit the connections to a list of users or known IP address sets.

Another technology consideration when deploying an SSRS server internally is wireless access. Wireless has its own level of encryption through the use of WEP, but not all default installations have this setting enabled by default. It is always best practice to have a server certificate installed on the SSRS server with a `SecureConnectionLevel` set to 2 or higher when working with any confidential data.

As you can see in Figure 9-27, the internal deployment allows for secure connection within many points of the company. Administrators can control access to the server via standard Windows domain authentication policies while maintaining limited and secure external access from known sources.

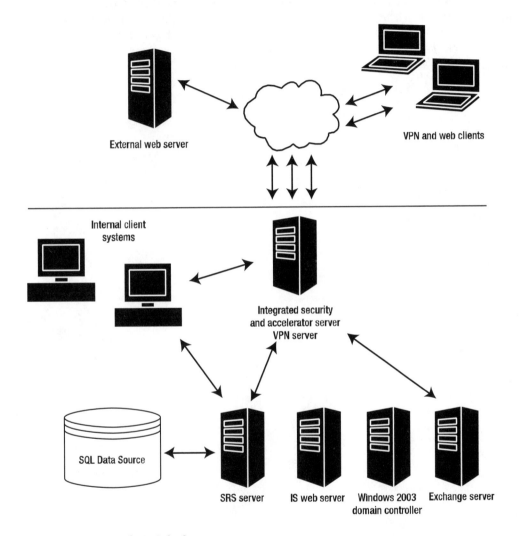

Figure 9-27. *Internal SSRS deployment*

Summary

In this chapter, you examined three of the security tasks essential to secure SSRS deployment: encrypting, authenticating, and auditing. You looked at how we chose to implement SSRS, both internally to intranet users and externally to Internet clients through a hosted application. In both models, the threat of confidential data falling into the wrong hands is real. When data is transmitted over a public network such as the Internet, you should make sure the three components are properly configured and thoroughly tested. Internally, only employees who need access to confidential data should have it, and you can ensure this by applying a special filter for a report deployment. As a software provider for health-care organizations that store confidential patient information, we are required to conform to the regulations imposed by HIPAA. However, in other industries, many similar regulations exist. Having security policies and procedures in place for any company is good practice, even when not working under stringent regulations. Fortunately, SSRS is designed to use the core-level security mechanisms that already exist in your organization through Windows authentication and can be extended, when required, to support other means of custom authentication.

CHAPTER 10

■■■

Delivering Business Intelligence with SSRS

Most companies accumulate business data that, if analyzed correctly, could provide insights into what direction the company could take to achieve ultimate success. The aim of BI is to provide data in such a way that it can be immediately utilized to make important decisions. Microsoft's BI platform comprises many services and applications that work together to facilitate the analysis and delivery of critical business data. SQL Server is at the heart of the BI model, providing data storage, data transformation, notification, scheduling, analysis, and now reporting services.

Having the right data available is just the first part of the challenge in building an effective BI system. The second part is to ensure that this data is delivered in an effective and accessible way to all the people who need to see it in order to make the right decisions. This is where SSRS comes into play. In our health-care company, we found that by integrating SSRS with many of the other components of the BI platform, we were able to dramatically improve our overall business strategy by making necessary information available to our employees wherever they were and whenever they needed it.

In this chapter, you will examine the following four applications that we have extended to include the SSRS reports for our software development company:

Microsoft CRM: We had been using Microsoft CRM to track sales leads, correspondence, and marketing efforts. However, the basic reports delivered with Microsoft CRM were limited in the information they provided to assist us in making business decisions. Using SSRS, we were able to extend the functionality of Microsoft CRM. In addition to the custom report that we designed for our company, we will show the report pack released for Microsoft CRM. This report pack includes several SSRS reports and also includes a sample Microsoft CRM database.

Microsoft Project: Developing software is an ongoing process of adding new functionality, assessing the risk of migrating to new technologies, and testing. To make this process efficient, our development team uses Microsoft Project 2003 to track every milestone. Falling behind schedule at any point in the project affects release dates, which has a cascading effect on all other departments. When we decided to migrate all the existing reports to SSRS, we used SSRS as a project management tool to track each report as it was migrated. We will show how we built the report to track the progress of the migration so that we could use it both in conjunction with Microsoft Project 2003 and as a stand-alone report to show delivery time frames.

Analysis Services: Having the ability to "slice" through dimensions of data often renders unexpected and meaningful results. When OLAP Services was introduced with SQL Server 7.0, we were asked to build a data warehouse, transforming our OLTP data into an OLAP cube. We maintained this project using Analysis Services that shipped with SQL Server 2000 and had some new functionality, such as data mining models.

SharePoint Portal Server: Part of Microsoft Office, SharePoint Portal Server provides our company with an intranet portal that we have departmentalized. Any information relevant to the company as a whole or to the individual departments is indexed and searchable. Integrating SRS reports with SharePoint lets our employees easily find the data they require to do their jobs. We will show how to add SSRS reports to SharePoint. Since SSRS builds on Windows SharePoint Services, the work you will do in this chapter will also be applicable to Windows SharePoint Services included with Windows Server 2003.

Most companies have similar applications to the ones we are describing. We are providing these examples to give you some ideas of how, with a modicum of effort, SSRS can easily enhance these types of business applications. Our purpose is not necessarily to provide a step-by-step guide but to show how your company might use SSRS. If you use any of the applications mentioned in this chapter, such as Microsoft CRM or SharePoint Portal Server, you can easily integrate this chapter's ideas into your own environment. The Microsoft CRM reports used in this chapter are available on the Apress Web site.

Extending Microsoft CRM with SSRS

Customer relationship management (CRM) applications have been around for many years. These products facilitate communication with customers, both before and after a sale. A successful business understands its market segment and maintains a good relationship with its customers by delivering products that meet the customers' changing needs. This is especially true for a software development company, such as ours, that develops a specialized application. Our customers must meet strict governmental guidelines imposed by the HIPAA, which means we must modify our software to accommodate those guidelines. If we did not, we would have many fewer customers. But aside from required modifications, we also value customer feedback about how to make our software better. Often, a sale depends on one or two key features. Knowing what a potential customer needs—and, even more important, why a customer decided to purchase other software—is the type of information that, if tracked and analyzed, can assist in making business decisions about the direction of the company.

We began using Microsoft CRM almost immediately after it was released. It falls under the Microsoft Business Solutions platform and has the distinction of being the first Microsoft business solution that was designed and built internally. It is a .NET application and uses SQL Server for database storage. It provides much of the functionality we needed for tracking our sales goals as well as communicating with our customers and contacts through integration with Microsoft Exchange Server.

However, it does have a few shortcomings, and one of these is with its reporting capabilities. Microsoft CRM uses a Crystal Reports–based reporting engine. (Bear in mind that Microsoft CRM was released before SSRS.) The real issue is that the standard reports do not provide enough of the kinds of information we needed to track, such as which customers had subscribed to our industry newsletters or how companies learned about our software. This is important information to us, as it dictates how our advertising money is allocated. If we know that a large percentage of our sales in the last 12 months were generated from Web searches, for example, we would want to improve our Web presence.

Not long after the initial release of SSRS, Microsoft released a report pack for its CRM product that not only extended the basic reports of Microsoft CRM but was also the first step toward migrating the existing reporting technology used for Microsoft CRM, which is Crystal Reports, to SSRS. In the following sections, we will demonstrate the custom reports that we designed as well as the reports included in the Microsoft CRM report pack.

Using the Report Pack for Microsoft CRM 1.2

The report pack for Microsoft CRM 1.2 may not include an overwhelming amount of reports, six to be exact, but it provides basic reports in SSRS that can be extended or modified to add value to Microsoft CRM. Microsoft has provided similar report packs to other applications, such as PeopleSoft, IIS, Exchange, SAP, and SharePoint Portal Server. Another great benefit of the Microsoft CRM report pack is that it contains a sample Microsoft CRM database that you can attach to an instance of SQL Server, 2000 or 2005, and can use to create and test reports, which we will do to demonstrate the sample reports. The six reports in the Microsoft CRM report pack are as follows:

- Account Chart

- Account Details

- Customer Account Details

- Knowledge Base List

- Lead Summary

- Pipeline

If you would like to download and install the Microsoft CRM report pack, it is available at `http://www.microsoft.com/downloads/details.aspx?FamilyId=619EEF04-DDDA-4811-A8E9-A7147A446624&displaylang=en`.

Once downloaded, the entire report pack can be installed, and the path that is created—typically, `C:\Program Files\Report Packs\CRM`—contains everything needed to load and deploy the six reports and sample database. The database file, called `Adventure_Works_Cycle_MSCRM`, is in the `Sample DB` folder. It is a standard SQL Server database file with an `.mdf` extension. You can find detailed instructions for attaching the database file in the `MS CRM 1.2 ReportPack Readme.htm` file in the root folder with the caveat that the instructions are for SQL Server 2000 (for which the report pack was released). Attaching the database to SQL Server 2005 is also possible using the `.mdf` file mentioned. We will show how to use SSMS to attach the sample Microsoft CRM database.

Open SSMS, connect to your SQL Server 2005 database engine, navigate to the `Databases` folder in the Object Explorer, right-click, and select Attach. This will open the Attach Databases dialog box. Click Add, and navigate to the `Adventure_Works_Cycle_MSCRM.mdf` file, as shown in Figure 10-1. The file in this case is stored in `C:\Pro_SSRS_Project\CRM`. Click OK.

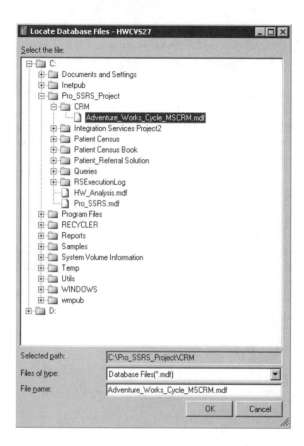

Figure 10-1. *Attaching the Microsoft CRM sample database*

When no log file with an `.ldf` extension exists, it is important to remove the log file reference in the Database Details section of the Attach Databases dialog box so that only one file type is there, Data and not Log. The attach process may ask to find the full-text catalogs for the database. If that is the case, simply click No, and the process will complete successfully.

When you have attached the database successfully, you can expand the various objects within SSMS to see the database structure. For example, Figure 10-2 shows all the tables in this database.

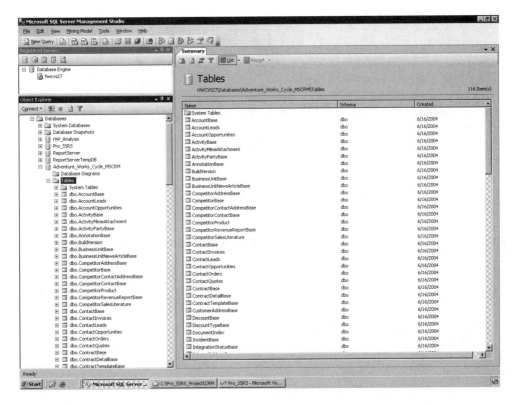

Figure 10-2. *Microsoft CRM sample database structure in SSMS*

Once you have attached the database, you can move on to loading the sample reports into the VS or BIDS project. The project is in the C:\Program Files\Report Packs\CRM\ Report Definition Files folder and is named CRM Report Pack.rptproj. If you have been using the Pro_SSRS solution throughout the book, you can simply add this project to the Pro_SSRS solution by right-clicking the Pro_SSRS solution in Solution Explorer and selecting Add an Existing Project. Navigate to the CRM Report Pack.rptproj file, and click Open.

With the project open, you can see one data source and six reports. The data source, Adventure_Works_Cycle_MSCRM.rds, points to local host by default, so if your Microsoft CRM sample database was attached to the local instance of SQL Server, you should not have to change it. If your database is on another server, you will have to double-click the data source and change the Data Source value to point to your server by name.

Let's open one of the sample reports, Lead Summary, and look at what it offers. When you double-click the Lead Summary.rdl file in the CRM Report Pack project, the first thing you should notice is a dialog box informing you that the report must be converted to the current report definition format and that the report cannot be edited in previous versions of Report Designer, as shown in Figure 10-3.

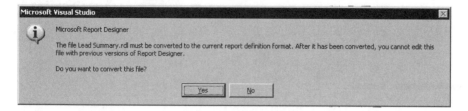

Figure 10-3. *Notice about converting the sample report file*

Click Yes to convert the file. The Lead Summary report contains a pie chart and table that lists detailed sales by salesperson and by company, as shown in Figure 10-4.

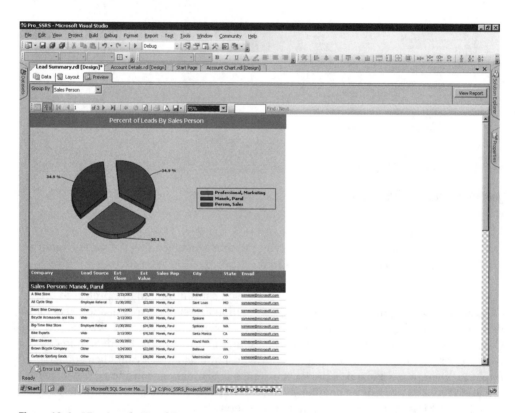

Figure 10-4. *Viewing the Lead Summary report*

One interesting note about this report is that it uses a navigation item for e-mail addresses. By adding a simple Jump to URL hyperlink action to this field, whose value is `mailto:someone@microsoft.com`, the report takes on an interactive property, which is one of the key benefits of a Web-based reporting application. We will show how to do something similar for the Microsoft CRM report covered in the "Creating Custom SSRS Reports for Microsoft CRM" section, where we will show how to link to Microsoft CRM forms and pass in parameters. This type of interactivity extends the base application as well.

You will use these reports in the "Incorporating SSRS with SharePoint Portal Server" section, where we show how to tie these and other BI reports together using SSRS Web Parts.

Creating Custom SSRS Reports for Microsoft CRM

In this section, we will show two custom Microsoft CRM reports that we developed and deployed with SSRS: the Sales Projections Chart report and the Lead Conversion report. Both of these reports are available for download at the Apress Web site and can be used directly with any Microsoft CRM version 1.2 database.

Though Microsoft CRM is not the easiest database to work with, once you understand where to retrieve description information that relates to CRM entities, such as opportunities, leads, lead sources, and industry codes, you've won half the battle. The values related to these entities are stored in the StringMap table. Both reports are based on the same basic query, as shown in Listing 10-1; you can see that StringMap.Value returns the lead source and is joined to the LeadBase table.

Listing 10-1. *CRM Query for the Sales Projection Chart Report*

```
SELECT
     OpportunityBase.EstimatedCloseDate,
     OpportunityBase.Name,
     OpportunityBase.StatusCode,
     OpportunityBase.EstimatedValue,
     RTRIM(CAST(DATEPART
       (yyyy, OpportunityBase.EstimatedCloseDate) AS char(5)) +
        DATENAME(m, OpportunityBase.EstimatedCloseDate)) AS Estimate_Close,
     OpportunityBase.CreatedOn,
     StringMap.Value AS [Lead Source],
     LeadBase.NumberOfEmployees,
     LeadBase.SIC,
     LeadBase.FullName AS [Lead Contact],
     LeadBase.IndustryCode.
     CAST(OpportunityBase.OpportunityId AS nvarchar(80)) AS
        OpportunityID
FROM
     OpportunityBase INNER JOIN
     LeadBase ON
     OpportunityBase.OriginatingLeadId = LeadBase.LeadId LEFT OUTER JOIN
     StringMap ON LeadBase.LeadSourceCode = StringMap.AttributeValue
     AND StringMap.AttributeName = 'leadsourcecode'
WHERE
     (OpportunityBase.StatusCode NOT IN (4, 5)) AND
(OpportunityBase.EstimatedCloseDate BETWEEN GETDATE() AND @SixMonthDate)
ORDER BY OpportunityBase.Name
```

■**Caution** Microsoft does not support accessing the Microsoft CRM database directly for reports.

Creating the Sales Projections Chart Report

The Sales Projections Chart report is a fairly simple and compact chart that shows at a glance the projected sales for the next six months. Several reports are available within Microsoft CRM, called *pipeline reports*, that deliver good sales forecasting information. However, if any key information is not included in the Crystal Reports CRM reports, modifying the reports is no easy feat. In fact, we needed one piece of information that the Microsoft CRM pipeline reports did not seem to have, and that was a chart of sales projections based on the lead source, such as through a Web search or partner.

We created the Sales Projections Chart report with SSRS to add the lead source information using steps similar to the ones used in Chapter 3, adding 3D effects and a nondefault color scheme. You can see that the layout of the chart has the Lead Source field applied to the series of the chart and the Estimated Close Date is defined for the category. The Estimated Value field makes up the Data section of the chart. This report has a parameter called SixMonthDate that is used as a query parameter in the WHERE clause of the query to provide a date range for the EstimatedCloseDate field between the current date and six months in the future. Any CRM leads or opportunities that are expected to close the sale within that date range will show in the chart. In Figure 10-5, you will also notice that the report's title section contains a parameter value expression for the SixMonthDate parameter. The default value for the SixMonthDate is six months, but because the user could change the default parameter to, say, three months into the future, the report title would need to change to reflect the user's date range. Adding the parameter value to the report title will dynamically change when the parameter value changes.

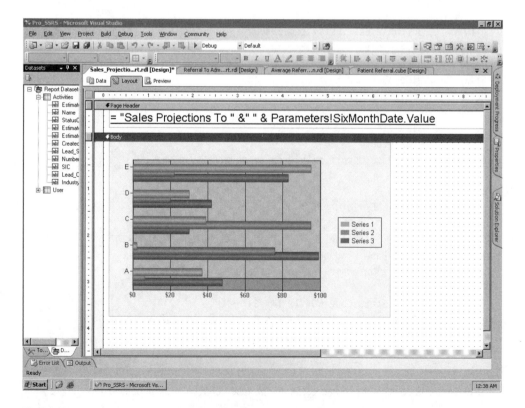

Figure 10-5. *Creating a chart to show projected sales*

To set the default parameter value for the date range of six months in the future, you can use an expression that takes the current date and adds six months to it, as follows:

```
=FormatDateTime(DateAdd(DateInterval.Month,6,Date.Today),DateFormat.ShortDate)
```

By combining several functions and .NET class library property values into a single expression, you can create a date range with desired formatting. In the preceding expression, the `FormatDateTime` function sets the output of the `DateAdd` function to a short date, which does not include the neutral time of 00:00:00 that would have been returned from the `DateAdd` function. Finally, the `DateInterval.Month` enumeration uses the value of 6 to add six months to the current date.

Creating the Lead Conversion Report

When a lead is converted to opportunity, which in CRM means there is a potential interest in the purchase of a product, it is important to be able to report that information to ensure that someone regularly follows up with this potential customer and sends important product information.

To this end, we decided to create the Lead Conversion report to show only opportunities so that a marketing employee could easily view this information. Further, by having a link within the report to the actual Microsoft CRM Opportunity form, the employee could then open the form without having to open the Microsoft CRM application and navigate to the form manually to update the information related to opportunities. You can do this by adding a URL link to the navigation sections of the report.

In this case, we designed the report, which lists all the companies that comprise the projected sales from the chart, with the intention of having the report essentially be an extension of Microsoft CRM itself. The report contains detailed information for each opportunity, including the opportunity name. We added a Jump to URL link to the report on the Navigation tab for the textbox that holds the opportunity name. The link will use the URL-addressable syntax for Microsoft CRM so that when the opportunity name is clicked in the report, the Microsoft CRM form associated with that opportunity displays. A sample expression to add to the Jump to URL field is as follows:

```
="http://hwcs03/SFA/opps/edit.aspx?id={"& Fields!OpportunityId.Value &"}"
```

This link will open the Opportunity form and pass in the field value of `OpportunityID` when the opportunity name is clicked in the report. One note of interest here is that the `OpportunityID` field value is a globally unique identifier (GUID) data type, and SSRS does not work well with GUIDs. In the SQL query, you can use the `CAST` function to convert the field to be a data type of `NVARCHAR`, as follows:

```
CAST(OpportunityBase.OpportunityId AS nvarchar(80)) AS OpportunityID
```

Then you can pass in the braces in the expression for the URL link. Figure 10-6 shows the report and the hyperlink to the Microsoft CRM form in the bottom-left corner of the browser. Notice also the pointing finger icon, indicating a hyperlink.

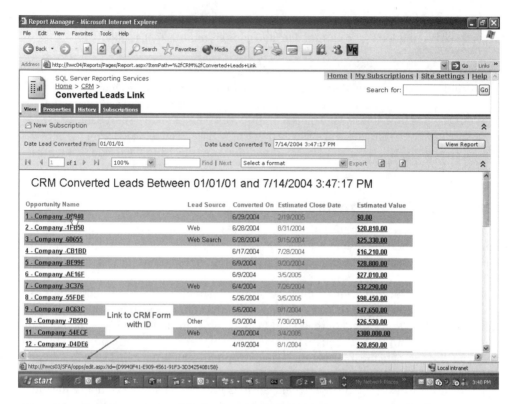

Figure 10-6. *Creating a Microsoft CRM opportunity listing with link*

■**Note** In the code download for this chapter, we have not only included the two Microsoft CRM reports mentioned here, the Sales Projections Chart report and the Lead Conversion report, but have also included two other complete, full-featured reports, Opportunities Without Activities and Opportunity and Lead Activities. The Opportunity and Lead Activities report uses an advanced query to combine the two entities in the same report, with hyperlinks directly to their respective activities. All that is required is to configure each report is to connect to your Microsoft CRM database.

Managing Projects with SSRS

In this section, we'll show how to integrate SSRS within a BI model before moving on to Analysis Services and SSRS. When SSRS was first announced as an add-on product to SQL Server 2000, we knew, as we said previously, that we would incorporate it into our base application, primarily to standardize our reporting on a single platform and move away from Crystal Reports and other applications we had used over the years. When I (Rodney) was tasked with migrating nearly 200 reports from the current system to SSRS, I was a little overwhelmed. On one hand, I needed a period of time to learn the new product, and on the other hand, I had to implement risk assessment for the new technology because SSRS is not simply a report designer; it is a full-blown report delivery system.

Coincidentally, at the same time we decided to move to SSRS, our development team had just begun to design an enhancement to our application. We thought the two projects could be developed in parallel, with me migrating the reports and with them delivering the new .NET enhancements. As a software development company, keeping on schedule through every aspect of a project is important for several reasons, mainly to stay on track with other departmental goals such as product testing, marketing, and creating documentation.

The development department uses Microsoft Project 2003 to record its project and task milestones throughout each phase of a project, whereas my work as an engineer and data analyst does not always require this degree of granular detail and planning.

I proposed a compromise solution (and this was probably because I really did not want to have to use Microsoft Project): I would develop a project management report using SSRS. In the report, I would track every report that was slated for migration to SSRS. My project report would provide timelines and status information similar to those provided by Microsoft Project (though on a much more limited basis than what Microsoft Project can deliver). As I migrated the reports from other reporting solutions, I would update a SQL database table that contained the project information, which would then be reflected in my SSRS report. Developers could use my report to incorporate the report project information into their own projects so that they could account for my development time.

In hindsight, developing this report of reports, as it were, was probably the best first SSRS project that I could have undertaken because it forced me to design a report that was flexible enough for everyone in the company to use for different purposes: my supervisor needed to know how much time I was devoting to the task of writing reports per week, the support and testing departments could use the list in their jobs as they worked with the application and answered customer questions, and finally the development department could see where I was in relation to their projects.

The first step was to extract the list of reports from the current SQL Server database that our application used. We store each report's name, base query, description, file name, and format in a table within the health-care database. I used Data Transformation Services (DTS), now SSIS, to pull this information into a single table, along with other crucial pieces of information for which I would have to create custom fields. I categorized and subcategorized each report according to its location within the application (for example, financial or clinical), and I added several tracking fields that were in line with a project management application, such as Status, In Progress, Completion Date, Estimated Time, and Date Last Updated.

It was important to know which reports would be new, which would be replacements, and which would be removed entirely. By using a combination of filters and parameters, I was able to deliver the report so that it would show only the reports that were being completed in SSRS, and I used color formatting to distinguish them from the previous report formats. One of the features that I wanted was the ability to link to each of the reports so that they could then, from one location, be printed as samples to include in product literature and customer newsletters. I added a Jump to URL hyperlink for each report name as well as a document map for easy navigation. Because I was new to SSRS at the time, I completed many of these tasks via trial and error, and I encountered lots of syntax errors, or other errors, that needed to be debugged. (Chapter 4 demonstrated many of the features that I added to this report.) Figure 10-7 shows the reports with the document map, parameters, color coding, and estimated completion time used to track deliverable dates. The single table, HWReports, that contains the project data used to create this report is included in the Pro_SSRS database, and the RDL report file itself, HW_Reports, is in the code download on the Apress Web site. We are including this report as a sample not so much for its content but more for many of the advanced features of report design that you can add to any report.

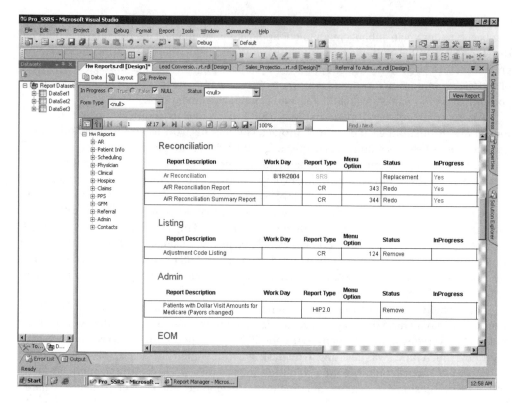

Figure 10-7. *Features of the report HW Reports*

Building SSRS Reports for SQL Analysis Services

When I (Rodney) began the journey of building an OLAP solution for our health-care application with SQL Server 2000 Analysis Services, I was really eager to jump right in and start analyzing data the first morning. I had become the resident expert at developing SQL queries to interrogate our OLTP database, and since this was the source database from which I was going to build the warehouse, I thought it would be a simple case of adding a few queries and processing the cube. It did not turn out to be quite that easy. In retrospect, however, the process of creating an OLAP data cube from a known source of data was worthwhile because I was able to apply the skills I learned to many other projects. With each new version of Analysis Services, more and more features are delivered; this at first can seem overwhelming simply because of the volume of enhancements and the time required to not only become familiar with the technology but also to master it to gain the most benefit. However, while adding new features, Microsoft also adds many new tools that simplify time-consuming tasks. In the case of Analysis Services 2005, these new tools include a graphical MDX query builder and a cube wizard that automates many of the steps that create the intricate parts of an Analysis Services solution.

In this section, we will show how to use a simple Analysis Services cube as the data source to build and deploy SSRS BI reports. The cube is based on a SQL Server database that serves as a data warehouse for the health-care application you have been using throughout the book. The cube is populated with data relevant to patient admissions for a health-care agency. Though we designed the report to analyze many aspects of patient admission history, such as patients with multiple recurrent admissions, changing diagnosis and patient referral sources, we will show how to create a report that specifically delivers analytical information about the length of time between when a patient is referred to the agency and when they are actually admitted. Over time, the data that is collected can help assist decision makers isolate problem areas and improve the processes that may be causing inefficient patient referral times. First, let's look at the database and cubes on which the report you create will be based.

The data warehouse database you will use as a source for the Analysis Services project is called HW_Analysis. It is a simple database containing only eight tables and is populated with data using SQL Server Integration Services (SSIS). The typical process for preparing a data warehouse database with SSIS is to export data from the source OLTP database, transform the data to make it more conducive to analysis by SSAS, and finally load this transformed data into the data warehouse.

We have already built both the Hw_Analysis database and the SSAS cube called Patient Referral, and we have included the required files for deploying these two key components and detailed installation instructions in the code download for this book. Once you have restored the HW_Analysis data warehouse database, you can open the Pro_SSRS project, which contains the Patient Referral cube. Figure 10-8 shows the simple Patient Referral cube structure in BIDS. The cube has six dimensions and two measures.

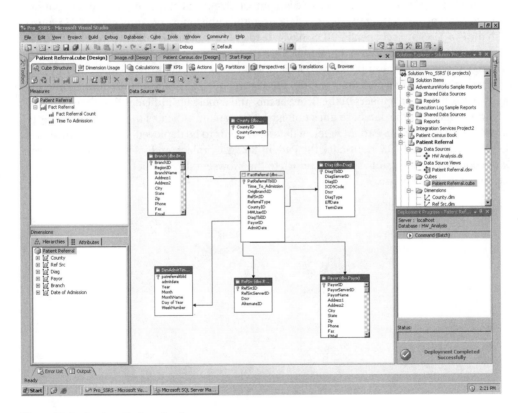

Figure 10-8. *Patient Referral cube structure*

Of the six dimensions, several of them should be familiar to you because you have worked with them in other chapters of the book. You can think of a dimension in a cube as preaggregated groups or categories of data that can be associated with one or more measures. Measures, such as Time to Admission and Fact Referral Count, are calculated values at each level in a dimension. Multidimensional data stored in a cube consists of both dimensions and measures that, when queried using MDX, can be analyzed not just two-dimensionally like rows and columns of a T-SQL query but can be drilled into and sliced at many dimensions. These are the dimensions you will use in the Patient Referral cube:

- County

- Referral Source

- Diagnosis

- Payer

- Branch

- Data of Admission

Since the starting point in this exercise is a prepopulated and processed cube, it is important to make sure you are getting the desired data from the cube before creating your SSRS reports. With the Pro_SSRS project open in BIDS, navigate to the Patient Referral SSAS project in Solution Explorer, expand to Cubes, and double-click Patient Referral.cube. This will open the cube in design mode. Once the cube is open, select the Browser tab. Figure 10-9 shows the opened cube with the combined measures and dimensions ready to be dragged and dropped into the query pane. If no data appears in the Browser tab, and a message indicates that there is a permission problem or the database does not exist, this usually indicates that the cube needs to be processed or the SSAS Patient Referral database needs to be deployed. To deploy the Patient Referral database in BIDS, right-click the Patient Referral project, and select Deploy. Once you have deployed it successfully, you can return to the Browser tab, and click the available link to reconnect to the database.

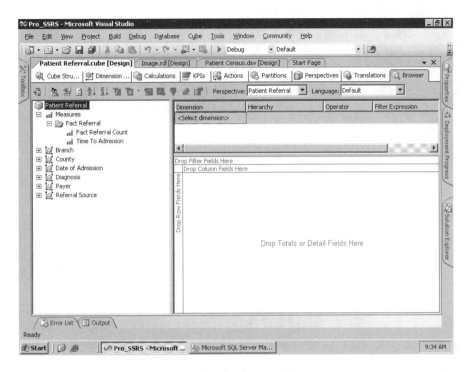

Figure 10-9. *Viewing the Patient Referral cube in BIDS*

You can begin by expanding Measures and then Fact Referral in the cube object window. Next, drag the Time of Admission measure to the Drop Totals or Detail Fields Here section of the query pane. You should see an average time of 14.095 minutes. This calculation was done at the time the cube was originally loaded and processed and represents a total average of time to admission for all dimensions combined. Figure 10-10 shows the Time to Admission measure in the query pane.

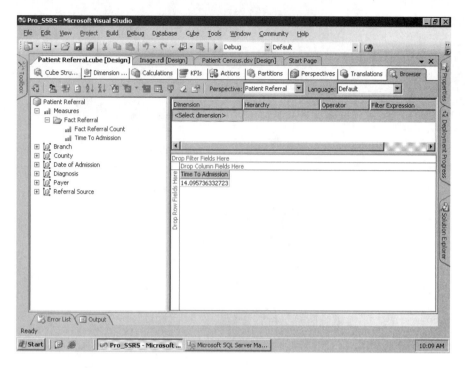

Figure 10-10. *Viewing the overall Time to Admission measure's average for all dimensions*

Now drag two dimension objects onto the query pane, one for fields and one for rows. Under the Branch object, drag and drop the BranchName field onto the Drop Column Fields Here section of the query pane. Next, under Date of Admission, drag and drop Year, MonthName, and admitdate to the Drop Row Fields Here section. Because this particular data store contains anomalies in some patient admission history left over from a data conversion, you know that the years 2000 and 2001 contain data that you will not be interested in for this query. You can therefore access the drop-down list on the Year header in the query pane and unselect 2000 and 2001. When finished, the cube browser should look like Figure 10-11. You can now see the overall average has dropped to 6.09 by removing the years you are not interested in and not the 14.095 that included the years 2000 and 2001. In addition, you can see the gradual decline in admission time from 2002 to 2005 at each branch level.

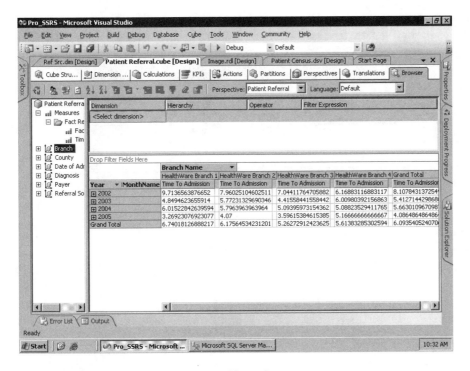

Figure 10-11. *Cube browser with year and branch*

You can drill down to the month and then to the actual admission day if you choose to do so. However, you now know that you are indeed getting data from the cube, so it is time to move on to SSRS and create the report you will deploy to the portal.

Using Analysis Service Cube with SSRS

Now that you have determined that the Patient Referral cube is working as it should, the next step is to create an SSRS report. In the Pro_SSRS project, you will find two completed reports, the Average Referral to Admission report and the Referral to Admission Chart report, that are both based on the Patient Referral cube. We will not go through the procedure of building these reports step by step; however, we will demonstrate the following through the Average Referral to Admission report:

- Setting up a data source to use Analysis Services

- Using the graphical MDX query builder that is new to SSRS for SQL Server 2005

Setting Up the Analysis Services Data Source

With the Pro_SSRS project open, navigate to the Reports folder, and open the Average Referrals to Admission report. Next, click the Data tab. In the Dataset list at the upper-left corner of the Data tab, notice that there are two datasets for this report, Patient_Referral and DateofAdmissionYear, as shown in Figure 10-12.

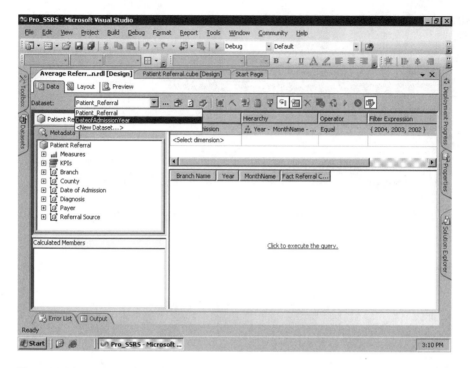

Figure 10-12. *Viewing the two datasets for the Average Referrals to Admission report*

Select the Patient_Referral dataset, and then click the ellipsis button to the right of the Dataset drop-down list. The data source for this dataset is PatRef_DS. If you click the ellipsis button on the Dataset drop-down list and then click the Edit button, you can see that the connection string that points to the cube Patient Referral on server hwcvs26, one of the servers used for the book. We did not set PatRef_DS to localhost, as we did with other data sources, so that we could show you how to set up the dataset and how to change the connection string. The type of data source is Microsoft SQL Server Analysis Services. You will need to change the data source server from hwcvs26 to your SSAS server name or localhost if you are running SSAS locally. You can do that easily by clicking the Edit button and changing the Server Name field to your server in the Connection Properties dialog box, as shown in Figure 10-13.

Figure 10-13. *Connection properties of the* PatRef_DS *data source*

With the datasets configured properly for your SSAS environment, you will next look at how you build the MDX queries.

Working with the Graphical MDX Query Builder

One of the great new features in SSRS for SQL Server 2005 is the graphical MDX query builder. MDX is a fairly large, complex language that is prone to syntactical errors. You must innately understand it to truly deliver precision data from SSAS cubes. Having and using a graphical query tool to form the base MDX query, in much the same way that developers use the graphical query designer for T-SQL, reduces common syntax errors and speeds development of the query.

With the Average Referral to Admission report open to the Data tab, notice that you have several dimensional elements listed: BranchName, Year, MonthName, Time To Admission, and Fact Referral Count. By default the report will open in the graphical design mode, as shown in Figure 10-14, and not the generic query designer. The design modes are toggled with the Design Mode button on the right of the toolbar. In the graphical design mode, the dimensional elements were dragged and dropped directly in the window from the Metadata pane where the elements are listed. If the Auto Execution button is selected, which it is by default, whenever elements are dragged and dropped, the query executes, and the data results are displayed.

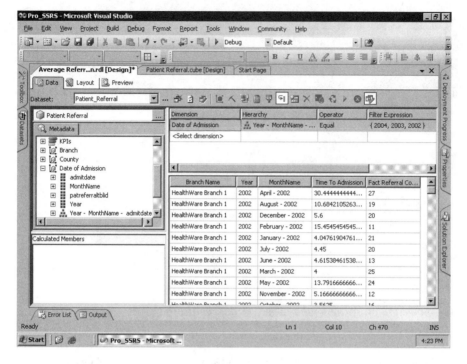

Figure 10-14. *Output from graphical query builder*

Instead of a multidimensional view of the data, as you saw when you queried the same cube in the Patient Referral cube browser, SSRS sees the data two-dimensionally, with rows and columns. An SSRS report can access data from a cube; however, it is necessary to arrange the data two-dimensionally because this is how the report will aggregate the data when it sums and totals the measured values, in this case Time to Admission and Fact Referral Count. We have also applied a filter to the query so that only the years from 2002 through 2005 will be selected.

You can use several buttons on the toolbar to modify the properties of the query, such as showing empty cells or adding calculated members. A calculated member is part of the MDX query that is created by combining one or more elements into an value that can be used independently as a new element. You could, for example, create calculated members to not only show that the average time to admission for each dimensional elements such as BranchName and Year but also show the minimum time to admission, using the MIN function, or the maximum time to admission, using the MAX function. The calculated members would become part of the overall query that could be used as new measures with data values returned at each dimensional level.

With the graphical query built and working, let's now look at the MDX that was created behind the scenes. You can do this by clicking the Design Mode toolbar button. Figure 10-15 shows the MDX query that returns the selected dimensional elements and measures for the report.

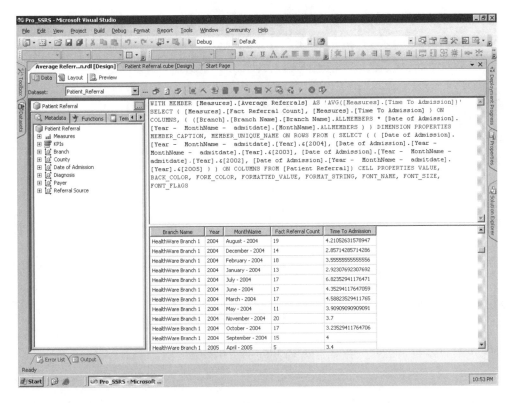

Figure 10-15. *MDX query generated graphically*

Caution If you modify the MDX query while in text mode and try to return to design mode, you could potentially lose any changes you made to the query manually, as shown in Figure 10-16.

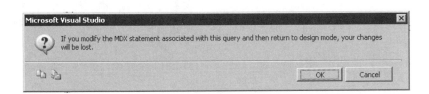

Figure 10-16. *Warning message displayed when altering MDX query*

Because both reports, Average Time to Admission and Referral to Admission Chart, will be displayed in a compact Web Part in SharePoint, which we will show how to do in the next section, we intentionally sized the reports small, with 8-point Arial font and narrow cells. Figure 10-17 shows the Layout tab for the Average Time to Admission report.

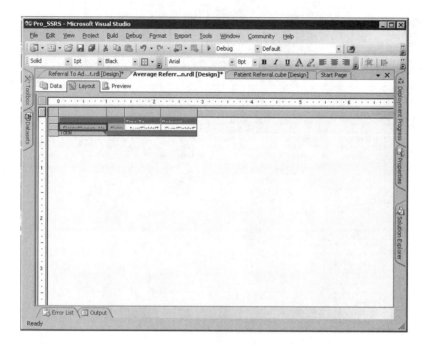

Figure 10-17. *Layout tab for Average Time to Admission report*

Finally, let's preview and then deploy both reports to the report server. With the Pro_SSRS report project set to the correct target URL for both the server and folder for the project properties, you can right-click each report in Solution Explorer and select Deploy. If you are unsure of how to configure the report's target URL, refer to Chapter 3 where you initially configured the Pro_SSRS report project. In our case, the target URL will be http://hwcvs26/ReportServer, and the folder will be Pro_SSRS. Figure 10-18 shows the Average Time to Admission report displayed in the browser with the URL you will use to place the report in SharePoint Portal Server. The extra whitespace will be removed in the portal.

		Time To Admission	Referral Count
HealthWare Branch 1	2002	8.98	227
	2003	4.70	186
	2004	5.71	197
	2005	3.25	52
HealthWare Branch 2	2002	7.85	478
	2003	5.76	549
	2004	5.77	555
	2005	4.03	200
HealthWare Branch 3	2002	6.63	136
	2003	4.37	154
	2004	5.12	149
	2005	3.66	52
HealthWare Branch 4	2002	5.74	77
	2003	5.61	102
	2004	5.06	102
	2005	4.45	66
Total		5.73	3282

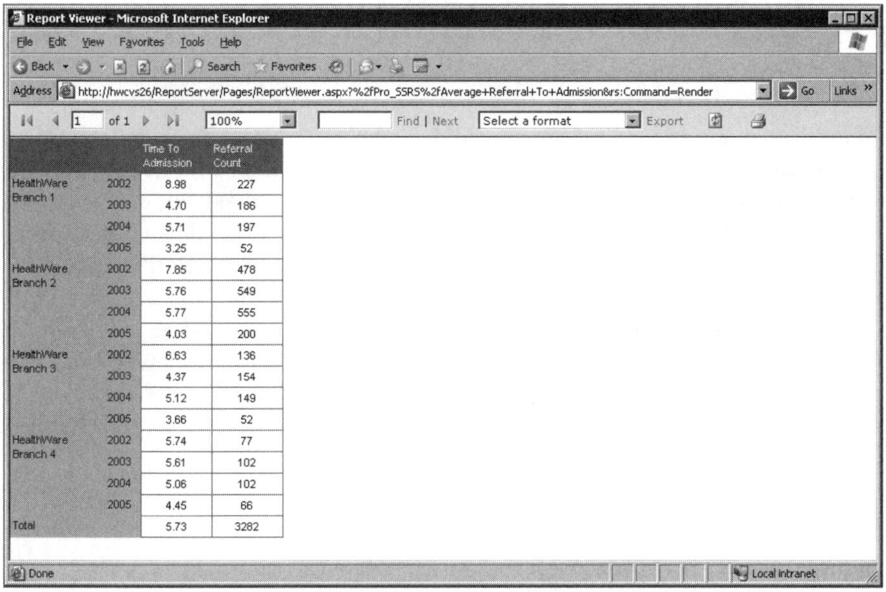

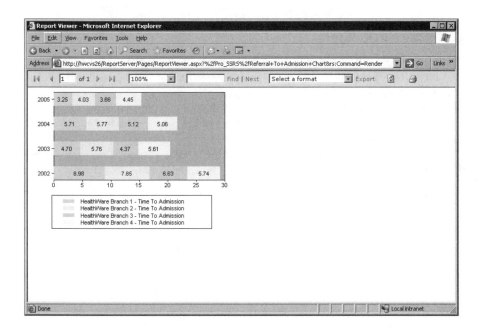

Figure 10-18. *Previewing Average Time to Admission in a browser*

Now let's look at the Referral to Admission Chart report that is based on the same Patient Referral cube but displays the data graphically using a stacked bar chart as opposed to the matrix style of the Average Time to Admission report. Figure 10-19 shows the Referral to Admission Chart in the browser.

Figure 10-19. *Previewing Referral to Admission Chart in a browser*

Incorporating SSRS with SharePoint Portal Server

SharePoint Portal Server and Windows SharePoint Services (which are components of Microsoft Office and Windows Server 2003, respectively) are important additions to the BI platform, because they serve as an intranet portal site, providing document management, collaboration, subscription services, and extensibility through custom *Web Parts*. Web Parts encapsulate Web content and services, such as news feeds, shared documents, or even other Web sites. Microsoft realized the need for custom SSRS Web Parts that link directly to reports and included these Web Parts for SSRS for SQL Server 2000 Service Pack 2, and they are also included with SSRS for SQL Server 2005. Prior to the release of the SSRS Web Parts, you could still add reports to a SharePoint page, but the procedure was not as simple and lacked properties specific to the configuration of the report URL. In the following sections, we will show how to use the SharePoint Web Part to embed a link to the two SSRS reports created in the previous section, Average Time to Admission and Referral to Admission Chart, that will become part of an over-all health-care portal page.

■**Note** In our environment, we have a Windows SharePoint Services virtual server called hwcvs21 where we will create the Web Parts. Assuming you have a Windows SharePoint Services or SharePoint Portal Server system in your domain, all that is required is to follow the installation procedure to add the SSRS Web Parts to the SharePoint server. You just need to execute the following from a command prompt on the SharePoint Server, ensuring that the paths to the STSADM utility and the rswebparts.cab file are correct for your environment: C:\Program Files\Common Files\Microsoft Shared\web server extensions\60\BIN\ STSADM.EXE -o addwppack -filename "C:\Program Files\Microsoft SQL Server\90\Tools\ Reporting Services\SharePoint\RSWebParts.cab".

Creating a Web Part Page

The first step to prepare to add the custom SSRS Web Parts is to create a Web Part Page by navigating to the portal home page (http://hwcvs21/default.aspx in this case) and clicking Create on the toolbar, as shown in Figure 10-20.

This will open the Create Page Web page, which lists the many types of pages you can create. You are interested in the Web Pages link at the bottom of the page, which includes the Web Part Page creation link. Click Web Part Page, and follow the steps to name the page and select the layout. Enter **Patient Referral** as the name, and select the Header, Footer, 2 Columns, 4 Rows option as the layout template, as shown in Figure 10-21. Then click Create.

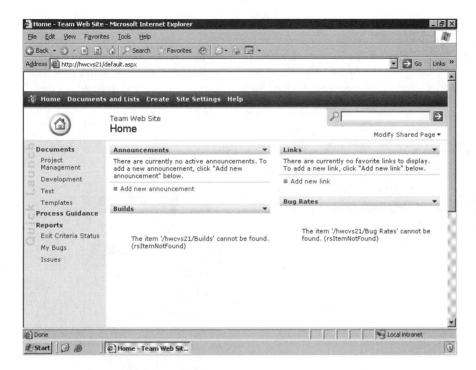

Figure 10-20. *Viewing the SharePoint home portal page*

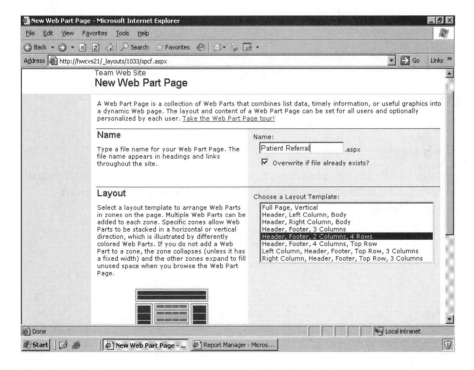

Figure 10-21. *Entering the name and layout for the Web Part Page*

We chose to save the Web Part Page in a document library called Manage Point; however, you can choose to save the page in whichever document library you choose. The document library is typically displayed as a link on the home page. As you can see in Figure 10-22, you are taken to the design layout of the page where you can view all the available Web Parts that are installed on the SharePoint server as well as the design area where the Web Parts will be placed.

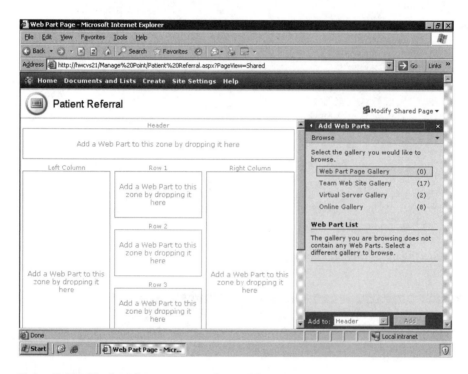

Figure 10-22. *Blank Web Part Page ready to add SSRS Web Parts*

Adding Web Parts

Clicking the Virtual Server Gallery shows the two available SSRS Web Parts that were installed from the RSwebparts.cab file, as shown in Figure 10-23. These two Web Parts are Report Explorer and Report Viewer.

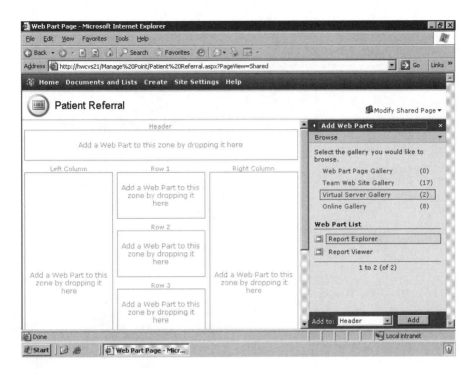

Figure 10-23. *Report Explorer and Report Viewer Web Parts*

You can use the Report Explorer Web Part to link directly to the Report Manager Web page and to a specific folder. Add the Report Explorer Web Part to the top portion of the Patient Referral page by dragging and dropping it directly into the Add a Web Part to This Zone by Dropping It Here area. To modify the properties of the Report Explorer Web Part to link to the report server URL, select the drop-down arrow on the Report Explorer window, and then click Modify Shared Web Part. You can set several properties for the Report Explorer Web Part; the two most important are the Report Manager URL and the Start Path properties. We have filled in these property values for our server and start path in Figure 10-24. Once the values are filled, click Apply; the Report Explorer displays the contents of the Pro_SSRS folder on the report server. The two reports, Average Referral to Admission and Referral to Admission Chart, are listed and can be executed from within the Report Explorer Web Part. The report, when clicked, will open in a new browser.

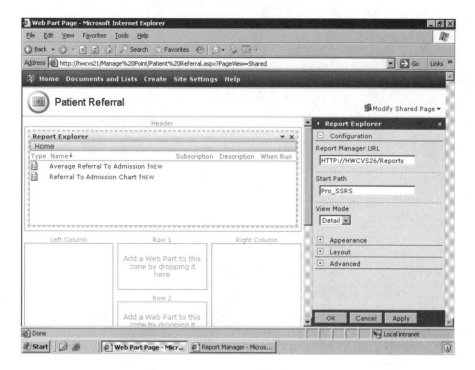

Figure 10-24. *Report Explorer URL and Start Path properties*

When you click OK to complete the modification, the full page with the Report Explorer will be displayed. To add the other Web Part, the Report Viewer, you need to click Modify Shared Page in the upper-right corner of the Patient Referral page, choose Add Web Parts, and then click Browse. Next, click Virtual Server Gallery, and then drag one Report Viewer to the left column on the page and one to the first zone in the first middle row so that it looks like Figure 10-25.

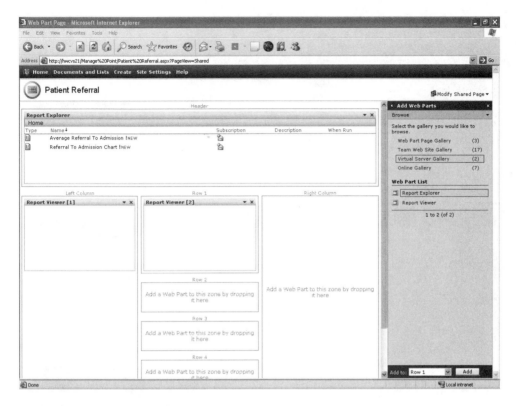

Figure 10-25. *Adding Report Viewer Web Parts*

Next, use the drop-down arrow on the Report Viewer [1] Web Part, and select Modify Shared Web Part. Again, enter the Report Manager URL property, and this time enter the path to the Average Referral to Admission report, remembering to include a slash (/) in the path, as shown in Figure 10-26. Also, choose None for the Toolbar Size option. Finally, expand the Appearance section, and set the Height and Width properties to 4 and 4.5 inches, respectively. When you click Apply, the report expands to fit in the first column as it should.

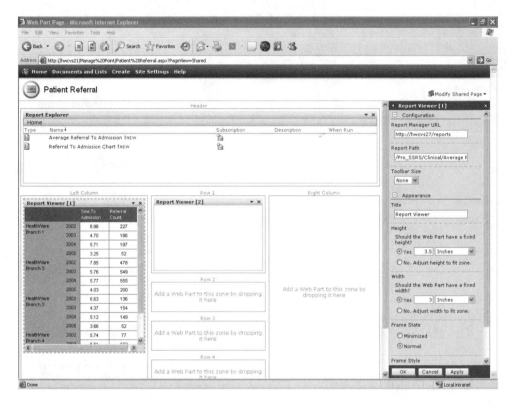

Figure 10-26. *Setting the Report Viewer URL and Report Path properties*

Leave the title as Report Viewer because even if you changed the title, SharePoint sees the Report Viewer Web Part as a single item and will continually rename it sequentially as Report Viewer [X], where X is the number of the individual Report Viewer control on the page. Since you are adding two Report Viewer controls ultimately for the example, the names will be Report Viewer [1] and Report Viewer [2]. This is a limitation of SharePoint.

Next, follow the same steps to add the Referral to Admission Chart report, replacing the height and width to be 4.1 inches by 4.5 inches and set the toolbar to Small instead of None. This will allow users to export the chart to Microsoft Excel if they so desire.

The end result appears in Figure 10-27.

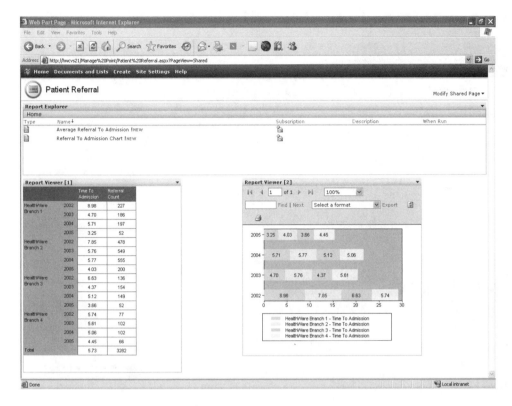

Figure 10-27. *Web Parts added to SharePoint*

One final feature of SSRS Web Parts is that they can be connected. In other words, you can connect Report Explorer and Report Viewer so that when a report is clicked inside the Report Explorer, it is displayed in the connected Report Viewer. We mentioned earlier when working with Microsoft CRM that you can add the sample CRM reports to SharePoint to tie both technologies together in a single portal. We will show how to do that now and take advantage of the connectable Web Parts.

To begin, modify the Patient Referral page that you have been working with by clicking Modify Shared Page, clicking Add Web Parts, and then clicking Browse. On the Virtual Server Gallery, drag another Report Explorer Web Part to the space beneath the first Report Explorer you added originally so that the page looks like Figure 10-28.

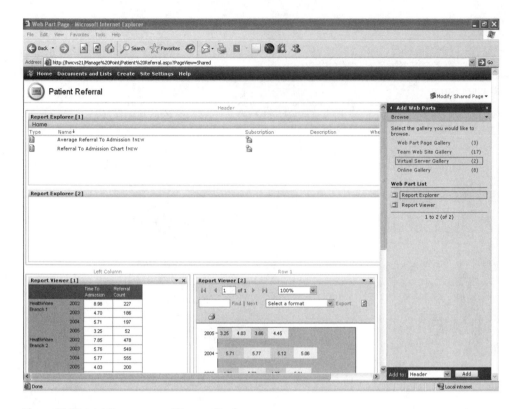

Figure 10-28. *Adding a second Report Explorer*

Next, modify the newly added Report Explorer Web Part, and add the link to the published Microsoft CRM sample reports. Notice in Figure 10-29, if you leave the View mode of Report Explorer set to Detail, you can see not only the reports, in this case Customer Account Details and Lead Summary, but also the description of the reports if one exists.

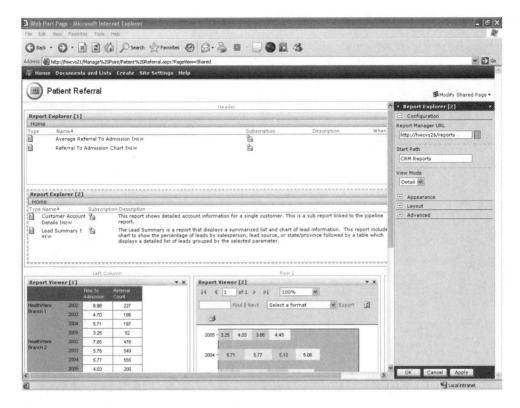

Figure 10-29. *Linking Report Explorer to CRM reports*

The next step to join the Web Parts is to click Modify Shared Web Part in the drop-down list on Report Viewer [1]. Once in design mode, the Connections property for the Report Viewer Web Part is available, as shown in Figure 10-30. Report Viewer [2] has been minimized for a better view. Notice that the Report Viewer can get a report from either Report Explorer [1] or Report Explorer [2], as these both now exist on the page. Choose Report Explorer [1].

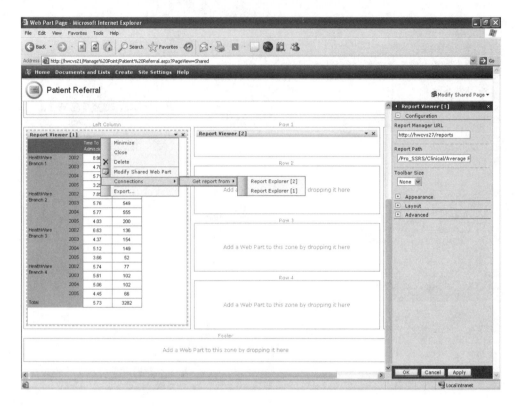

Figure 10-30. *Adding a Report Explorer connection to Report Viewer*

Follow the same steps to add a connection to Report Explorer [2] for Report Viewer [2]. When you click OK to refresh the page and return to Shared View mode from design mode, you will notice that each Report Viewer still launches its default reports that were assigned to it in previous steps; however, they now both have the ability to contain other reports that are listed in each of the Report Explorer Web Parts. As Figure 10-31 shows, Report Viewer [2] will contains the Lead Summary report launched from Report Explorer [2], and Report Explorer [1] contains the Referral to Admission Chart report from Report Explorer [1]. Also, the Web Parts do not automatically resize to fit the report they contain. It is possible to set the size of the Report Viewer Web Part to automatically fit the zone it is in, but even this will not guarantee a perfect fit for a report. When designing SSRS report for Web Parts, it is important to consider the size and placement of the reports on the page.

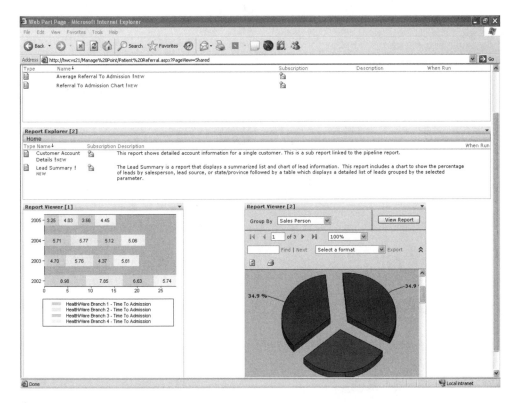

Figure 10-31. *Launching reports to the Report Viewer Web Parts from Report Explorer*

Summary

In this chapter, we showed how to incorporate SSRS into a BI model, specifically covering the business model of a software development company and health-care agency deploying a custom BI portal. Understanding how to transform and analyze the data that drives your business will help you make important business decisions. Delivering that data to decision makers is a pivotal link in the BI chain. With SSRS, Microsoft has provided organizations with another tool that can easily tap into and extend the reach of crucial data. From business applications such as Microsoft CRM to custom project management solutions, SSRS easily utilizes many types of data and can deliver it in a variety of formats. Working with other applications and products in the Microsoft BI platform—such as SharePoint Portal Server, Analysis Services, and Office—SSRS will prove to be an invaluable BI tool now and in the future.

CHAPTER 11

■■■

Performing Ad Hoc Reporting Using Report Builder

If you follow newsgroups like we do, then you have most likely noticed the prodigious number of postings asking whether SSRS offers a report builder application with enough functionality to let users design their own reports without knowing the underlying data structure or being proficient with full development environments such as Visual Studio or BIDS. When SSRS was released for SQL Server 2000, such a tool, also known as *ad hoc reporting*, was available only in third-party applications, such as ActiveViews. The alternative to purchasing a product for ad hoc reporting was to create your own; in fact, Microsoft offered several white papers on the topic with code samples and step-by-step guidelines. Fortunately for everyone, Microsoft decided to include a full-blown ad hoc report builder in SSRS for SQL Server 2005. Further, Microsoft decided to include it in the Workgroup and Standard editions of SQL Server, when it was originally slated to be included only in the Enterprise edition.

In this chapter, you will explore Report Builder and its components. As you will see, even though the user compiling the report needs to do some design work, the administrator still needs to design the report model that provides data to the Report Builder client application. We will walk you through the process of using Report Builder from two vantage points—developing and publishing a report model based on user input and then creating your own ad hoc reports based on that model. The three steps we will cover are gathering user feedback, creating and publishing the report model, and finally testing the report model by creating reports with Report Builder.

Getting feedback: Since we have worked alongside developers for many years, we know that one of the biggest problems with delivering a new application is that sometimes users get the application and expect it to do more than it does, or expect it to do something in a different way. The expectation from a user's vantage point is that the system should do exactly what they need. But for a developer, if it doesn't do it in version 1, it will have to do it in version 2. You can avoid this conflict by implementing standard design practices, which always take user feedback into consideration up front. This process is especially important when the same application will be delivered to different companies with users from different backgrounds, each with their own interpretations of how a process should work. In the past few decades, a system analyst would take information from groups of users and translate this to a technical diatribe that the developer could slowly digest. Today, most system analysis work is done directly by the developer, who interacts with users during the design phase of the project. Before we cover how to build a report model to be used by report designers, we will provide a sampling of some of the feedback we have received about the kinds of reports users would like to see.

Building the report model: The report model is the heart of Report Builder. Report models serve as semantic descriptions of the underlying data source. Because the report model can simplify a potentially complex overall database schema by selecting individual tables, fields, and values, it can be likened to a SQL Server view. Indeed, a key component of the report model, as you will see in this chapter, is a data source view. Once DBAs or developers have created a report model that contains the data to meet the requirements of the users, they can publish it to the report server where it can be used by Report Builder, which is the client-side report designer. All the data provided to Report Builder comes from published report models. We will show how to create and publish models in this chapter based on user feedback.

Using Report Builder: Report Builder is the design application used to create and publish SSRS reports, without requiring a full development environment such as Visual Studio or BIDS. Report Builder relies on prepublished report models as its data sources. As you will see, the interface for Report Builder is intuitive; in fact, it is ideal for users who need to quickly create reports based on predefined report templates. Report Builder not only allows users to design reports but also serves as the publishing tool to deploy the completed report directly to the report server.

Getting User Feedback

At this point in the book, you have built a report, Employee Service Cost, that breaks down the cost of health-care visits at several levels. You designed this report using BIDS, and it contains several grouping levels, interactive sorting, and drill-down functionality. The data source for this report is a stored procedure that provides the desired fields from several tables in the Pro_SSRS database. Like the reports you will build with Report Builder, this stored procedure and report were created based on feedback from users who needed it. One objective when creating the stored procedure was to design it not only to address the requirements for one report but to be versatile enough to be reused for other similar reports. We will cover this issue when we show how to build a report model to meet the needs of the users and the report designers who will be creating and publishing the reports with Report Builder.

In the health-care industry (namely, in post-acute care such as home health and hospice), you have to follow many reporting requirements for state and federal agencies. From cost reports to patient admission and discharge information, different reports are needed by different departments for different reasons. One group of reports that is used by every department is the patient census. This report shows all the patients who are currently admitted to the health-care facility and who are receiving services. The report can be as simple as an alphabetized listing of patient names or as detailed as all the demographic information about each patient, such as where they live and who to contact in case of an emergency.

Since the patient census is the most frequently requested report for customization, we will use it as the example in this chapter for the report model, making sure we provide enough data to meet both current and future needs.

For the patient census report example, imagine that users have requested to see a daily total of patients who have been admitted to the facility. Such patients all have common data associated with them that is important when looking at a census. The information answers these types of questions:

- What is the patient's primary diagnosis?

- What branch office is the patient currently admitted to?

- What is the patient's length of stay in the facility?

- How many active patients are in each branch currently?

- What is the patient's address, phone number, and other key demographic information? (This type of census report, often referred to as a *face sheet*, shows a lot of information about a patient in a compact location.)

- If the patient was discharged, when did that occur and what was the reason? Is it because they became well, or did they transfer to a hospital?

■**Note** The type of information we are discussing in this chapter is considered to be PI data, which, thanks to HIPAA, needs to be tightly guarded and accessible only to those who are permitted to use it. Chapter 9 covers how to secure access to data delivered through SSRS.

You can answer all these questions and more with a single query, which can form the foundation of the report model. So, in the `Pro_SSRS` database, you will join several tables into a single data source view to provide the information needed to deliver the patient census. You have used most of these tables already when developing other reports, but we will review the database schema of the associated tables before showing how to build the report model. These are the tables you will use in this chapter's example:

- `Admissions`

- `Branch`

- `Diag`

- `Discipline`

- `DocumentImage`

- `PatEMRDoc`

- `Employee`

- `PatDiag`

- `Dischg`

- `Patient`

Each table contains specific information that is relevant to the individual patient's admission history, and together they will provide enough data to create many kinds of census reports for many departments within the health-care agencies. You know the kinds of questions you will need to answer, and the tables have been designed to deliver that information based on direct feedback and requests for users. Now let's move on to designing the query and building the report model.

Introducing the Report Model

Just because you don't understand the intricacies of putting all the parts of a car engine together does not mean you can't drive, right? The same can be said for report designers who will design and publish reports using the ad hoc Report Builder. In this case, you have little need to understand the pieces and parts of the database structure in order to build reports. It is unavoidable, though, that *someone* must understand the database schema, just as mechanics must understand brake pads and fan belts. Building a versatile report model, which the report designer will use to create reports, will most likely fall under the authority of the DBA or data analyst, who will have an intimate understanding of the data sources. In this section, we will show how to use the feedback gathered from the report consumers to develop a report model for the patient census reports that will serve to make the data easily accessible with logical and intuitive field names.

You will perform the following procedures to create the report model for the Patient Census report model:

1. Add a report model project to the existing Pro_SSRS solution using BIDS.

2. Create a data source.

3. Create a data source view.

4. Create the Patient Census report model based on the data source view.

5. Publish the Patient Census report model to the SSRS server.

The process of building a report model consists of many individual steps, many of which are controlled entirely by stepping through available wizards. A report model can be complex or simple, based on your individual needs. For the sake of brevity, we will keep the sample model as simple as possible; you will be able to answer the feedback questions for the patient census, and you will be able to create and publish your own report model without any issues.

Adding a Report Model to BIDS

In this section, you will add a report model project to the Pro_SSRS solution that you have been working with throughout the book. When you open the solution, you will notice an already created report model called Patient Census Book. If you would like to publish the Patient Census Book report model as it is in the project to your SSRS server and begin working with the client-side Report Builder application, that is fine. (In that case, just skip to the "Using Report Builder" section.) To follow the steps to create each piece of a report model, from adding data sources and data source views to publishing the completed model, read on.

Open the Pro_SSRS solution you have been using thus far. In the Solution Explorer, right-click the Pro_SSRS solution, and select Add ➤ New Project. As you can see in Figure 11-1, you can use several available project templates. Choose the Report Model Project template, name it Patient Census, add the appropriate location (in this case C:\Pro_SSRS_Project\Patient Census), and click OK.

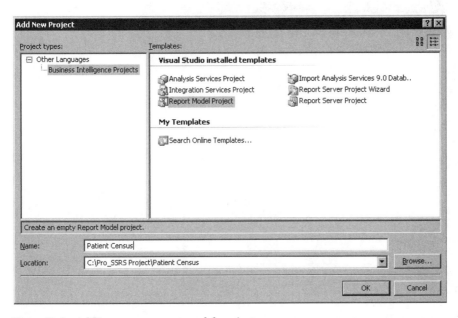

Figure 11-1. *Adding a new report model project*

A report model project has three main components: data sources, data source views, and report models, each one relying on the previous one. In other words, a data source view requires a data source, just as a report model requires a data source view. If you have successfully added the Patient Census report model project, you can expand the Patient Census project and see these three components, as shown in Figure 11-2.

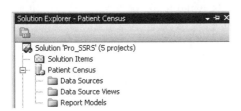

Figure 11-2. *Viewing the new Patient Census report model*

Adding a Data Source

Logically, the first step is to create a data source. Right-clicking the Data Sources folder in the Solution Explorer and selecting Add ➤ New Data Source instantiates the Data Source Wizard, which, by the way, is the only way to create a data source for a report model. Figure 11-3 shows the first page of the Data Source Wizard. Fortunately, you can select to not display the first page every time you open the wizard by checking Don't show this page again.

Figure 11-3. *Using the Data Source Wizard*

You have two options when creating a data source through the wizard, as shown in Figure 11-4. You can either create a new one based on an existing or a new connection or create a data source based on another object such as a data source already defined in another project. For this example, choose to create a new data source based on a new connection, and click New to open the Connection Manager.

In the Connection Manager, select localhost as the server name, leave the Use Windows Authentication button checked, and change the database name to Pro_SSRS, as shown in Figure 11-5. On the next and final screen of the wizard, leave the default data source name of Pro_SSRS, and click Finish to create the data source.

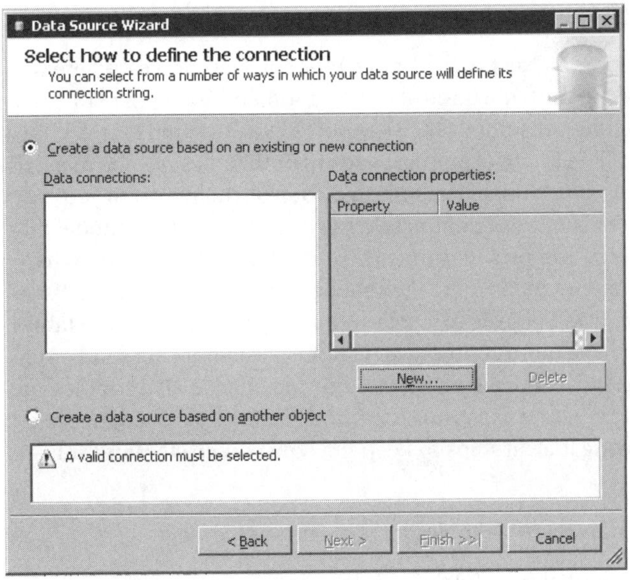

Figure 11-4. *Defining a connection*

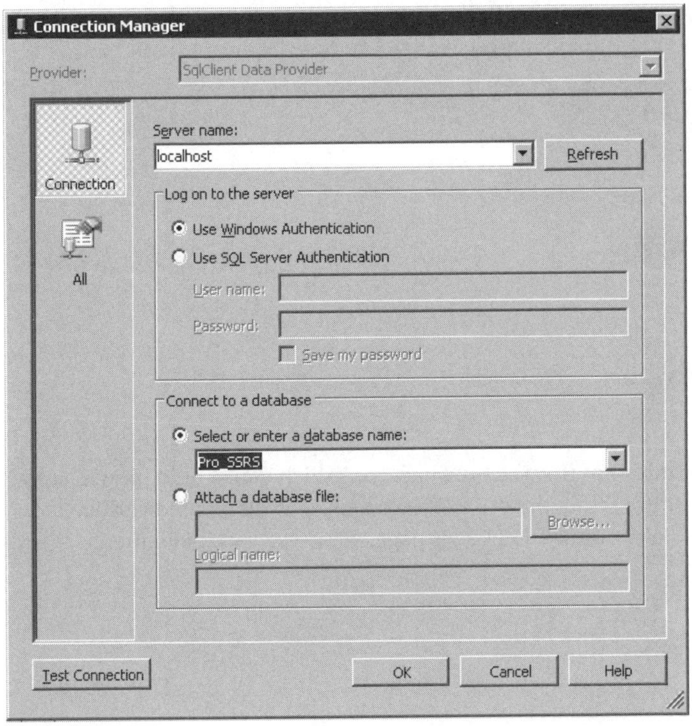

Figure 11-5. *Setting the server name and database*

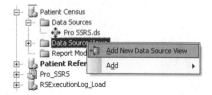

View

...ort model project from relational data sources, where you
...ed to form the basis of the data source view. In the Pro_SSRS
...d tables are joined by column ID fields; the Admissions table
...ne PatID field, for example. Fields in both tables may be relevant
...; however, superfluous data may just confuse them. Part of your job
...to remove the complexity of the schema but also provide a model that
..."friendly" names and provides only the data that will be useful. Why
...r for a diagnosis code, when you really should just make it Diagnosis Name,
...ice it is also possible to add objects to a data source view that are derived tables
...ustom queries, you will have more control over creating a custom data source view
...ate much of the work of removing the extraneous fields included in all the tables you
...g. This will become more evident to you as you step through the process. For now we
...now how to perform the following logical steps to keep the data source view and subse-
...ent model simple but effective:

- Building a query instead of many multiple tables for the data source view

- Selecting only relevant and potentially useful fields for the report designers, based on their requests

- Using friendly names for data source view fields and values

The first step in creating the view, like with the data source, is to open the wizard by right-clicking the Data Source Views folder and selecting Add New Data Source, as shown in Figure 11-6.

Figure 11-6. *Adding a data source view to the project*

On the first page of the wizard (not the welcome page, on which you should immediately check Don't show this page again), select the Pro_SSRS data source you created earlier, and then click Next to move to the Select Tables and Views page. As you can see in Figure 11-7, you can choose from many tables.

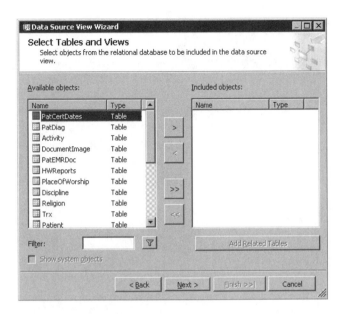

Figure 11-7. *Related tables in the* Pro_SSRS *data source*

You could add all the tables from the list of required tables for the patient census reports you are going to create; however, knowing that you will have too many unnecessary fields to work with, simply select Next and then Finish to close the wizard without including any objects. This will create the Pro_SSRS data source view with no tables defined. Why, you may ask, did you not select any relational objects, since this seems like a crazy way to start? The reason is that you will add your own single object, called a *named query*, that is like a view in a SQL Server database. It is an object derived from a query of other objects. Assuming you had chosen one or more tables, you would have graphically defined the relationships for the tables based on primary keys, if they existed or by using related column ID values, and these tables would become the source for the report model. The end result is the same, whether you use real table objects with relationships or you use named query tables that contain only the fields you want. The difference is that this way you gain the benefit of one simple and concise table, instead of using many tables with the potential downside of adding more data than is needed for the model.

Once you have created the data source view, which defaults to a name of Pro SSRS based on the data source, you can double-click to open it in the design environment. It will appear empty, as it should. You can add the source query, or more accurately, the named query, by clicking the New Named Query button on the toolbar, as shown in Figure 11-8.

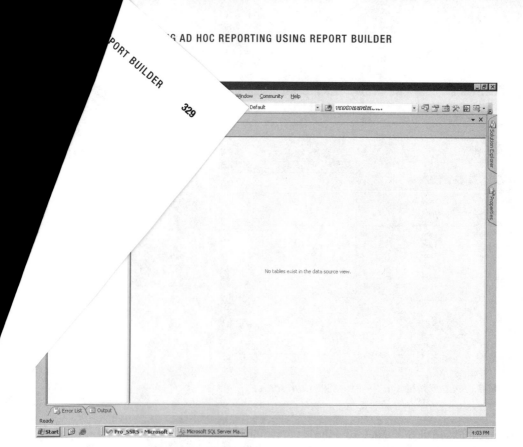

Figure 11-8. *Pro SSRS data source view*

In this case, you have already designed the query; however, Report Builder includes its own graphical query builder, so it is possible to develop the query on the fly so to speak. The graphical query designer is standard fare, with standard diagram, grid, SQL, and result panes. Clicking the New Named Query button opens the Create Named Query window. In the SQL pane, paste the preexisting Patient Census query from Listing 11-1, and click in the blank diagram pane to automatically load the graphical representation of the query. If you need to provide aliases for any fields, such as distinguishing the common LastName fields from the employee and patient table, you can do that in the grid pane, as shown in Figure 11-9, which also shows the query and all the joined tables. Alias the lastname field as Pat_LastName for patient and as Emp_LastName for employee. Otherwise, if there were common references to lastname, the default alias would have been ExprX where X is the number of common references. You can do the same for the ubiquitous DSCR, used for descriptions, as in the Diag and PatEMR tables.

Listing 11-1. *Patient Census Query*

```
SELECT
    Admissions.PatProgramID, Employee.EmployeeID,
    Employee.LastName AS Emp_LastName,
    Employee.FirstName AS Emp_Firstname,
    Discipline.Dscr AS Discipline, Branch.BranchName,
    Patient.PatID, Patient.LastName AS Pat_LastName,
    Patient.FirstName AS Pat_FirstName,
    Diag.DiagID, Diag.Dscr AS Diagnosis, PatDiag.DiagOnset, PatDiag.DiagOrder,
```

```
    Admissions.StartOfCare, Admissions.DischargeDate, Patient.MI,
    Patient.Address1, Patient.Address2, Patient.City,
    Patient.HomePhone, Patient.Zip, Patient.State, Patient.WorkPhone,
    Patient.DOB, Patient.SSN, Patient.Sex, Patient.RaceID, Patient.MaritalStatusID,
    PatEMRDoc.DateEntered, PatEMRDoc.Dscr AS EMR_Document,
    Dischg.Dscr AS [Discharge Reason],
    DATEDIFF(dd, Admissions.StartOfCare, Admissions.DischargeDate) + 1
    AS [Length of Stay]
FROM
    Admissions INNER JOIN
    Patient ON Admissions.PatID = Patient.PatID INNER JOIN
    Branch ON Branch.BranchID = Patient.OrigBranchID LEFT OUTER JOIN
    PatDiag ON Admissions.PatProgramID = PatDiag.PatProgramID INNER JOIN
    Diag ON PatDiag.DiagTblID = Diag.DiagTblID LEFT OUTER JOIN
    Employee ON Admissions.EmployeeTblID = Employee.EmployeeTblID LEFT OUTER JOIN
    Discipline ON Discipline.DisciplineTblID = Employee.DisciplineTblID
    LEFT OUTER JOIN
    PatEMRDoc ON Admissions.PatProgramID = PatEMRDoc.PatProgramID LEFT OUTER JOIN
    DocumentImage ON DocumentImage.DocumentImageID = PatEMRDoc.DocumentImageID
    LEFT OUTER JOIN Dischg ON Admissions.DischargeTblID = Dischg.DischgTblID
WHERE
 (PatDiag.DiagOrder = 1) AND (PatDiag.DiagEnd IS NULL)
```

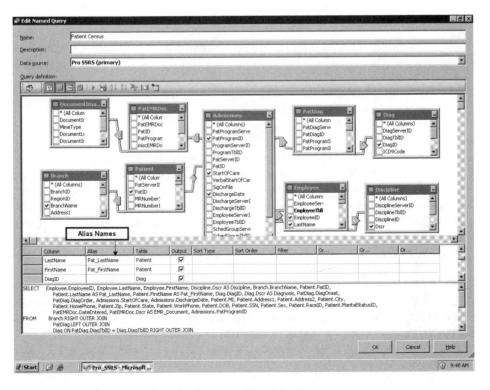

Figure 11-9. *Named query displayed graphically with alias names*

Finally, name the query Patient Census. When you click OK to complete the named query, your simple data source view consists of one object, `Patient Census`, that contains the desired fields for the model. You can see in Figure 11-10 that 32 fields will be supplied to the model.

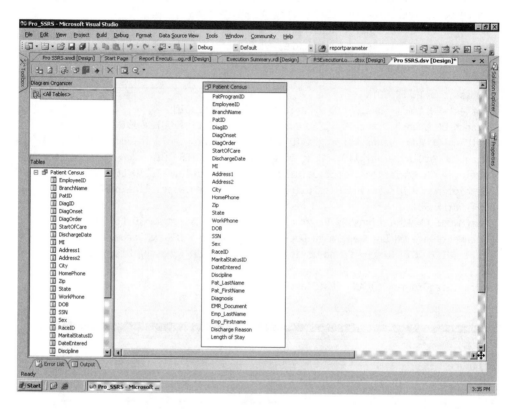

Figure 11-10. *Data source view with one object*

The next step in the process is to add a logical primary key to the Patient Census named query because the report modeler requires a primary key when it generates the model. Because the query is driven from the `Admissions` table, which contains the `PatProgramID` field that you know will contain unique values, you can use this field as the logical primary key for the Patient Census query. The `PatProgramID` field, in the example database, controls the admission and discharge records for a patient over time. It is typical that the same patient will be admitted to two separate service lines, referred to as *programs*; hence, you have `PatProgramID`. Without the `PatProgramID` field, the records would not be unique with the patient's identification number, `PatID`, alone.

To set the logical primary key for the `Patient Census` object to be `PatProgramID`, simply right-click the `PatProgramID` field either in the Tables list or in the Patient Census diagram, and select Set Logical Primary Key, as shown in Figure 11-11.

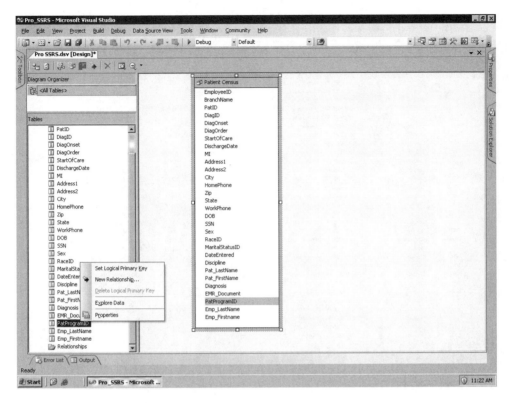

Figure 11-11. *Setting the logical primary key*

At this point, you can save the data source view and then create the report model. Before you do, however, let's take a look at a really great feature in the design environment, which is the ability to explore the data. Right-click anywhere in the Patient Census object—on EmployeeID, for example—and select Explore Data. As you can see, many records are returned from the entire Patient Census object, which you will use for the report you create later. However, also notice the three additional tabs beside Table, as shown in Figure 11-12. The Pivot Table, Chart, and Pivot Chart tabs show up here like finding a really valuable trumpet shell unexpectedly on the beach. (Not that this will help you greatly when developing the report model, but we just thought it was worth showing.)

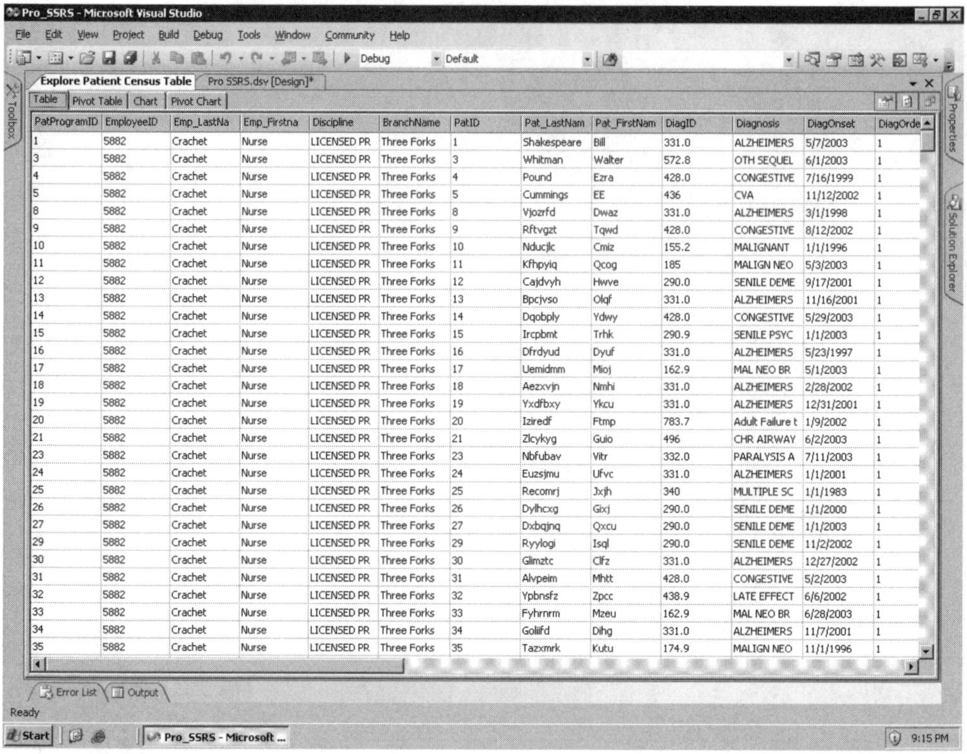

Figure 11-12. *Additional tabs when exploring data*

Now that you have determined that the Patient Census data source view is returning data as you expected, you will save it and move on to the real heart of Report Builder, the report model.

Creating a Report Model

The report model will add a layer of separation between report designers and the underlying data source, simplifying the process of designing reports by allowing them to focus on report design and not query design. Now that you have the data source view, which is a requirement for building a report model, you will now learn how to create the model. The process is straight-forward, thanks to autogeneration methods that analyze the data source view in two passes and produce the end result—a publishable report model that would have otherwise taken much time and effort to produce its constituent elements, as you will see. The goal in this section is to walk you through the wizard so you can pay attention to the generation methods and finally deploy your completed model to the SSRS server.

You will again utilize the right-click procedure to initiate the Report Model Wizard from the Report Models folder in Solution Explorer. After navigating past the first welcome page to the Select Data Source View page, you are presented with the Pro SSRS data source view selection, as shown in Figure 11-13.

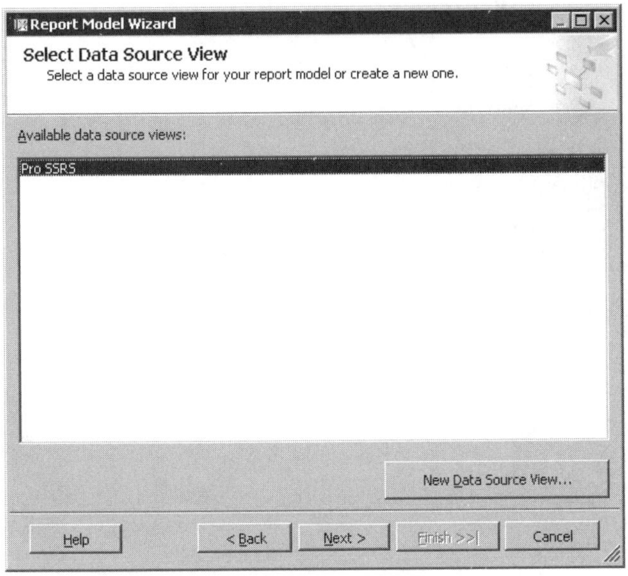

Figure 11-13. *Selecting a data source view*

After selecting Pro SSRS, click Next, where you can now select the report model generation rules. You will see two sets of rules, one for each pass on the data source view. Several rules exist, and most of them are selected by default. Many of the rules are self-explanatory; however, two are not selected by default, Create Entities for Nonempty Tables and Create Attributes for Non-empty Columns. These two rules instruct the generation process to create entities and attributes only for tables that contain data. Entities are the report model's table equivalent, and attributes are conceptually the fields or columns defined within the entities.

The following are all the rules for the first pass of generating the model and are selectable in the Report Model Wizard:

- Create Entities for All Tables

- Create Entities for Non-empty Tables

- Create Count Aggregates

- Create Attributes

- Create Attributes for Non-empty Columns

- Create Attributes for Auto-increment Columns

- Create Date Variations

- Create Numeric Aggregates

- Create Date Aggregates

- Create Roles

The next set of rules are applied automatically during the second pass of the generation process:

- Lookup Entities

- Small Lists

- Large Lists

- Very Large Lists

- Set Identifying Attributes

- Set Default Detail Attributes

- Role Name Only

- Numeric/Date Formatting

- Integer/Decimal Formatting

- Float Formatting

- Date Formatting

- Discourage Grouping

- Dropdown Value Selection

We said that there are two passes during the autogeneration process for the model. The first pass processes all rules up to Create Roles, and the second pass begins with Lookup Entities and completes with Dropdown Value Selection. You will also see a helpful description for each rule, as shown in Figure 11-14.

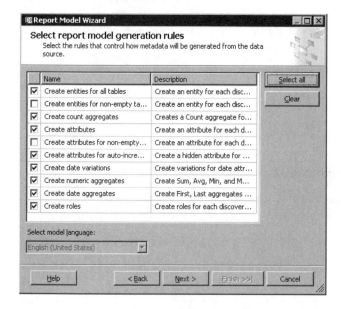

Figure 11-14. *Model generation rules with descriptions*

For this example, leave the default selections, as these will give you features such as automatic aggregations for any numbers and dates and also create date variations so that for every DateTime data type in the data source view, you will have Day, Month, and Year created. You can click Next and choose to update statistics before generating, as shown in Figure 11-15. This is important if any data has changed significantly in the source tables.

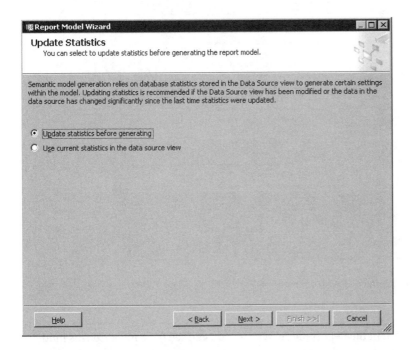

Figure 11-15. *Update Statistics page*

On the next page in the wizard, select Run to begin the two passes of the rules to generate the model. Figure 11-16 shows the output after clicking Run, and the process has completed successfully. You can see the details at each rule level of exactly what the rule did based on the data in the data source view. Notice that for Create Date Variations, for example, the rule discovered and created dates for DiagOnset, which is the date on which the patient was diagnosed with a disease. Other attributes that were created were Sum, Avg, Min, and Max for the Length of Stay column. The length of stay, usually an average, is the amount of time between the patient being admitted and being discharged from a long-term health-care facility. The DateDiff function calculates the length of stay.

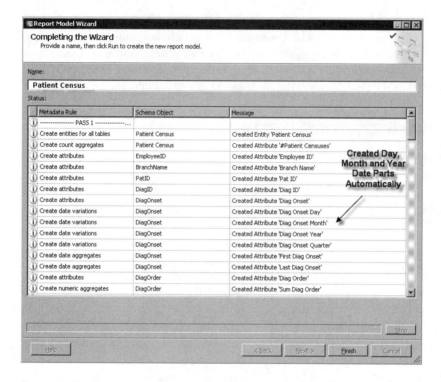

Figure 11-16. *Rules completed successfully*

After you click Finish in the Report Model Wizard, you can see the Patient Census model has been created with the expected attributes. At this point, you can deploy the model directly to the report server by right-clicking the model in the Solution Explorer and selecting Deploy. You can control where the model will be deployed in the project's properties pages, as shown in Figure 11-17, by clicking Project ➤ Project Properties on the toolbar. In this case, the project will be deployed to the Models folder on the report server, which has a target server URL of http://localhost/ReportServer. The data sources for the model will be published in the Data Sources folder.

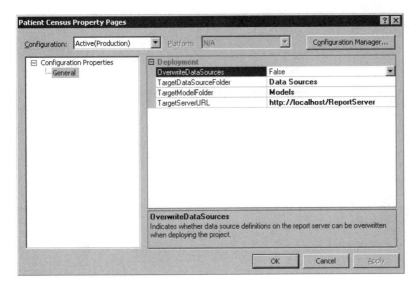

Figure 11-17. *Project properties for the report model*

■Note We should mention that report models are created with Semantic Model Definition Language (SDML), which is an XML-style grammar similar to RDL. Where RDL defines reports and report properties, SMDL defines models objects, such as the entities and attributes that you are creating here.

After you deploy the model, you can see in Report Manager the two folders that were created, Data Sources and Models. The Data Sources folder contains the Pro_SSRS data source, and the Models folder houses the Patient Census report model. Figure 11-18 shows the properties of the Patient Census report model. Just as with a standard data source, it is possible to view which reports have been created using the model.

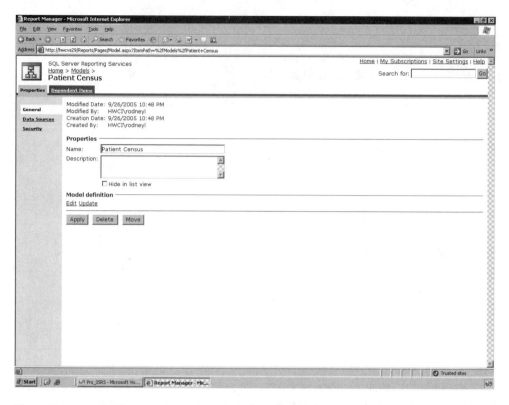

Figure 11-18. *Patient Census report model properties*

Before you begin creating reports with Report Builder, it is important to note that users who will need permissions to use Report Builder must have item-level role assignments for various tasks associated with creating reports with Report Builder. SSRS includes a new Report Builder role for this purpose, as shown in Figure 11-19. Users assigned to the Report Builder role have all the required permissions to access the report models, folders, and published reports. To publish reports, however, they will need to have the ability to manage report content before they can successfully publish their reports to the report server. The Content Managers role has all the required permissions for full report creation and publishing capabilities.

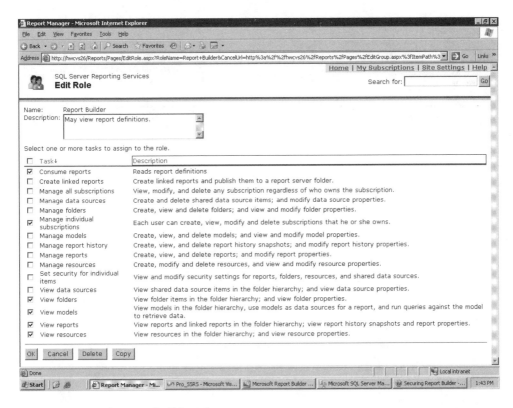

Figure 11-19. *SSRS Report Builder role*

Using Report Builder

To this point you have created all the requisite pieces for using Report Builder—you have created the report model Patient Census and deployed it to the report server. It is now waiting to be used as a source for the front-end Report Builder application. Report Builder provides some of the same functionality of a full report development environment, such as BIDS or Visual Studio, including the ability to drag and drop data elements to the design area with Matrix, Table, and Chart data regions as well as the ability to deploy finished reports to the report server. However, before you dive in, we should state that Report Builder serves the purpose of allowing end users to design their own reports. It was designed to be intuitive and friendly, and because it is not a full-featured IDE, it may at first seem limited.

In this section, you will explore Report Builder and uncover the features that are available to the report designer such as adding functions, similar to adding expressions in BIDS, and providing filtering, grouping, and sorting capabilities. The goal in this section is show you how to create and deploy, step by step, the requested census reports from the Patient Census model created earlier in this chapter.

To launch Report Builder, first open Report Manager by navigating to `http://Servername/Reports`. On the main toolbar of the Report Manager home page, you should see the Report Builder button, as shown in Figure 11-20. Click the Report Builder button to initialize the Report Builder installation if it is not already installed or to open the installed application.

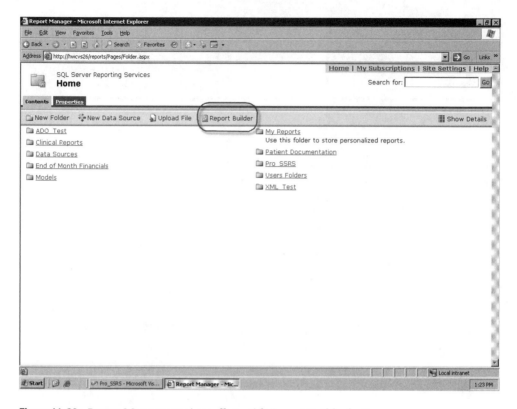

Figure 11-20. *Report Manager main toolbar with Report Builder button*

■Note It is also possible to launch Report Builder directly from the `ReportServer` URL such as
`https://mySSRSserver/ReportServer/ReportBuilder/ReportBuilder.application`.

Report Builder uses ClickOnce technology to install itself from the Web site. The code is
downloaded and installed to the local machine from the browser, assuming there are no issues
with missing prerequisites, one of which is .NET Framework 2.0. If this is not installed, it will
issue a warning message that Report Builder requires .NET Framework 2.0 before it can be
installed. If all the requirements are met, Report Builder initiates and completes installation.
Figure 11-21 shows the installation progress.

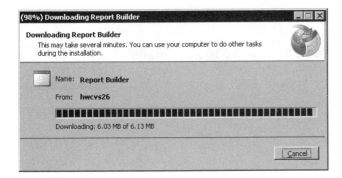

Figure 11-21. *Report Builder installation progress*

After Report Builder is installed, it launches automatically. The first step to begin design-ing a report is to select a source of data, as shown in Figure 11-22. The source will be a report model, in this case the Patient Census report model you have already published. So, select it, and click OK to continue.

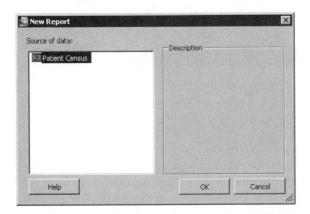

Figure 11-22. *Selecting the report model*

At first glance, it is easy to see that Report Builder has the look and feel of other Microsoft design products in the Office suite, such as FrontPage. You will see a simple design area, a Report Data area, and a Report Layout area that contains templates that can be used for each report. The three available templates are familiar versions of data regions available for SSRS reports: Table, Matrix, and Chart. Each template has predefined areas such as a title, a total column, and a fil-ter description column, as shown in the table report in Figure 11-23. You can also see the fields of the Patient Census report model in the Report Data tab on the left.

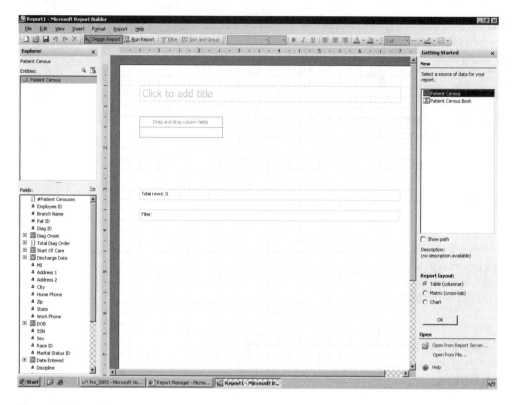

Figure 11-23. *Table report template in Report Builder*

Creating a Table Report

To address many of the report requests received from user feedback, you can use the table report. One item to note, which may fall into the category of a limitation of Report Builder, is that you can use only one data region per report. In other words, unlike the full IDE of BIDS, users who build reports with Report Builder are limited to one Table, Matrix, or Chart data region per report. You cannot add a second data region. In fact, reports are not only limited to a single data region, but they are relegated to using the controls that have been defined for each template. It is not possible to add textboxes, for example, or any other type of design element, other than the data from the fields. You will work within this limitation to produce your first report, a *patient face sheet* (as it is commonly called), which displays demographic information about each patient. With the table report still open, you will drag several fields onto the table where it says Drop Column Fields so that the report looks like Figure 11-24. The fields that you will use are Branch Name, Pat ID, Pat First Name, Pat Last Name, Diagnosis, Start Of Care, Address 1, Address 2, City, State, and Zip. At this point, you can also add a title in the Click to Add Title textbox. Notice also that as the fields are added, Pat Last Name, for example, they become bold in the Fields tab on the left indicating they have already been used.

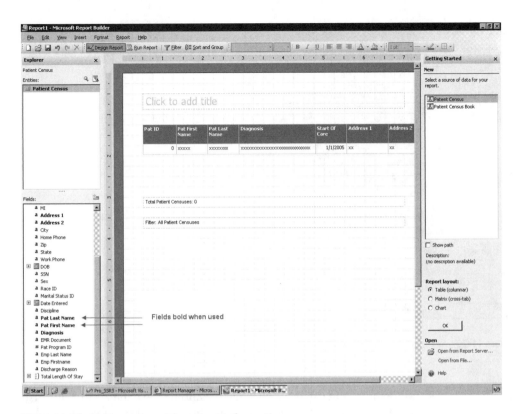

Figure 11-24. *Table report with patient information*

Once you have added all these fields to the report, you could click Run Report to preview the report; however, at this point, you must perform some tasks to make the report fit on a printed page. In its default page setup, the report is set to Portrait; however, the fields you have added extend beyond 8.5 inches across. To fix this, right-click in the design area, and select Page Setup so that the Page Setup dialog box appears, as shown in Figure 11-25. Set the Orientation property to Landscape, and click OK.

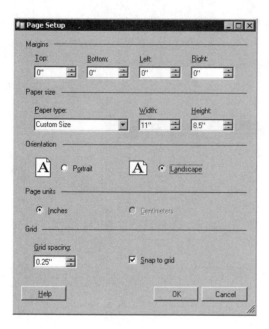

Figure 11-25. *Setting the page orientation*

To make even more room, you can use a formula to combine the patient's first and last names. To do this, simply right-click the Pat First Name data cell, and select Edit Formula. This will open the Define Formula window. Formulas in Report Builder are like expressions in BIDS. Here is where you can combine report fields and built-in functions to produce the desired value. Figure 11-26 shows the Define Formula dialog box with several available functions. Notice the formula used to concatenate the Pat First Name and Pat Last Name fields, which uses report data fields and an ampersand (&) to add a literal comma character to separate the names. You can also use the RTRIM function to remove trailing spaces. You could have done much of this work in the report model, where it most likely should have been done. However, we had you leave the names this way so we could now demonstrate the use of a simple formula. Once the formula is in place, rename the field to Patient Name, and click OK.

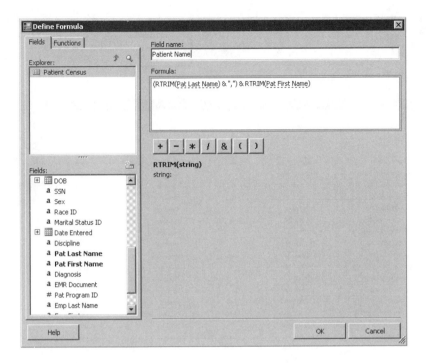

Figure 11-26. *Define Formula window*

Now that you have the patient's full name combined, you can delete the Pat Last Name field by clicking the data cell and pressing the Delete key. One task remains before previewing the report, and that is to resize the fields so that each record will fit on a single line. Of the fields you have used for the report, the Diagnosis and Address fields have the potential to be the largest, as they are variable-length fields that usually contain between 20 and 50 characters. For this example, size the Pat ID field to about .5 inches, expand the Diagnosis, Address 1, and Address 2 fields to approximately 1.5 inches, and preview the report, as shown in Figure 11-27. There will be as many *x* characters representing the data as there are characters found in the largest value in the database field, which makes it easy to determine how much to resize each column. The reason that the Address fields display NA is because this information was either scrambled, in the case of the patient names, or modified to be NA to remove identifiable information. Notice also in Figure 11-27 that each field automatically contains an interactive sorting icon at the column heading level. Though clicking the icon will rerender the report, no actual sorting will be performed until you configure it to do so. You will do that next.

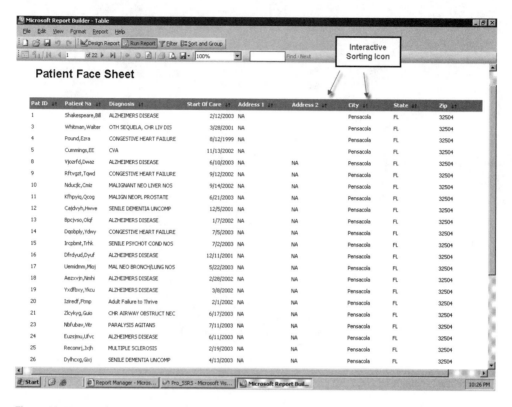

Figure 11-27. *Previewing the Patient Face Sheet report*

Return to the design area of the report by clicking the Design Report button on the toolbar. Next, right-click the Pat ID data cell, and then select Sort and Group on the toolbar. This will open the Sort dialog box. With the Patient Census group selected, choose to first sort by Pat ID, then by Patient Name, and finally by Diagnosis, as shown in Figure 11-28. You also have the ability to put a page break after each group as a group option. Do not add a page break at this time. Once you click OK, you can preview the report and see that the sorting for each of the defined columns is working correctly.

We should mention one more thing about dragging fields to the table area of the report: groups are automatically defined from left to right. In other words, dragging and dropping fields to the right of another field keeps the field in the same group, in this case the Patient Census group; however, if you have already dragged a field to the table and then drag another one to the left of it, another group is created based on the name of the field that is dropped. You can see this in Figure 11-29, where you dragged the Branch Name field to the left of the Pat ID field. If you are going through these steps, go ahead and drag the Branch Name field to the report to see the automatic grouping.

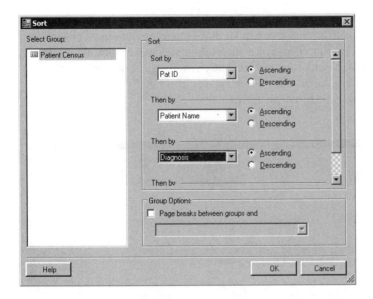

Figure 11-28. *Sorting and grouping options*

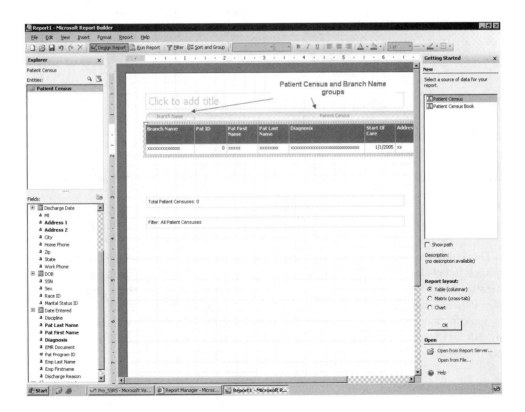

Figure 11-29. *Automatically created groups*

You can preview the report one last time before saving it to the report server. Notice in Figure 11-30 that the newly added branch group hides duplicate values automatically and groups each record from the Patient Census group under their assigned branch names. You could, at this point, use standard formatting features such as adding a border or changing the background color of cells or even the font size, color, and justification if you so desired, but the base report meets your needs, so go ahead and deploy it.

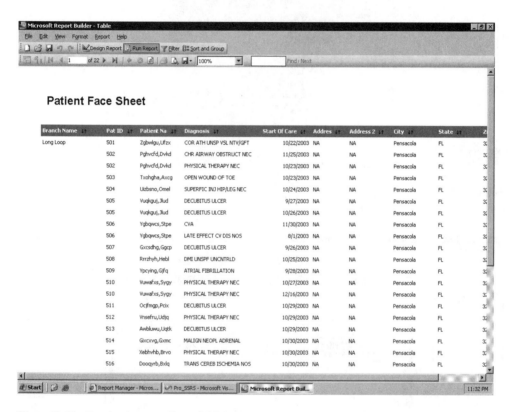

Figure 11-30. *Previewing new Branch Name group*

Deploying the report to the report server is as simple as clicking the Save button on the toolbar. After clicking Save, a Save Report dialog box appears that allows you to navigate to an accessible folder on the report server; in this case, open Pro_SSRS to save the report. Name this report Patient Face Sheet, as shown in Figure 11-31, and click the Save button.

You can navigate to the Report Manager later to make sure the report was saved successfully, but for now, you will move on to the next type of report you will learn how to create, a matrix report.

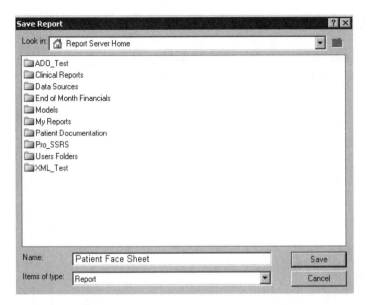

Figure 11-31. *Saving a report to the server*

Note Though you will save the report to the report server and can load it back into Report Builder for modification, it is possible to open a Report Builder RDL file from a file location as well. Opening a report from a file is a choice in the task pane, accessible by selecting View ➤ Task Pane or by pressing Ctrl+F1.

Adding a Matrix Report

Unlike a table report, a matrix report displays aggregated values two-dimensionally with column groups as well as row groups. The totals, whether they are sums, averages, or counts, intersect at the grouping levels for columns and rows. This creates a cross-tab report similar to a pivot table in Microsoft Excel. One of the requests for the report was to show the length of stay for patients, from the time they were admitted to the time they were discharged. Also, it is a requirement that the discharge reason show on the report. You can combine these two requests perfectly into a single matrix report.

So, return to the Report Builder design area, and click the matrix report in the Report Layout tab. This opens a new blank matrix template where you can drag and drop fields onto the Matrix data region, just as you did with the table report. The template is nothing more than a predefined Matrix data region to which you will add several fields, as shown in Figure 11-32.

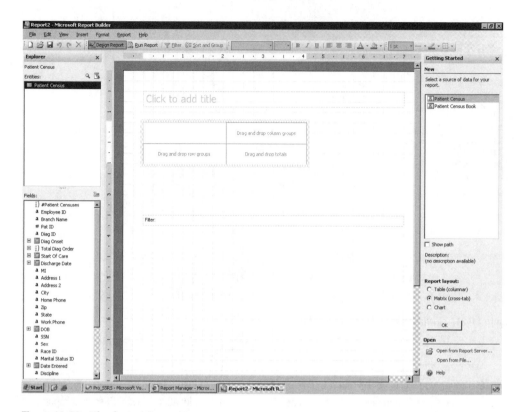

Figure 11-32. *Blank matrix report*

To the totals area, drag and drop the Avg Length of Stay under the Length of Stay attribute that was calculated when the model was generated. For the row grouping, add the Discharge Reason field. Finally, drag the MaritalStatus ID field to the column grouping area so that the matrix report resembles Figure 11-33. It will be necessary to resize the Discharge Reason field and center-justify the MaritalStatus ID field. You will also at this time add a title to the report: Average Length of Stay.

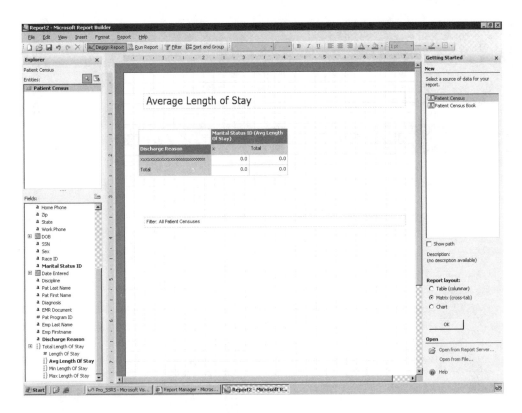

Figure 11-33. *Matrix report with data*

When previewed, the report is already taking shape, as shown in Figure 11-34; however, you need to address some anomalies. First, the number format is not what you expected or wanted. A general number, which by default is the data type assigned to the Avg Length of Stay field, is not desired. You will need to add formatting to the number. Second, you will see rows and columns with empty values. This is happening for two likely reasons. First, you are including patients who have not been discharged yet, in other words, active patients. Second, marital status is not a required field, so some records will not have values.

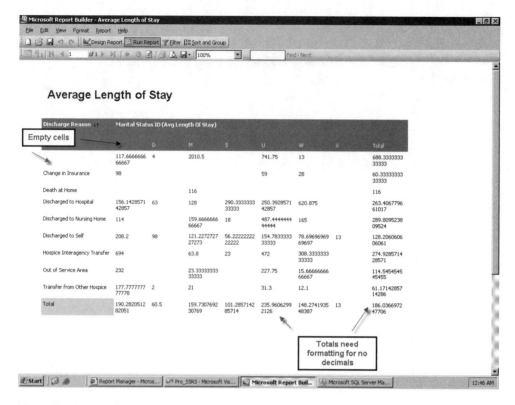

Figure 11-34. *Initial preview of a matrix report*

You can take care of the number formatting by returning to the design area, right-clicking the last column, which is the total, and selecting Format. In the Format dialog box, change the defined format from General to 1234.56, and change the decimal places from 2 to 0, as shown in Figure 11-35. Then click OK.

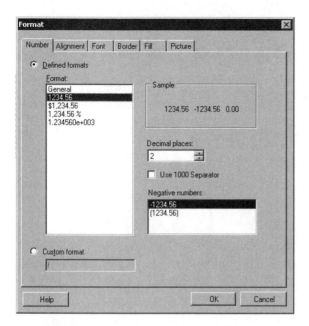

Figure 11-35. *Changing the number formatting*

To address the empty columns, add a filter to the report to limit the data to only discharged patients with discharge reasons and to patients who have a marital status defined. The Filter button on the toolbar will launch the Filter Data dialog box. In Figure 11-36 you can see that you can add four filter conditions: where MaritalStatusID, Discharge Date, and Discharge Reason are not empty and where the Discharge Year is greater than or equal to 2003. (We added the last filter to demonstrate that it is possible to have the report prompt the user for a value as a parameter that is tied to a filter.)

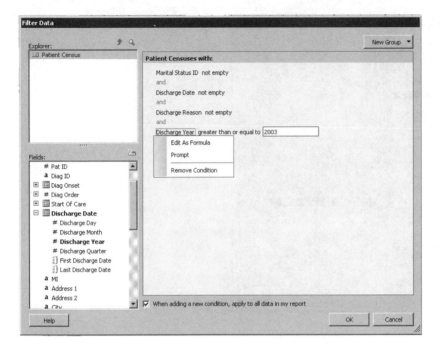

Figure 11-36. *Setting up report filters*

Now, when you preview the matrix report in Figure 11-37, you can see that the numbers have been cleaned up and all empty fields are gone; also, you are prompted for the discharge year. Save the report now to the Pro_SSRS folder on the report server, just as you did the table report, and move on to create the final report, the chart.

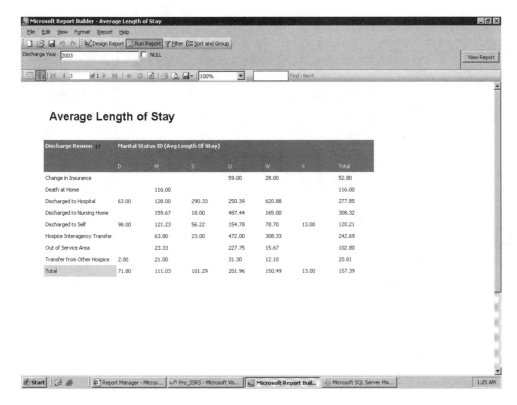

Figure 11-37. *Preview of matrix report*

Adding a Chart Report

The last report type available in Report Builder is the chart report. Thus far, you have created and saved table and matrix reports to address many of the report requests for the Patient Census report. Now, we will show one of the most important reports to answer the question of the number of patients on the census, meaning they are currently receiving services and have not been discharged. In the database you are using, a patient is considered active if their discharge date is Null, or, in Report Builder vernacular, *empty*. The chart you create will be a simple bar chart showing a count of active patients by their branch association.

Return to the design area of Report Builder, and click the chart report in the Report Layout tab. The blank report template has a single Chart data region, as shown in Figure 11-38. As you did with the two previous reports, table and matrix, you will add a title: Active Patient Census.

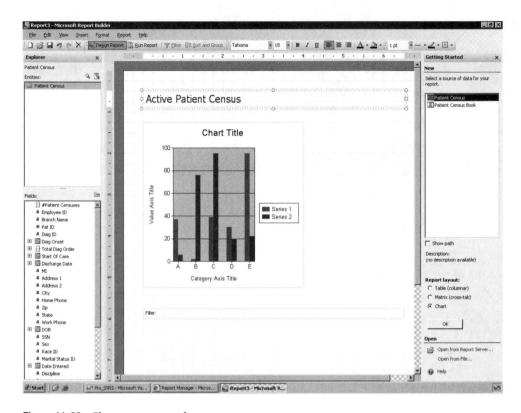

Figure 11-38. *Chart report template*

The chart has three areas to which you can drag and drop data: Series, Category, and Data. You want to be able to show an active patient count, so you could drag the Pat ID field to the Data area; however, because the Pat ID field is not seen as a field that can have an aggregated function applied to it, unlike Avg Length of Stay, you cannot drag it directly to the Data area. The chart simply won't accept it to be dropped there. Since you know you will need both a count value and a filter to get only active patients, you can take care of both at the same time by adding a new field to the field list. Click the New Fields button in the Report Data tab, and name the new field Patient Count, as shown in Figure 11-39. The formula you can use for the Patient Count field is COUNTDISTINCT(Pat ID). Notice that in the Define Formula dialog box that the Pat ID field, when added to the Formula textbox, has a dotted line beneath it indicating a link. You can click the field and add a filter while defining the formula for the new field, which you will do next.

Click the No Filter Applied link, and select Create New Filter to open the Filter Data dialog box. You can see the filter you need to apply to show only active patients in Figure 11-40, where you have set Discharge Date to "empty," which will force only patients who do not have discharge dates to be used in the formula. Call the filter Active Patients, and select OK. Once the Patient Count field is created and shows up on the Fields tab, you can drag and drop it in the Data area of the chart.

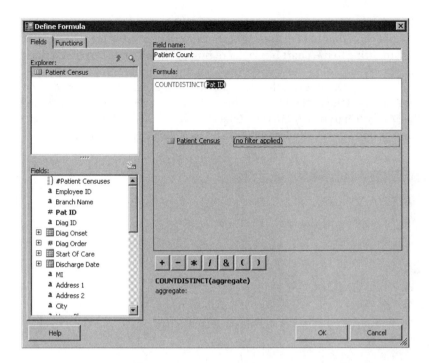

Figure 11-39. *Defining formula for new field,* Patient Count

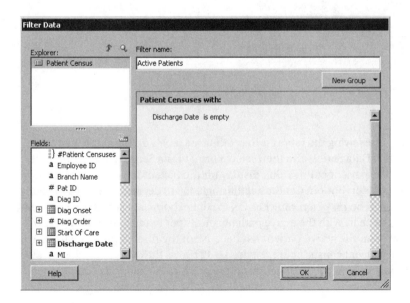

Figure 11-40. *Adding the Active Patients filter*

Next, drag the Branch Name field to the Series area of the chart. You could add further series items or categories to the chart, but to keep the chart simple and to address the request, you will just apply some formatting to the chart by way of removing the chart title so that it does not say *Chart Title* on the report. Leave the report title. To modify the chart properties, right-click the chart, and select Chart Options. On the Titles tab, delete the text for the chart and the Category X and ValueY titles. On the Legend tab, set the position to Bottom Center. Finally, on the 3D tab, check the Display Chart with 3-D Visual Effect box, set Horizontal Rotation to 25, set Vertical Rotation to 10, and select Cylinder as the shape, as shown in Figure 11-41.

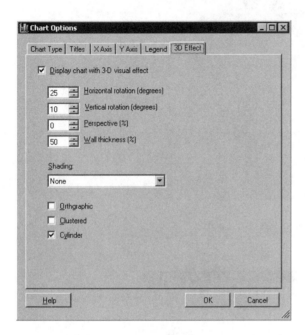

Figure 11-41. *Setting 3D visual effects*

The last task before previewing the report is to set the data labels on the chart. To do this, right-click the chart, select Data Series, and then select Format Data Series–Patient Count. If you would like to have the patient count value display on the bars of the chart, select Show Point Labels. Make the position Bottom Center, set the angle to -10 degrees, and click the Font button to set the font size to be 16. When you click OK to set the point labels and then preview the report, you can see the chart with the active patient counts per branch. As patients are discharged, they will drop from the active patient list because of the filter, and the chart will automatically reflect the current census count. Figure 11-42 shows the completed chart. Now you can save the chart report as Active Patient Census to the Pro_SSRS folder, as you did the other two reports.

Active Patient Census

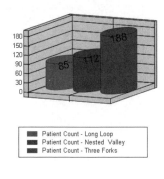

All Patient Censuses

Figure 11-42. *Preview of Active Patient Census chart report*

The reports are deployed as standard RDL report files with the exception that their data source is a report model and not a standard RDS data source object. You can see the three newly published reports in Report Manager, as shown in Figure 11-43.

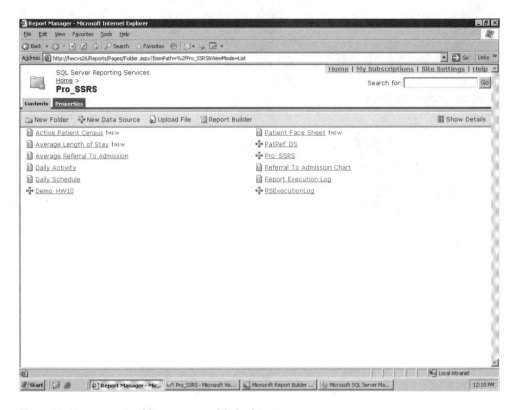

Figure 11-43. *Report Builder reports published in Report Manager*

Summary

Ad hoc reporting, giving users the ability to create their own reports on the fly, has been a highly requested feature for SSRS, so much so that Microsoft decided to deliver its first incarnation in SQL Server 2005. Though it lacks the true versatility of BIDS or Visual Studio, the functionality serves its purpose as a front-end report builder. DBAs and data analysts still need to be involved to produce the report model, which contains the metadata layer separating the report designer from the complicated structure of the underlying data source. But Report Builder will continue to develop in complexity and features and will become better equipped to design more sophisticated reports. In this chapter, you learned about some of its benefits and many of its limitations, and you probably have come away with an answer to the question of whether Report Builder is something your users will want. If so, then the good news is that it is included as a standard feature.

Index

You Need the Companion eBook

Your purchase of this book entitles you to its companion eBook for only $10.

We believe this Apress title will prove so indispensable that you'll want to carry it with you everywhere, which is why we are offering the companion eBook for $10 to customers who purchase this book now. Convenient and fully searchable, the eBook version of any content-rich, page-heavy Apress book makes a valuable addition to your programming library.. You can easily find, copy, and apply code—and then perform examples by quickly toggling between instructions and the application. Even simultaneously tackling a donut, diet soda, and complex code becomes simplified with hands-free eBooks!

Once you purchase this book, getting the $10 companion eBook is simple:

❶ Visit **www.apress.com/promo/tendollars/**.

❷ Complete a basic registration form to receive a randomly generated question about this title.

❸ Answer the question correctly in 60 seconds and you will receive a promotional code to redeem for the $10 eBook.

2560 Ninth Street • Suite 219 • Berkeley, CA 94710

Offer valid through 7/01/06.